Alyce Alexandra is the best-selling author of seven thermo cooker cookbooks. She has her own range of thermo cooker accessories, runs her own thermo cooker cooking school and is creator of The TM Shop, selling all things thermo cooker related.

Alyce is passionate about every avenue of food, from seedling to stomach. Her mission is to get people cooking, more often and from scratch, by showing how easy, achievable and rewarding home cooking can be. Her unpretentious, work-every-time recipes have made her a much-loved figure in the thermo cooker community. She lives, gardens, writes, cooks and eats in Victoria, Australia.

www.alycealexandra.com
@alycealexandracookbooks

# everyday thermo cooking

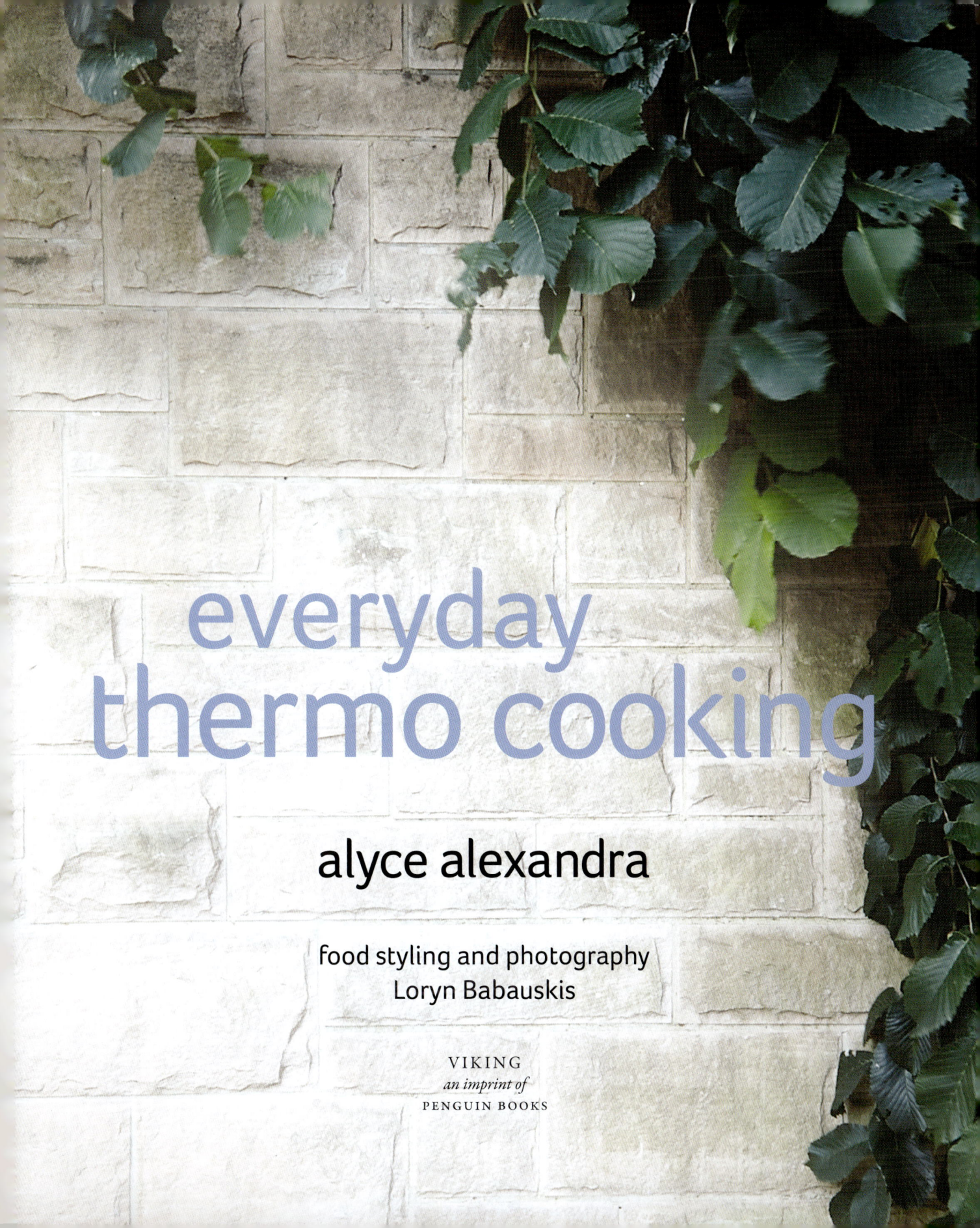

alyce alexandra

food styling and photography
Loryn Babauskis

VIKING
*an imprint of*
PENGUIN BOOKS

This book is dedicated to my mum Janene.

These pages are far richer for her inspiration,
contribution and support, as am I.

# contents

| | |
|---|---|
| introduction | 1 |
| the basics | 4 |
| symbols | 5 |
| thermo cookers and terminology | 7 |

## break the fast — 9

| | |
|---|---|
| pink chia puddings | 11 |
| crunchy maple pecan clusters | 12 |
| crispy kale fritters | 15 |
| lazy breakfast loaf | 16 |
| macadamia milk | 18 |
| honey porridge | 21 |
| breakfast latte | 22 |
| coconut yoghurt | 24 |
| smoothie bowl | 27 |
| mexican hollandaise | 28 |

## snacks on — 31

| | |
|---|---|
| chocolate cookie dough balls | 32 |
| sweet and spicy nuts | 35 |
| extra-punchy hummus | 37 |
| apricot delights | 38 |
| cheese and vegemite scrolls | 40 |
| green olive dip | 43 |
| cranberry and hazelnut crackers | 44 |
| lavender coffee tonic | 46 |
| loryn's tropical 'juice' | 48 |
| fudgy chocolate fig slice | 51 |
| creamy tomato and basil spread | 52 |
| savoury summer tart | 54 |
| chilli soy oysters | 56 |

## quick fix meals — 59

| | |
|---|---|
| korean rice bowl | 60 |
| vietnamese trout salad | 62 |
| one-bowl mushroom spaghetti | 65 |
| garlic and white wine mussel pots | 67 |
| creamy zucchini soup | 68 |
| potato, mint and fried egg salad | 71 |
| lamb with herby yoghurt lentil salad | 75 |
| garlic chilli sardines on toast | 76 |
| rice and black bean burritos | 78 |
| moreish meatballs | 80 |
| + well stocked | 82 |

## meatless mondays — 87

| | |
|---|---|
| thai pumpkin soup | 88 |
| mushroom bolognaise | 90 |
| fresh green curry | 93 |
| chilli olive spaghetti | 94 |
| sushi mash-up | 96 |
| curried lentil 'sausage' rolls | 98 |
| beetroot burgers | 100 |

## low and slow — 103

| | |
|---|---|
| rich brisket ragù | 105 |
| korean beef ribs | 106 |
| lamb shoulder with salsa verde | 108 |
| massaman beef curry | 111 |
| + bones about it | 114 |

## super sides — 117

- mashed potato — 118
- crunchy salad with ranch dressing — 121
- garlic pull-apart — 122
- pickled salad — 124
- soft polenta — 126
- focaccia — 129
- fresh charcoal pasta — 130
- mexican corn salad — 133

## easy entertaining — 135

- chickpea curry — 138
- slow beef curry — 140
- roti bread — 143
- tamarind mint raita — 144
- spiced coconut rice — 145
- spiced cauliflower — 146
- mango chutney — 148
- coconut mango lassi — 149
- chai panna cottas — 151

- + timeline — 152
- + ingredients list — 153
- + how to make entertaining easy — 155

## waste not want not — 157

- almond coconut macaroons — 158
- ricotta cheese — 160
- tuna mornay bake — 163
- anything goes baos — 165
- herb vinaigrette — 168
- clean green smoothie — 171
- frugal frittata — 175
- roast potatoes — 178
- noodle curry soup — 180
- 'the' risotto — 183
- money-saving minestrone — 187
- stock concentrate — 190

## homemade is best — 195

- individual dark chocolate cakes — 196
- butterscotch ice cream — 198
- matcha passionfruit chia parfait — 201
- anzac biscuits — 202
- choc macadamia cookies — 204
- individual 'baked' cheesecakes — 206
- cheat's vanilla slice — 208
- peach and mango sorbet — 211
- yoghurt cheesecake — 212
- peanut butter choc pops — 215
- boozy berry fool — 216
- after-dinner mint hot chocolate — 219

- + pretty as a picture — 220

## flavour makers — 223

- healthy hoisin — 224
- herbed mayo — 226
- lemon myrtle dukkah — 229
- facon — 230
- satay sauce — 233
- barbecue sauce — 234
- easy kimchi-kraut — 236
- corn and mustard chutney — 239
- tomato chutney — 241
- rhubarb and ginger relish — 242
- caramelised orange balsamic — 243
- flavour bomb salt — 246
- garlic cubes — 248
- meyer lemon infused oil — 250
- salad seed sprinkles — 251
- quick toffee caramel sauce — 252
- coconut caramel — 254
- raspberry, rhubarb and vanilla jam — 255

## acknowledgements — 257

## index — 260

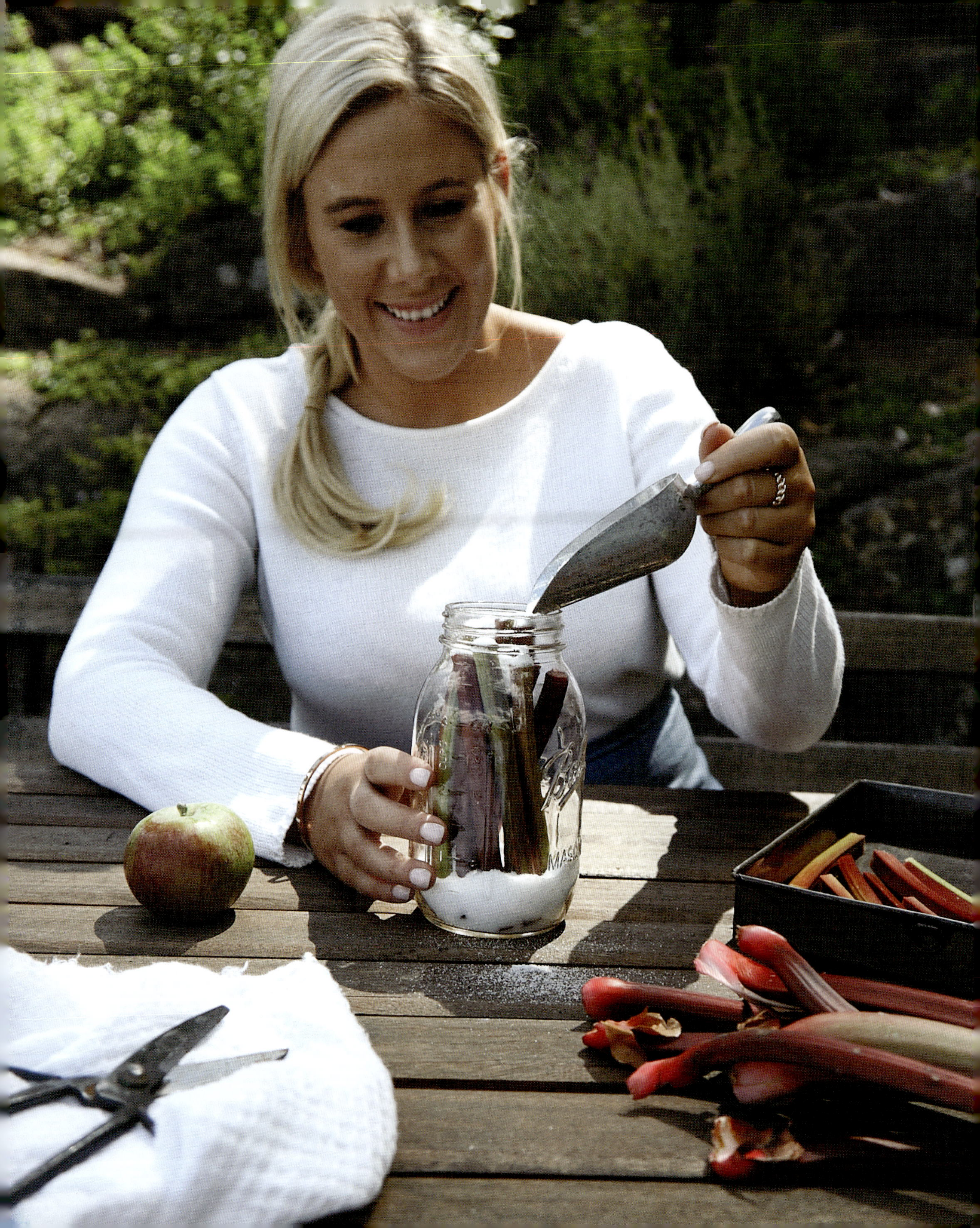

# introduction

This is the book I've always wanted to write, my manifesto of sorts through food. This is what I cook, what I eat, what I do, and what I think about it all. Like you, I am a busy home cook who doesn't have all day to spend in the kitchen. And truthfully, even if I did have all day, I'm not sure the kitchen is where I'd choose to spend it. But I love food. I love everything about it – the growing, the purchasing, the cooking, the eating, the nourishment, the connection, the celebration. To me, food is central to everything that's important in life – how we eat and how we feed others is such a strong reflection on who we are, our values and how we live. And we get to enjoy this ritual three times every single day! I want to have my cake and eat it too, and it is this conundrum that has ultimately defined me – how can we cook and eat from scratch while living in the busy modern world?

I'm not sure which came first – my love of cooking or my love of thermo cookers. My thermo cooker opened a whole new world of possibilities, making life in the kitchen quicker, easier and much more enjoyable. I can cook more than I ever could without it, in a whole lot less time. I truly believe that, regardless of skill level or time constraints, anyone with a thermo cooker can cook nourishing and delicious food they are proud to serve and share.

This book is a collection of what I cook in my thermo cooker every day – real-life recipes for real-life cooks. Let me show you how to get the most out of your thermo cooker, using it to prepare breakfast, lunch and dinner, and everything in between. There is nothing complicated or cheffy about my recipes; simple yet satisfying is my motto, and in today's world simple is often exactly what we need.

In many ways the structure of this book reflects how I approach my own home cooking – I've got the Monday to Friday rush covered with pre-prepared breakfasts, tasty lunchbox options and quick meals. Then, for when you've got a little more time on the weekends, there are slow cooks, baked goods and investment flavour makers to stock up on. There's also my entertaining menu, creative ways to use up leftovers and, of course, sweet treats when a celebration or little indulgence is in order. You'll be cooking more in less time, wasting less food, eating more sustainably and entertaining without the hassle.

The recipes in this book include variations enabling you to cater for a wide variety of dietary preferences, including vegetarian, vegan, dairy free, gluten free, nut free and refined-sugar free. Many can be completed in less than 30 minutes, qualifying as a 'quick fix'. The rest do take longer, but the actual hands-on time is usually minimal. For the most part I use unprocessed ingredients – things you'd find at a market or around the perimeter of the supermarket, although occasionally convenience sneaks in.

In spite of being a blueprint of my culinary life, ultimately that's not what this book is about. Rather it's about getting you to use and love your thermo cooker, cook more often and cook from scratch. It isn't prescriptive or aspirational, it's about what you like, what you have on hand, and how to make your life that little bit easier. I sincerely hope you read it, use it and love it, and that you become a more proficient thermo cook along the way.

Happy cooking,

*alyce xo*

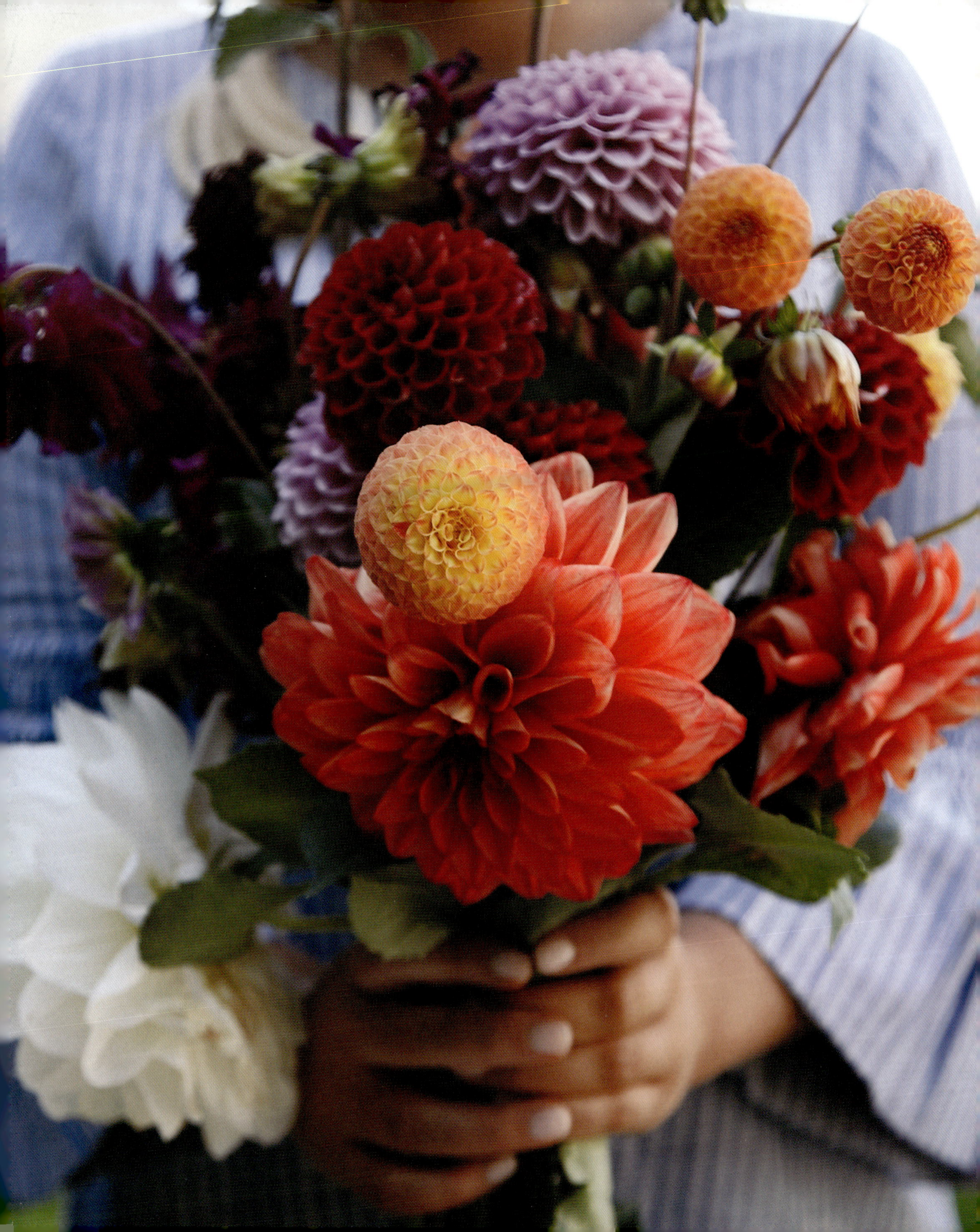

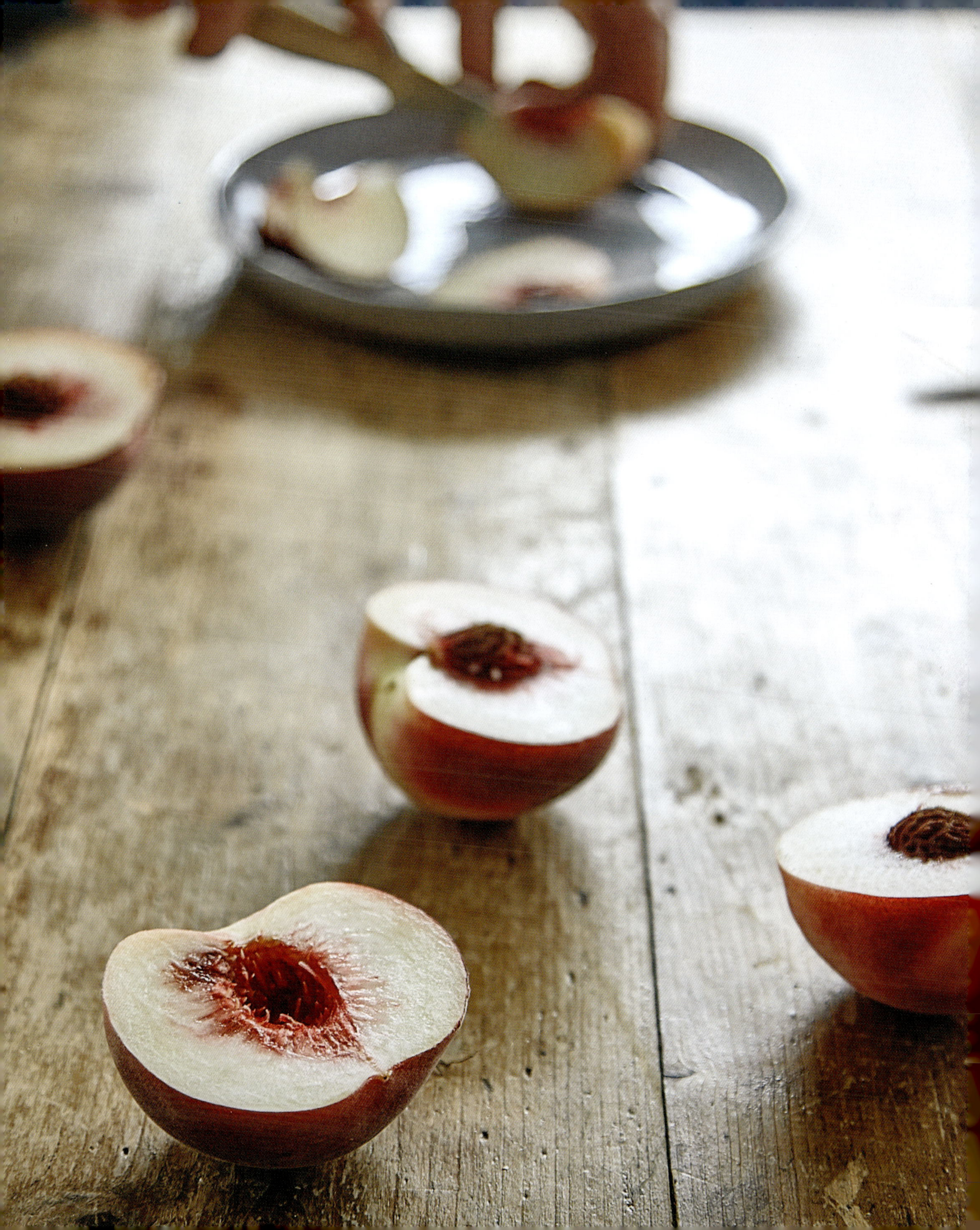

# the basics

- **OIL**  I use extra virgin olive oil for all raw applications and in the thermo cooker to temperatures up to and including 100°C. For anything hotter than that, such as on the stove and in the oven, I use macadamia or coconut oil as they have a higher smoke point. There are many great quality and ethical brands of all three.

- **SALT**  I recommend using a good-quality, pure, unrefined salt. Salt is not simply for saltiness; it acts as an enhancer, highlighting all the flavours in the dish. If something tastes bland, it probably needs a little salt. Often it is fine to add salt to taste, but if an exact measure is specified I will always indicate the type of salt used. This is important as one teaspoon of fine salt is saltier than one teaspoon of coarse salt or flakes! I recommend always using fine salt for baking, but for general seasoning salt flakes can also be used.

- **FLOUR**  For the best bread, it is essential to use baker's flour, also known as bread flour or strong flour. This has more gluten than regular plain flour, and therefore more protein. As a general rule, 9–10% protein content is a soft flour ideal for cakes, whereas 12–14% protein is a stronger flour ideal for bread.

- **EGGS**  Always free range. But not all free range is equal, with stocking densities and other policies fluctuating dramatically between brands. Check the rules of the individual certifying bodies, and if in doubt price is usually a good indicator of quality. Many good brands are now including outdoor stocking densities on the carton – look for 1500 birds per hectare or less.

- **DAIRY**  I always use full-fat dairy products, not only because I like to cook with unrefined ingredients wherever possible, but simply because they taste better! Low-fat products just don't cut it, in my book (pardon the pun!).

- **FRUIT AND VEGETABLES**  While organic is great where possible, I believe that buying local, seasonal produce is just as important. Shop at farmers' markets and browse online for co-ops – some of them even do home delivery. Better yet, grow some of your own! Herbs, rocket, zucchini and tomatoes would be my pick to start.

- **BEEF AND LAMB**  Where possible I cook with beef and lamb that is locally grown, and grass fed and finished. To me, it doesn't make sense to grow food to feed food. Buying meat directly from the farmer is a great way to get quality products at reasonable prices, and you have a much better chance of knowing how the animal lived, and how it died. Don't be afraid to ask questions; people who care will be happy to share the answers.

- **SEAFOOD**  My preferred seafood picks are always the most sustainable ones, such as oysters, mussels, sardines, mackerel, whiting, bream, crab, calamari, squid and octopus. Buy local wherever possible, and diversify your choices to spread the impact of fishing pressures.

- **WEIGHTS**  The weight specified for each ingredient is the weight after the ingredient has been prepared per instruction (for example, pumpkin, peeled, seeds removed). Please factor this in when shopping.

- **TEASPOONS**  I use Australian metric measurements, meaning 1 teaspoon = 5 ml and 1 tablespoon = 20 ml.

- **OVEN**  All oven temperatures are for a fan-forced setting, unless otherwise stated. My experience is that oven temperatures can vary dramatically, so I recommend you get to know your own oven and adjust the temperatures accordingly. You may also need to rotate baking trays during the cooking time to ensure even cooking and browning.

# symbols

For recipes catering for specific dietary requirements look for the symbols:

| | | |
|---|---|---|
| | Dairy free | Dairy free |
| | Dairy-free option | Follow the variation for a dairy-free option |
| | Gluten free* | Gluten free |
| | Gluten-free* option | Follow the variation for a gluten-free option |
| | Vegetarian | Vegetarian |
| | Vegetarian option | Follow the variation for a vegetarian option |
| | Vegan | Vegan |
| | Vegan option | Follow the variation for a vegan option |
| | Quick Fix | The entire recipe can be completed and on the table in less than 30 minutes |
| + FREEZING | Quick Fix + | The total hands-on time is less than 30 minutes, but the recipe also requires baking, marinating, soaking, proving, chilling or freezing time, as indicated after the QF symbol |

* While every effort has been made to indicate gluten-free ingredients, make sure you read the ingredients list of all food products to ensure they are suitable for a gluten-free diet.

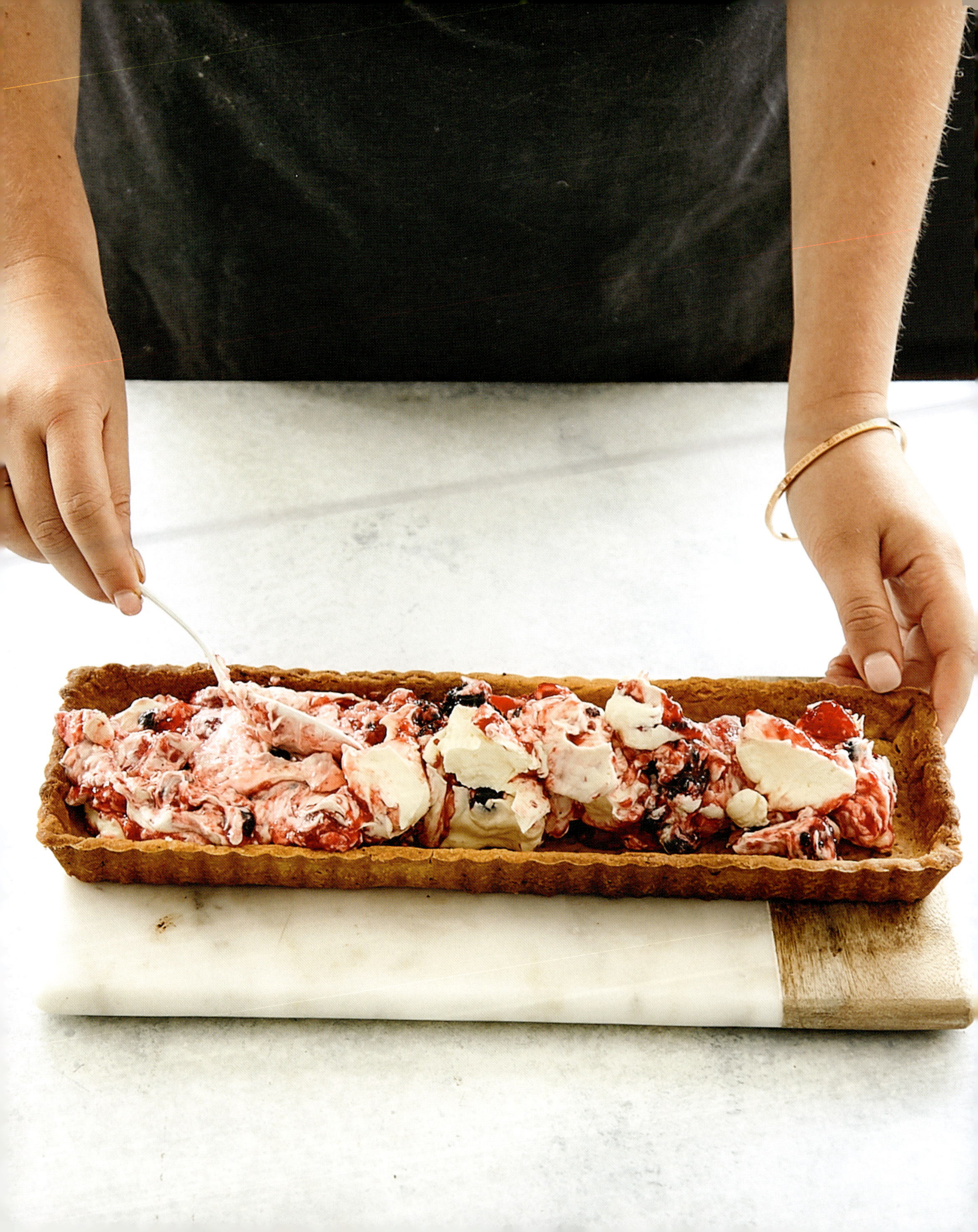

# thermo cookers and terminology

The recipes in this cookbook have been developed and tested in the Thermomix TM31 and Thermomix TM5 models; however they are suitable for use across many thermo cookers, including:

- Thermomix TM5
- Thermomix TM31
- Thermochef Natura
- BioChef MyCook
- Optimum ThermoCook
- Intelli Kitchen Master
- Supercook
- HotmixPRO
- SuperChef
- ThermoPro
- ThermoBlend
- Mistral Professional Ultimate Kitchen Machine

Some recipes will also be suitable for high-speed food processors and blenders.

It is natural to expect some variation between brands of thermo cooker, and slight adaptations to the method may be required, depending on your machine.

## TERMINOLOGY

**TC:** Thermo cooker

**MC:** Measuring cup that sits in the top of the thermo cooker lid

**STEAMING TEMPERATURE:** Many machines have a special steaming function (in the Thermomix this is called Varoma temperature), but if yours doesn't, use 110°C

**STEAMING BASKET:** This basket sits inside the thermo cooker bowl and needs to be inserted before securing the lid

**STEAMING TRAY:** This attachment sits on top of the thermo cooker bowl and needs to be placed on top after securing the lid

**DOUGH FUNCTION:** Many machines have a special dough function (in the Thermomix this is called interval speed), but if not, start at speed 6 for 10–20 seconds, then drop to a lower speed until a dough is formed

**ASSISTING WITH SPATULA:** This requires you to put the spatula in the hole in the lid and stir while the thermo cooker is in operation

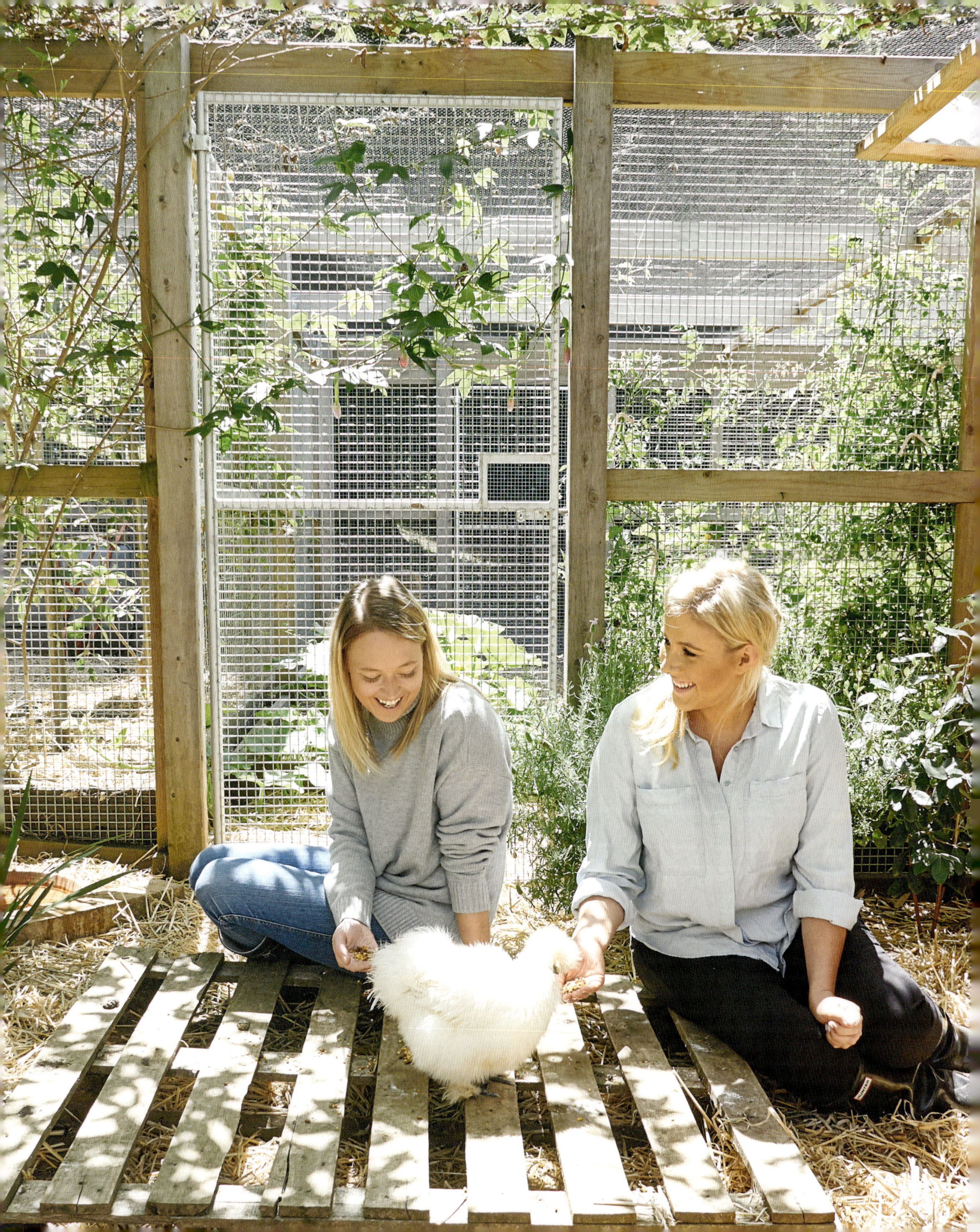

# break the fast

If breakfast is the most important meal of the day, then I believe we should treat it with the respect it deserves and make something delicious and nutritious from scratch. Don't worry, it's much easier than it sounds! Convenience still tops the agenda, so in this chapter we offer recipes that can be partly or entirely prepared in advance or take just minutes to whip up in the morning. Protein and healthy fats are a regular feature as they will help sustain you right through to lunch time. If you've ever studied the ingredients lists on prepackaged breakfast fare you'll agree that what we include in our meals is just as important as what we leave out ...

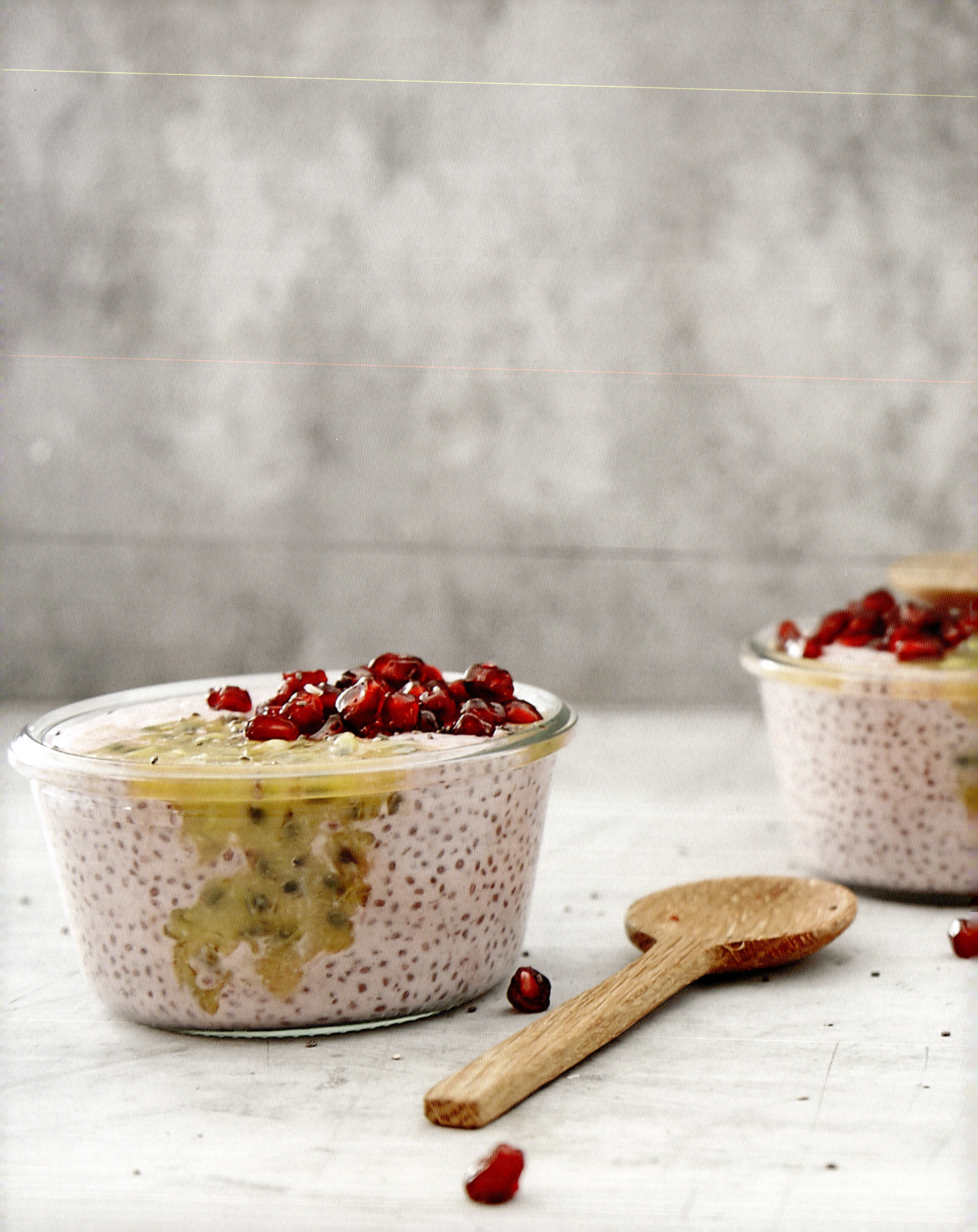

# pink chia puddings

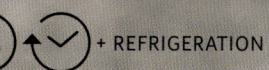

+ REFRIGERATION

SERVES 4

I am a big fan of anything that can be made in advance, especially when it comes to breakfast! This one is a favourite of mine, particularly during the week. Make it before bed and enjoy a healthy breakfast on the go in the morning. Chia seeds are full of protein and fibre so they really keep you full 'til lunch.

100g fresh or frozen raspberries
20g raw sugar or xylitol (optional)
400g can coconut milk
60g chia seeds
Your choice of toppings (fresh fruit, dried fruit, coconut, nuts, seeds, buckwheat groats, cacao nibs etc)

1 Place raspberries and sugar or xylitol in TC bowl, pulverise for 10 seconds, speed 9.

2 Add coconut milk, mix for 5 seconds, speed 6.

3 Add chia seeds, mix for 5 seconds, reverse speed 4.

4 Divide coconut mixture among 4 jars or bowls. Sprinkle with toppings. Refrigerate overnight.

Enjoy straight out of the jar or bowl in the morning.

VARIATION: Replace raspberries with mango or banana for a tropical twist.

# crunchy maple pecan clusters

**MAKES 8 CUPS**

These sweet, toasty golden clusters have expanded their reach beyond the first meal of the day, finding their way into my afternoon repertoire and even occasionally making an appearance before bed! Consisting predominately of nuts and seeds, they are full of protein and healthy fats, and as a result will keep you feeling full and satisfied for much longer than most other breakfast cereals.

120g pure maple syrup or coconut nectar
50g coconut oil
2 teaspoons vanilla extract
Pinch fine salt
200g slivered almonds
150g pecans
100g coconut flakes
100g sunflower seeds
100g pumpkin seeds
80g buckwheat groats
20g sesame seeds
150g rolled oats

1. Preheat oven to 140°C. Line 2 large roasting tins or baking trays with baking paper or baking mats.

2. Place maple syrup or coconut nectar, coconut oil, vanilla and salt in TC bowl, melt for 3 minutes, 50°C, speed 2.

3. Add almonds, pecans, coconut flakes, sunflower seeds, pumpkin seeds, buckwheat groats, sesame seeds and (lastly) oats. Mix for 1 minute, 70°C, reverse speed 2.5, assisting with spatula if necessary. Spread mixture evenly over the lined tins or trays, but keep mixture touching with no gaps.

4. Bake for 20 minutes, then turn off oven. Allow mixture to cool completely in the oven – do not open the door during this time.

5. Once cooled, mixture should be golden and set in 2 sheets. Break into rough chunks ('clusters') and store in airtight jar. They will keep for up to a month.

Serve clusters with yoghurt, milk and/or fruit, or just enjoy them on their own.

VARIATION: For a gluten-free option, omit the rolled oats.

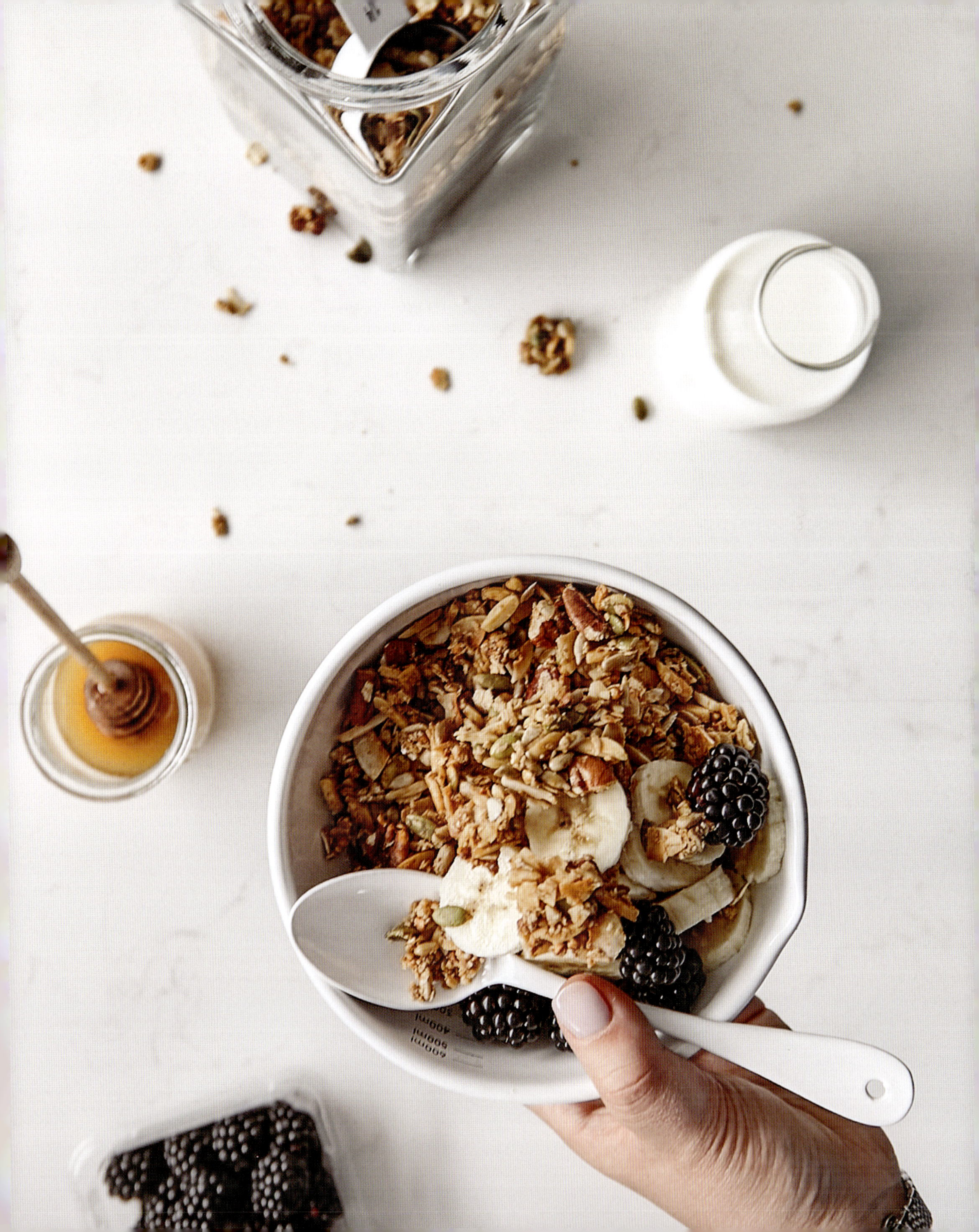

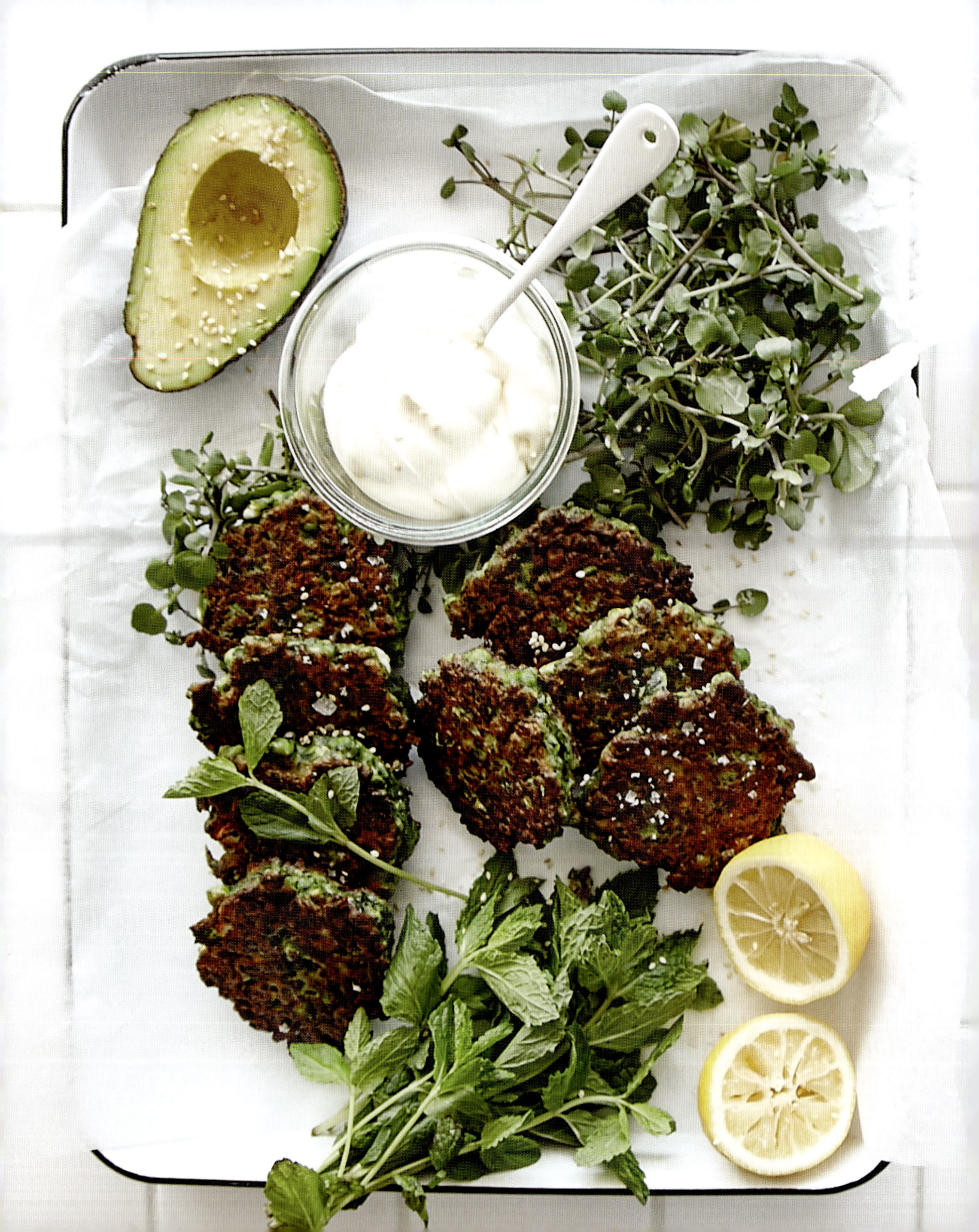

# crispy kale fritters

**MAKES 8**

I just love the crispy-creamy-salty-sweet combination of fried kale, feta and peas, plus a little zing from the fresh herbs. You will be surprised by how many vegetables I've crammed into these fritters – they definitely don't taste healthy! Kale is so densely nutritious and easy to grow year-round, so I'm thrilled to have a new way to cook with it. This recipe is probably weekend fare as it takes a little more time than most of my breakfasts, but the fritters are still super easy and any leftovers are great cold in lunchboxes.

1 zucchini, quartered
1 teaspoon fine salt
½ bunch kale, spines removed (approx. 120g)
Handful fresh mint
Handful fresh parsley
200g frozen peas, defrosted
150g plain flour
2 eggs
100g Greek feta, crumbled
50g buttermilk or milk
Macadamia oil, for frying

1. Place zucchini and salt in TC bowl, chop for 2 seconds, speed 6. Transfer to steamer basket or colander to drain. Press down with the back of a spoon or spatula.

2. Meanwhile, place kale, mint and parsley in TC bowl, chop for 5 seconds, speed 6, assisting with spatula, or until finely chopped.

3. Add peas, flour, eggs, feta, milk and drained zucchini, mix for 30 seconds, reverse speed 3, or until well combined.

4. Heat a tablespoon of macadamia oil in a large fry pan over medium heat. Add as many tightly compacted spoonfuls of mixture as will fit and flatten with the back of a spatula. Cook for 3 minutes each side, or until dark brown, crispy and cooked through. Transfer to a baking tray and keep warm in a low oven while you cook the rest. Repeat with remaining mixture, adding additional macadamia oil as needed.

Serve topped with a soft poached egg, Mexican hollandaise (see page 28), sour cream or chutney (see pages 239 to 240), or just a squeeze of lemon and slices of avocado.

NOTE: Don't be tempted to undercook these – you want them dark brown and crispy, not just golden.

# lazy breakfast loaf

**MAKES 1 LOAF**

My favourite Sunday mornings start with a warm, crusty slice of fresh bread straight out of the oven. However, I don't want to wait hours for the dough to prove! Here's my solution, born out of necessity: start this recipe after dinner the night before, and by the time you wake up in the morning the dough will be ready for baking. Not only is this recipe oh so convenient, it is also super easy – you don't have to shape or even handle the dough.

570g filtered water
750g baker's flour, plus extra if needed
2½ teaspoons fine salt
⅔ teaspoon dried yeast

1. Place water, flour, salt and yeast in TC bowl, mix for 6 seconds, speed 6.

2. Knead for 30 seconds, dough function.

3. Invert TC bowl over 900g jumbo bread tin and twist the blades, allowing dough to drop into the tin. If you can't move the blades, then the mixture is too wet. Add 2 heaped tablespoons of flour and knead on dough function for another 10 seconds. Cover with a clean tea towel and set aside overnight to prove (approx. 8–14 hours).

4. In the morning (or when you are ready to cook), preheat oven to 230°C. The dough is ready to cook when it has risen approx. 2cm from the top of the tin.

5. Place tin in oven and bake for 30 minutes.

6. Using oven mitts, turn tin on its side and shake to release loaf. Continue cooking loaf on oven rack for 10 minutes, or until bread is browned and the crust is hard when knocked.

Cool on a wire rack for about 30 minutes before serving.

NOTE: Avoid extremes of temperature while your dough is proving. Very hot weather will mean the dough may overprove by morning, and very cold weather may mean that the dough will not rise sufficiently by breakfast (but might be ready for lunch or dinner!). Store your dough overnight at ambient room temperature – perhaps on top of the hot water system in winter or in a cool room in summer.

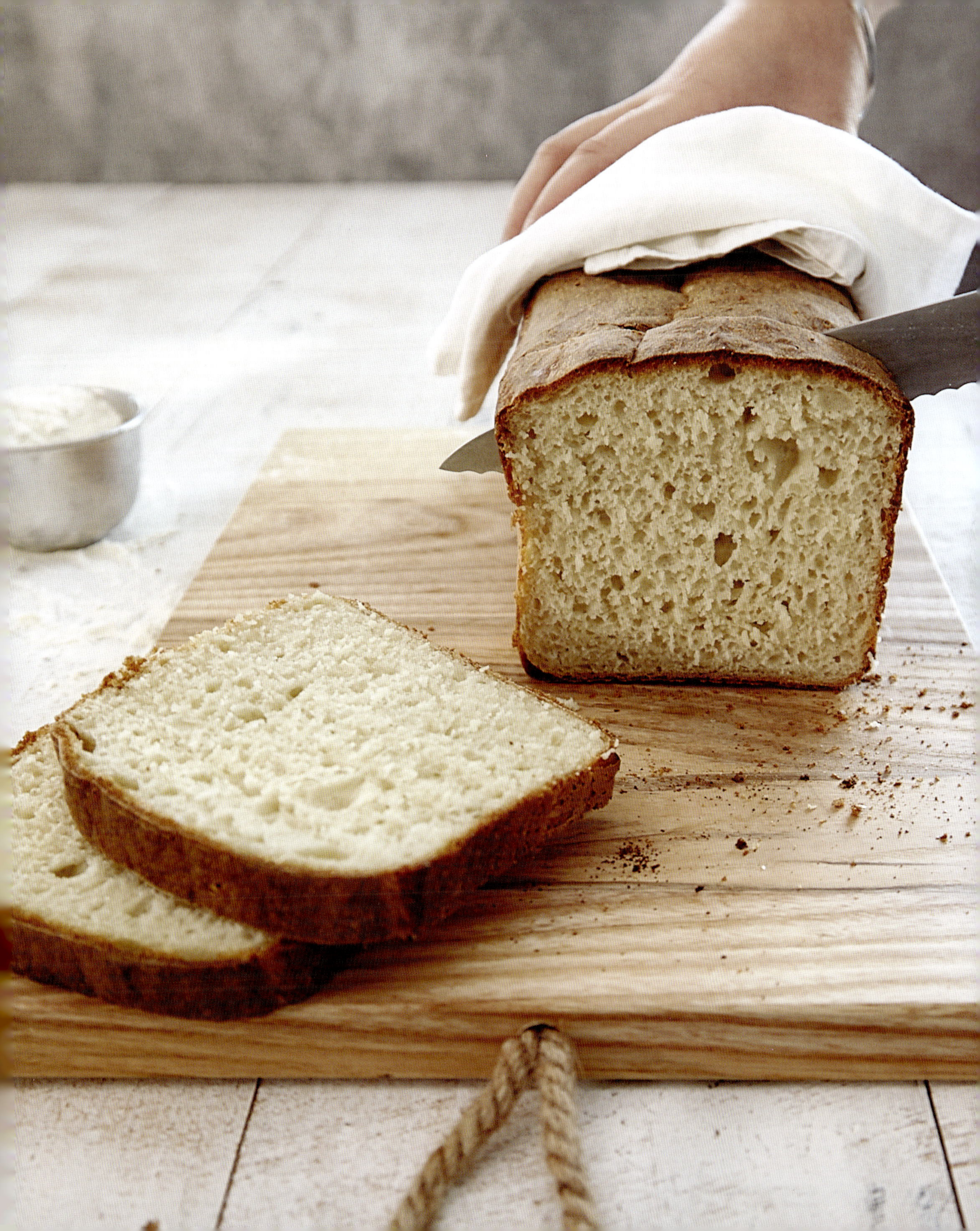

# macadamia milk

**MAKES 1 LITRE**

This is definitely my nut milk of choice – quick and easy. No soaking, no straining and no wastage. Use macadamia milk to make smoothies or coffee, pour over cereal or muesli, or use wherever you would usually have cow's milk. It's creamy and delicious with just a hint of sweetness.

900g water
150g raw macadamia nuts
½ vanilla bean
100g ice
20g pure maple syrup, or to taste
Pinch fine salt

1. Weigh out 800g water. Set aside.

2. Place nuts and vanilla bean in TC bowl, mill for 8 seconds, speed 7.

3. Add ice, maple syrup, salt and remaining 100g water and purée for 30 seconds, speed 9.

4. Continue on speed 9 for 1 minute, while slowly pouring the reserved 800g water onto the TC lid.

Pour macadamia milk into glass bottles and refrigerate for up to 4 days. Shake or stir before serving. Pictured with crunchy maple pecan clusters (see page 12).

VARIATION: For a richer milk, reduce the quantity of water to 700g or increase the nuts to 200g.

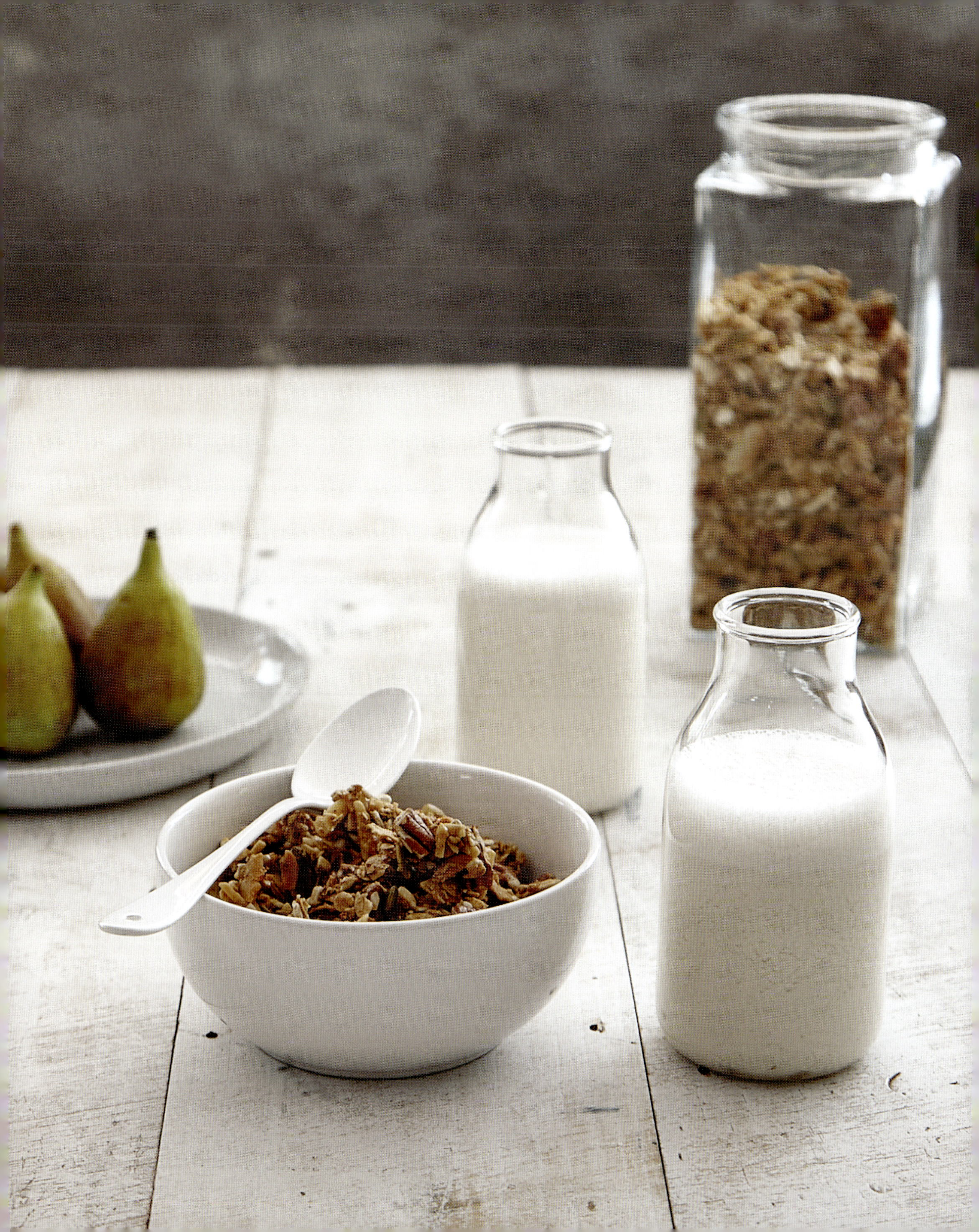

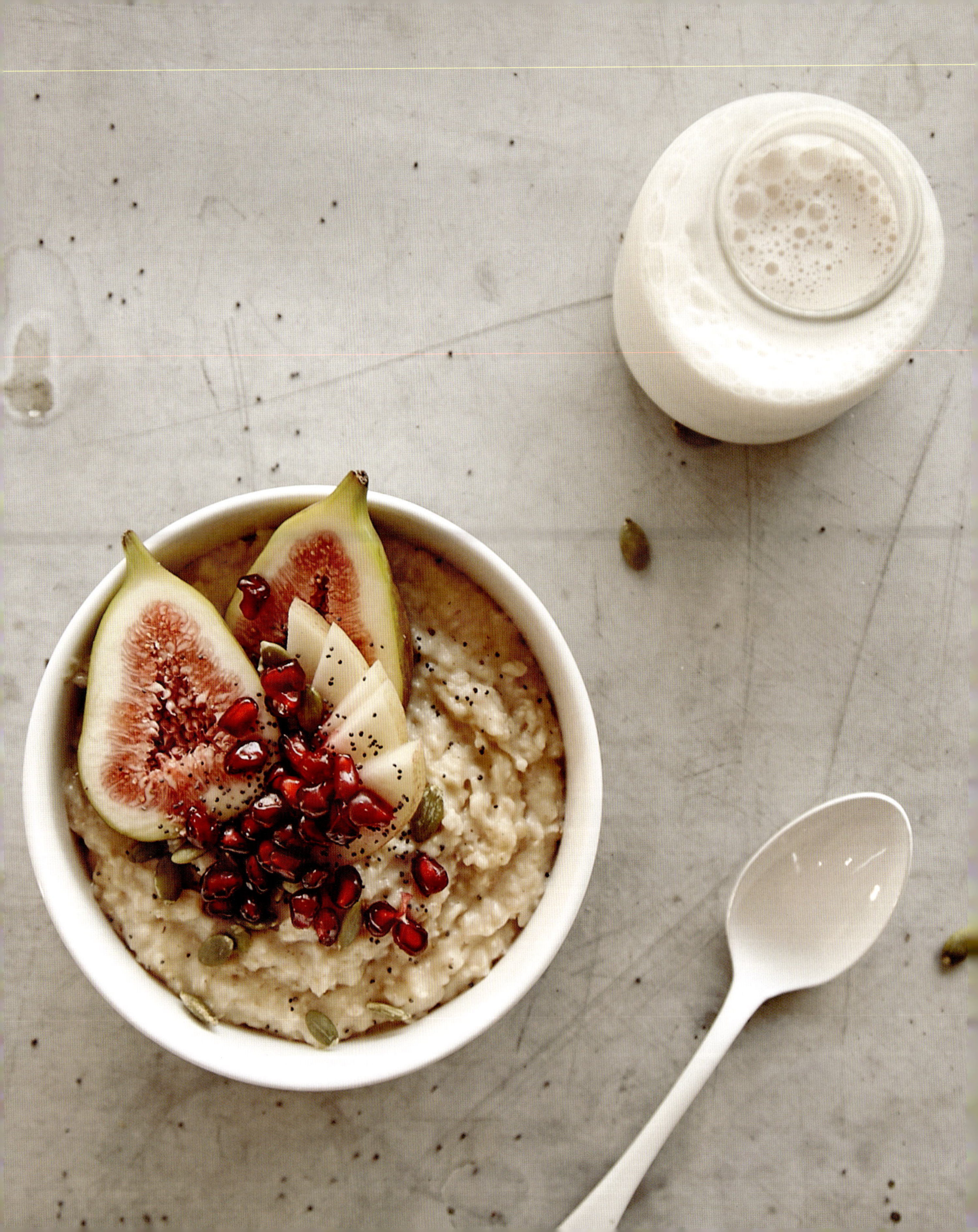

# honey porridge

**SERVES 2**

Often people cook a very basic porridge and then load the toppings on at the end, but to me that's going about it the wrong way! By cooking the porridge with the honey and butter, every grain gets a glistening coat of sweet silky goodness.

100g rolled oats (not instant)
300g water
100g milk
40g butter, or to taste
30g honey, or to taste
½ teaspoon vanilla bean paste
Pinch fine salt
Your choice of toppings (fresh fruit, nuts, seeds or yoghurt)

1. Place oats, water, milk, butter, honey, vanilla and salt in TC bowl, cook for 11 minutes, 90°C, reverse speed soft. For a thicker porridge, allow to stand in TC bowl for 5 minutes before serving.

Delicious on its own or serve with your choice of toppings.

NOTE: You can use any proportion of milk and water in this recipe – just ensure the combined total is 400g.

VARIATION: For a vegan and dairy-free alternative, replace the milk with all water or a vegan milk, the butter with coconut oil and the honey with maple syrup.

# breakfast latte

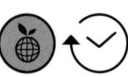

SERVES 1

My weekday breakfast is often something in a flask sipped as I'm rushing around, but sometimes a green smoothie just doesn't cut it – especially in the colder months! My breakfast latte is creamy, warm, nourishing and delicious, and ready in no time, making it the perfect on-the-go meal. I've kept the ingredients intentionally vague so no matter what your dietary and flavour preferences are, this recipe is sure to suit.

| INGREDIENT: | WHY NOT TRY: |
| --- | --- |
| 250g milk | Cow's, almond, macadamia, coconut, soy |
| 1 tablespoon booster | Protein powder, collagen hydrolysate or gelatine, cream, butter |
| 2 teaspoons flavouring | Instant coffee, cocoa powder, turmeric blend, chai spice blend, matcha green tea powder |
| 1 teaspoon sweetener (optional) | Sugar, honey, pure maple syrup, xylitol |

1. Place all ingredients in TC bowl, heat for 5 minutes, 70°C, speed 3.
2. Mix for a further 30 seconds, slowly increasing from speed 1 to 9.

Pour into a travel mug or jar and head out the door. Turmeric latte pictured.

BREAK THE FAST

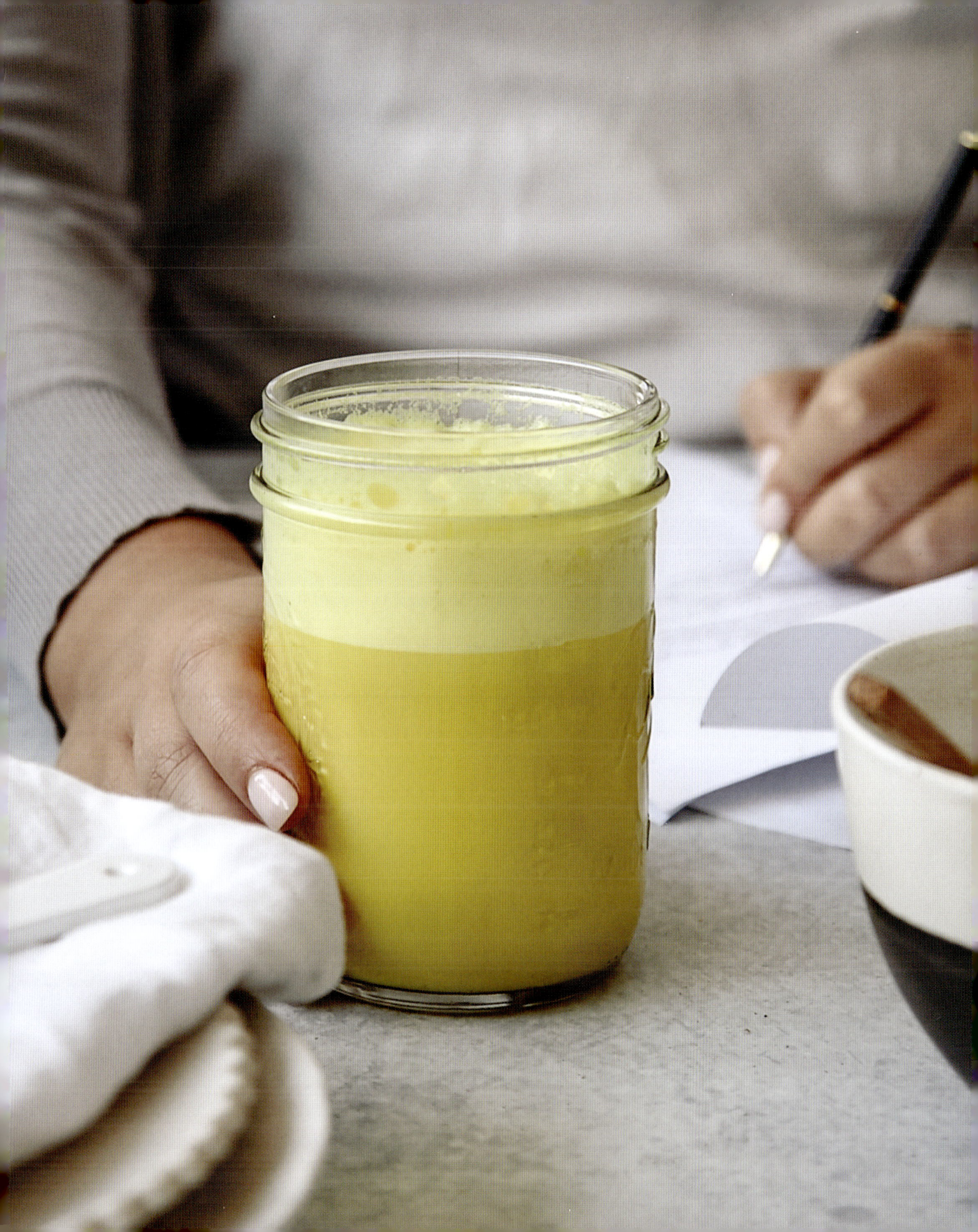

# coconut yoghurt

**MAKES 800G**

Coconut yoghurt is suddenly so popular it's sprouting up everywhere! However, it often seems to be exorbitantly priced, so it's a good thing we can make it economically at home. Like the cow's milk original, it has so many uses in both sweet and savoury dishes, from breakfasts, smoothies and desserts to dips, sauces and dressings. But unlike the original, it's great if you are lactose intolerant, paleo or vegan ... or perhaps you just want to give the cows a break. This version is particularly thick and creamy, replicating a Greek-style yoghurt. Special thanks to my mum Janene for becoming the doyenne of coconut yoghurt – she's tested every conceivable method and variation, and this is the version that consistently comes out on top.

30g kuzu (see note page 254)
800g canned coconut cream (see note)
20g pure maple syrup (optional)
2 probiotic capsules, powdered contents only

1. Place kuzu in TC bowl, mill for 10 seconds, speed 10. Scrape down sides and lid.

2. Add coconut cream and maple syrup (if using), cook for 10 minutes, 90°C, speed 3. Leave in TC jug to cool – remove jug from TC cradle to speed up the process. It may take a couple of hours, depending on room temperature.

3. Once mixture is below 37°C (there should be no temperature registering), add probiotics, mix for 5 seconds, speed 4.

4. Warm for 10 minutes, 37°C, speed 3. Meanwhile, fill a 1 litre food thermos with boiling water.

5. Pour out hot water, then pour coconut mixture into thermos. Seal and leave undisturbed at room temperature for 24 hours.

6. Transfer to glass jar and refrigerate for a minimum 24 hours before serving.

Serve with fresh fruit and crunchy maple pecan clusters (see page 12).

NOTE: It is important to use a good-quality coconut cream, one without any additives or thickeners. In my experience, organic brands are best.

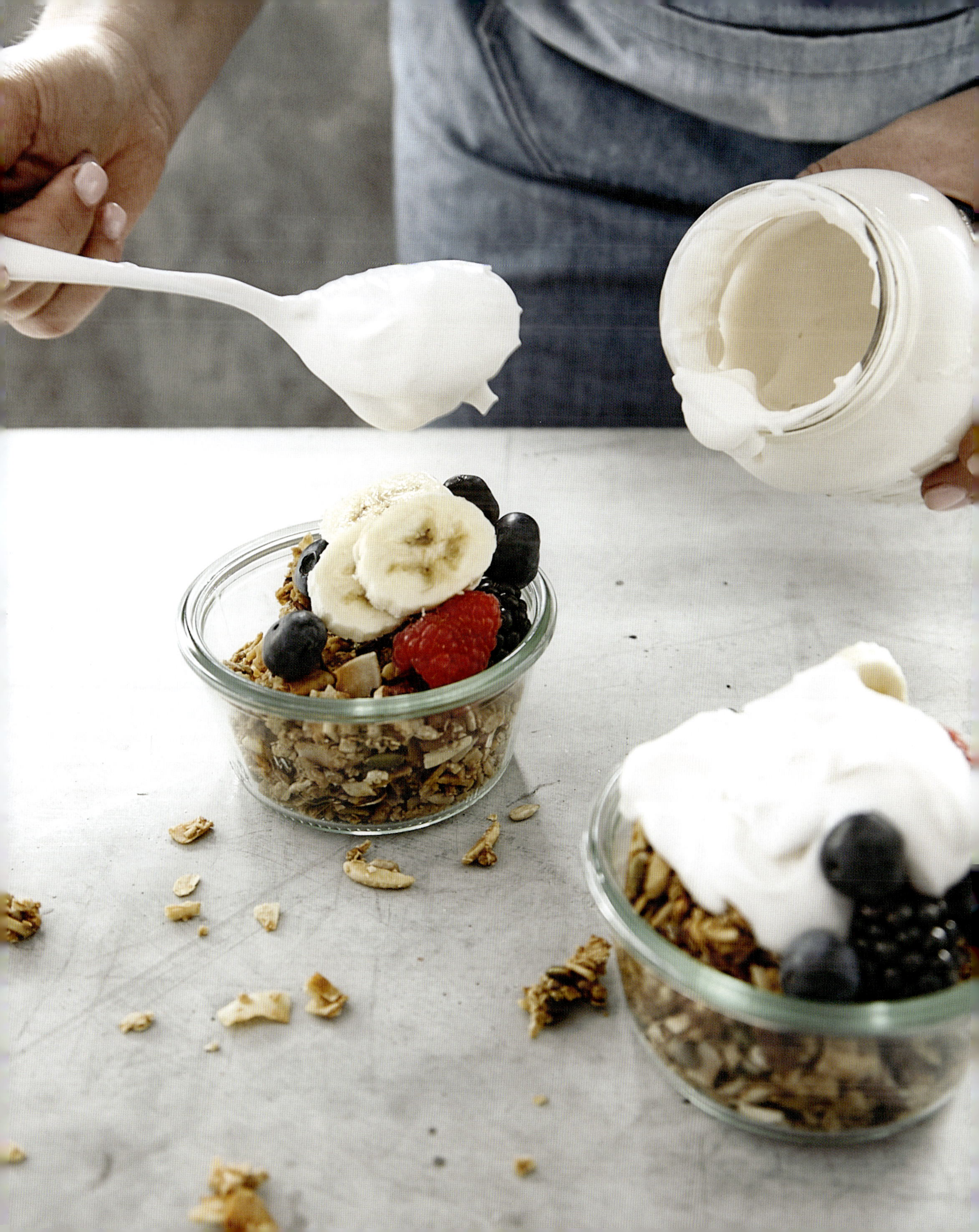

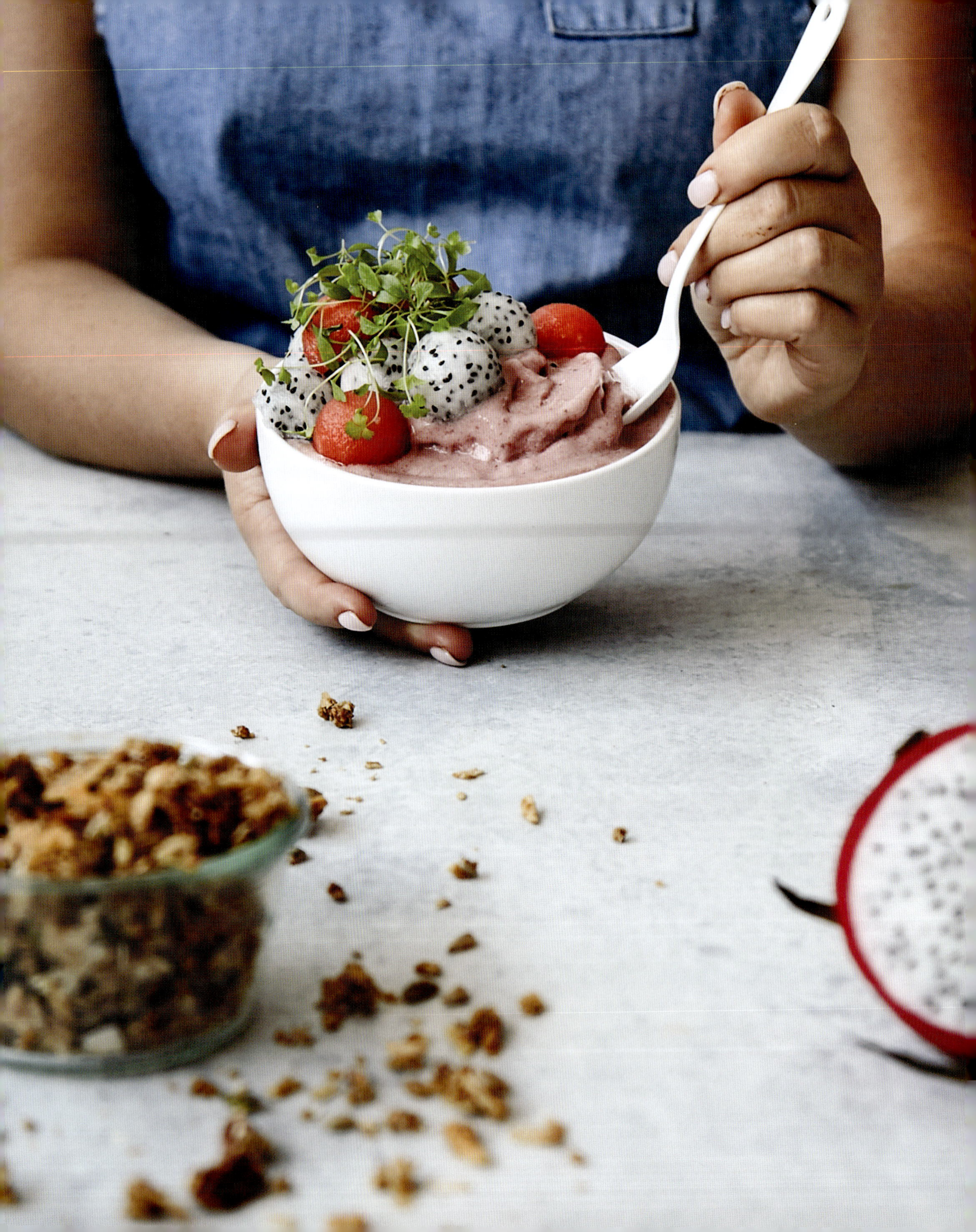

# smoothie bowl

SERVES 2

A delicious way to start the day that really doesn't feel like breakfast at all! I love this recipe, especially in summer, when I feel like a smoothie just isn't going to cut it. While it may be the same ingredients, there is something satisfying about a bowl and spoon. Smaller portions make a great afternoon snack, or even dessert!

400g can coconut cream, chilled (see note)
3 bananas, halved and frozen
100g frozen berries
100g coconut water or plain water
Your choice of toppings (fresh fruit, coconut, nuts and seeds)

1  Insert butterfly into TC bowl. Carefully open coconut cream without shaking. Place the thick coconut cream collected at the top of the can in TC bowl. Whip for 20 seconds, speed 4, or until smooth. Remove butterfly and set whipped coconut cream aside.

2  Without cleaning TC bowl, add bananas, berries, water and the remaining liquid in the coconut can. Purée for 1 minute, speed 9, assisting with spatula. Divide mixture between 2 serving bowls.

Decorate each bowl with whipped coconut cream and toppings and serve immediately.

NOTE: Ensure your coconut cream is high quality and contains only coconut and water, with no emulsifiers or other additives, otherwise you won't be able to separate it. In this event (or to save time), skip step 1 and add the entire can of coconut cream at step 2, omitting the water.

# mexican hollandaise

**MAKES 1 CUP**

It was hollandaise sauce that first had me fall in love with the thermo cooker. I still can't believe that a sauce so renowned for its difficulty can be whipped up in six minutes, absolutely no skill required! I love this Mexican-inspired variation which is punchier than the classic, adding a whole new dimension to Sunday-morning eggs. Invest in a great-quality smoked paprika – it will make all the difference.

120g butter, roughly chopped
2 eggs (see note)
2 egg yolks
½ lime, juice only
50g white balsamic vinegar
¼ teaspoon fine salt
¼ teaspoon smoked paprika, or to taste

1. Insert butterfly into TC bowl. Add all ingredients, cook for 6 minutes, 70°C, speed 4. Allow to stand in TC bowl for 5 minutes before serving.

Serve with toast, grilled asparagus and facon (see page 230), or poached eggs and your favourite fritters. It's particularly good with my crispy kale fritters (see page 15).

NOTE: We've used 2 whole eggs and 2 egg yolks in this recipe to reduce the amount of egg white left over, but you can use 4 egg yolks if preferred. Next time you make a meringue, freeze the leftover egg yolks in a small container or ziplock bag. When you want to make hollandaise, simply defrost them in the fridge before use.

VARIATION: For the classic hollandaise sauce, omit the smoked paprika and use lemon juice instead of lime.

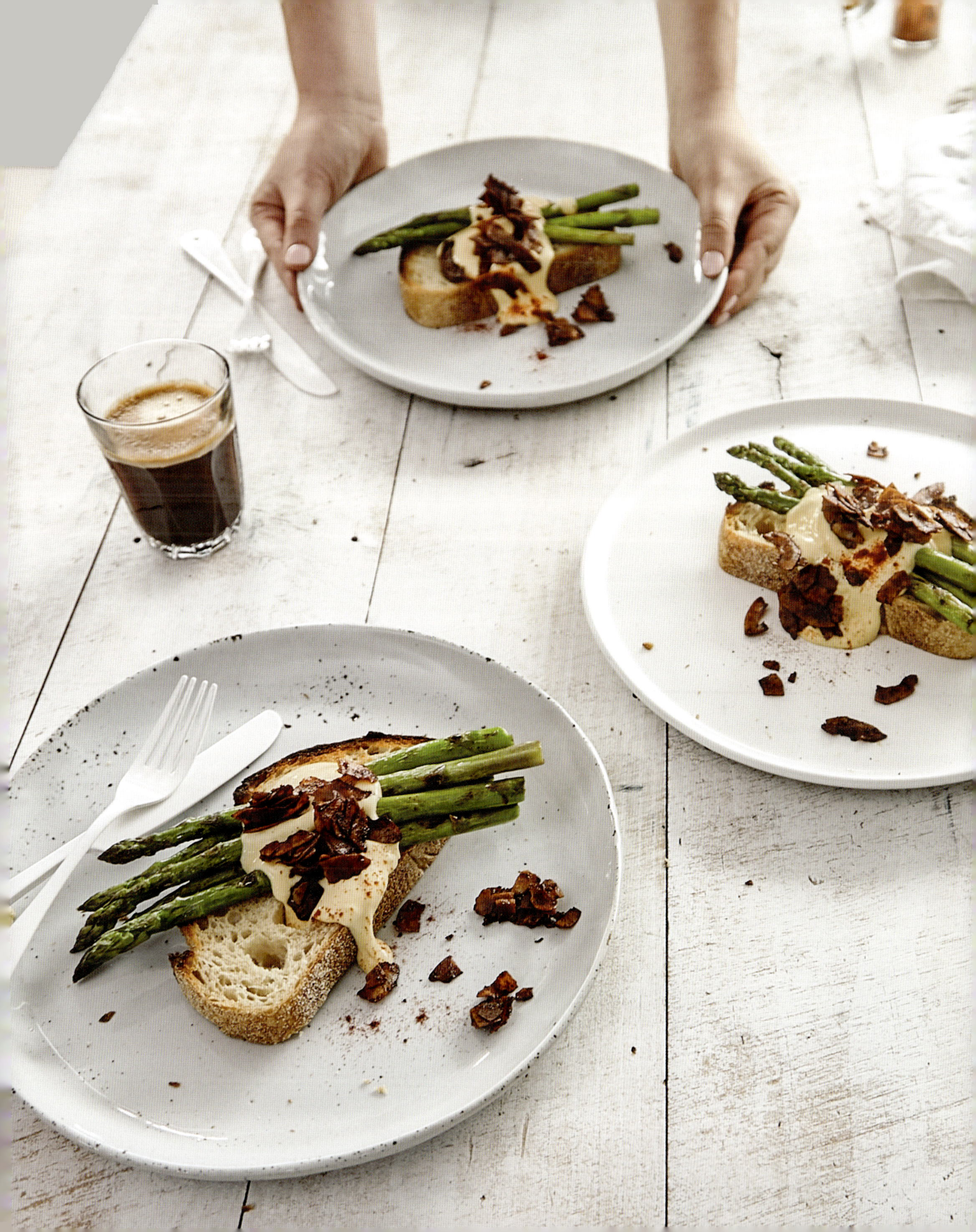

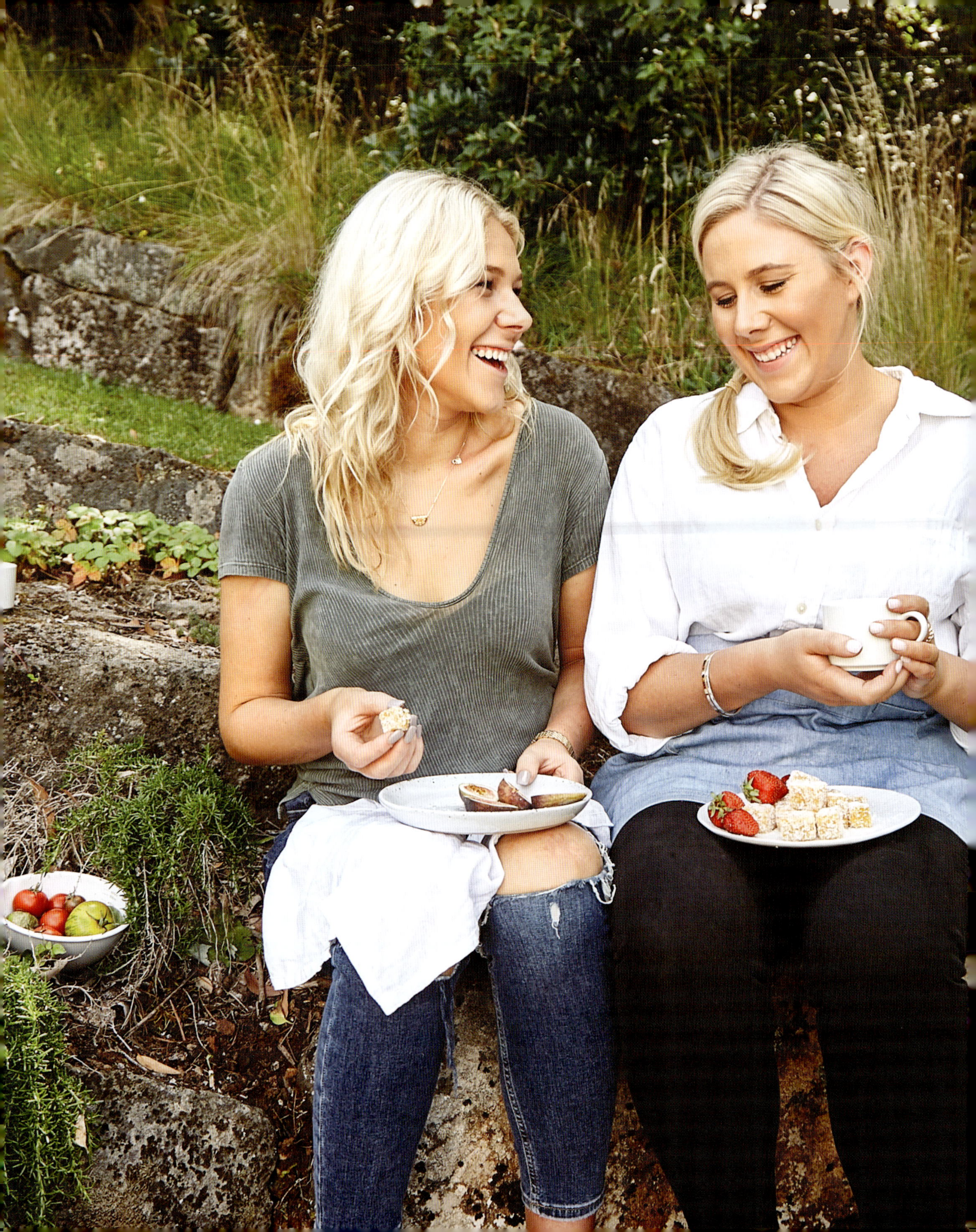

# snacks on

Snacks are often one of the first things people buy ready-made, but there's really no need as they are so easy to make at home! Here are some of my favourite afternoon pick-me-ups, ranging from sweet to savoury, and a couple in between. Some recipes can be whipped up in mere minutes and enjoyed on the spot, while others require a little forward-thinking – make these on the weekend and stock up for the week ahead. Come Friday, you'll be very glad you did!

# chocolate cookie dough balls

**MAKES 10**

Super simple and made with ingredients you're likely to already have in the pantry, this is one snack recipe you'll want in your repertoire. Whip up a batch for the kids' lunchboxes or to cure your afternoon sugar craving… so satisfying you'll be able to avoid reaching for the real chocolate!

150g roasted unsalted cashews
10 medjool dates, pitted
50g cocoa powder
20g pure maple syrup
1 teaspoon vanilla extract
Pinch fine salt

1. Place all ingredients in TC bowl, chop for 15 seconds, speed 9, or until very finely chopped.
2. Squeeze tablespoons of mixture together and roll into balls.

Store in the fridge (or in the freezer if you want to keep them for longer).

VARIATION: For a raw sweet treat, use raw cashews instead of roasted and raw cacao powder instead of cocoa.

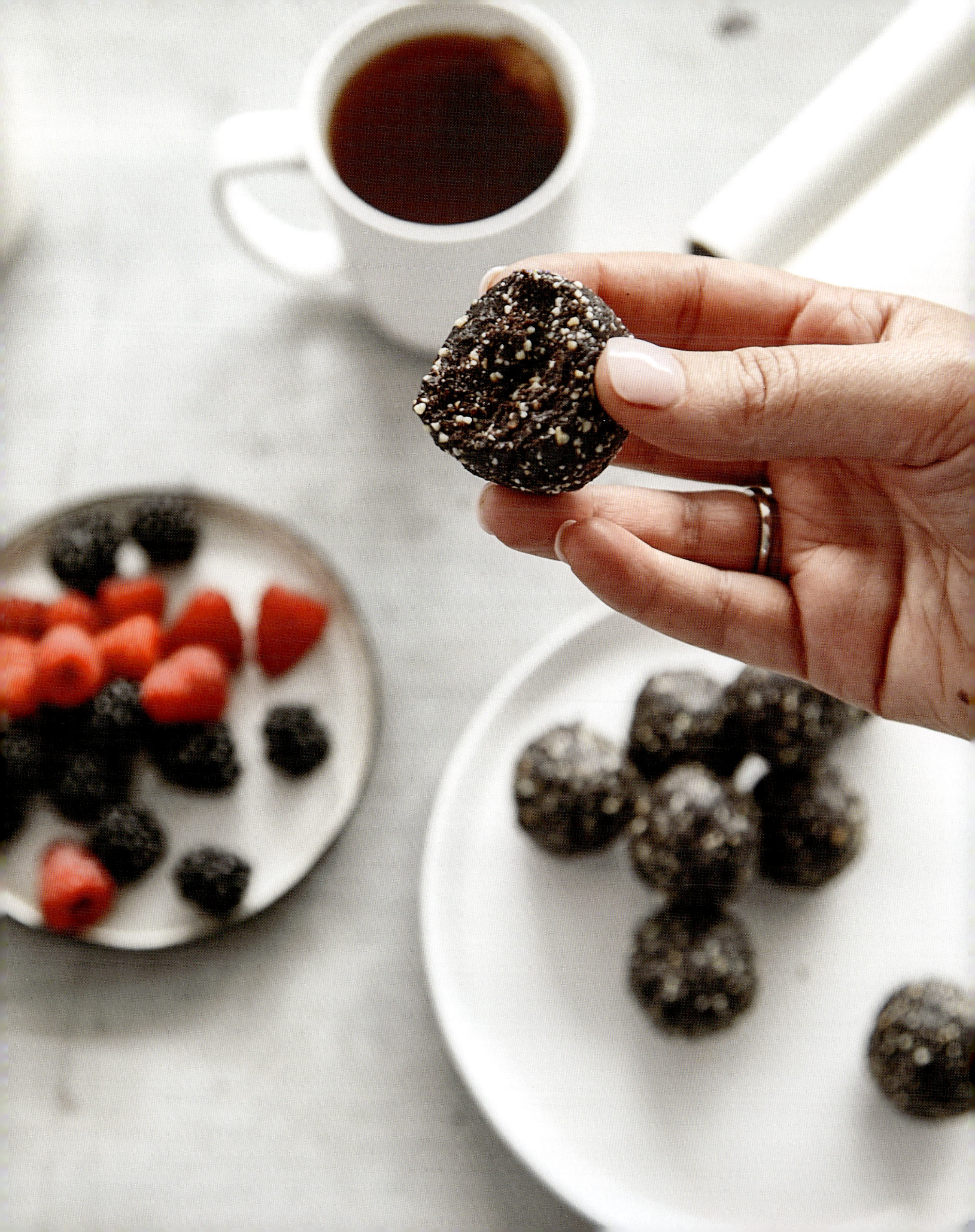

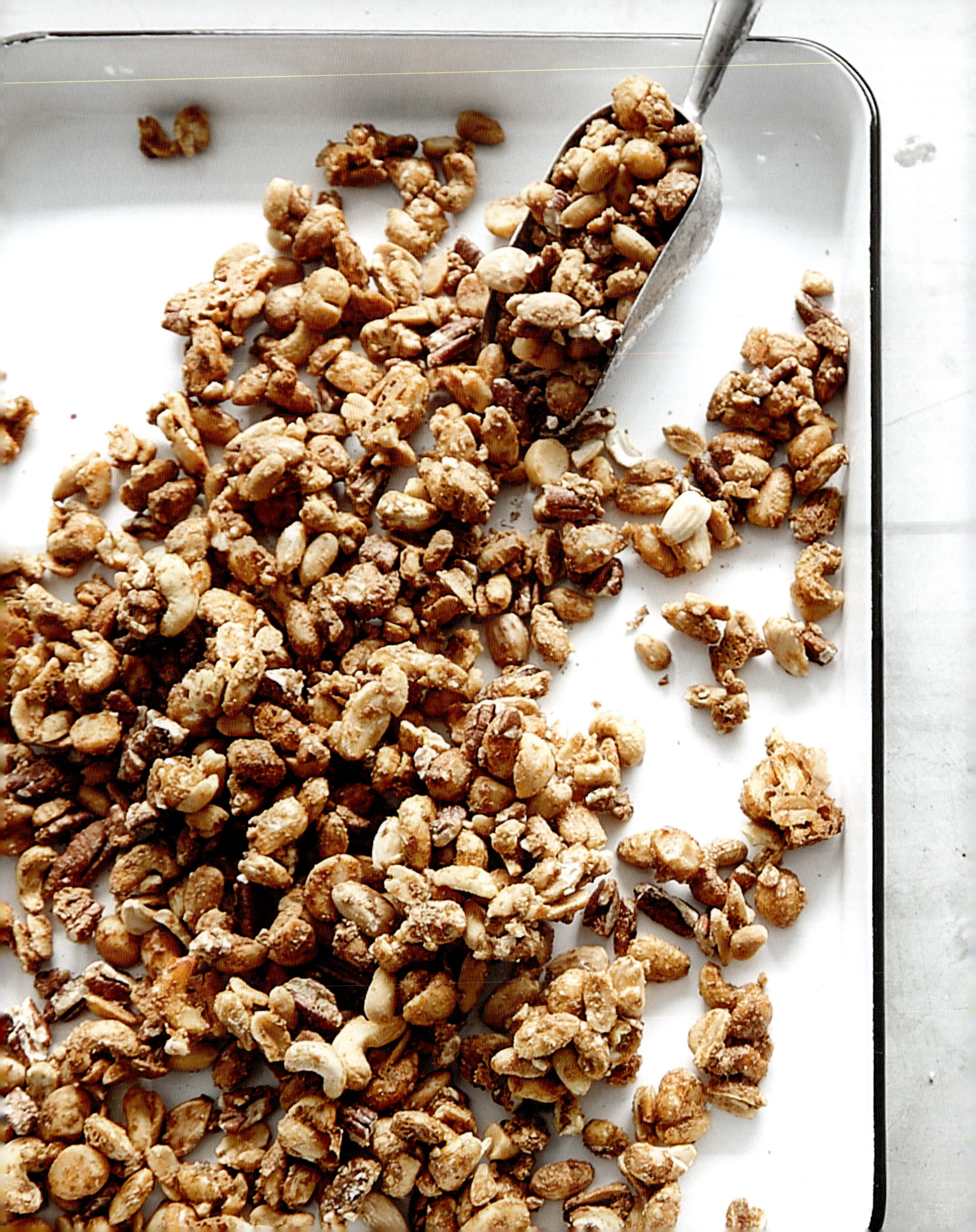

# sweet and spicy nuts

**MAKES 1KG**

These nuts need rationing – they are so addictive! They make the perfect portable snack, being a little sweet, a little salty and a whole lot satisfying.

25g coarse salt
6 sprigs fresh rosemary, leaves only
2 teaspoons garlic powder
2 teaspoons sweet paprika
1 teaspoon cayenne pepper
100g rice malt syrup
20g macadamia oil
1kg mixed raw nuts (such as walnuts, cashews, almonds, brazil nuts, pecans or macadamia nuts)

1. Preheat oven to 160°C. Line 2 baking trays with baking paper or baking mats.
2. Place salt, rosemary, garlic powder, paprika and cayenne pepper in TC bowl, mill for 20 seconds, speed 9.
3. Add rice malt syrup and oil, heat for 2 minutes, 60°C, speed 1.
4. Add nuts, mix for 10 seconds, reverse speed 3, or until all nuts are coated in spices.
5. Spread out nuts in a single layer on the lined trays and toast for 20 minutes, or until golden, stirring occasionally if they are cooking unevenly. Allow nuts to cool completely on trays before transferring to an airtight container for storage.

For prolonged freshness, store in the fridge.

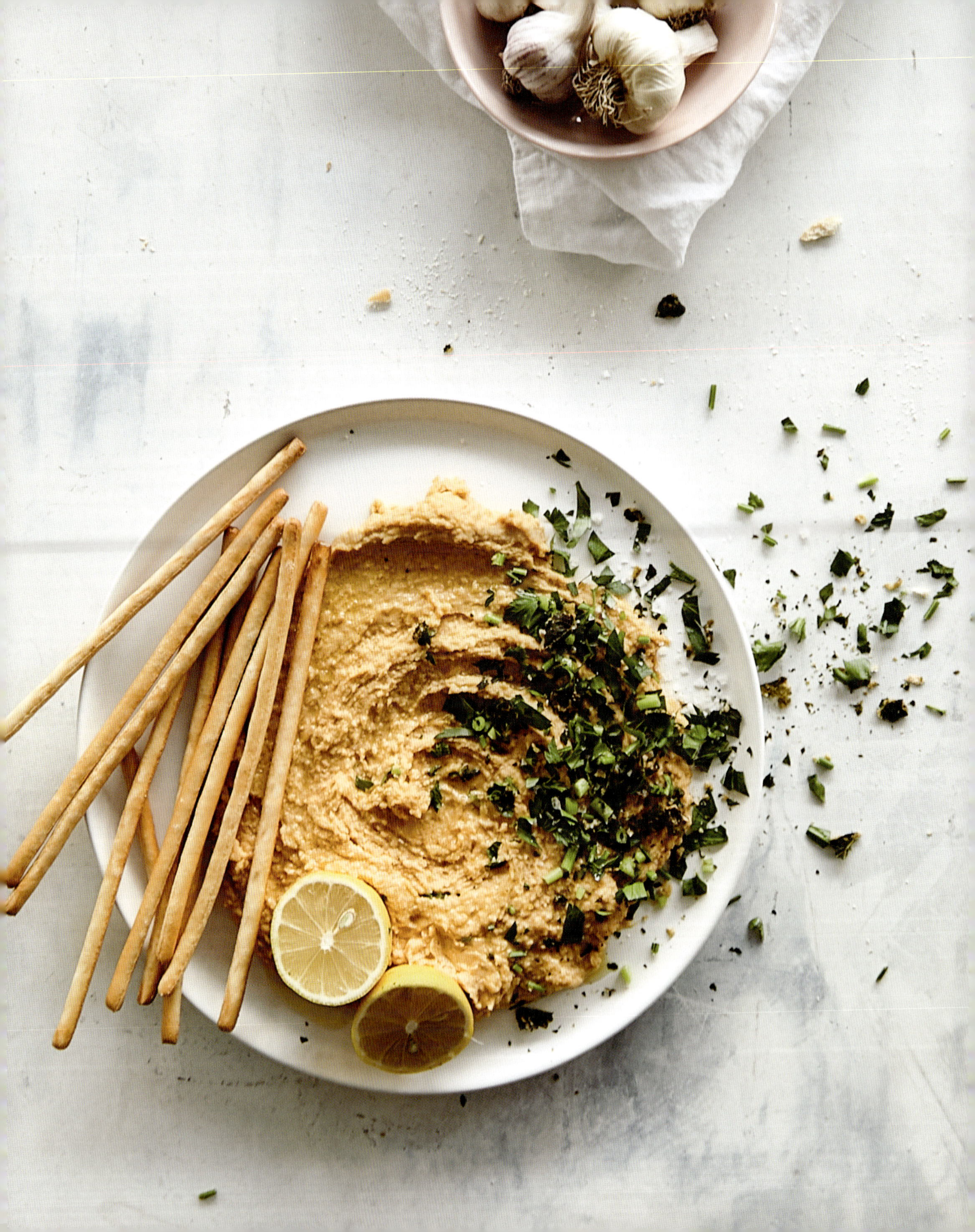

# extra-punchy hummus

**MAKES 1 CUP**

Words cannot express 'hummus' I love this recipe (and a pun)! Hummus gets a bad rap from the flavourless, watery varieties often sold commercially, but when you make it yourself with quality ingredients it is punchy and full of flavour. It's a good thing to make at the start of the week to have on hand – not only is it a healthy dip to snack on, it can be spread on toast for breakfast or sandwiches for lunch and dolloped on any Middle Eastern dish or salad for dinner.

1 garlic clove, peeled
400g can chickpeas, rinsed and drained
1 lemon, juice only
50g tahini
50g olive oil
1 teaspoon fine salt
½ teaspoon ground cumin
½ teaspoon smoked paprika

1. Place garlic in TC bowl, chop for 5 seconds, speed 5.
2. Add chickpeas, lemon juice, tahini, oil, salt, cumin and paprika, chop for 10 seconds, speed 6. Scrape down sides and lid.
3. Mix for a further 1 minute, speed 4, or until combined but still has some texture.

Garnish with fresh parsley, salad seed sprinkles (see page 251) or extra smoked paprika. Serve with crackers, bread or vegetable crudités, flatbread or any Middle Eastern dish.

# apricot delights

+ REFRIGERATION

**MAKES 40**

My whole family has always loved the commercial variety of these, so I decided I had to develop a homemade version. Just between friends, I think mine is better (and certainly healthier!).

250g dried apricots
100g desiccated coconut, plus extra to coat
60g rice malt syrup
1 tablespoon lemon juice
10g white chia seeds

1. Place apricots, 100g coconut, rice malt syrup, lemon juice and chia seeds in TC bowl, chop for 30 seconds, speed 6.

2. Tip mixture out onto a piece of baking paper or a baking mat and form into a block using wet hands. Fold the baking paper or mat up and over apricot mixture and refine shape further. Refrigerate overnight.

3. Remove apricot block from fridge and open baking paper or mat. Cut into 40 little cubes and toss in extra coconut.

Store in an airtight container in the fridge for 2–3 weeks. The squares will continue to firm up over time.

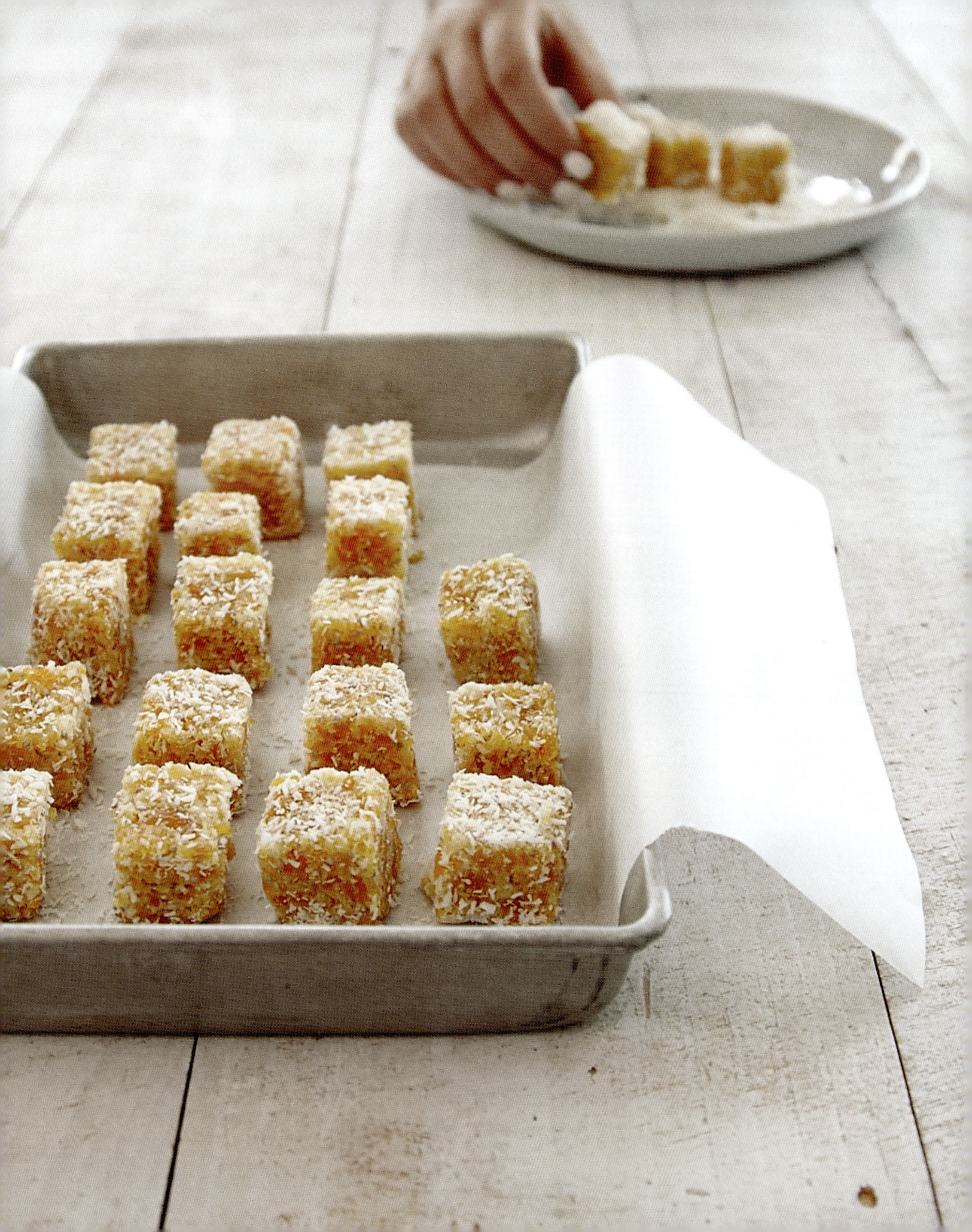

# cheese and vegemite scrolls

**MAKES 12**

Just like a cheese and Vegemite sandwich, only much, much better! Soft, buttery dough layered with melted cheese and the saltiness of Vegemite. So good I've even converted Vegemite sceptics – who could resist one of these beauties still warm from the oven?

600g baker's flour, plus extra for rolling
1½ teaspoons dried yeast
1½ teaspoons fine salt
430g filtered water
Oil, for proving bowl
250g tasty cheese, roughly chopped
100g butter
1 tablespoon Vegemite, or more to taste

1. Place flour, yeast, salt and water in TC bowl, mix for 6 seconds, speed 6.

2. Knead for 2 minutes, dough function. You are looking for a sticky consistency where the dough adheres to the bottom of the TC bowl, but releases from the sides of the bowl. Add more flour if necessary.

3. Turn TC bowl upside down over an oiled bowl, allowing dough to drop out. Using a spatula, tuck the dough under itself to form a ball, turning to coat dough in oil. Cover and position in a warm place for 1–2 hours, or until doubled in size.

4. Once dough has doubled in size, place cheese in clean TC bowl, chop for 5 seconds, speed 8, or until finely grated.

5. Add butter and Vegemite, mix for 1 minute, 37°C, speed 4, or until mixture is whipped and spreadable, scraping down sides if necessary. You don't want the mixture melted.

6. Lightly flour bench or baking mat. Roll dough into a rough 50×30cm rectangle, sprinkling flour if dough is sticky. Spread Vegemite cheese mixture evenly on top.

7. Starting at the long length of the dough furthest from you, tightly roll the dough towards you, finishing seam side down. Cut into 12 portions, work each into a round shape and arrange in a roasting tin lined with baking paper or a baking mat, allowing 3cm between each scroll. Cover loosely with a tea towel and set aside in a warm place for 30–60 minutes, or until scrolls are almost touching.

8. Preheat oven to 180°C.

9. Bake scrolls for 25 minutes, or until golden.

Allow to cool in the tin for 10 minutes, then serve warm. These are best eaten on the day of baking, although leftovers can be warmed through in a moderate oven and enjoyed the next day.

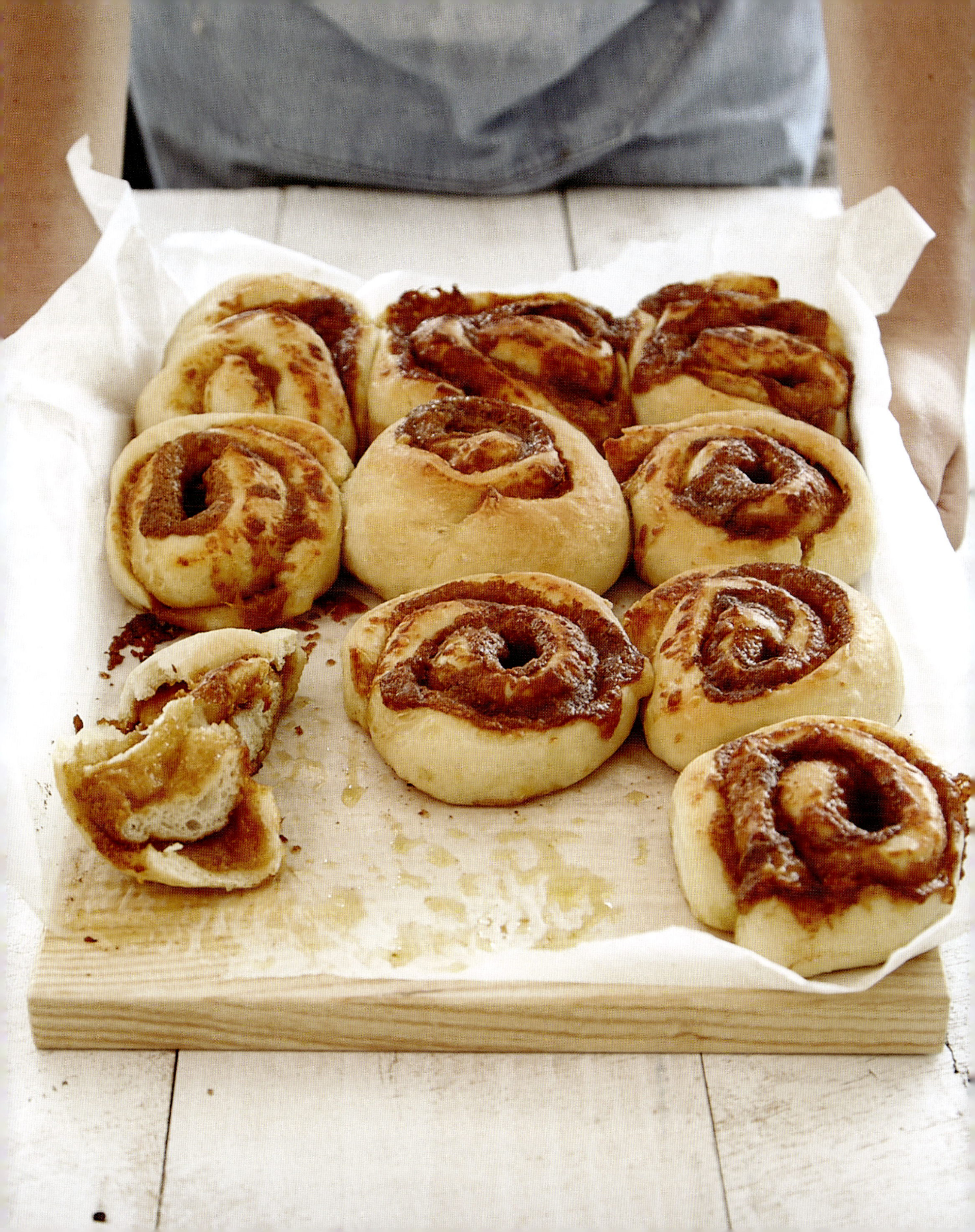

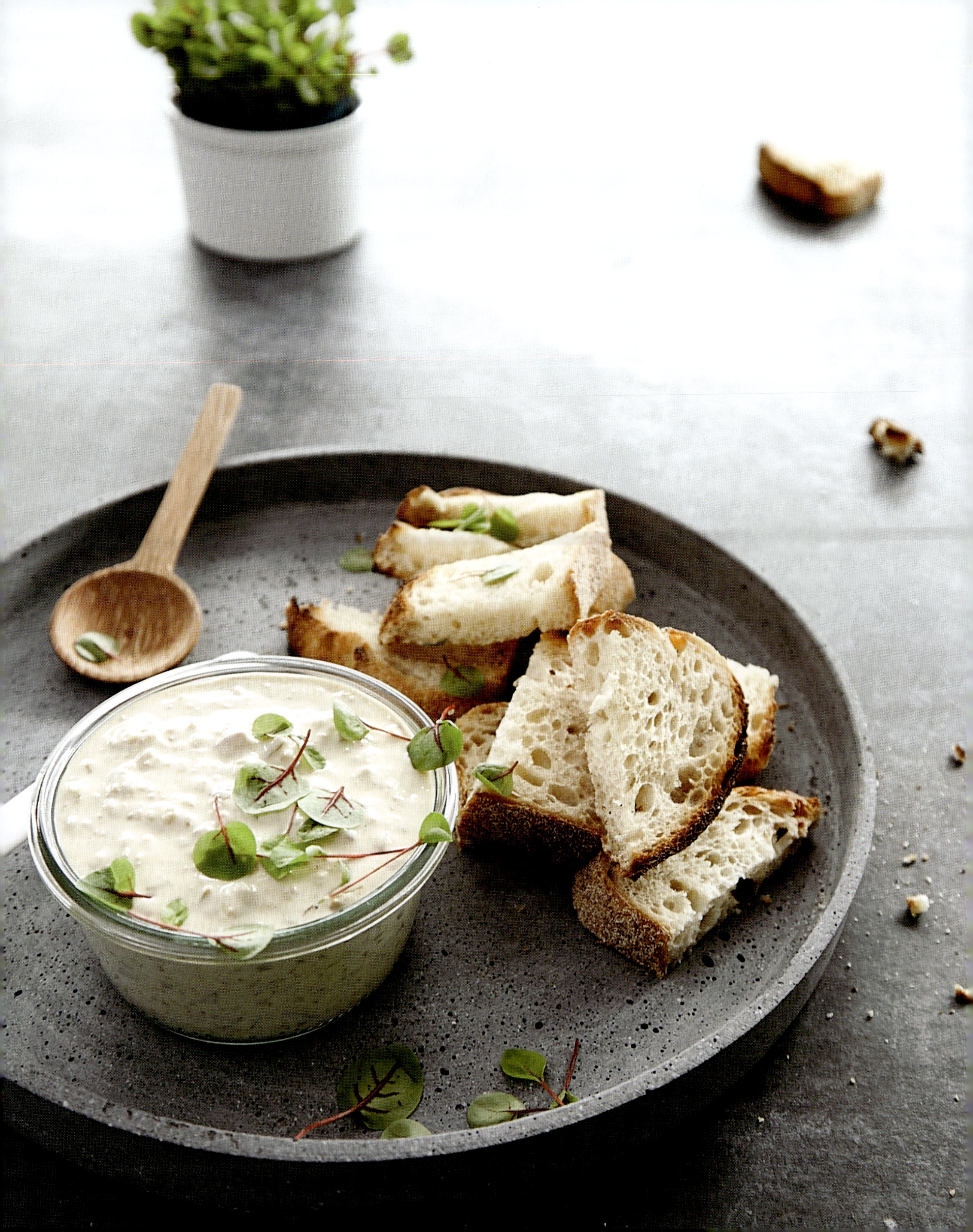

# green olive dip

**MAKES 2 CUPS**

My favourite childhood dip was zesty olives stirred through a creamy mayonnaise base and I just had to recreate it. It's just like the supermarket versions, only with better flavours (and ingredients!).

150g grapeseed oil
50g olive oil
250g green olives, pitted and drained
1 egg yolk
30g apple cider vinegar
50g Dijon mustard
1 teaspoon fine salt
1 teaspoon onion powder
1 teaspoon garlic powder

1. Weigh grapeseed and olive oils into a small jug. Set aside.

2. Place olives in TC bowl, chop for 2 seconds, speed 6, or until finely chopped. Set aside.

3. Without cleaning bowl, add egg yolk, vinegar, mustard, salt, onion powder and garlic powder, mix for 10 seconds, speed 4.

4. With blade continuing to run on speed 4, slowly drizzle the oils over the TC lid. Continue to mix for 2 minutes, speed 4, until thickened.

5. Add olives, mix for 10 seconds, reverse speed 3. Refrigerate until ready to serve.

Serve with bread, crackers or vegetable crudités, spread on sandwiches or toast, or enjoy as an accompaniment to grilled lamb.

NOTE: To ensure the dip has a good thick texture, make sure you drain the olives well before chopping. It will also continue to thicken as it chills.

# cranberry and hazelnut crackers

**SERVES 6**

To me, these are the perfect crackers – crunchy, a little sweet and a little salty. I first tasted a similar combination in San Francisco and as soon as I got home, I headed straight to the kitchen to recreate it. They are particularly good served with a soft cheese such as goat's feta or brie, but really, they are so delicious you can just as easily enjoy them on their own.

50g roasted hazelnuts
200g plain flour
1 teaspoon baking powder
35g olive oil
1½ teaspoons fine salt
20g pumpkin seeds
10g sesame seeds
10g flaxseeds
30g brown sugar
60g dried cranberries
100g water

1. Place hazelnuts in TC bowl, mill for 1 second, speed 6.
2. Add all remaining ingredients, mix for 2 seconds, speed 5.
3. Knead for 1½ minutes, dough function, or until dough is formed.
4. Wrap dough in cling wrap or a baking mat and refrigerate for a minimum of 1 hour or freeze for 15 minutes.
5. Preheat oven to 220°C.
6. Divide dough in half. Place half the dough between 2 sheets of baking paper or baking mats and, using a rolling pin, roll out to approximately 3mm thick. Try to maintain an even thickness across the dough, being careful not to roll it thinner at the edges. Remove top piece of baking paper or mat and place dough (on remaining baking paper or mat) on a baking tray. Repeat with remaining mixture and place on second baking tray.
7. Bake for 10–12 minutes, or until golden. Transfer to a chopping board and, while still warm, use a large knife to cut into rough wedges. Allow to cool completely.

Serve as they are or with cheese and/or dips. Store in an airtight container for up to 2 weeks.

NOTE: It is essential to roll out the dough very thinly before baking to get a crunchy cracker; remember it will rise slightly when cooked.

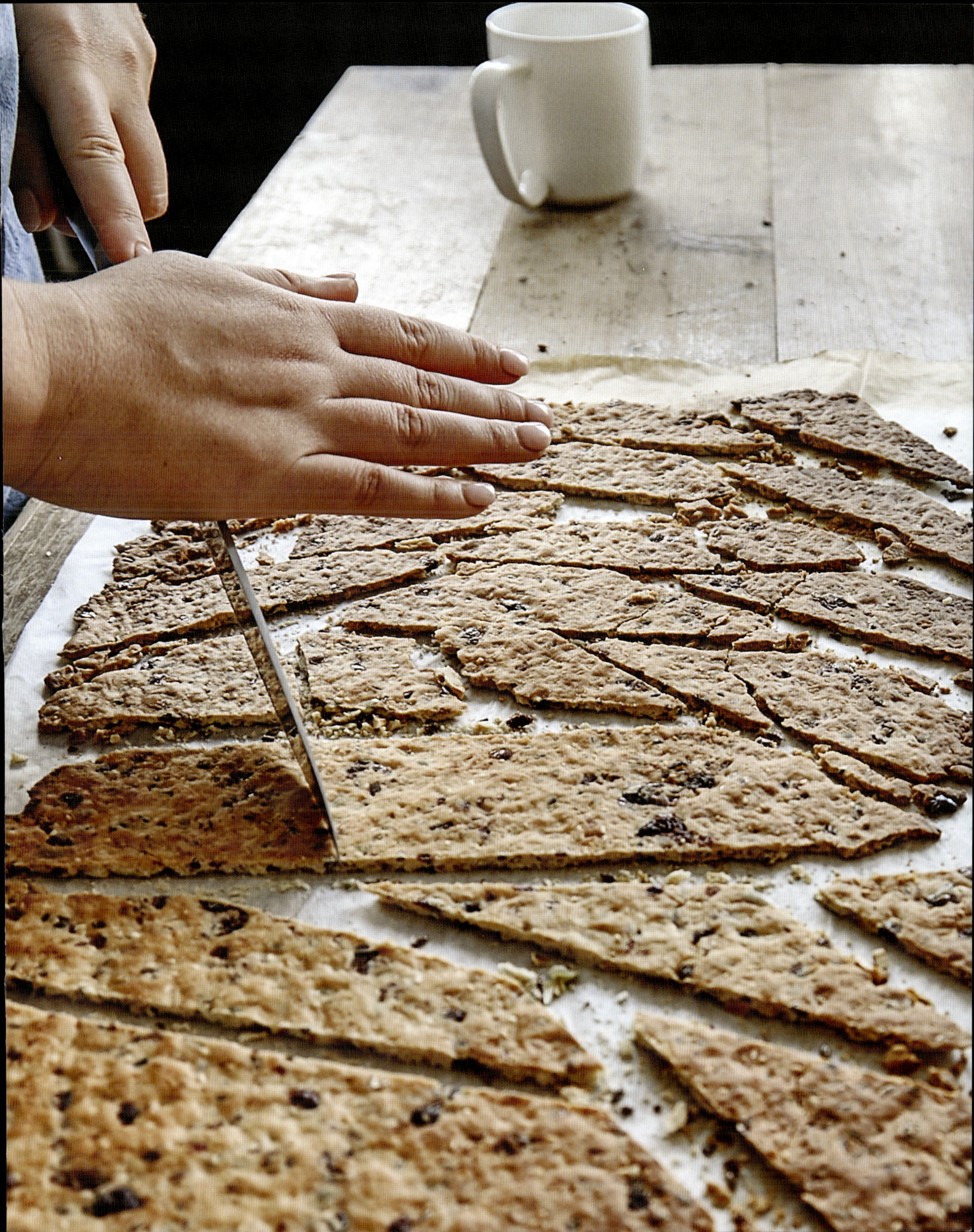

# lavender coffee tonic

+ REFRIGERATION

SERVES 4

A surprising combination, but one that the AA team swears by – especially on photoshoot days! Bubbly and refreshing with sweet, floral flavours and a welcome little hit of caffeine, it's the perfect afternoon pick-me-up.

40g coffee beans
2 tablespoons dried lavender flowers
60g raw sugar
400g water
Ice
Soda water, to serve

1. Place coffee beans, lavender and sugar in TC bowl, mill for 10 seconds, speed 10.

2. Add water, heat for 5 minutes, 70°C, speed 2. Allow to stand in TC for minimum 10 minutes, before straining through a fine sieve or coffee filter. Refrigerate until cold.

To serve, fill 4 glasses with ice. Divide coffee syrup evenly among glasses and top with soda water.

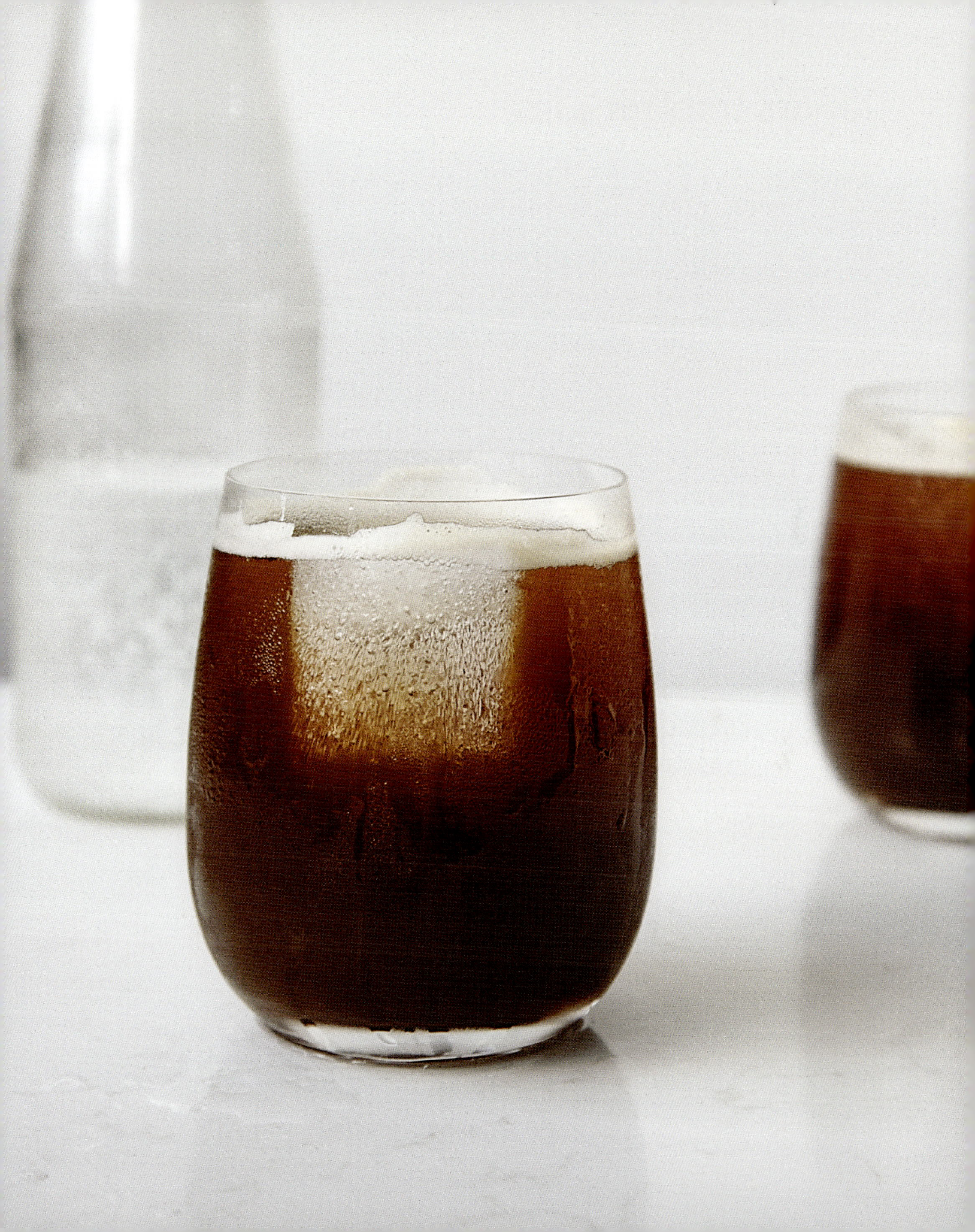

# loryn's tropical 'juice'

SERVES 3

My sister Loryn created this recipe years ago, and boy are we glad she did! Since then it's been a summer favourite, deliciously sweet and refreshing but still retaining all the fibre and goodness by using the whole fruit. The pineapple offers tropical sweetness, the watermelon gives juiciness and the banana makes it smooth and creamy – the perfect combination. We never measure the ingredients and it always turns out perfectly, so don't worry too much about the weights.

1½ bananas, halved and frozen (approx. 150g)
½ pineapple, roughly chopped (approx. 300g)
⅛ watermelon, roughly chopped (approx. 600g)
1 lime, juice only (optional)

1  Place all ingredients in TC bowl, blend for 1 minute, speed 9.

Pour into tall glasses and enjoy. Can be refrigerated for up to 2 days, then simply shake or stir before serving.

NOTE: For a chilled drink, refrigerate the pineapple and watermelon before blending.

VARIATION: For a creamier smoothie, add a frozen mango or frozen strawberries. For an extra dose of goodness, add baby spinach, fresh mint or cucumber.

SNACKS ON

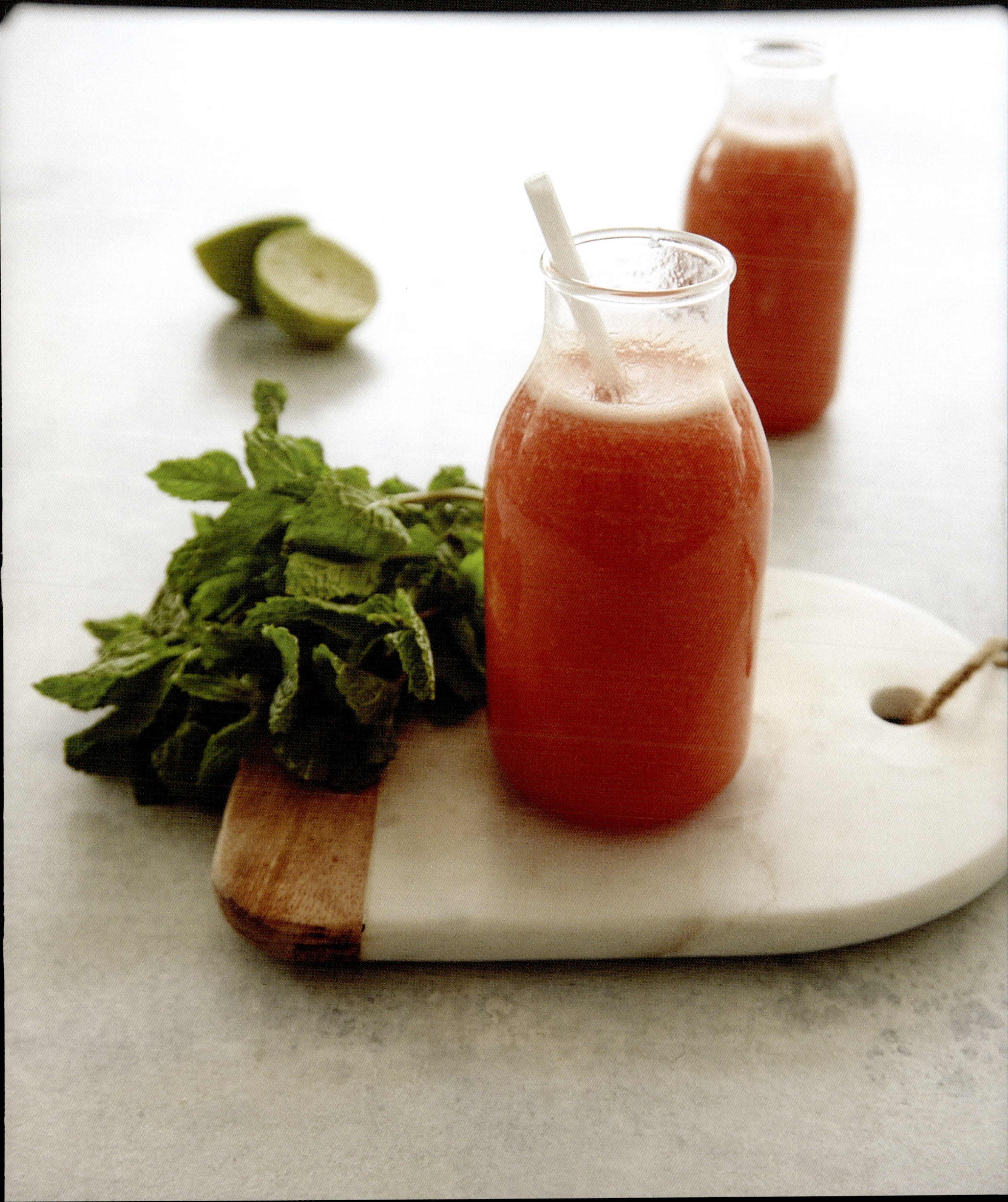

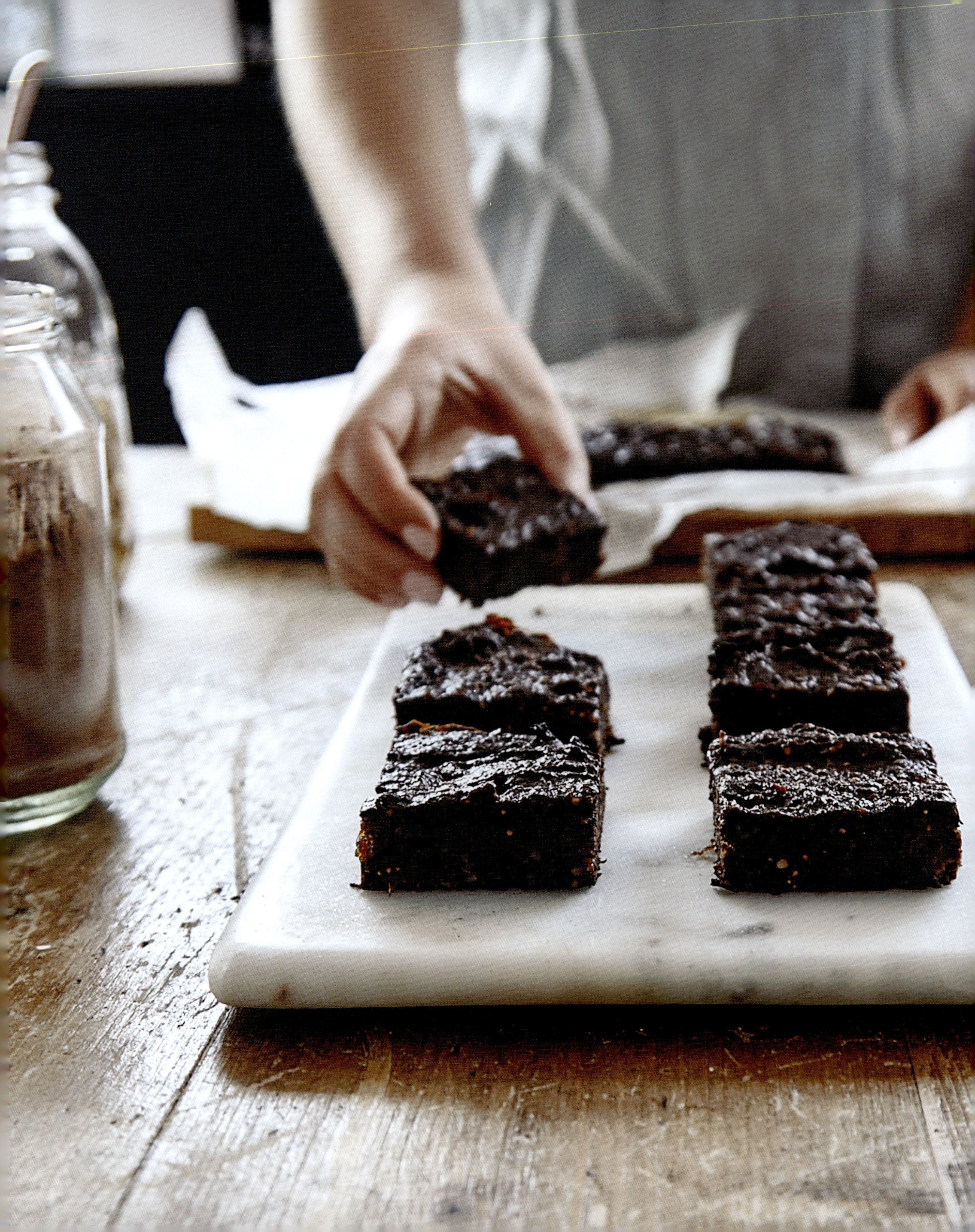

# fudgy chocolate fig slice

+ BAKING

**SERVES 16**

Ironically, this slice has no chocolate in it at all! And no refined sugar, dairy or gluten. It is simply fruit and nuts blended together with cocoa to create a rich chocolate-y treat. A slice of this and a cup of tea and I am completely set for the afternoon.

8 dried figs, halved and stems removed
250g raw cashews
200g dates, pitted
3 very ripe bananas, halved
60g macadamia oil
40g cocoa powder
2 teaspoons vanilla extract

1. Preheat oven to 160°C. Line a 24cm square cake tin with baking paper.

2. Place figs in TC bowl, chop for 3 seconds, speed 8, or until finely chopped. Set aside.

3. Without cleaning TC bowl, add cashews, dates, bananas, oil, cocoa and vanilla, purée for 45 seconds, speed 9, assisting with spatula if necessary, until almost smooth.

4. Add chopped figs, mix for 5 seconds, reverse speed 4. Transfer mixture to lined tin and spread out evenly.

5. Bake for 40 minutes. Allow to cool in tin for 30 minutes before removing and slicing.

Store in an airtight container in the fridge for up to a week.

VARIATION: I prefer macadamia oil in this recipe as it gives a subtle buttery flavour, but you can use any oil you like, including coconut or olive.

# creamy tomato and basil spread

**MAKES 1 CUP**

Super simple and full of flavour, this spread makes a fresh addition to any sandwich. It also doubles as a delicious dip for vegetable crudités and crackers. While my pick is basil, feel free to try it with any of your favourite fresh herbs.

Handful fresh basil
150g cream cheese, roughly chopped
150g semi-dried tomatoes in oil
20g olive oil
Salt, to taste

1. Place basil in TC bowl, chop for 2 seconds, speed 5.

2. Add remaining ingredients, chop for 5 seconds, speed 5. Scrape down sides.

3. Mix for a further 30 seconds, speed 4, or until smooth and creamy. Refrigerate until ready to serve.

Spread thickly on bread as a base for sandwiches, top with your favourite salad ingredients, avocado, deli meats or smoked salmon.

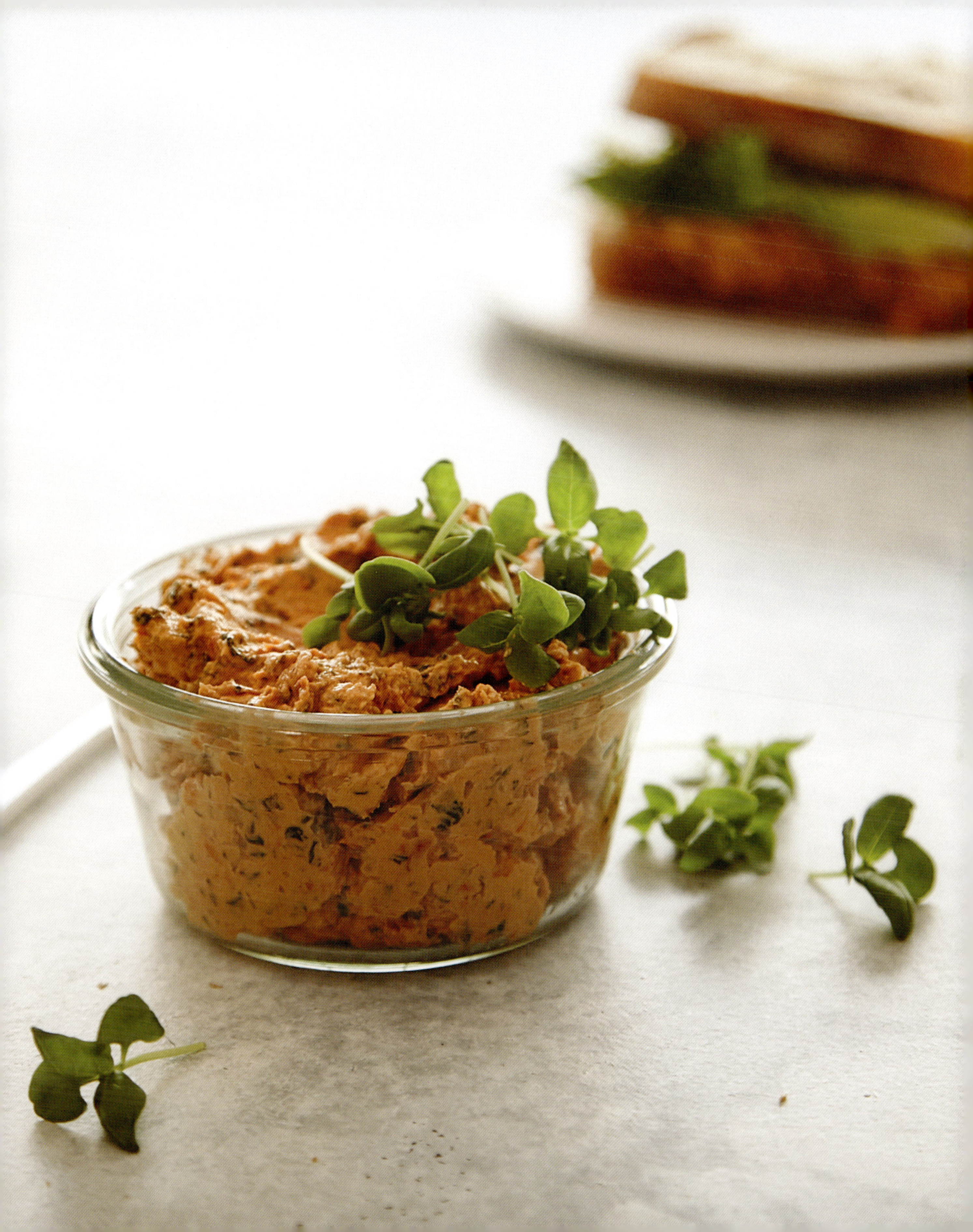

# savoury summer tart

**SERVES 8**

To me, this tart embodies summer. Fresh flavours, produce at its finest, all beautifully presented and ready for enjoying in the sunshine. The recipe is deceptively simple, allowing the quality of the ingredients to shine. If you can, choose a variety of heirloom tomatoes in different shapes, sizes and colours; these will not only add visual interest but also a diverse range of flavours and textures with pops of sweet and sour. Buy your ricotta fresh from the deli and use it as quickly as possible, or, even better, make your own (see page 160).

170g butter, roughly chopped
130g cream cheese, roughly chopped
300g plain flour
2 teaspoons fine salt
¼ teaspoon baking powder
1 lemon, rind only
Handful fresh basil
300g fresh ricotta
80g crème fraîche
500g heirloom tomatoes, roughly chopped
Olive oil, to serve
Thin honey, to serve (optional)
Micro basil, to serve

1. Preheat oven to 200°C.
2. Place butter in TC bowl, melt for 3 minutes, 50°C, speed 2.
3. Add cream cheese, mix for 5 seconds, speed 5. Scrape down sides.
4. Add flour, 1 teaspoon salt and baking powder, mix for 10 seconds, speed 3. Scrape down sides.
5. Mix for a further 10 seconds, dough function, or until mixture no longer looks floury but rather crumbly.
6. Push pastry firmly into the base and up the sides of a 36×12cm loose-bottom tart tin. Prick base all over with a fork.
7. Bake tart shell for 20–25 minutes, or until pastry is golden.
8. Allow pastry to cool for a minimum of 15 minutes before removing from tin and placing on serving board.
9. Meanwhile, in a clean TC bowl place remaining 1 teaspoon salt and lemon rind. Mill for 10 seconds, speed 8. Scrape down sides.
10. Add basil, chop for 2 seconds, speed 8. Scrape down sides.
11. Add ricotta and crème fraîche, mix for 8 seconds, speed 3, or until just combined. Spread mixture into pastry case and top with tomatoes, pressing lightly into ricotta mixture. Drizzle with olive oil and honey (if using) and scatter with micro basil.

Serve immediately or refrigerate for up to 4 hours.

NOTE: You can bake the tart shell and whip the ricotta mixture up to 3 days in advance. Store the tart shell at room temperature and the ricotta mixture in the fridge. Chop the tomatoes and assemble the tart shortly before serving.

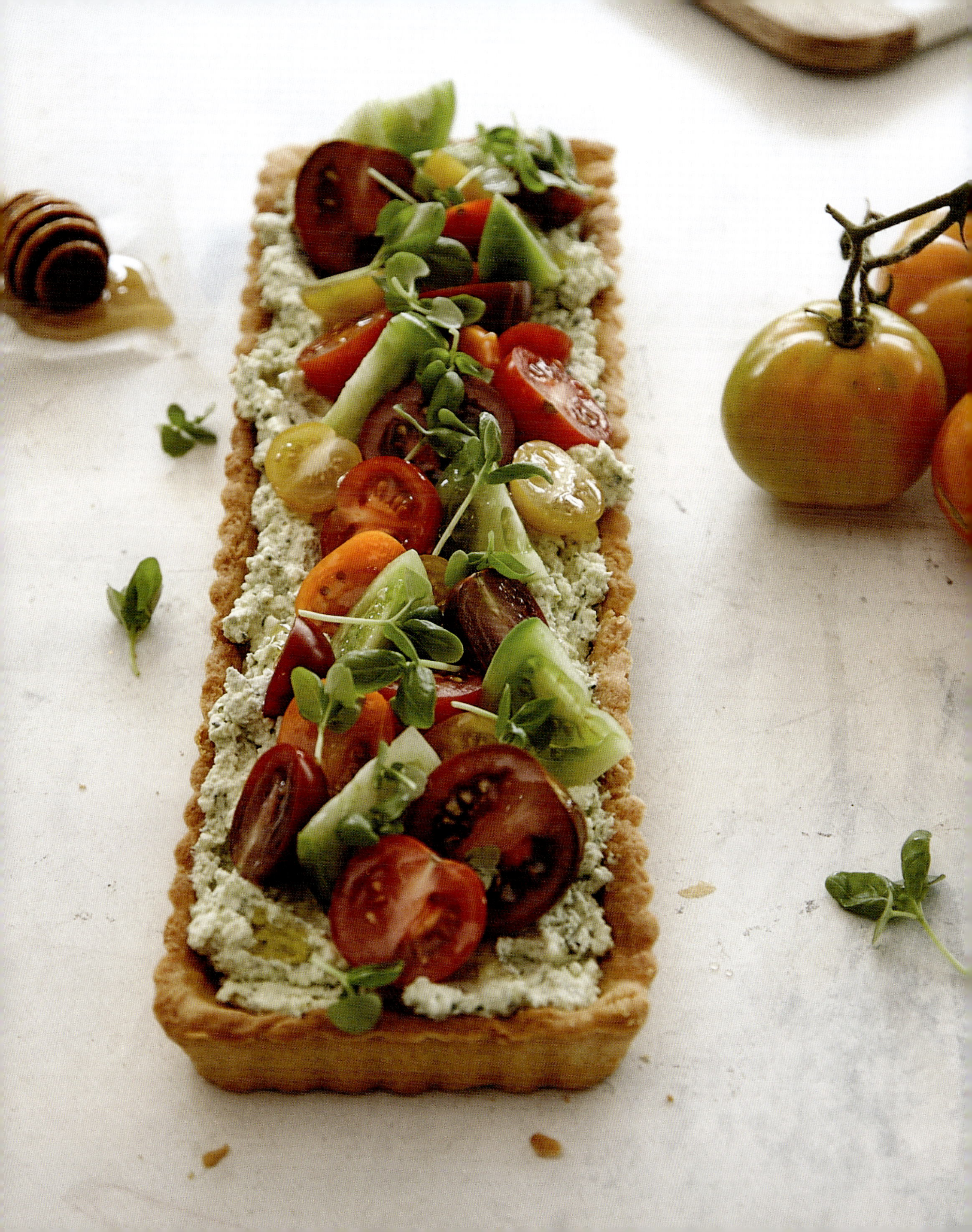

# chilli soy oysters

**MAKES 48**

I first made this dish for my dad's birthday party, as it's a combination of some of his favourite flavours – spicy chilli, tangy vinegar and salty tamari; however, it turns out that this is a lot of people's favourite way to eat oysters! The punchy flavours balance well with the creamy oysters, making them agreeable even to oyster sceptics. Oysters are one of my favourite seafood options as their farming has very little impact on the ocean and environment. They are also incredibly high in iron, higher gram for gram than red meat, making them a healthy inclusion for women in particular.

2 red Asian shallots, peeled
1 long red chilli
2 teaspoons white sugar
100g rice wine vinegar
25g tamari
48 freshly shucked oysters

1. Place shallots, chilli and sugar in TC bowl, chop for 3 seconds, speed 8.
2. Add vinegar and tamari, mix for 3 seconds, speed 3.

Fill each oyster with a spoonful of dressing and serve.

NOTE: The sauce will keep for a month in the fridge, so there's no need to serve all 48 oysters at once!

VARIATION: Tamari can be replaced with soy sauce, but please note that the recipe will no longer be gluten free.

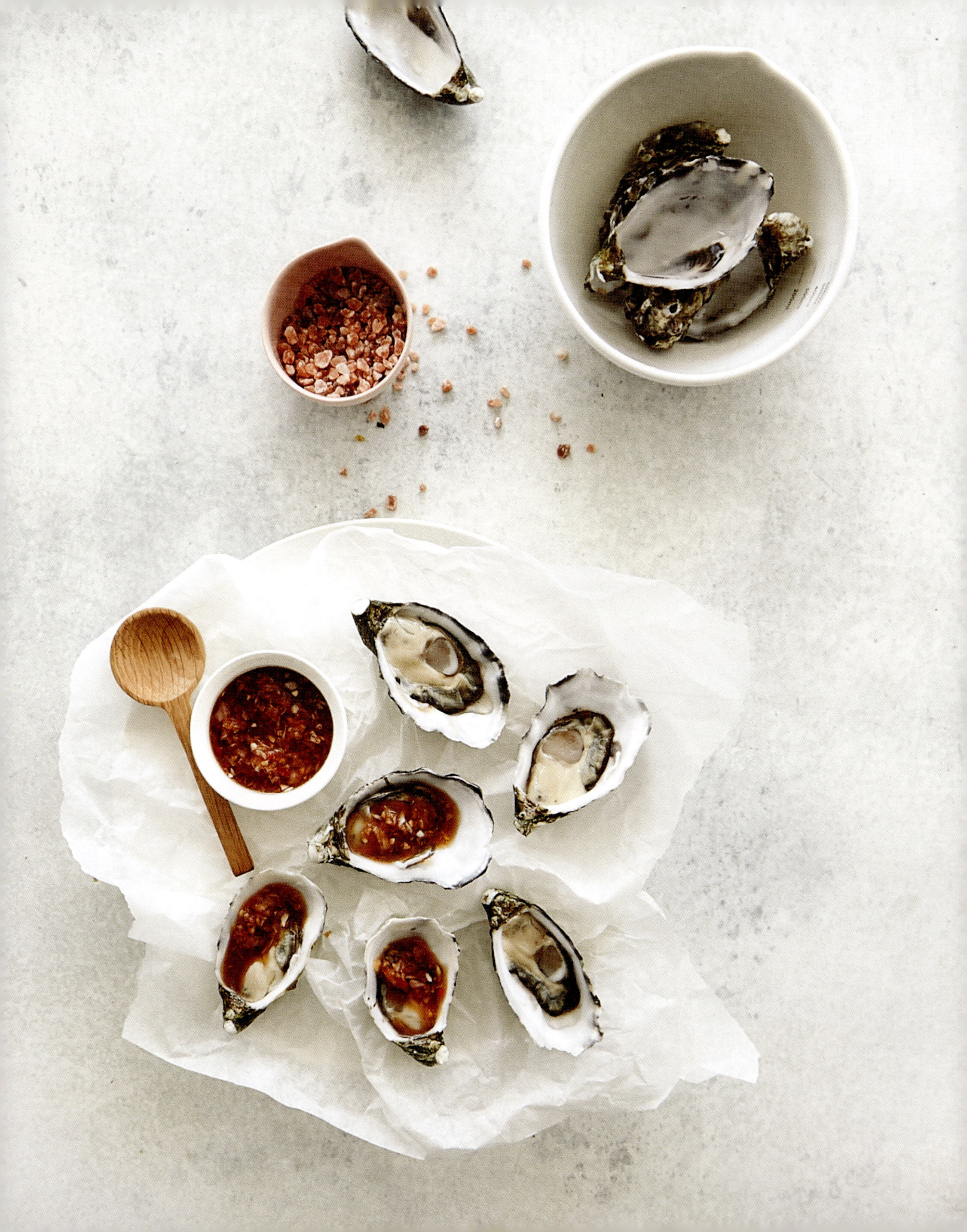

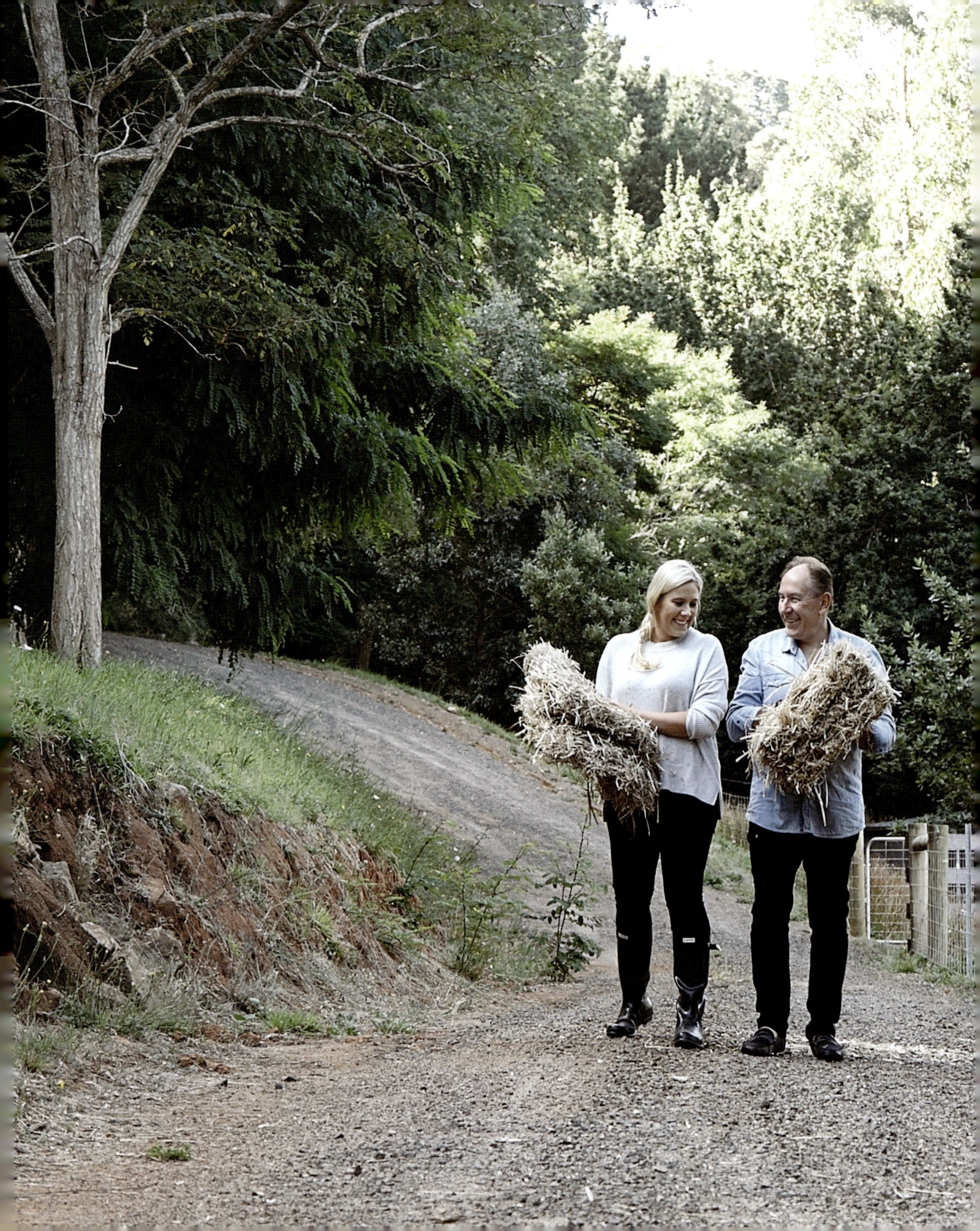

# quick fix meals

Life is busy, and sometimes it feels like a juggling act trying to fit everything in. Which is why most of my meals, especially during the week, are 'quick fix', meaning I can get them on the table in under 30 minutes – less time than it would take to get takeaway! No jars of pasta sauce, cans of soup or microwave required, and no ridiculous clean up either. Just quality ingredients, brought together by the magic of the thermo cooker. Some recipes are best served immediately, making them ideal for dinner, while others are great packed into lunchboxes and served cold. To me, this is having your cake and eating it too – enjoying home-cooked meals, but also having time for all the other important things in life.

# korean rice bowl

**SERVES 4**

It looks like a stir-fry, it tastes like a stir-fry, but it's a whole lot easier and a lot less mess! The entire dish is steamed, making it fresh and light. It's also super speedy to make; if you start with boiling water you can have this delicious meal on the table in less than 20 minutes.

3 garlic cloves, peeled
3cm piece ginger, peeled
1 long red chilli, halved (optional)
30g toasted sesame oil
400g beef rump steak, thinly sliced
80g dark soy sauce
800g boiling water
300g medium-grain white rice
2 carrots, cut into matchsticks
200g snow peas, ends trimmed
1 red capsicum, thinly sliced
kimchi-kraut (see page 236) or kimchi, to serve
Sesame seeds, to serve

1. Place garlic, ginger and chilli in TC bowl, chop for 5 seconds, speed 5. Scrape down sides.

2. Add oil, sauté for 5 minutes, 100°C, speed 1.

3. Add beef and soy sauce, mix for 1 minute, 100°C, reverse speed 1. Transfer to a bowl.

4. Without cleaning TC bowl, add 800g boiling water. Place rice in steamer basket and rinse under running water. Insert in TC bowl. Place steaming tray on top and fill with marinated beef – some of the marinade will drip down onto the rice. Steam for 6 minutes, steaming temperature, speed 3.

5. Add carrot, snow peas and capsicum to steaming tray and combine with beef using tongs. Steam for a further 5 minutes, steaming temperature, speed 3.

6. Check rice, beef and vegetables are cooked. If not, steam for a further 2 minutes, steaming temperature, speed 3.

To serve, divide rice, beef and vegetables among 4 bowls. Top with kimchi-kraut or kimchi and sprinkle with sesame seeds.

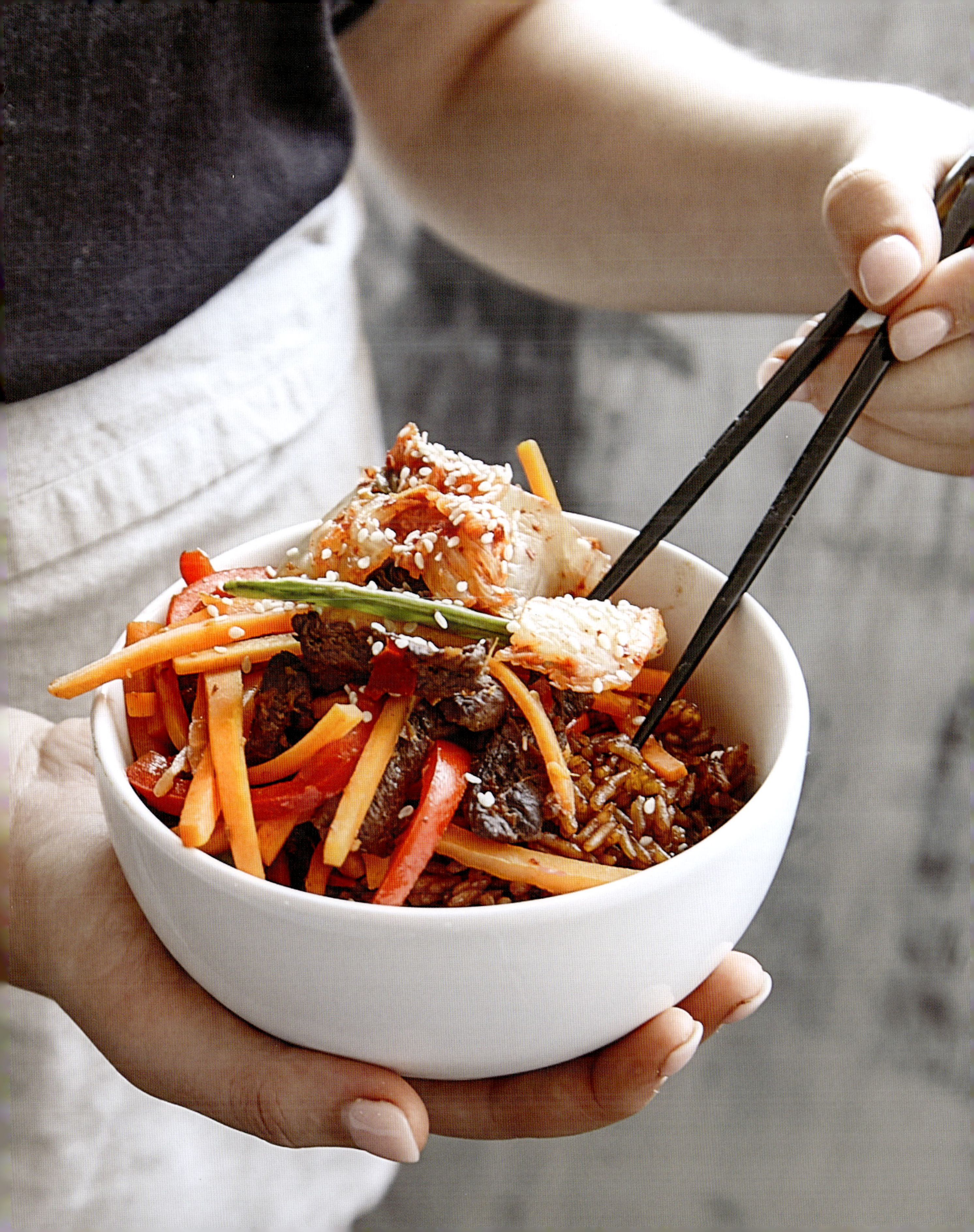

# vietnamese trout salad

SERVES 3

This fresh salad has it all: vibrant herbs, crunchy vegetables, delicate flakes of trout and a beautiful sweet/sour/spicy dressing to bring it all together. It's the ultimate light summer meal, and to top it all off you can have it in a bowl and ready to eat in 10 minutes!

1 long red chilli, halved
2 garlic cloves, peeled
20g toasted sesame oil
40g coconut sugar
50g rice wine vinegar
50g fish sauce
1 lime, juice only
½ Chinese cabbage (wombok), cut into 8 pieces
Handful fresh mint, leaves only
Handful fresh Thai basil, leaves only
2 carrots, julienned
1 cucumber, julienned
300g smoked trout, skin and bones removed, flaked (approx. 1 fish)
Fried shallots, to serve
Lime cheeks, to serve
Chilli sauce, to serve (optional)

1. Place chilli and garlic in TC bowl, chop for 3 seconds, speed 6. Scrape down sides.

2. Add oil, sauté for 4 minutes, 100°C, speed 1.

3. Add sugar, vinegar, fish sauce and lime juice, mix for 10 seconds, speed 4. Set aside.

4. Without cleaning TC bowl add half the cabbage, chop for 4 seconds, speed 4. Transfer to a large salad bowl.

5. Add remaining cabbage to TC bowl, chop for 4 seconds, speed 4. Transfer to salad bowl. Add mint, basil, carrot, cucumber, trout and dressing to the salad bowl, toss to combine.

Garnish with fried shallots and serve with lime cheeks and chilli sauce on the side (if using).

NOTE: To keep this salad fresh, dress it just prior to serving. For lunchboxes, pack the dressing separately in a small container.

VARIATION: You can toss through cooked rice vermicelli noodles – they will soak up the delicious dressing and bulk out the salad.

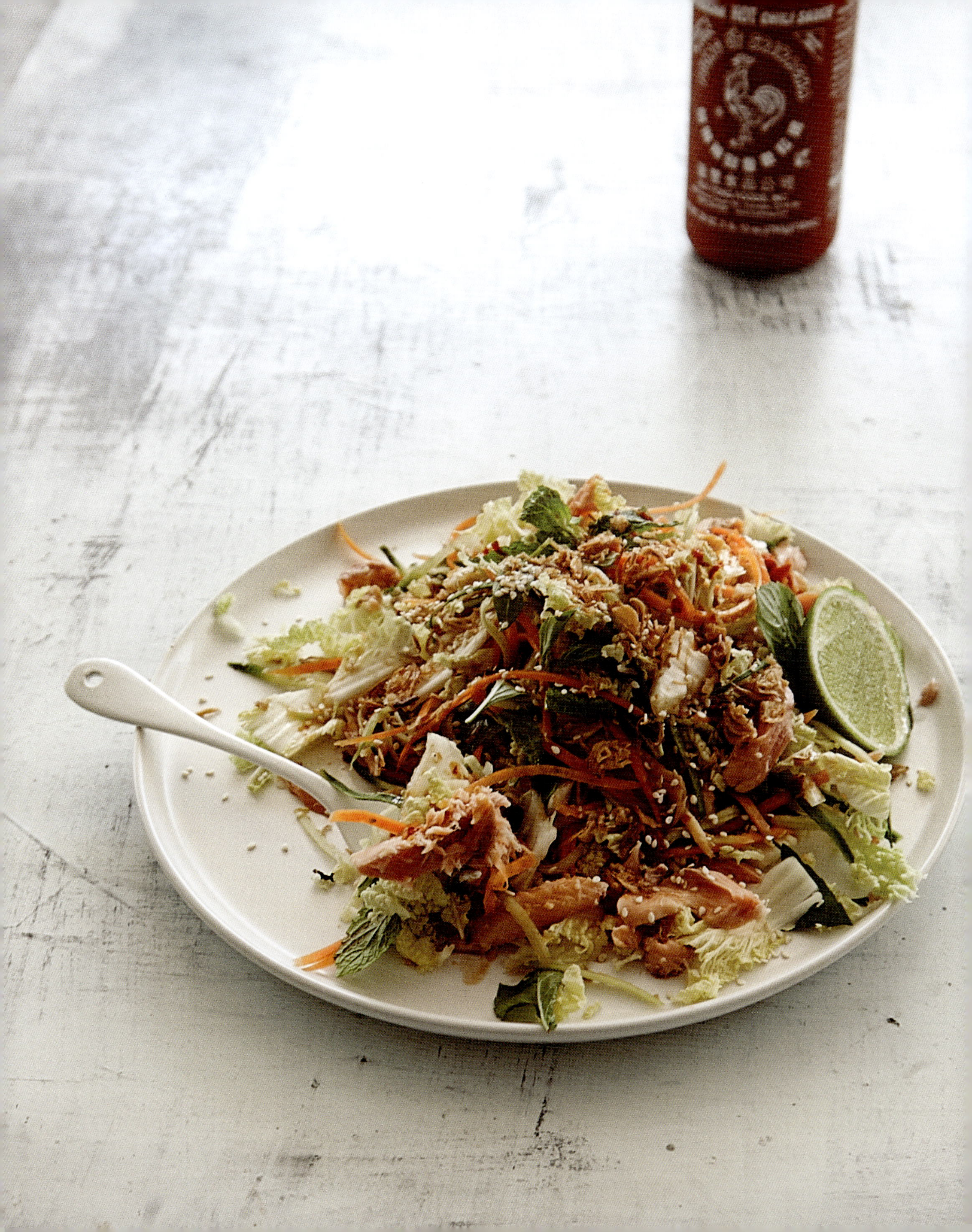

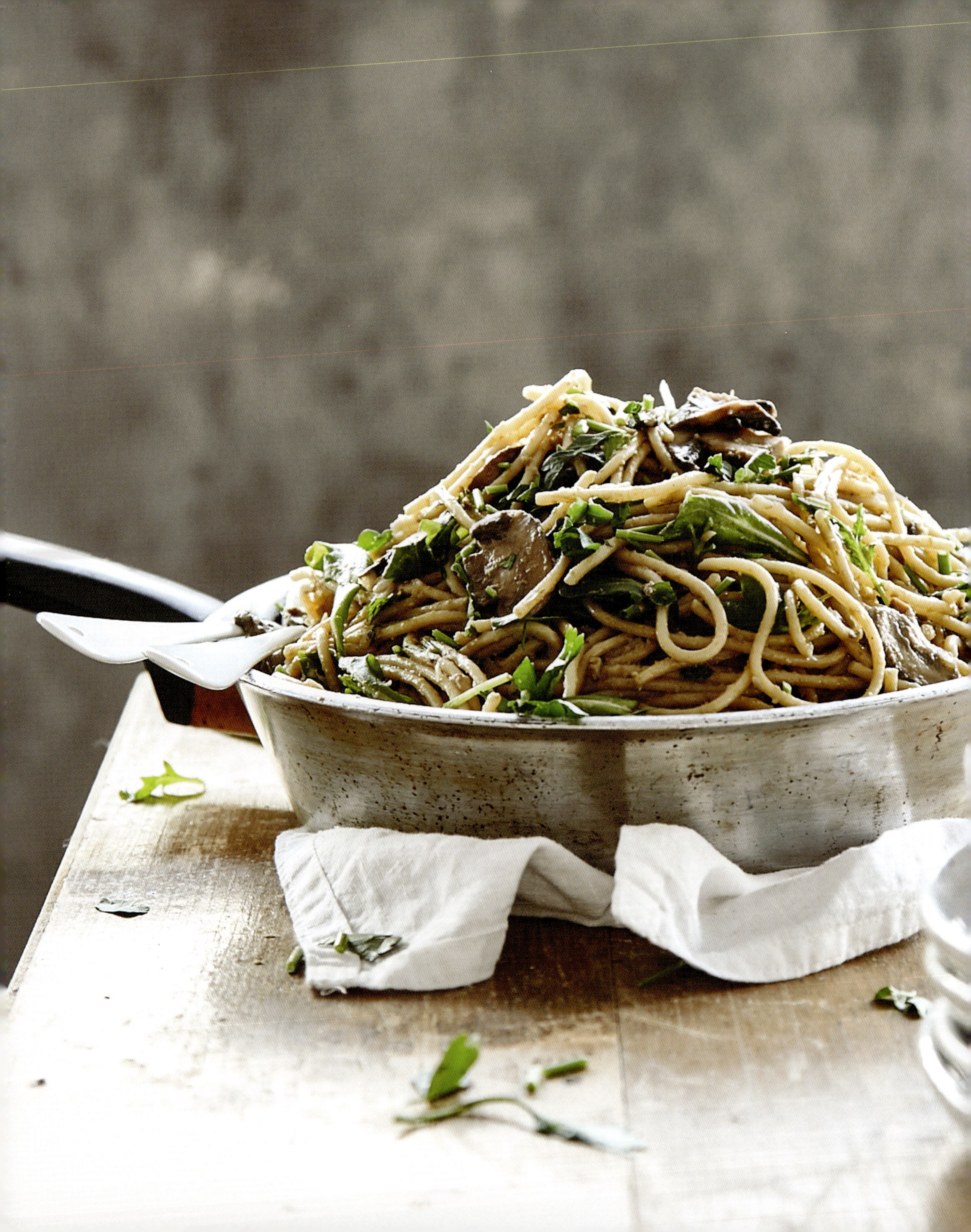

# one-bowl mushroom spaghetti

SERVES 4

This is ultimate 'bowl food' – speedy, simple and satisfying, cooked entirely in the thermo cooker bowl and eaten from a serving bowl (possibly while sitting on the couch). I think even Nigella would be impressed!

5g dried porcini mushrooms
2 garlic cloves, peeled
1 brown onion, peeled and halved
40g olive oil
250g mixed mushrooms, sliced
200g cream
1½ tablespoons stock concentrate (see page 190)
1 teaspoon Dijon mustard
½ teaspoon fine salt
600g water
400g spaghetti
50g rocket
Fresh parsley, to serve

1. Place porcini mushrooms in TC bowl, mill 10 seconds, speed 9.
2. Add garlic and onion, chop 5 seconds, speed 5. Scrape down sides.
3. Add oil, cook 5 minutes, 100°C, speed 1.
4. Add mushrooms, cream, stock concentrate, mustard, salt and water, cook for 8 minutes, 100°C, reverse speed 1.
5. Remove MC and add spaghetti through hole in lid. Cook for 4 minutes, 100°C, reverse speed soft.
6. Remove lid and submerge spaghetti into sauce using spatula. Replace lid and MC. Cook for 2 minutes, 100°C, reverse speed soft.
7. Gently stir spaghetti, folding the top spaghetti to the bottom. Replace lid and leave standing for 10 minutes in the TC bowl to complete cooking.

Serve topped with rocket and parsley leaves.

NOTE: The timing of this recipe must be precise for the pasta to be cooked al dente, so don't venture too far from your thermo cooker!

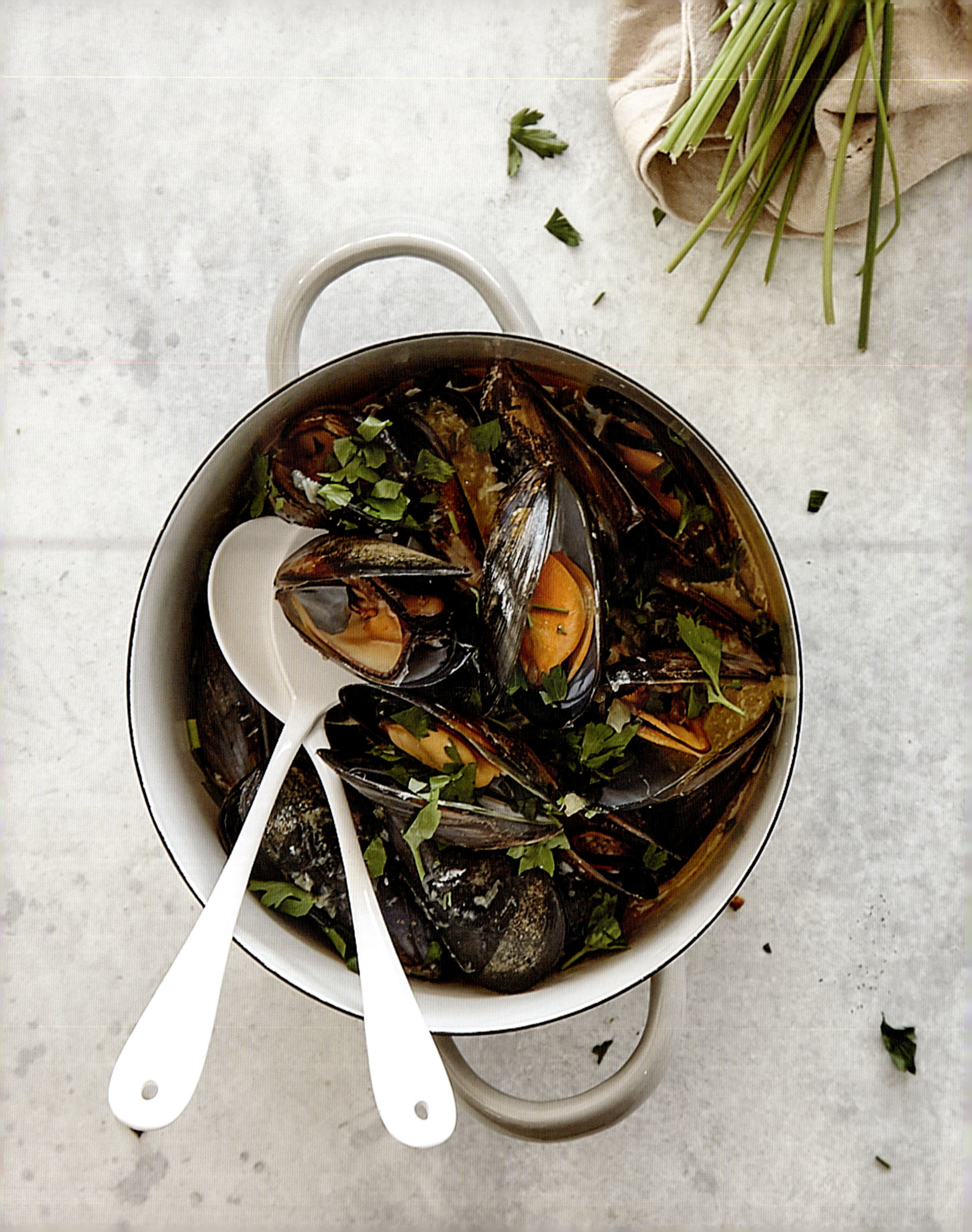

# garlic and white wine mussel pots

**SERVES 3**

Mussels are my number one choice when it comes to seafood – they are delicious, nutritious, sustainable and cheap! Mussel farming can even benefit the surrounding marine environment as, like oysters, they filter their food from the water and do not require additional feed. Mussels are a great addition to laksa, paella, risotto, pasta and chowder; you can even crumb and grill them. But I think the best pairing is with this rich and buttery garlic and white wine sauce. Just make sure you've got plenty of fresh bread on hand to mop up the gorgeous juices.

1 leek, white part only, quartered
4 garlic cloves, peeled
100g butter
300g white wine
20g stock concentrate (see page 190)
1kg mussels, scrubbed and debearded
Thyme or parsley leaves, to serve
Grilled or fresh bread, to serve

1. Place leek and garlic in TC bowl, chop for 3 seconds, speed 6. Scrape down sides.
2. Add butter, sauté for 5 minutes, 100°C, speed 1.
3. Add white wine and stock concentrate, cook for 7 minutes, steaming temperature, reverse speed 3, or until steaming temperature is reached.
4. Place mussels in steaming tray, steam for 6 minutes, steaming temperature, reverse speed 3. Remove any mussels that have opened.
5. Steam for a further 1 minute, steaming temperature, reverse speed 3. Again, remove mussels that have opened.
6. Steam for a further 1 minute, steaming temperature, reverse speed 3. Divide open mussels among 3 serving bowls and pour over garlic and white wine sauce. Discard any unopened mussels.

Garnish with thyme or parsley and serve with bread.

# creamy zucchini soup

**SERVES 4**

Zucchinis are one of the easiest vegetables to grow – so easy, in fact, that you can easily end up with too many! This recipe came to the rescue when we found ourselves harvesting 12 kilograms in just one week. If you can't grow your own, zucchinis are cheap and plentiful at the height of summer so look out for them at your local grocer. Make a few batches of soup at a time and freeze, then simply defrost, blend and reheat all at once in the thermo cooker for a quick fix meal full of nutrients.

1 brown onion, peeled and halved
2 garlic cloves, peeled
20g olive oil
1kg zucchini, roughly chopped
500g chicken or vegetable stock
1 tablespoon stock concentrate (see page 190)
150g cream
Toast, to serve (optional)

1. Place onion and garlic in TC bowl, chop for 5 seconds, speed 5. Scrape down sides.
2. Add oil, sauté for 5 minutes, 100°C, speed 1.
3. Add zucchini, chop for 6 seconds, speed 6, assisting with spatula, or until grated.
4. Add stock and stock concentrate, cook for 14 minutes, 100°C, speed 2.
5. Add cream, purée for 30 seconds, slowly increasing to speed 9, or until smooth.

Serve hot with a thick slice of buttered sourdough toast (if using). Garnish with toasted pine nuts (see note page 94), fresh parsley or dehydrated kale chips (pictured).

NOTE: When growing your own, it is very easy to end up with giant zucchinis! Unfortunately, these are often starchy and lack flavour, but they are perfect to use in puréed soups such as this.

VARIATION: Add some grated parmesan at step 5 for a cheesy zucchini soup.

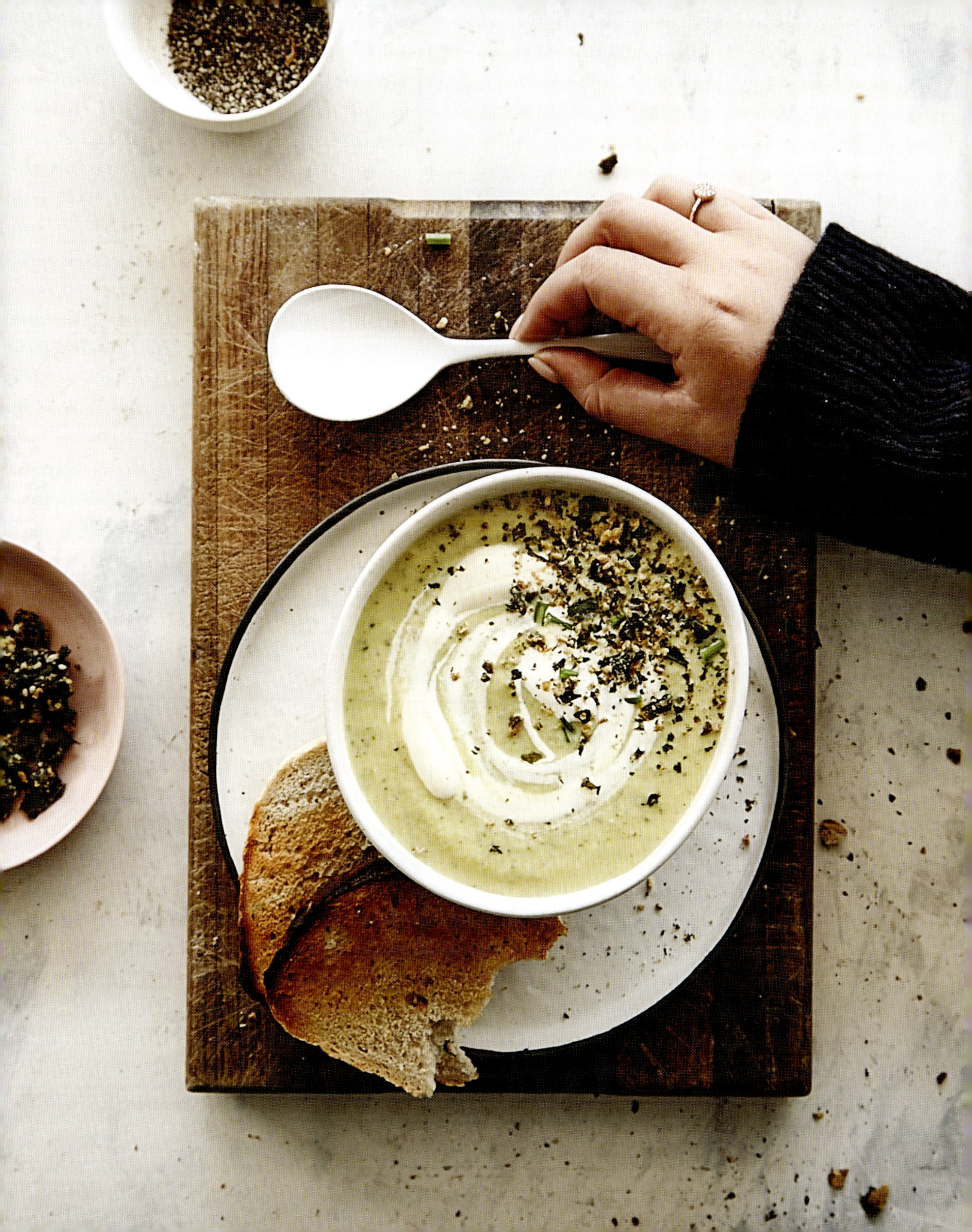

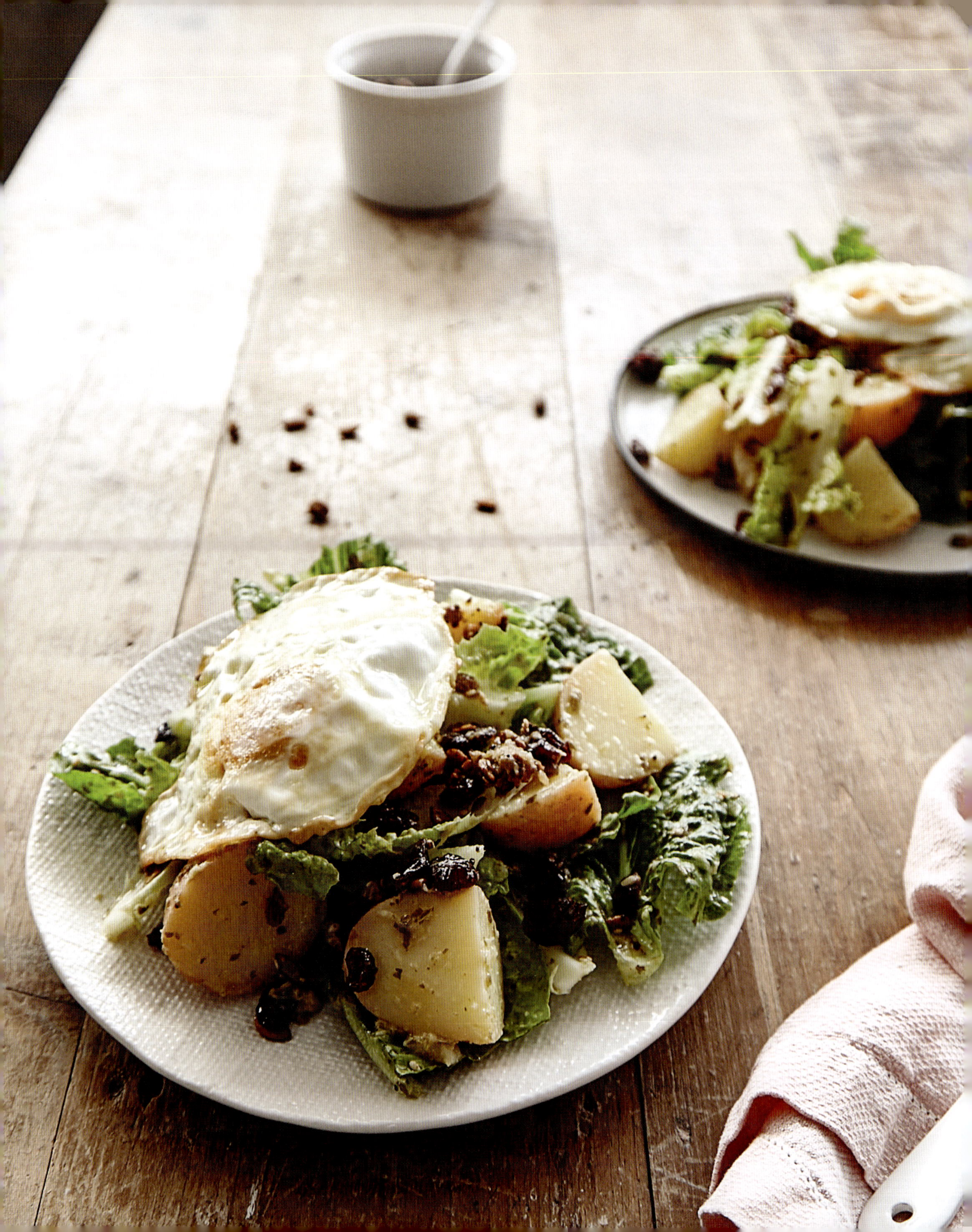

# potato, mint and fried egg salad

**SERVES 4**

My sister Loryn thought this was one of my stranger salad combinations, but then immediately fell in love when she tasted it. It is simple and fresh but unexpectedly satisfying as a quick meal – the warm potatoes soak up all the flavours of the dressing while the seeds and cos add crunch and the dried fruit gives a hint of sweetness. The fried egg on top seals the deal, and if you keep the yolk runny it acts as a second dressing. It's delicious warm or cold, making it the perfect lunchbox meal.

2 handfuls fresh mint
4 spring onions, ends trimmed, halved
80g white balsamic vinegar
80g olive oil
2 teaspoons Dijon mustard
1 teaspoon fine salt
800g boiling water
1kg baby red potatoes, quartered
Macadamia oil, for frying
4 eggs
1 baby cos lettuce, roughly chopped
120g salad seed sprinkles (see page 251) or mixed seeds
60g sultanas or dried cranberries

1. Place mint and spring onion in TC bowl, chop for 1 second, speed 8.
2. Add vinegar, olive oil, mustard and salt, mix for 10 seconds, speed 6. Set aside.
3. Without cleaning TM bowl fill with 800g boiling water. Place potatoes in steaming tray and steam for 17 minutes, steaming temperature, speed 3, or until tender.
4. Transfer potatoes to a large salad bowl and pour over mint dressing. Toss to combine while still hot.
5. Meanwhile, heat macadamia oil in a large fry pan over medium heat. Crack eggs into pan, keeping them separate. Cook for 2 minutes, then using a spatula flip eggs over. Immediately remove from pan and set aside (you want the yolk inside to be runny).
6. Add lettuce, salad seed sprinkles or mixed seeds and dried fruit to bowl with potatoes. Toss to combine, redistributing dressing. Divide among 4 serving bowls and top each with a fried egg.

Serve immediately or refrigerate for up to 24 hours.

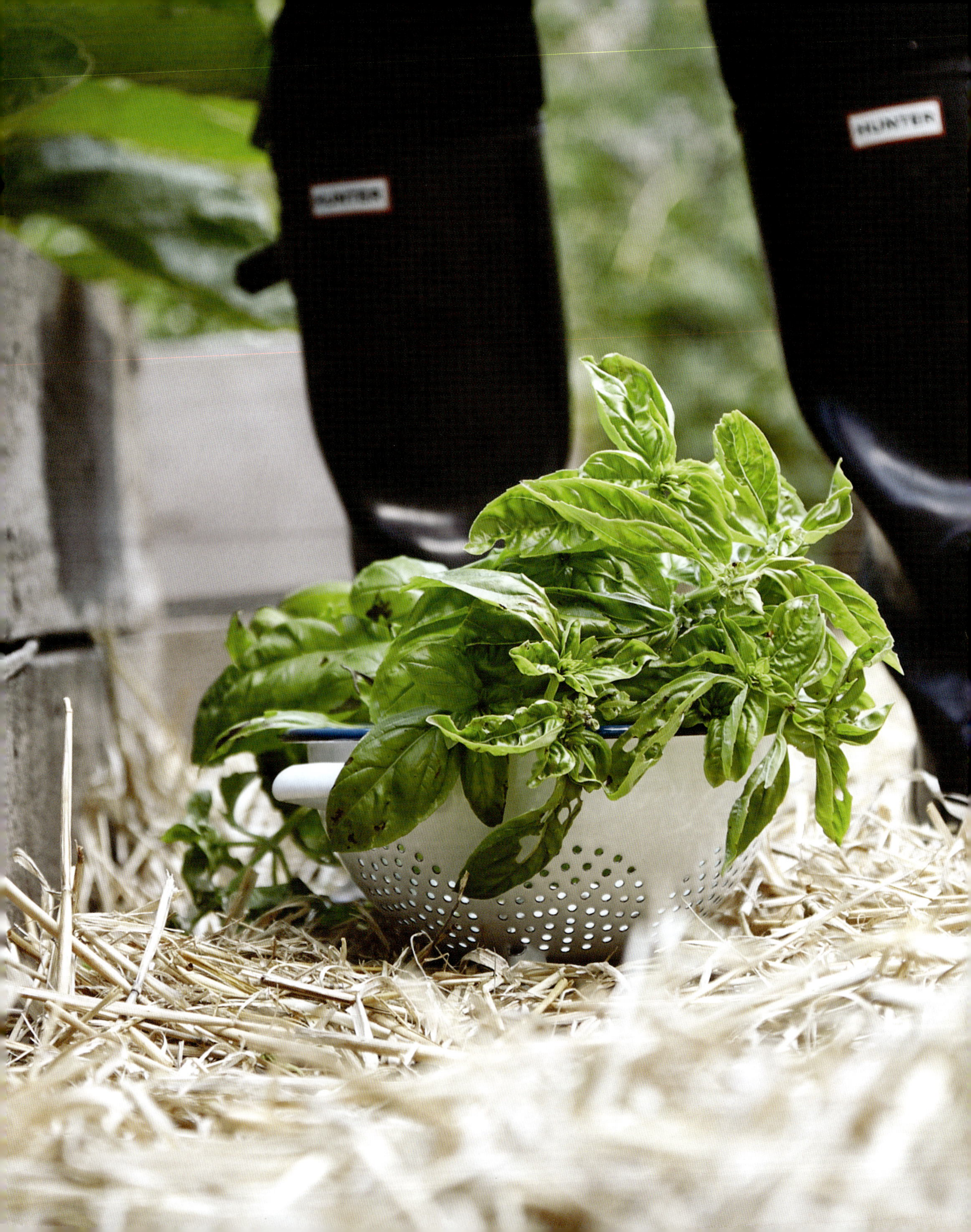
HUNTER
HUNTER

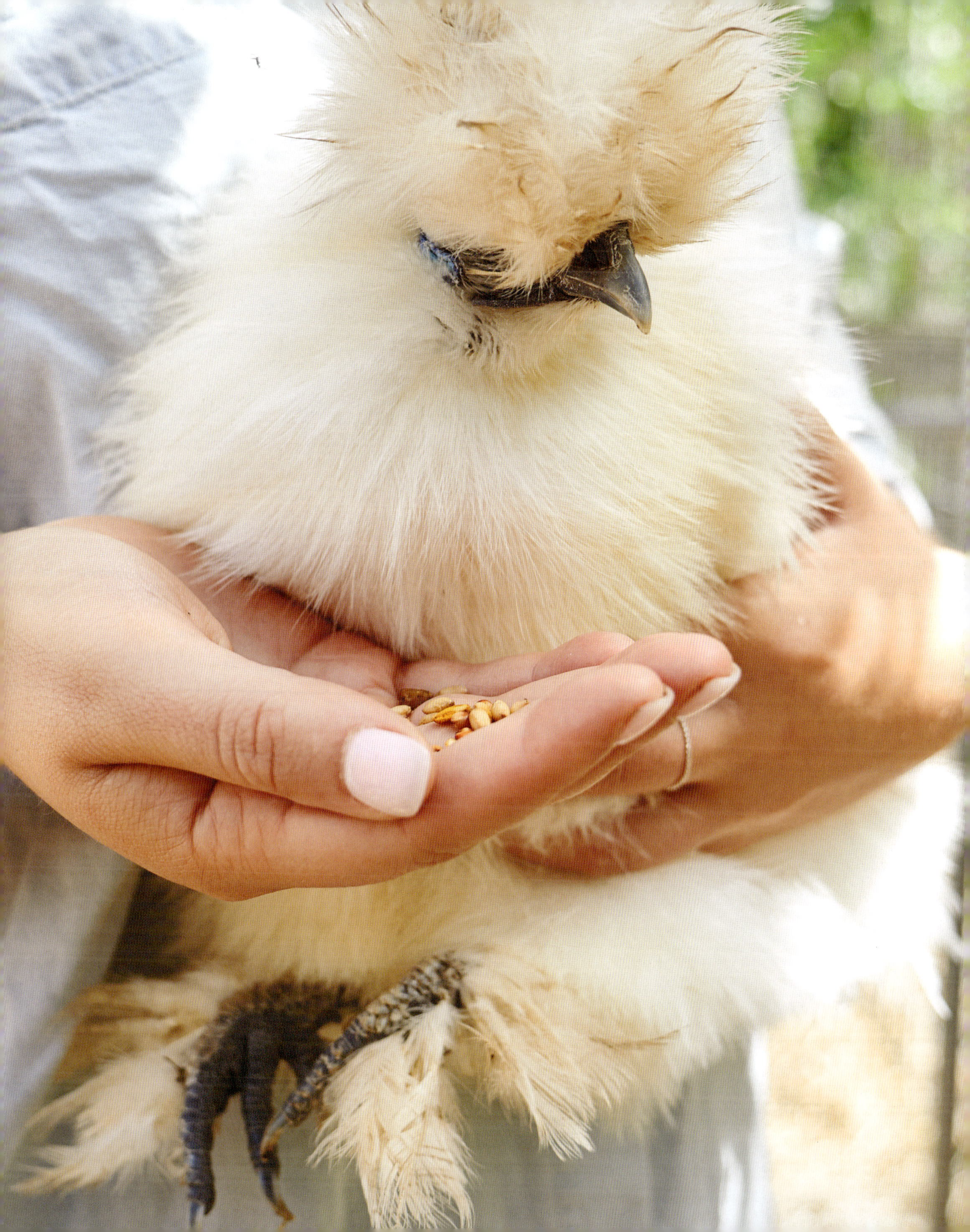

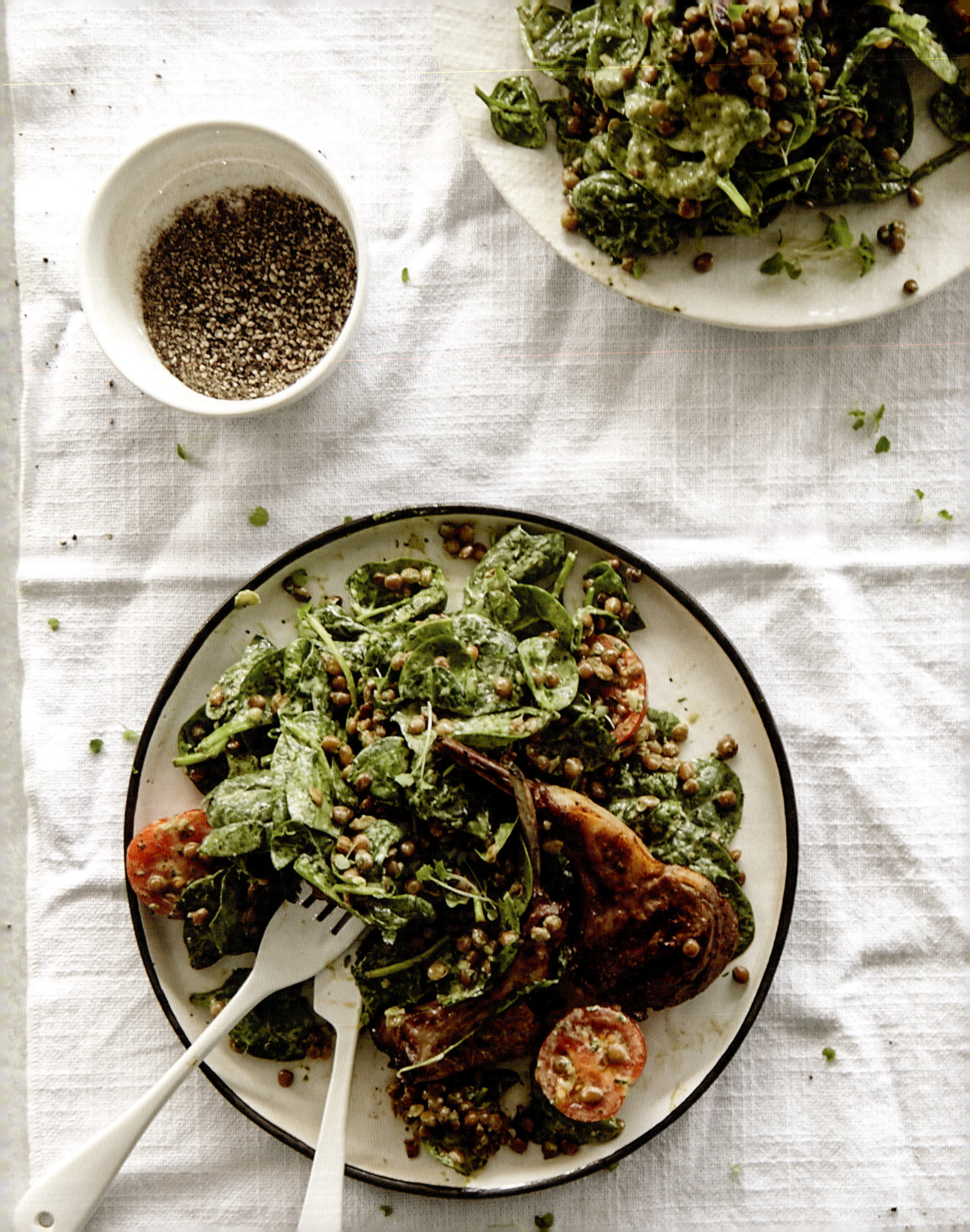

# lamb with herby yoghurt lentil salad

**SERVES 4**

Mint, yoghurt and garlic ... could there be a more perfect combination to accompany lamb? This dish makes an incredibly satisfying quick dinner, but ditch the meat, double the recipe and you've got a super-easy salad that really looks the part at your next barbecue or picnic. While this is 15-minute meal territory, you will need to make like Jamie and have everything ready to go.

2 handfuls fresh mint
Handful fresh parsley
2 garlic cloves, peeled
50g olive oil
8 lamb cutlets
Macadamia oil, for frying
1½ teaspoons fine salt, plus extra for seasoning
400g can brown lentils
2 litres boiling water
150g Greek yoghurt
20g white balsamic vinegar
10g Dijon mustard
250g cherry tomatoes, halved
100g baby spinach

1. Heat a chargrill pan over high heat.

2. Meanwhile, place mint and parsley in TC bowl, chop for 2 seconds, speed 8. Set aside.

3. Place garlic in TC bowl, chop for 3 seconds, speed 6. Scrape down sides.

4. Add olive oil, sauté for 4 minutes, 100°C, speed 1.

5. Meanwhile, brush lamb cutlets with macadamia oil and season with salt. Cook on chargrill pan 2 minutes each side, or until browned on the outside but still pink in the middle.

6. Meanwhile, place lentils in TC steamer basket and rinse with boiling water. Allow to drain.

7. Add yoghurt, vinegar, mustard, 1½ teaspoons salt and chopped herbs to TC bowl, mix for 5 seconds, speed 4.

8. In a large bowl, fold together tomatoes, spinach, lentils and yoghurt dressing. Divide among 4 serving plates and top each with 2 lamb cutlets.

VARIATION: Try lamb backstrap instead of cutlets.

# garlic chilli sardines on toast

**SERVES 2**

It is widely accepted that sardines are one of the most sustainable seafood options and one of the healthiest, yet they are so rarely utilised! We've got to break the sardine stigma, and I think the best way to do it is to show that sardines can be the star ingredient in a quick and delicious breakfast, lunch or dinner. Give this recipe a go – I think you'll be pleasantly surprised.

½ lemon, rind and juice
3 garlic cloves, peeled
1 long red chilli, halved and deseeded
220g canned sardines in olive oil (see note)
50g olive oil
4 thick slices bread
Micro salad, snow pea tendrils or rocket, to serve

1. Place lemon rind in TC bowl, zest for 10 seconds, speed 8. Scrape down sides.

2. Add garlic and chilli, chop for 6 seconds, speed 6. Scrape down sides.

3. Drain the oil from the sardines into TC bowl. Add olive oil and sauté for 5 minutes, 100°C, speed 1. Meanwhile, toast bread.

4. Divide sardines evenly among toast slices and drizzle with oil mixture from TC bowl.

Top with greens and a squeeze of lemon juice and serve.

NOTE: If possible, always try and buy Australian sardines.

VARIATION: Use gluten-free bread for a gluten-free option.

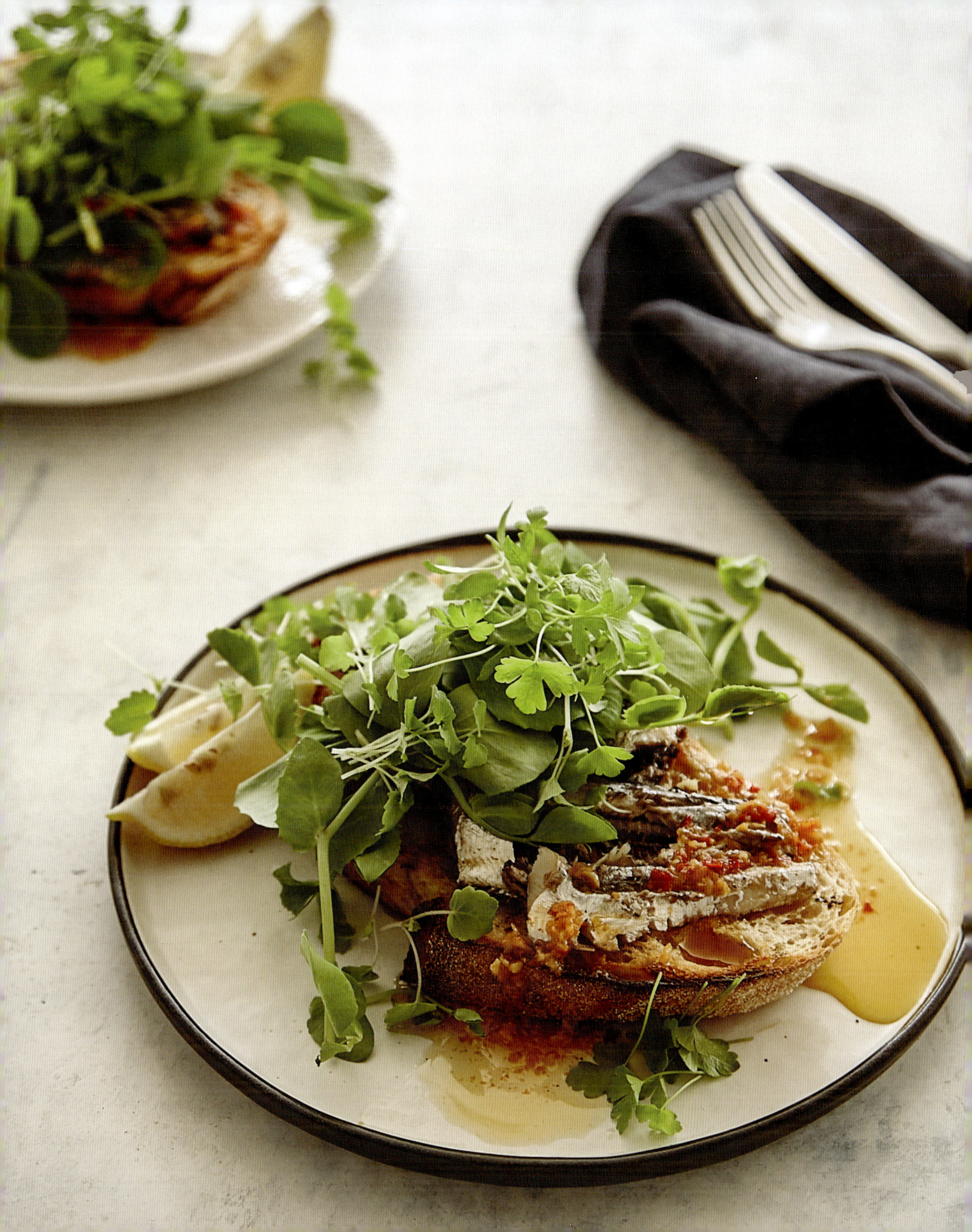

# rice and black bean burritos

**MAKES 18**

This is possibly the quickest, easiest and cheapest way to feed a crowd. Don't let the long list of ingredients fool you – you've probably got most of them at home already. I recommend keeping a supply of basmati rice, frozen veggies and stock concentrate at home, then you can always whip up a quick rice dish for dinner. Once you've got the basics, the flavourings and accompaniments can be substituted with whatever you've got on hand, and if you don't have tortillas simply serve this as a burrito bowl!

18 large flour tortillas
1 brown onion, peeled and halved
2 garlic cloves, peeled
40g olive oil
200g basmati rice, rinsed just prior to cooking
200g mixed frozen vegetables
400g can diced tomatoes
200g water
60g stock concentrate (see page 190)
800g canned black beans, rinsed and drained
1 lime, juice only
2 teaspoons sweet paprika
1 teaspoon ground chipotle chilli, or to taste
Salt, to taste
250g grated mozzarella
Greek yoghurt or sour cream, to serve
Coriander leaves, to serve
Lime wedges, to serve

1. Preheat oven to 150°C.
2. Once heated, wrap tortillas in foil and place in oven for 10 minutes.
3. Meanwhile, place onion and garlic in TC bowl, chop for 5 seconds, speed 5. Scrape down sides.
4. Add oil, sauté for 5 minutes, 100°C, speed 1.
5. Add rice, vegetables, tomatoes, water and stock concentrate, cook for 10 minutes, 100°C, reverse speed 1.5.
6. Add black beans, lime juice, paprika, chilli and salt, combine using spatula. Allow to sit in the TC bowl for 10 minutes before serving.

Serve as a DIY banquet with warm tortillas, cheese, yoghurt or sour cream, coriander and lime wedges, all in the middle of the table. Always goes well with a side of pickled salad (see page 124, pictured).

VARIATION: If black beans are unavailable, replace them with kidney beans or a four bean mix.

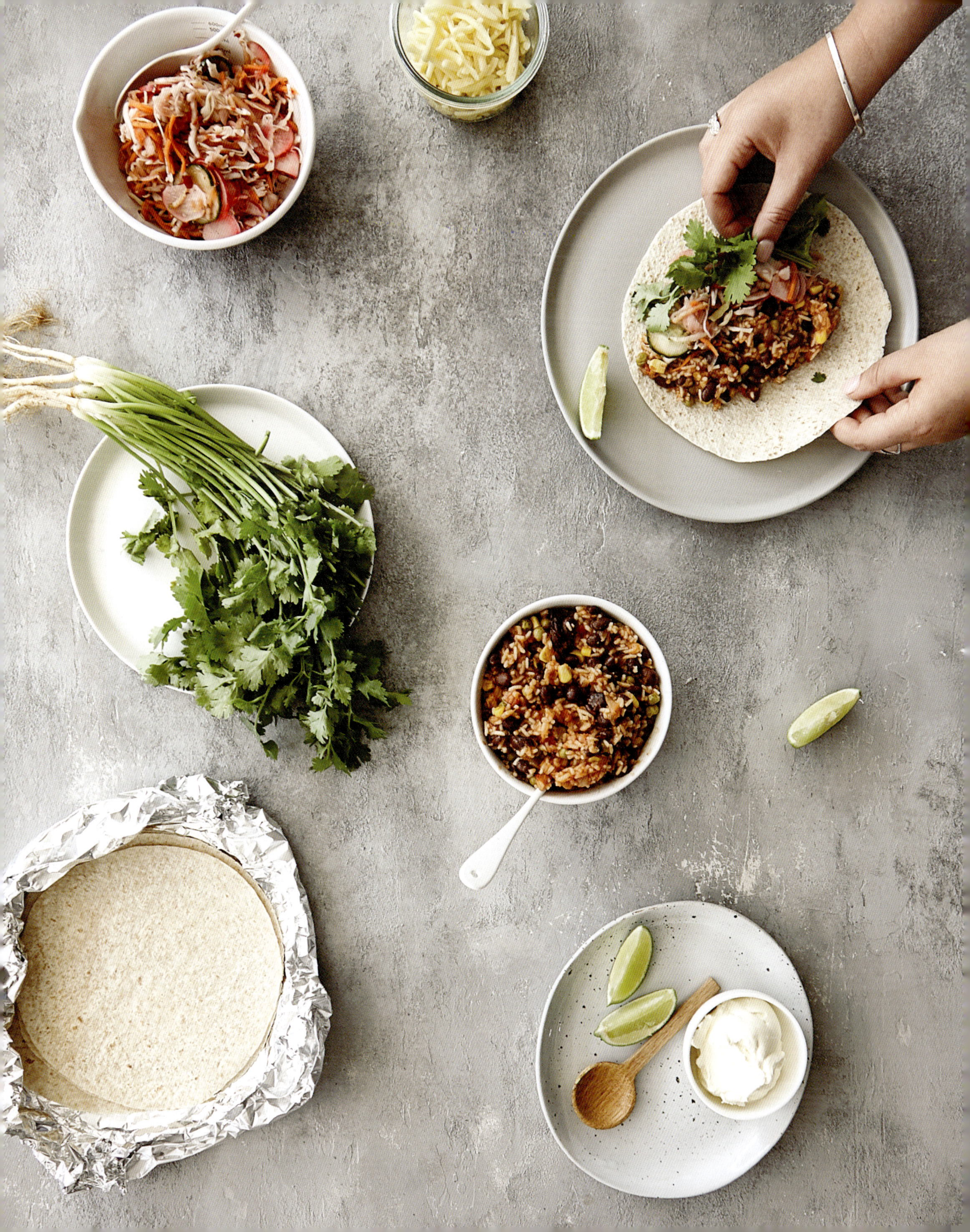

# moreish meatballs

**MAKES 24**

These meatballs are a complete meal-in-a-mouthful! You've got juicy meat, creamy feta, sweet currants, crunchy pine nuts, fresh herbs and even a nutritional dose of kale for good measure. All that mopped up with sourdough bread and bound together with egg. Pack in a lunchbox with fresh veggies, serve at a picnic or cocktail party with toothpick skewers, or wrap in pita bread. You can of course serve them with a dipping sauce such as hummus (see page 37), tzatziki, rhubarb and ginger relish (see page 242) or tomato chutney (see page 240), but they're so good they don't really need one.

40g kale, spine removed
2 slices sourdough or homemade bread, quartered and frozen
Handful fresh parsley
2 garlic cloves, peeled
750g minced beef (not lean), roughly broken
2 eggs
100g Greek feta, roughly crumbled
70g currants
70g pine nuts, toasted (see note page 94)
1 teaspoon flavour bomb salt (see page 246) or fine salt
Macadamia oil, for frying

1. Place kale, bread, parsley and garlic in TC bowl, chop for 6 seconds, speed 8, assisting with spatula if necessary.

2. Add beef, eggs, feta, currants, pine nuts and salt, mix for 15 seconds, speed 4, or until thoroughly incorporated. Squeeze spoonfuls of mixture into 24 firm golf-ball-sized meatballs.

3. Heat a liberal amount of macadamia oil in a large fry pan over medium heat. Once hot, add meatballs (as many will fit without touching) and cook for 8 minutes, or until golden all around and cooked through, rotating every couple of minutes. Repeat with remaining meatballs.

Serve warm straight from the fry pan or refrigerate and serve cold.

NOTE: Freeze uncooked meatballs on a flat tray. Once frozen, transfer to a plastic container or ziplock bag and freeze for up to 3 months. When ready to cook, allow the meatballs to defrost in the fridge before frying.

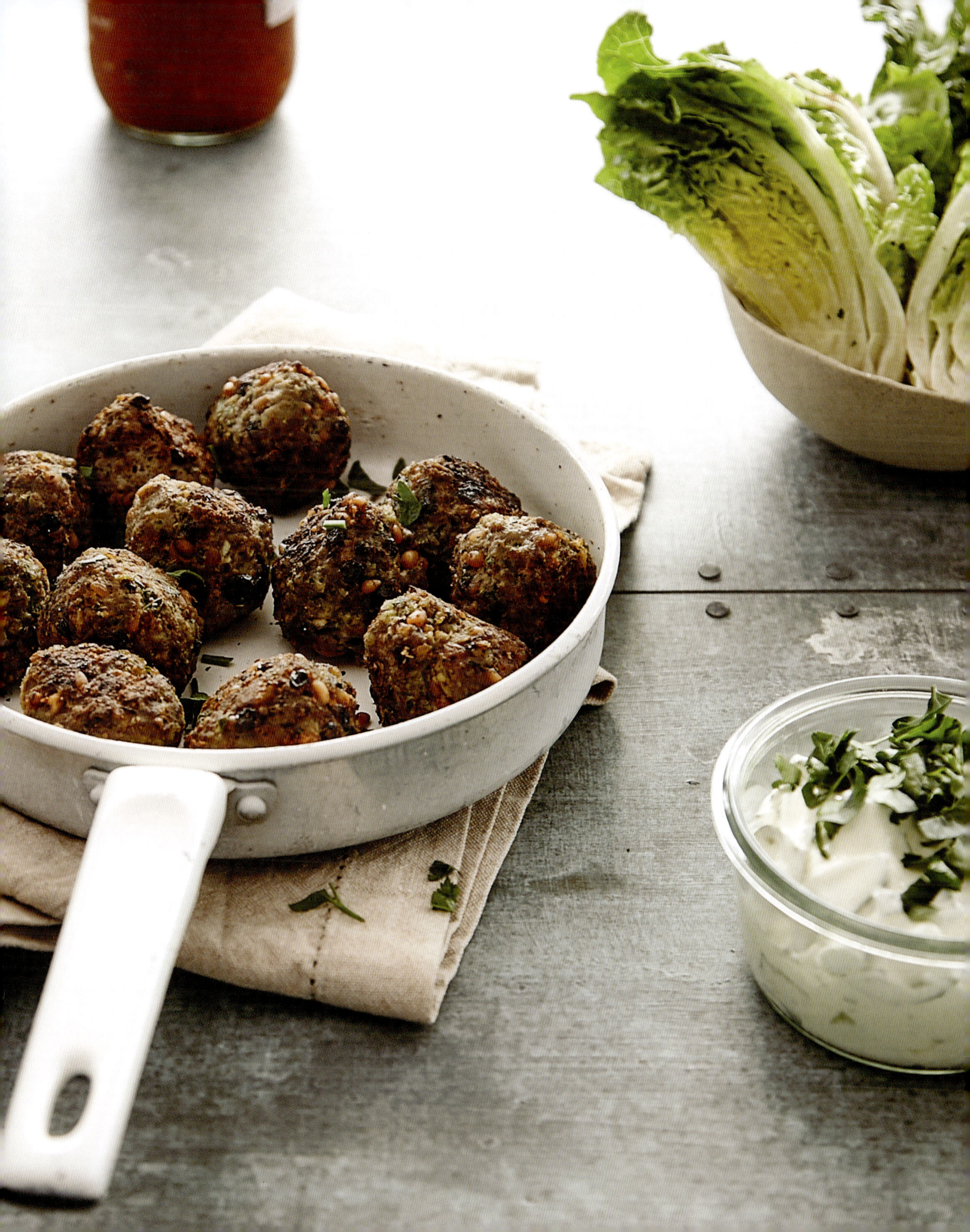

# well stocked

To cook quick fix meals, it is essential to have a well-stocked pantry, fridge and freezer. Whether you are pulling together a quick dinner, trying to find something for the lunchboxes or simply wanting a sweet treat, having the basics on hand will mean a nourishing and delicious morsel cooked from scratch is never far away. It may take a little investment at the beginning, but the long-term benefits more than make up for it as you will be saving time and money, buying quality ingredients in bulk, and whipping up meals in a flash without even leaving the house.

To get you started, here's a list of my essentials …

## PANTRY

I keep my pantry items in BPA-free plastic containers with airtight lids, each with a clearly visible label on the front. It's important that the containers are transparent so you can quickly gauge which items are running low. I love the idea of glass jars, but I find these can get quite heavy when full, making it difficult to carry several ingredients at once!

### Oils / Vinegars / Sauces
- Extra virgin olive oil
- Macadamia oil
- Coconut oil
- Balsamic vinegar
- Apple cider vinegar
- Tamari

### Fruits / Vegetables
- Sultanas
- Shredded coconut
- Coconut flakes
- Dried porcini mushrooms
- Vanilla beans
- Medjool dates
- Canned diced tomatoes
- Canned coconut cream
- Brown onions
- Garlic

### Sweeteners
- White sugar
- Raw sugar
- Coconut sugar
- Maple syrup

### Herbs / Spices
- Curry powder
- Chilli flakes
- Sweet paprika
- Smoked paprika
- Ground cinnamon
- Ground cumin

### Nuts / Seeds
- Raw almonds
- Raw cashews
- Raw macadamia nuts
- Roasted peanuts
- Pine nuts
- Sesame seeds
- Pumpkin seeds
- Chia seeds

### Grains
- Arborio rice
- Basmati rice
- Plain flour
- Baker's flour
- Cornflour
- Dried pasta
- Rolled oats

### Beans / Legumes
- Canned/dried chickpeas
- Canned/dried kidney beans
- Canned brown lentils
- Dried red split lentils

### Other
- Baking powder
- Dried yeast
- Cocoa powder
- Coarse salt

## FRIDGE

My fridge is organised into sections: dairy, deli, meat, condiments, leftovers, fruit and vegetables. This means that when I'm looking to see what ingredients I have at the ready to whip up a quick meal I know exactly which sections to go to and the order in which to investigate (leftovers first of course!). Organising the fridge in this way also means there is less chance of food being overlooked, and therefore less chance of spoilage. I also always try to have fresh baby spinach on hand, stored in special containers designed for that purpose. I can use it as the base for a salad, wilt it with eggs for breakfast, stir it through risottos, soups, stews and pastas, and finally, if there is any left over looking a little limp, I throw it straight into a green smoothie (see page 171)!

- Eggs
- Butter
- Yoghurt
- Dijon mustard
- Wholegrain mustard
- Stock concentrate (see page 190)
- Chutneys and sauces (see page 223)

## FREEZER

I keep my frozen items in labelled ziplock bags, which I continually use for the same item to avoid wastage. The exception here is liquid stocks which I do keep in plastic containers. When freezing items such as bananas, mango and bread, make sure you freeze them in the same form you wish to use them frozen – for example, I peel and halve bananas, and make sure all bread is sliced. This is important as frozen food becomes very hard and solid, making it both difficult and dangerous to chop. Chuck steak is my generic pick for slow cooking, but I'll often also have other secondary cuts in the freezer that I've bought in bulk direct from a local farmer.

Plus any leftovers that would otherwise spoil: milk, almond milk and macadamia milk frozen in ice-cube trays, cream, grated cheese, chillies, kaffir lime leaves, turmeric, galangal, both raw and cooked meats, steamed broccoli, roasted vegetables, watermelon, pineapple, cooked rice, uncooked pastry, egg whites, egg yolks, stewed fruit, curries, sauces, soups, stews, pesto …

- Peas and corn
- Spinach
- Raspberries
- Blueberries
- Mango
- Banana
- Garlic cubes (see page 248)
- Grated tasty cheese
- Crumbled feta
- Bread
- Chopped chuck steak
- Homemade stock (see page 190)
- Leftover meat fat (see page 178)
- Leftover bones for making broth (see page 114)

Remember, with a thermo cooker you can transform ingredients in under a minute, so there's no need to buy a supply of:

| | | |
|---|---|---|
| Almond meal | ⟶ | mill raw almonds, speed 8 |
| Fine salt | ⟶ | mill coarse salt, speed 9 |
| Self-raising flour | ⟶ | add 1 teaspoon baking powder to 100g plain flour |
| Caster sugar | ⟶ | mill white sugar, speed 10 |
| Icing sugar | ⟶ | mill white sugar, speed 10 |
| Breadcrumbs | ⟶ | mill frozen bread, speed 8 |
| Desiccated coconut | ⟶ | mill shredded coconut or flakes, speed 8 |
| Coconut milk | ⟶ | combine 100g water with 300g coconut cream |
| Grated cheese | ⟶ | grate pieces of cheese, speed 8 |
| Wholegrain flour | ⟶ | mill whole grains, speed 9 |
| Rice flour | ⟶ | mill rice, speed 10 |
| Besan (chickpea flour) | ⟶ | mill whole dried chickpeas, speed 10 |
| Ground coffee | ⟶ | mill coffee beans, speed 9 |
| Ground pepper | ⟶ | mill whole peppercorns, speed 9 |
| Stock cubes | ⟶ | use stock concentrate (see page 190) |

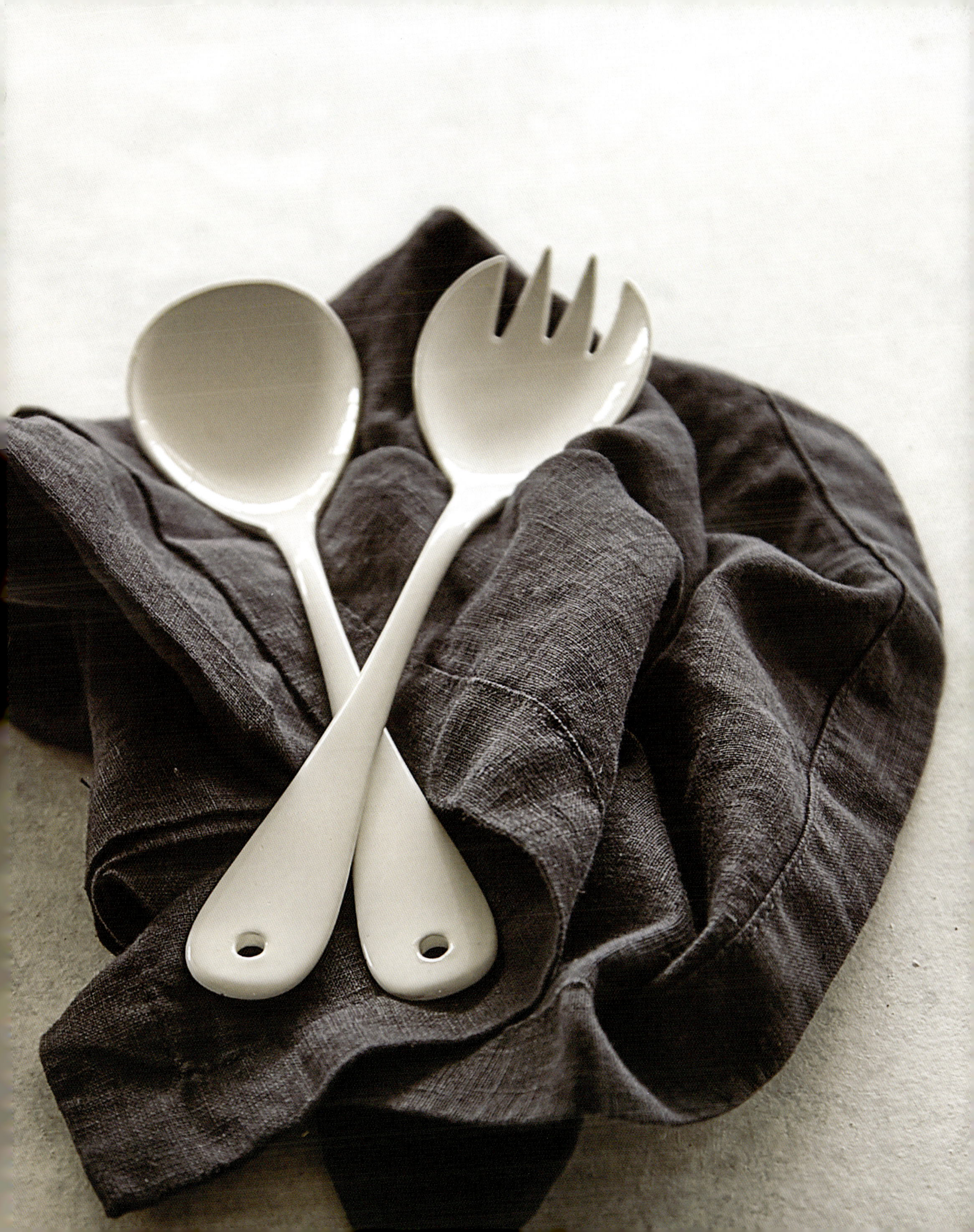

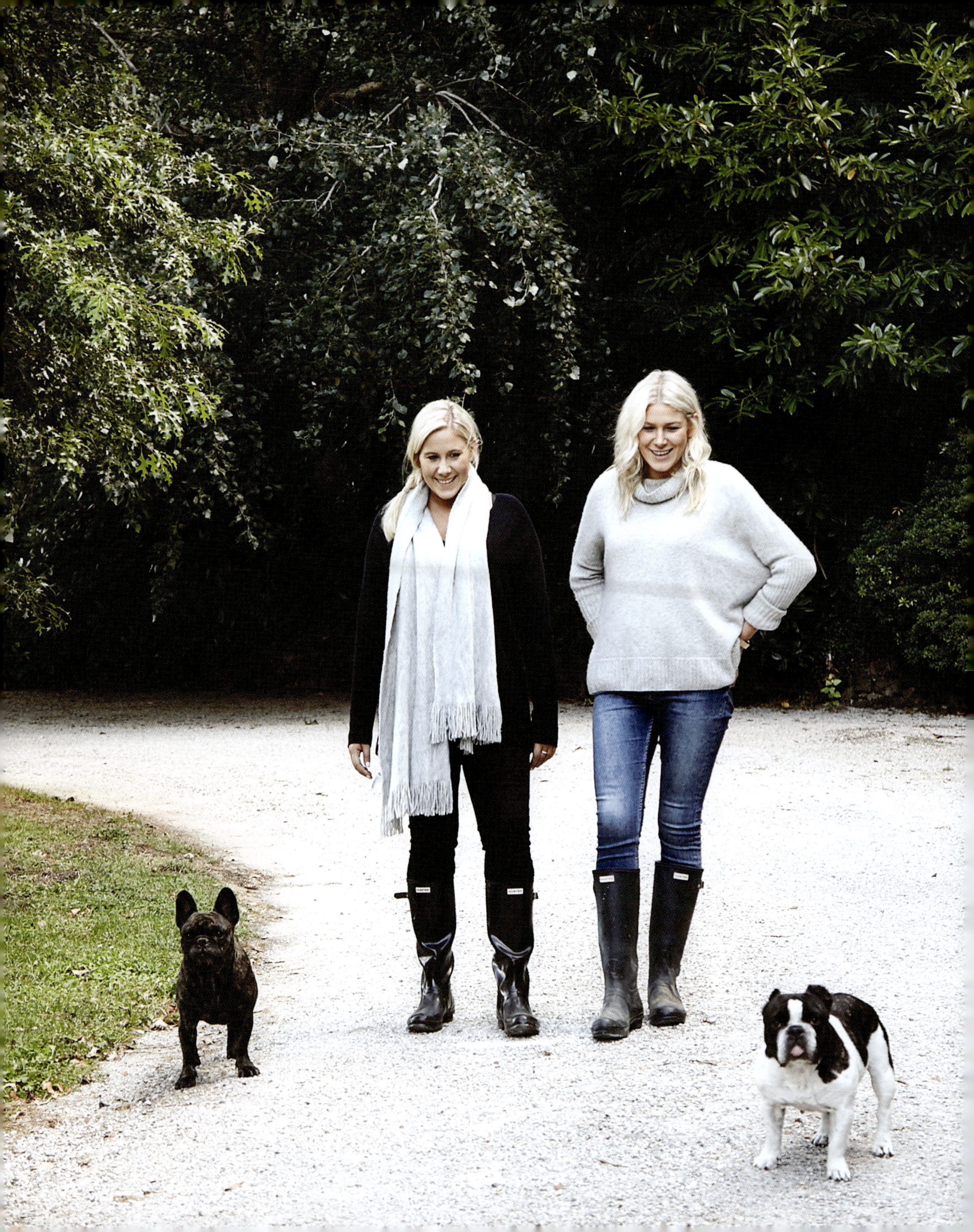

# meatless mondays

Many of us aren't vegan or vegetarian, but regardless of how we label ourselves I believe it is important for everyone to be a conscious consumer, and reduce the impact of our food choices on the creatures around us wherever we can. Try swapping a meaty dish for a vegetarian or vegan alternative once or twice a week, perhaps starting this Monday! The easiest way to achieve this is to incorporate tasty meals into your repertoire … that just happen to be vegan or vegetarian. It's not about deprivation, it's about embracing recipes that utilise all the delicious flavours the plant world has to offer. This chapter has some of my favourite vegan recipes, but there are plenty more vegetarian and vegan recipes throughout the book – look out for the symbols in the top right-hand corner of the page.

# thai pumpkin soup

**SERVES 4**

Classic pumpkin soup has been given a vegan makeover using coconut milk, and I can confidently say that it's not only the new version, it's definitely the improved version! Incorporating all the fresh flavours of Thai cooking – lemongrass, galangal, turmeric, chilli and kaffir lime – this soup is creamy, sweet, sour and spicy all at the same time. I generally prefer to make my own curry pastes, but a commercial jar will do just fine in this recipe. Remember that heat levels vary between brands so if you are feeding children opt for a milder curry paste.

1 brown onion, peeled and halved
2 garlic cloves, peeled
80g Thai red curry paste, or to taste (see note)
40g coconut oil
800g pumpkin, peeled, seeds removed and roughly chopped
400g coconut milk
200g water
40g stock concentrate (see page 190)
Fresh coriander, to serve (optional)
Lime wedges, to serve (optional)

1. Place onion and garlic in TC bowl, chop for 5 seconds, speed 5. Scrape down sides.
2. Add curry paste and coconut oil, sauté for 5 minutes, 100°C, speed 1.
3. Add pumpkin, grate for 10 seconds, speed 8.
4. Add coconut milk, water and stock concentrate, cook for 18 minutes, 100°C, speed 2.
5. Purée for 30 seconds, slowly increasing from speed 1 to 9.

Pour into soup bowls and serve with coriander and lime wedges (if using).

NOTES: The Asian flavours in this soup mean that it is perfect served with either roti bread (see page 143) or a traditional slice of toast.

Look for a vegan curry paste that doesn't contain shrimp or fish sauce, or make your own.

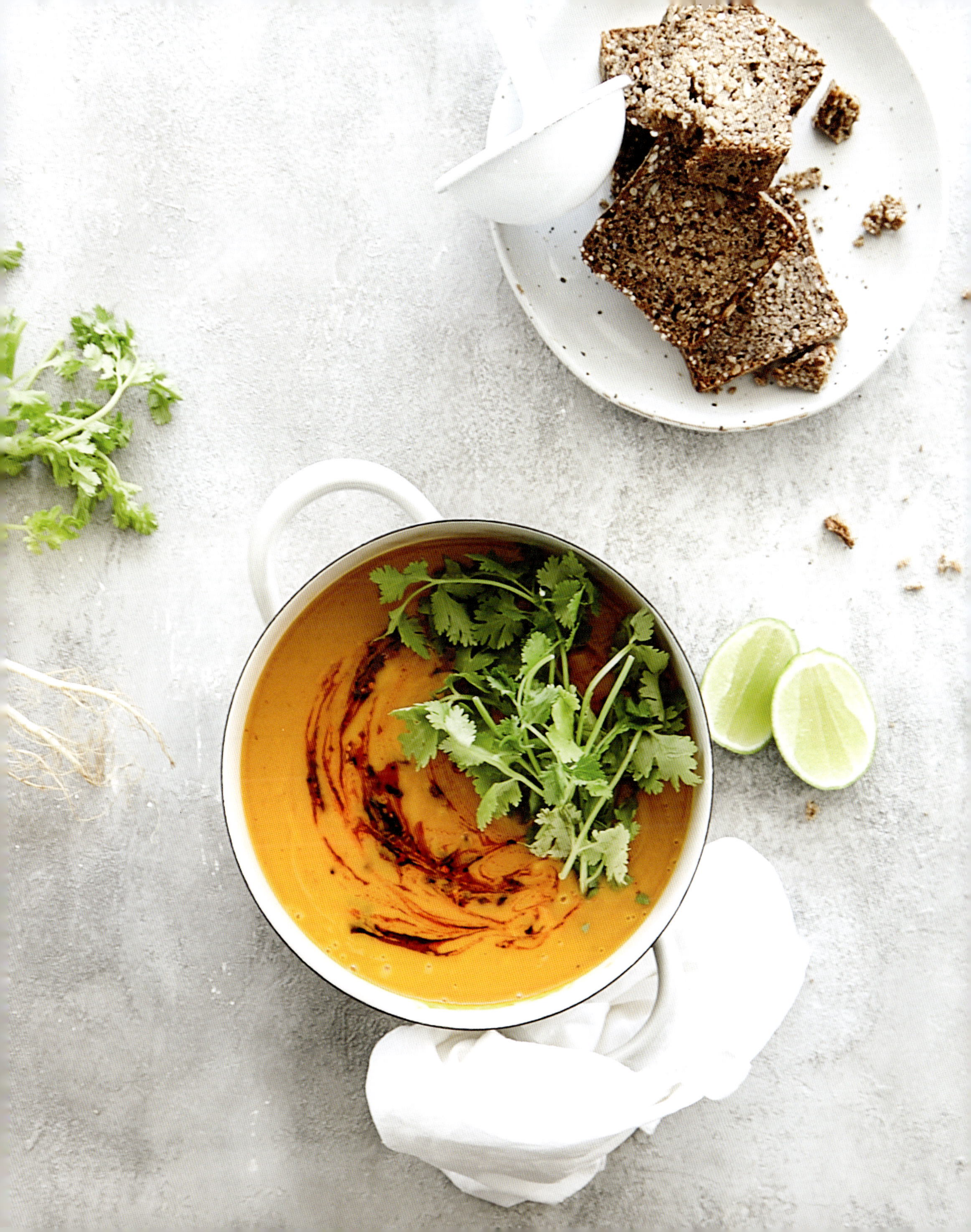

# mushroom bolognaise

**SERVES 8**

Rich and full of flavour, this sauce tastes deceptively meaty thanks to the mushrooms and miso. I always make a big batch so I can use it in various different meals throughout the week (see below for ideas). If you prefer, you can freeze it in serving-size containers, then defrost it as needed for super-speedy dinners. Easy.

- 1kg mixed mushrooms, roughly chopped into 1.5cm cubes
- 2 tablespoons macadamia oil
- 1 teaspoon flavour bomb salt (see page 190) or fine salt
- 4 garlic cloves, peeled
- 1 brown onion, peeled and halved
- 40g dried shiitake mushrooms
- 20g olive oil
- 700g tomato passata
- 400g can diced tomatoes
- 50g red wine
- 50g balsamic vinegar
- 1 tablespoon miso paste (see note)
- 1 tablespoon stock concentrate (see page 190)
- 1 teaspoon sweet paprika
- 1 teaspoon chilli flakes (optional)

1. Preheat oven to 200°C. Line 2 baking trays with baking paper or baking mats.
2. Toss mushroom with macadamia oil and salt and transfer to lined trays. Roast for 15 minutes, or until mushrooms are tender and golden.
3. Meanwhile, place garlic, onion and shiitake mushrooms in TC bowl, chop for 3 seconds, speed 6. Scrape down sides.
4. Add olive oil, sauté for 6 minutes, 100°C, speed 1.
5. Add passata, tomatoes, wine, vinegar, miso, stock concentrate, paprika and chilli (if using), cook for 10 minutes, 100°C, speed 1.
6. Fold together mushrooms and tomato sauce.

Serve in a lasagne, jacket potato or pot pie, as a pasta sauce, or over steamed vegetables.

NOTE: For this sauce to be gluten free, you'll need to use a miso paste made from soybeans, chickpeas, brown rice or adzuki beans.

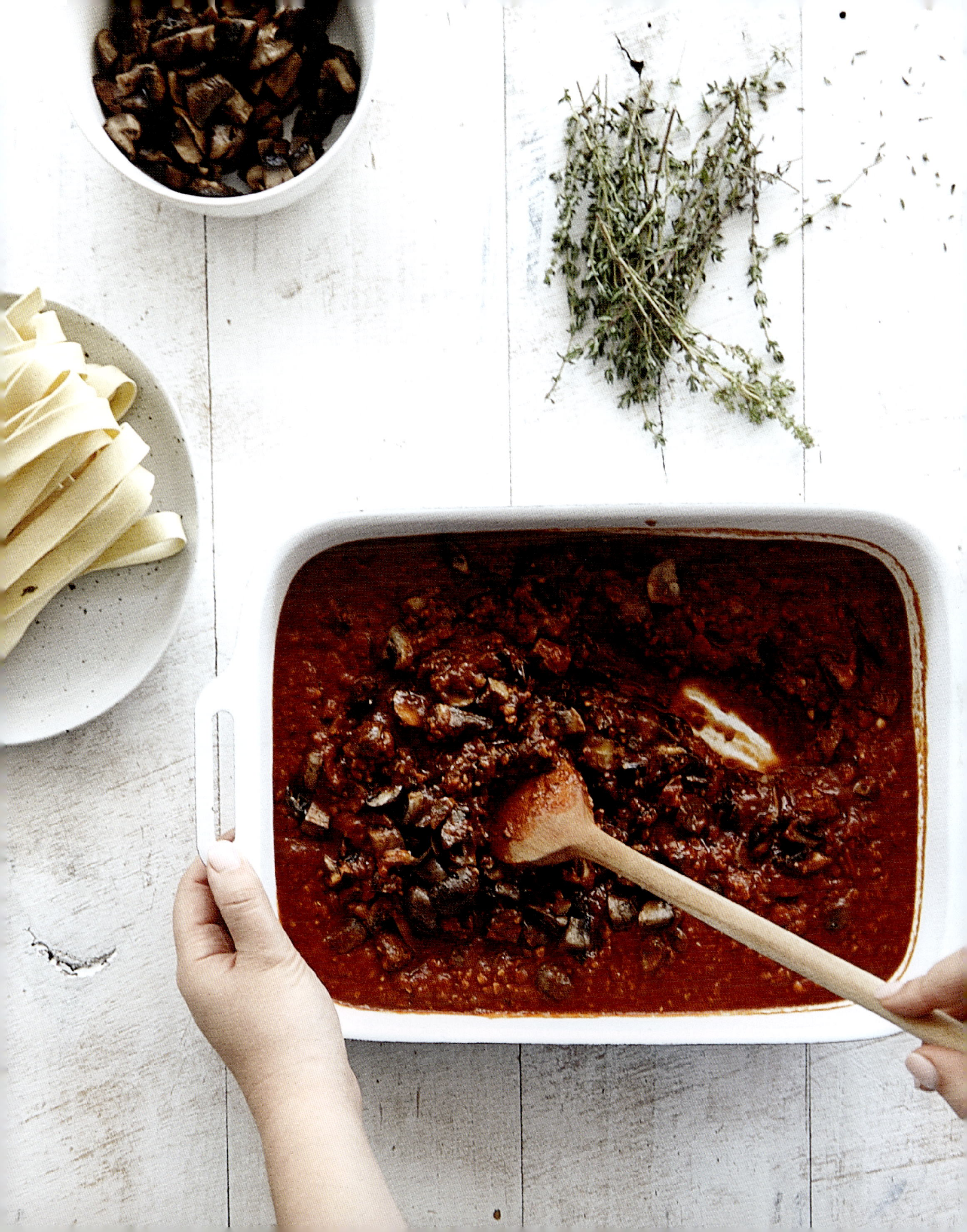

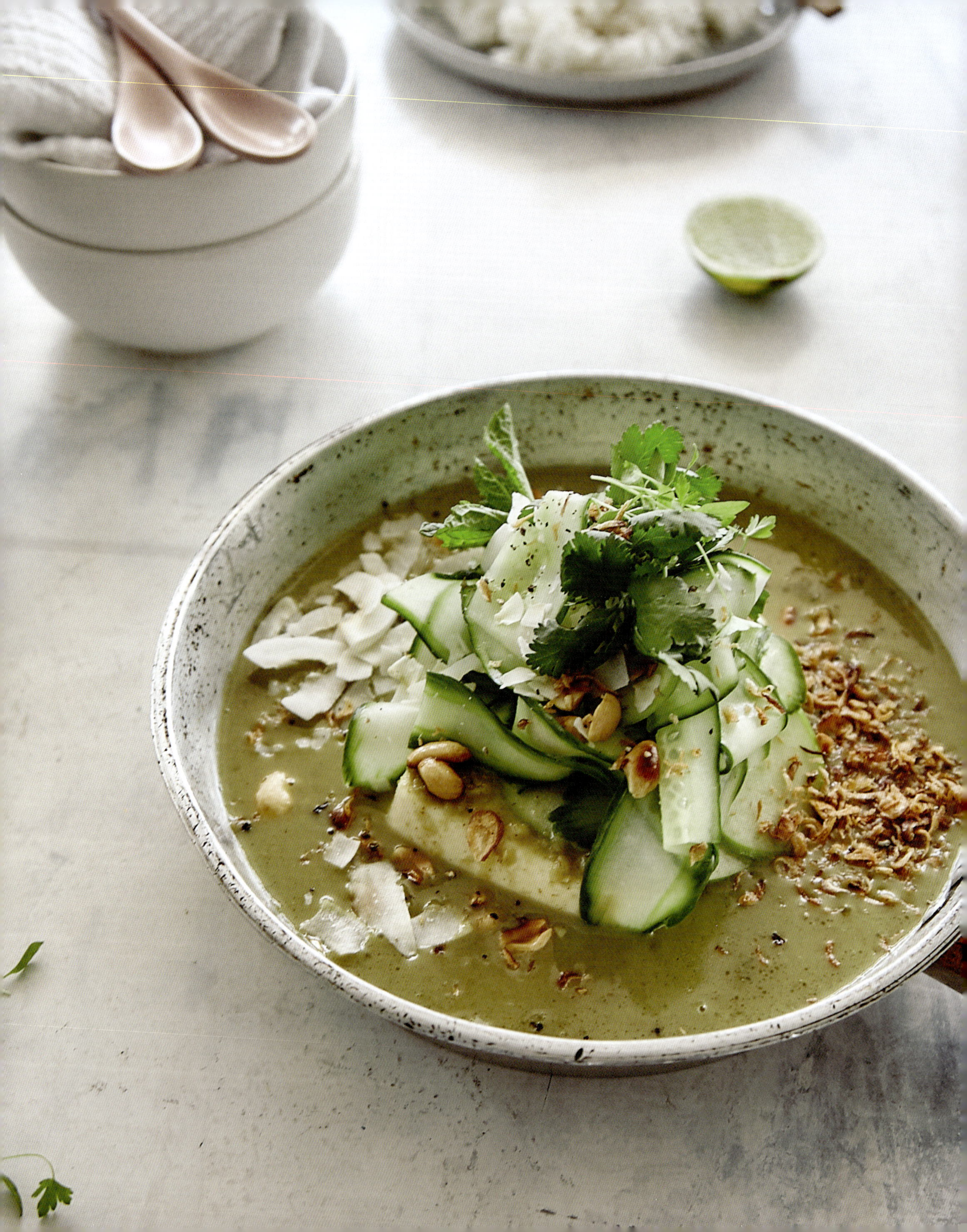

# fresh green curry

**SERVES 2**

This would have to be one of my favourite curries, and the fact that it is vegan is just an added bonus. Not to mention that it also happens to be super easy to make. You've got a creamy coconut base, silky tofu, crunchy toppings, a kick from the curry paste and a fresh burst from the apple, cucumber and lime, all mopped up with fluffy white rice.

1 brown onion, peeled and halved
2 garlic cloves, peeled
20g coconut oil
100g Thai green curry paste (see note)
400g can coconut milk
½ teaspoon fine salt
300g block silken tofu
200g jasmine rice
800g water
½ cucumber, shaved
½ green apple, cored and shaved
½ lime, juice only
50g roasted peanuts
30g coconut flakes
1 tablespoon fried shallots
Fresh coriander, to serve
Fresh mint, to serve

1. Place onion and garlic in TC bowl, chop for 5 seconds, speed 5. Scrape down sides.
2. Add oil and curry paste, sauté 5 minutes, 100°C, speed 1.
3. Add coconut milk and salt, heat for 6 minutes, steaming temperature, speed 2.
4. Place tofu block in food warmer or pre-warmed casserole dish. Pour over curry mixture and cover with lid. Set aside.
5. Place rice in steamer basket and rinse. Fill clean TC bowl with 800g water and insert steamer basket filled with rice. Steam for 15 minutes, steaming temperature, speed 3, or until rice is cooked.
6. Toss cucumber and apple in lime juice. Remove lid from food warmer or casserole dish and top with cucumber and apple mixture, peanuts, coconut, fried shallots and fresh herbs.

Serve with steamed rice.

NOTES: Use a standard vegetable peeler or mandolin to thinly shave slices of cucumber and apple.

Look for a vegan curry paste that doesn't contain shrimp or fish sauce, or make your own.

# chilli olive spaghetti

SERVES 4

This dish is an absolute favourite – on the table in 15 minutes and full of flavour. I am yet to find a person who doesn't love this recipe, herbivore or carnivore!

500g spaghetti
4 garlic cloves, peeled
2 long red chillies, halved
100g olive oil
250g black olives, pitted
1 bunch fresh basil, leaves picked
1 teaspoon fine salt
100g pine nuts, toasted (see note)
50g rocket

1. Cook spaghetti on stove according to packet instructions.
2. Meanwhile, place garlic and chilli in TC bowl, chop for 3 seconds, speed 6. Scrape down sides.
3. Add oil, sauté for 6 minutes, 100°C, speed 1.
4. Add olives, basil and salt, chop for 5 seconds, speed 6.
5. Heat for 3 minutes, 60°C, speed 1.

To serve, toss spaghetti with olive mixture, pine nuts and rocket.

NOTE: To toast pine nuts, cook them in a fry pan over medium–low heat, stirring frequently until golden brown. Keep a close eye on them as they can burn easily.

VARIATION: This recipe makes a delicious cold pasta salad perfect for the lunchbox – replace the spaghetti with a bite-sized pasta such as farfalle for easy eating. For a gluten-free option, simply use buckwheat pasta.

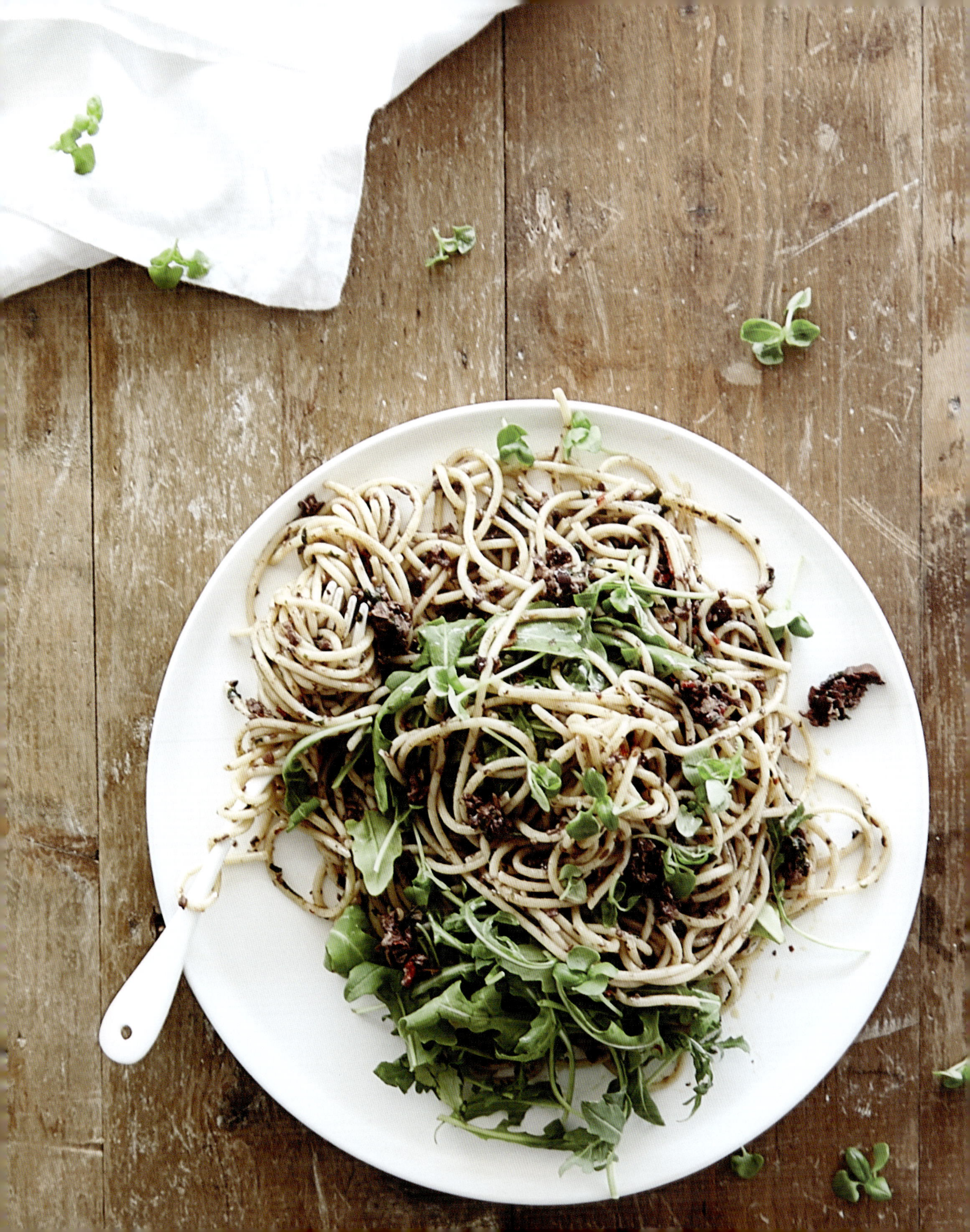

# sushi mash-up

SERVES 4

Sushi is always an easy takeaway option, but it's also pretty simple to make at home. Not to mention a whole lot cheaper. The rolling and shaping can be a bit fiddly, so I've simplified the entire process and whacked it all in a bowl, resulting in a fresh quick-fix dinner that also happens to be vegan. The edamame and avocado bulk it up so no one will miss the meat or seafood.

60g pickled ginger
150g rice wine vinegar
2 teaspoons white sugar
1 teaspoon fine salt
100g tamari
1 teaspoon wasabi paste, or to taste
400g sushi rice
500g frozen edamame (soybeans)
2 tablespoons toasted sesame seeds, plus extra to serve
2 sheets nori, thinly sliced (see note)
2 avocados, cubed
1 cucumber, finely shredded
2 carrots, finely shredded

1. Place ginger, 120g rice wine vinegar, sugar and salt in TC bowl, chop for 1 second, speed 9. Set aside.

2. Without cleaning bowl add remaining 30g vinegar, tamari and wasabi. Mix for 10 seconds, speed 4. Set aside separately.

3. Rinse TC bowl and add 900g water. Place rice in steamer basket, rinse under cold water and insert in TC bowl. Place edamame in steaming tray and place on top. Steam for 23 minutes, steaming temperature, speed 3, or until rice is cooked.

4. Set edamame aside. Transfer rice to a large bowl and pour over ginger mixture. Add sesame seeds and nori and fold through until everything is well combined. Once cool enough to handle, remove edamame beans from their pods.

Divide rice among 4 serving bowls and top each with edamame beans, avocado, cucumber and carrot. Garnish with extra sesame seeds and serve with tamari dressing.

NOTE: The easiest way to thinly slice the nori sheets is to fold them up and cut with scissors.

VARIATION: Add thinly sliced sashimi-grade raw salmon or tuna for a non-vegan alternative.

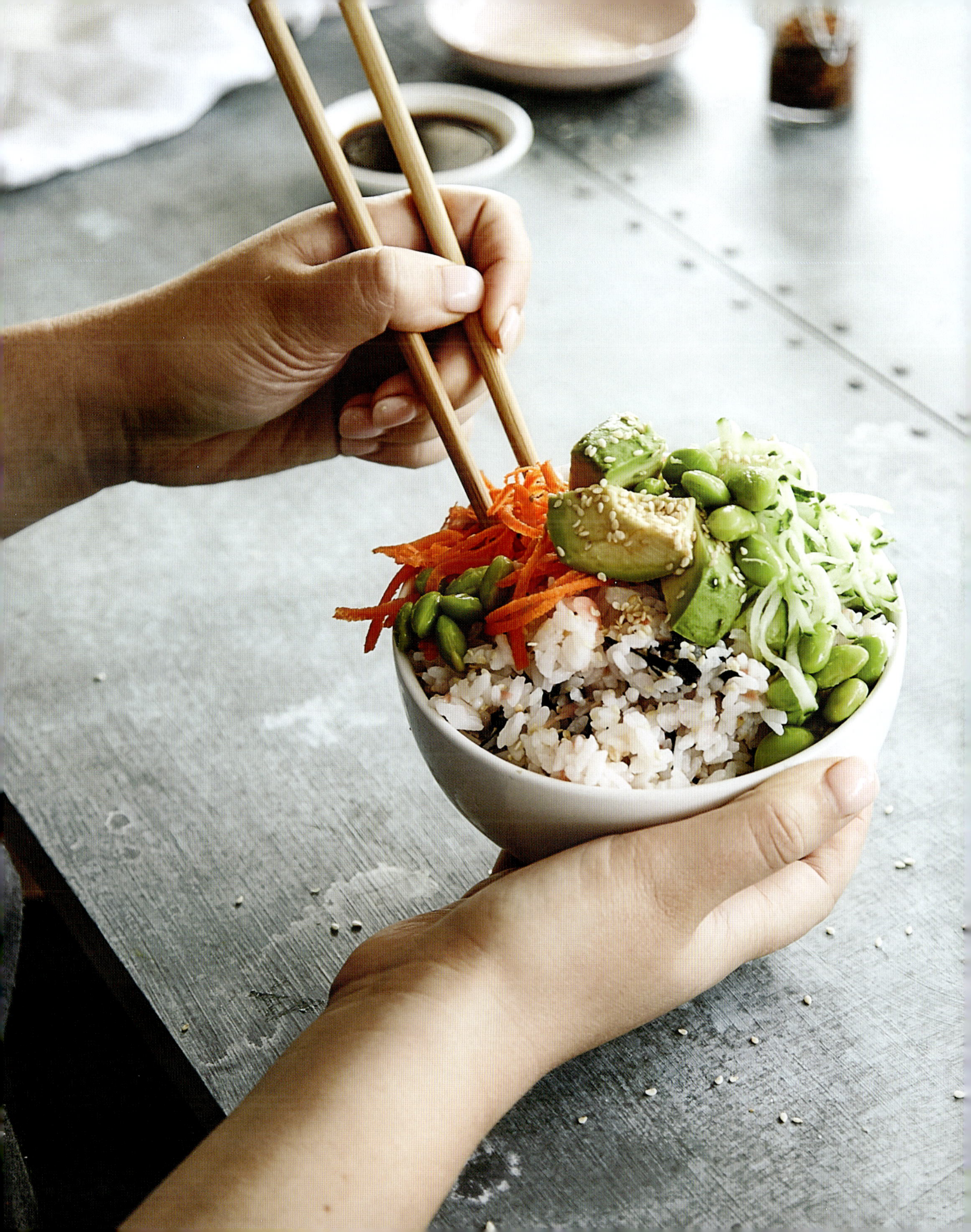

# curried lentil 'sausage' rolls

**MAKES 9**

I always try to create vegan dishes that everyone loves, not just the vegans! These sausage rolls hold their own with their bold curry flavours – definitely not a Clayton's version. You'll need to get started on this recipe a couple of hours ahead of time as the filling needs to be refrigerated, but this can work in your favour as it allows for some serious meal prep – you can make the filling up to three days in advance!

2 carrots, quartered
1 zucchini, quartered
1 brown onion, peeled and halved
3 garlic cloves, peeled
3cm piece ginger, peeled
50g coconut oil
1 tablespoon curry powder
2 teaspoons mustard seeds
1 teaspoon ground cumin
200g split red lentils, rinsed
400g water
2 tablespoons stock concentrate (see page 190)
1 tablespoon tomato paste
6 sheets puff pastry, defrosted if frozen

1. Place carrots in TC bowl, chop for 2 seconds, speed 6.
2. Add zucchini, chop for 4 seconds, speed 4. Set aside.
3. Place onion, garlic and ginger in TC bowl, chop for 3 seconds, speed 6. Scrape down sides.
4. Add oil, curry powder, mustard seeds and cumin, cook for 5 minutes, steaming temperature, speed 1.
5. Add lentils, water, stock concentrate and tomato paste, cook for 18 minutes, 100°C, reverse speed 2.
6. Add carrot and zucchini mixture, combine using spatula. Refrigerate mixture for a minimum of 2 hours.
7. Preheat oven to 210°C. Line a baking tray with baking paper or a baking mat.
8. Place one-third of the chilled mixture along the edge of a doubled-up pastry sheet and roll to form a log. Cut into thirds with a serrated knife. Transfer to the lined tray and place seam side down. Repeat with remaining mixture and pastry.
9. Bake rolls for 25 minutes, or until browned.

Serve hot out of the oven or allow to cool completely before packing into lunchboxes. Delicious served with chutney (see pages 148, 239 and 240).

NOTE: To make mini sausage rolls perfect for finger food, follow the same recipe but don't double up the pastry – roll up 6 individual sheets and cut each roll into 4–6 pieces.

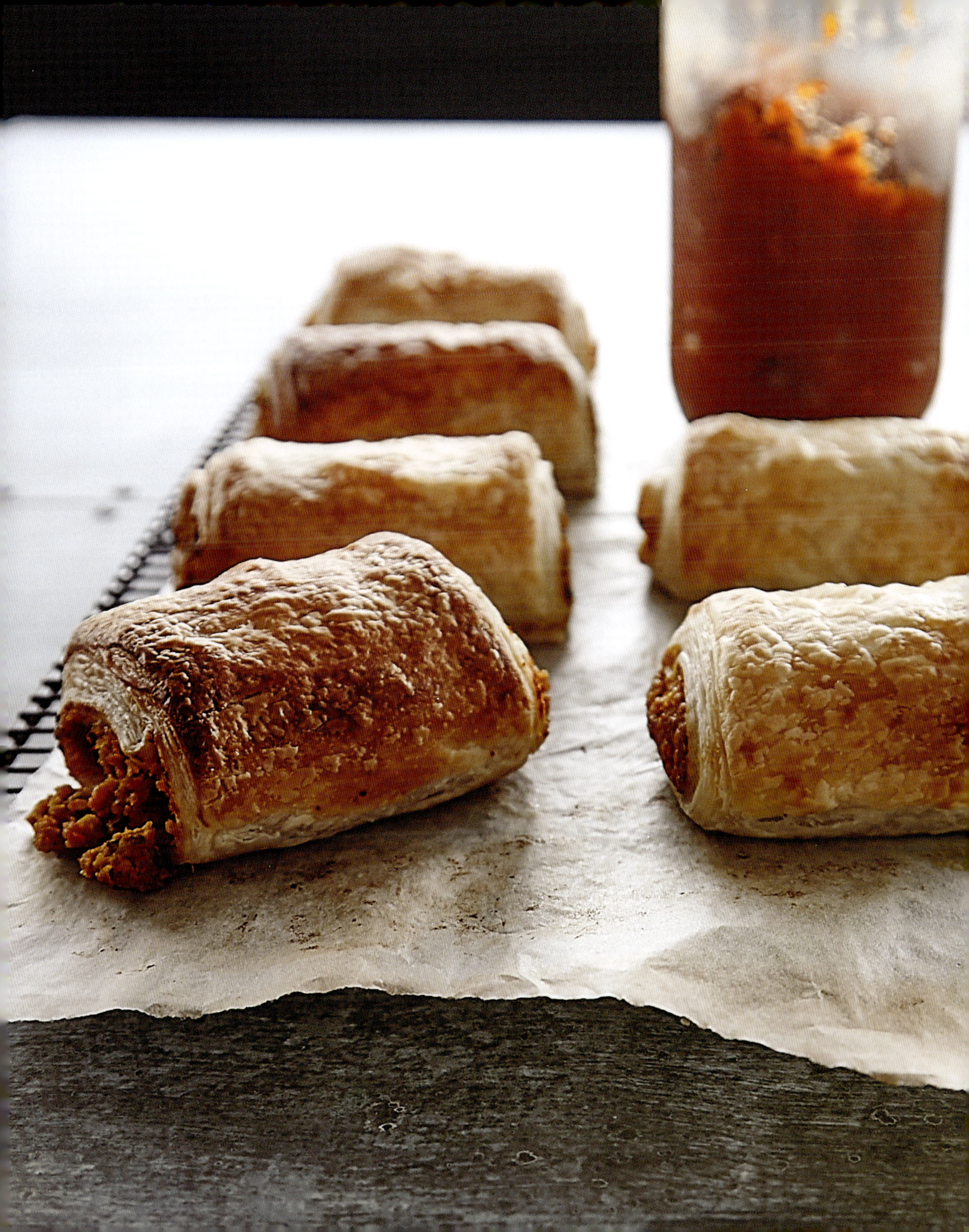

# beetroot burgers

**MAKES 8**

What I love about this burger is not just what's left out, but that it is full of healthy veggies, seeds and lentils. While the beetroot provides the bulk for this recipe, the flavour is certainly not earthy – it's actually very fresh and light. And unlike your average veggie burger, the patties are super moist with texture and crunch. My mum Janene developed this gem, and she's done herself proud.

100g rolled oats
100g split red lentils
1 red onion, peeled and halved
3 garlic cloves, peeled
15g macadamia oil, plus extra for frying
4 medium beetroot, peeled and quartered (approx. 500g)
1 carrot, quartered
1 handful fresh mint
10g coconut sugar
10g apple cider vinegar
1 tablespoon smoked paprika
¼ teaspoon ground allspice
2 teaspoons flavour bomb salt (see page 246) or fine salt
60g sunflower seeds
50g pumpkin seeds
40g chia seeds

1. Place oats in TC bowl, mill 4 seconds, speed 9. Set aside.
2. Place lentils in steamer basket and rinse thoroughly. Place 600g water in TC bowl and insert steamer basket. Cook lentils for 10 minutes, 100°C, speed 4. Set aside with oats.
3. Rinse TC bowl with cold water and dry. Add onion and garlic, chop for 5 seconds, speed 5. Scrape down sides.
4. Add oil, sauté 5 minutes, 100°C, speed 1.
5. Add beetroot, carrot and mint leaves, chop 5 seconds, speed 5, or until finely chopped but not puréed. Scrape down sides.
6. Add sugar, vinegar, paprika, allspice, salt, sunflower seeds, pumpkin seeds, chia seeds, reserved lentils and milled oats. Cook for 3 minutes, 70°C, reverse speed 2. Using wet hands, form mixture into 8 patties.
7. Heat a liberal amount of macadamia oil in a large fry pan over medium heat. Once hot, add as many burgers as will fit and cook for 5 minutes each side, or until golden brown and heated through. Repeat with remaining burgers.

Serve patties just as they are or inside burger buns along with lettuce, tomato, sauce and chutney. Pictured here with tomato chutney and hummus (see pages 240 and 37).

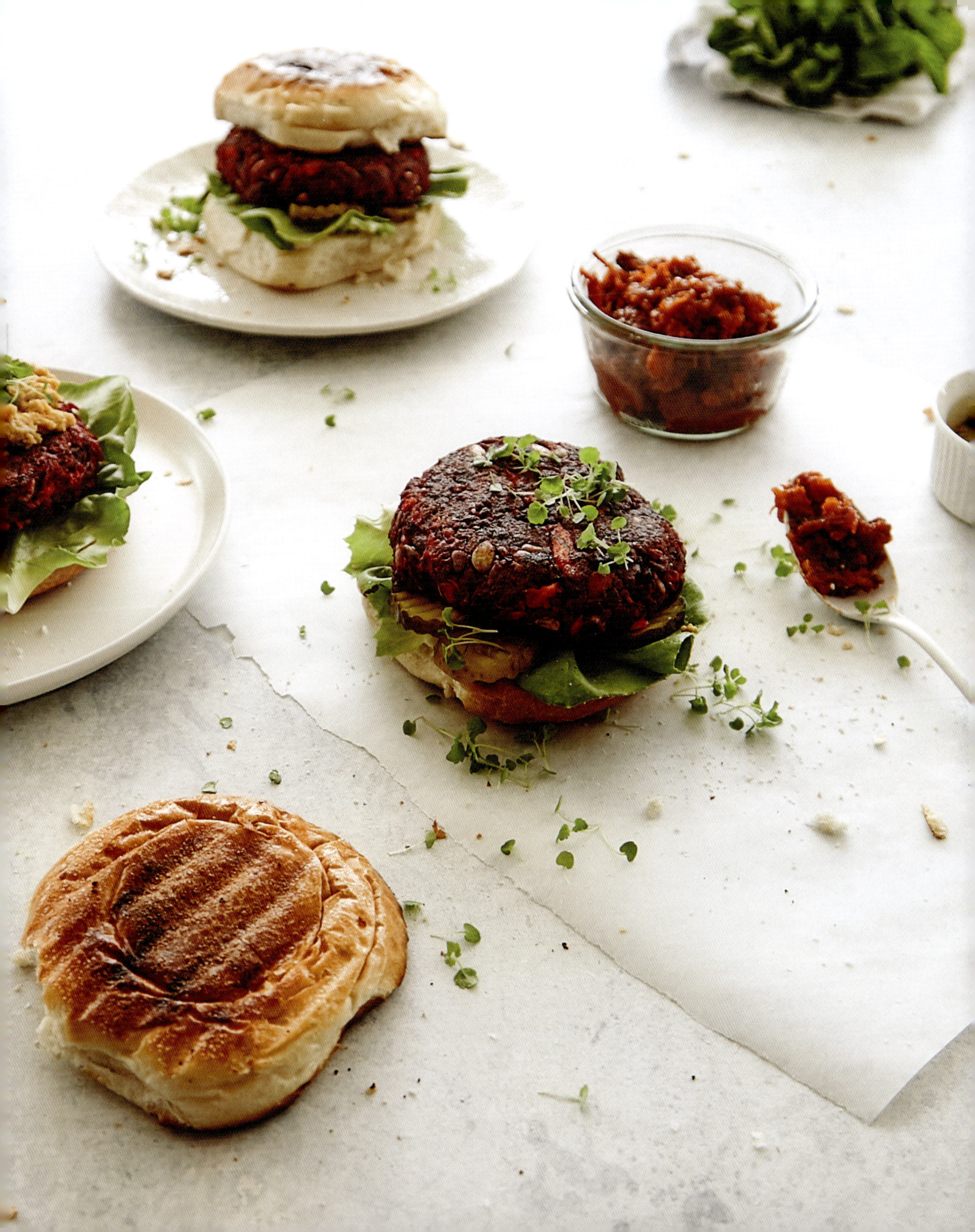

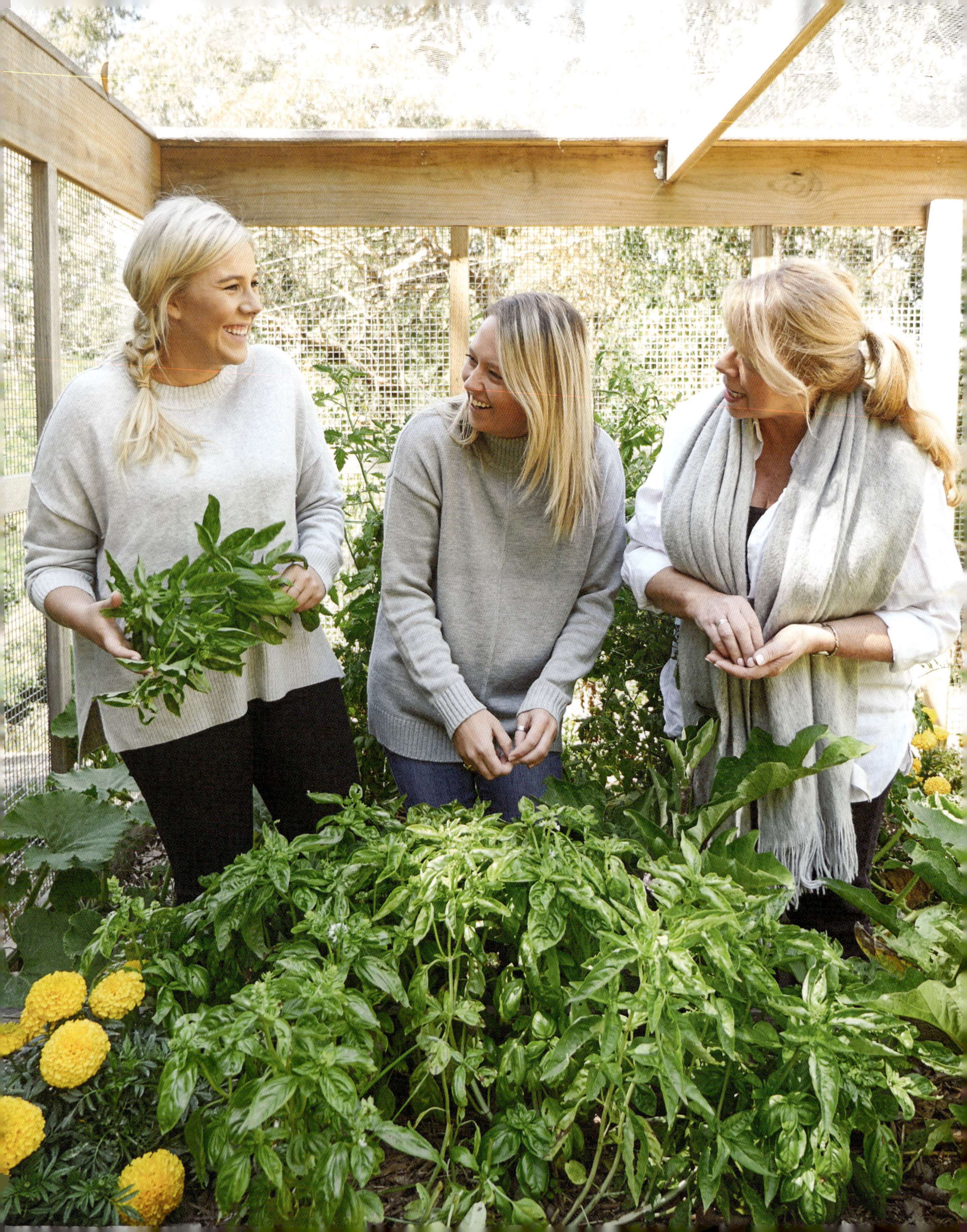

# low and slow

Slow cooking is my secret weapon in the kitchen. You can cook cheap cuts of meat to tender, melting perfection with little chance of it burning or drying out. It may take hours until the final dish is ready, but the hands-on time is minimal, making it a quick process … in a roundabout way! Get organised and do a slow cook on the weekend – you'll be enjoying the fruits of your labour throughout the busy week. While the thermo cooker itself cannot slow cook your meal, it can save you a whole lot of time in the preparation. View it as your own sous chef – a second set of hands to grind, mince, chop, sauté, heat and blend. Cooking low and slow also means your thermo cooker is free to do other things, like make the delicious sides and accompaniments in the other chapters.

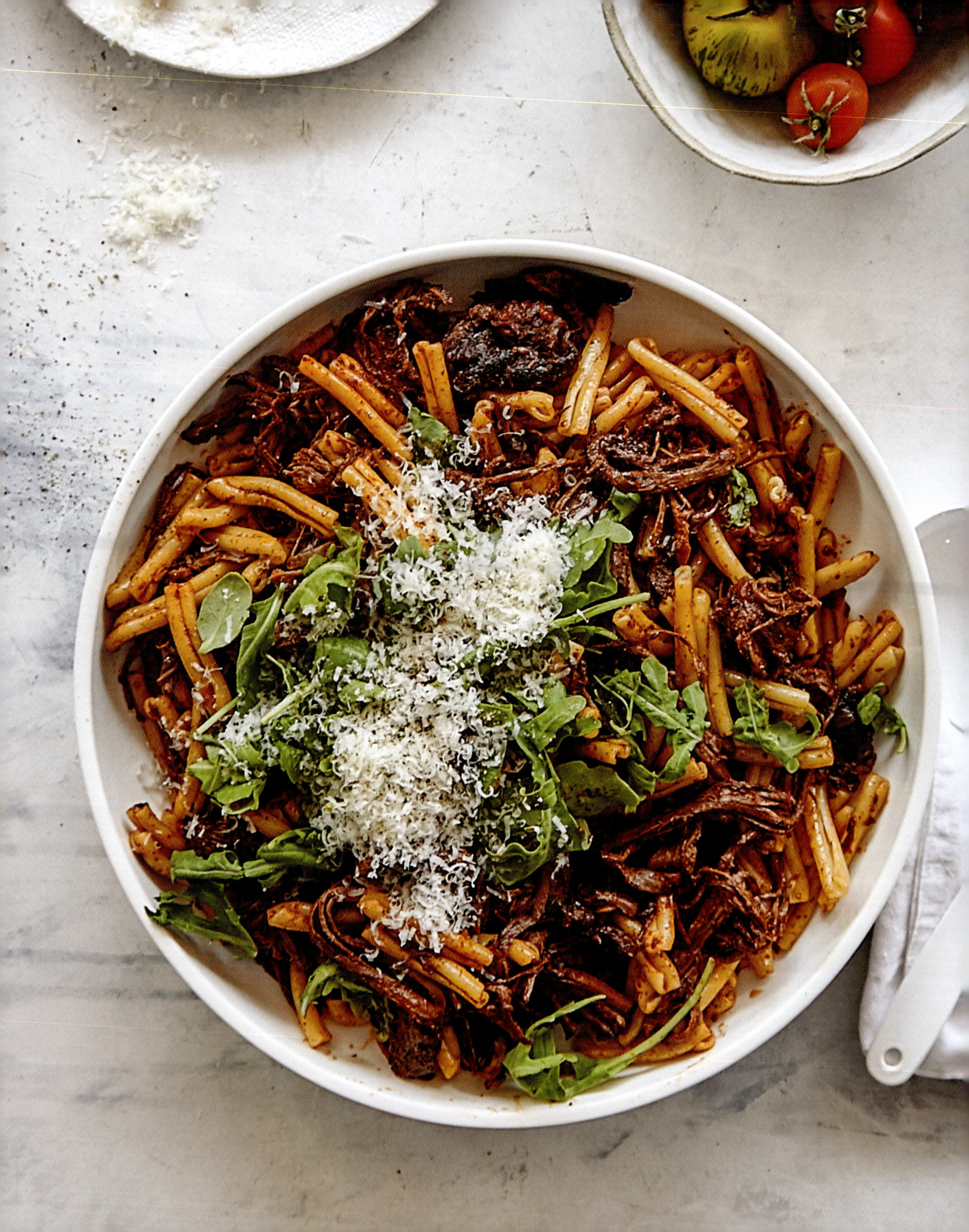

# rich brisket ragù

**SERVES 10**

When I lived in Texas I fell in love with beef brisket, and couldn't understand why this delicious cut of meat wasn't more popular in Australia. I put it down to people not knowing what to do with it. Because of all the thick connective tissue it has to be cooked very low and very slow, otherwise it is as tough as old boots. Cooked correctly, it simply melts in your mouth. You need to get started on this recipe well ahead of time, but the upside is that it makes a huge amount and tastes even better the next day. Serve it with fresh pasta for the most amazing meal of your life. (Big call, but my good friend Poppy made it!)

2kg boneless beef brisket
30g macadamia oil
6 sprigs fresh rosemary
2 brown onions, peeled and halved
4 garlic cloves, peeled
700g tomato passata
400g can diced tomatoes
250g red wine
60g stock concentrate (see page 190)
50g balsamic vinegar
20g Dijon mustard
20g brown sugar
100g rocket
100g pecorino or parmesan, shaved (optional)

1. Preheat oven to 200°C.

2. Place meat flat in a large casserole dish, fatty side up. Choose a dish that fits the meat snugly, but still allows it to lie completely flat. Rub meat with 10g macadamia oil and scatter with rosemary sprigs. Roast for 30 minutes, uncovered.

3. Meanwhile, place onion and garlic in TC bowl, chop for 5 seconds, speed 5. Scrape down sides.

4. Add remaining 20g macadamia oil, sauté for 6 minutes, 100°C, speed 1.

5. Add passata, tomatoes, red wine, stock concentrate, vinegar, mustard and sugar. Mix for 5 seconds, speed 4.

6. Cook for 10 minutes, 100°C, speed 1.

7. Remove meat from oven and pour over the tomato mixture, ensuring meat is submerged as much as possible. Cover with a tight-fitting lid or foil. Reduce temperature to 140°C and roast for 4 hours.

8. Remove lid or foil and cook, uncovered, for a further 1 hour, or until sauce is thick and reduced and meat pulls apart easily.

9. Remove meat from oven and set aside to rest for 30 minutes. Shred meat using two forks and stir through pan juices.

Serve ragù with fresh charcoal pasta (see page 130), dried pasta, soft polenta (see page 126) or mashed potato (see page 118). Top with rocket and cheese.

# korean beef ribs

+ SLOW-COOKING

**SERVES 8**

This is my favourite slow-cooked Asian beef recipe – meltingly tender meat falling off the bone in a rich soy sauce. It lends itself to so many serving suggestions, but my preference is to serve it simply with a big bowl of fluffy rice to soak up all the juices. Other than being home for three hours, there's really not much for you to do here – just let it gently bubble away, filling the house with delicious aromas while you get on with other things.

8 garlic cloves, peeled
3cm piece ginger, peeled
60g brown sugar
30g stock concentrate (see page 190)
3 teaspoons Korean red pepper flakes or chilli flakes
100g dark soy sauce
60g rice wine
3kg beef short ribs, cut into individual ribs
Toasted sesame seeds, to serve

1. Preheat oven to 140°C.
2. Place garlic and ginger in TC bowl, chop for 2 seconds, speed 6.
3. Add sugar, stock concentrate, red pepper or chilli flakes, soy sauce and rice wine, mix for 5 seconds, speed 4.
4. Place beef in large casserole dish and pour over sauce mixture. Cover and cook in the oven for 3 hours, or until meat is so tender it falls off the bone.

Serve ribs and juices sprinkled with sesame seeds. Accompany with kimchi-kraut (see page 236), sliced cucumber, baos (pictured, see page 165), steamed rice, Asian slaw, pickled salad (see page 124) or thick rice noodles.

NOTE: While 3kg of ribs sounds like a lot, bear in mind that this includes the bone weight – the quantity of meat will be far less after it falls off the bone.

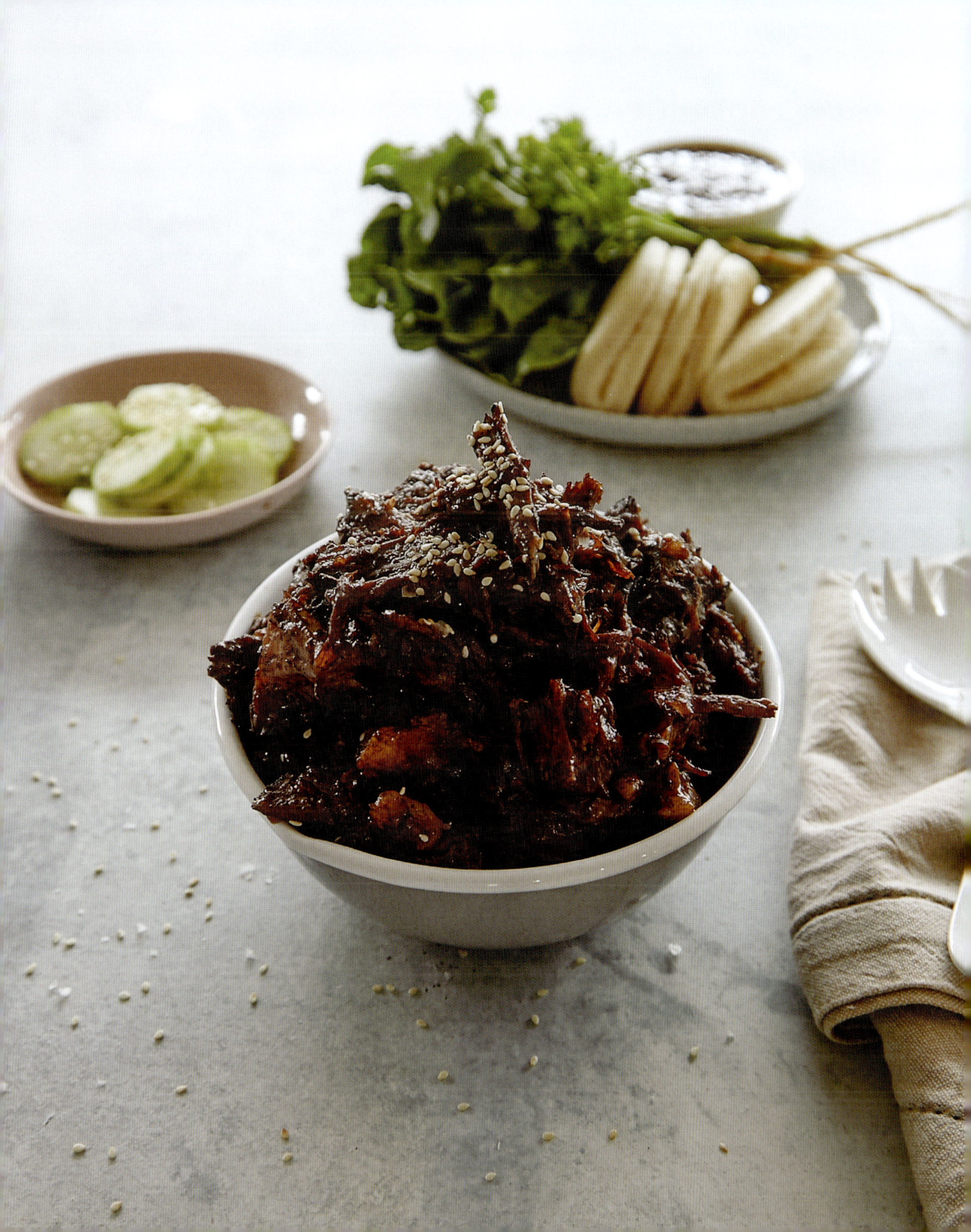

# lamb shoulder with salsa verde

**SERVES 8**

Warning: you must start this recipe first thing in the morning! It literally takes all day to cook, but the good news is there's hardly any hands-on time. The result is sweet and tender melt-in-your-mouth meat. The tangy freshness of the salsa verde and yoghurt really cuts through the richness, balancing this dish perfectly. Serve with roasted vegetables, rocket salad, warmed pita bread or a rice pilaf.

3 teaspoons coarse salt
2 teaspoons coriander seeds
2 teaspoons cumin seeds
1 teaspoon fennel seeds
6 garlic cloves, peeled
100g olive oil
1 lamb shoulder, bone in (approx. 2 kg)
1 lemon, rind of 1 and juice of half
Handful fresh mint
Handful fresh parsley
30g Dijon mustard
2 teaspoons capers, drained
Yoghurt, to serve (optional)
Micro herbs, to serve (optional)

1. Place 2 teaspoons salt, coriander, cumin and fennel in TC bowl, mill for 10 seconds, speed 10.

2. Add garlic, chop for 3 seconds, speed 6.

3. Add 40g oil, mix for 5 seconds, speed 8. Rub spice mix over lamb. Place lamb in a large casserole dish or roasting tin, fatty side up. Pour 1 cup (250 ml) of water into the dish (pour around lamb rather than on top). Cover with lid or foil and sit at room temperature for 2 hours.

4. Transfer lamb to oven and set to 120°C. Cook for 7 hours, or until meat is falling off the bone.

5. Allow meat to rest for 30 minutes before pulling apart with a fork.

6. Meanwhile, place lemon rind and remaining 1 teaspoon salt in clean TC bowl. Mill for 10 seconds, speed 8.

7. Add mint, parsley, mustard, capers, lemon juice and remaining 60g oil, mix for 8 seconds, speed 9.

Serve warm or cold with salsa verde, yoghurt and micro herbs (if using).

NOTE: Freeze any leftover lamb fat for later use (see page 178).

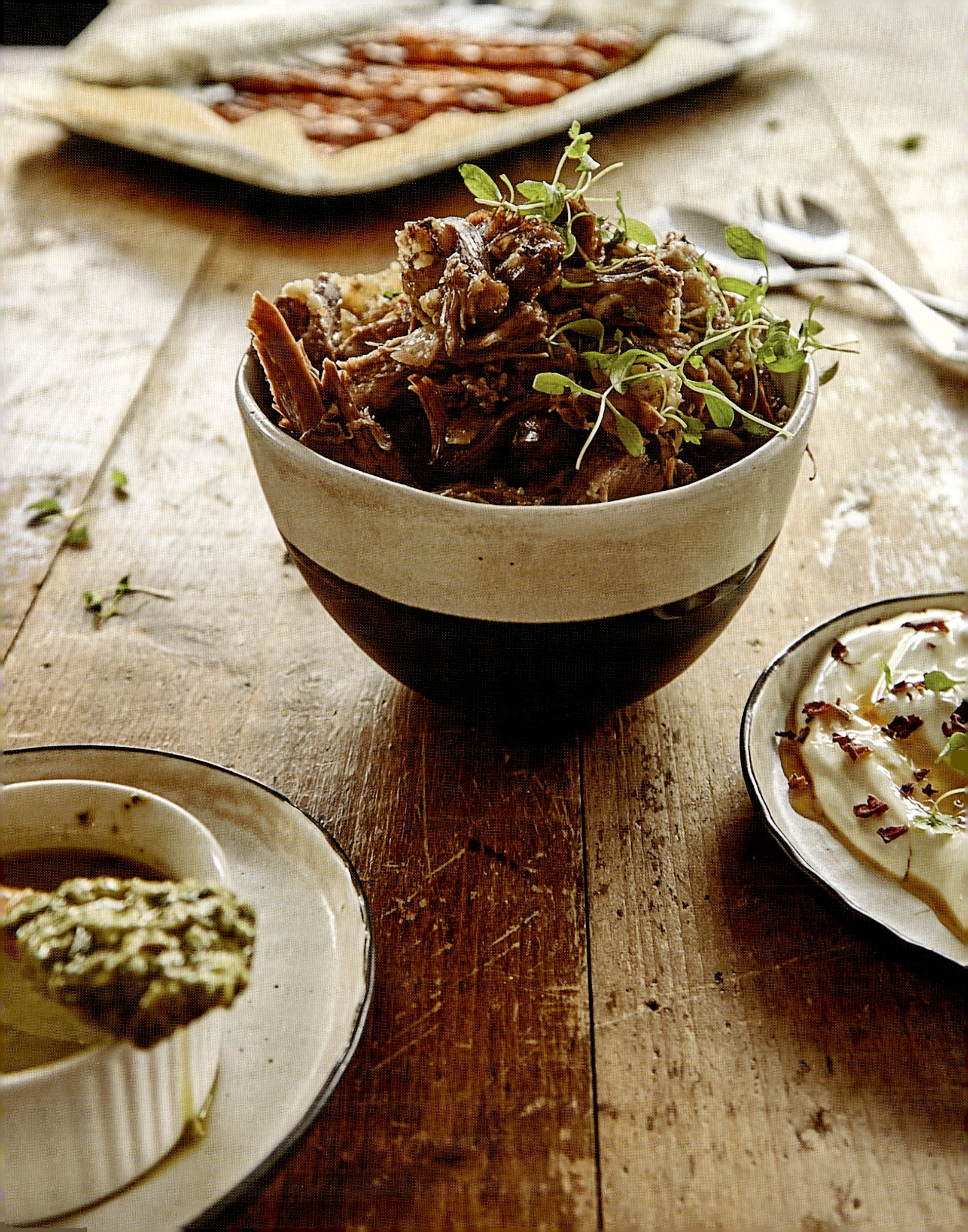

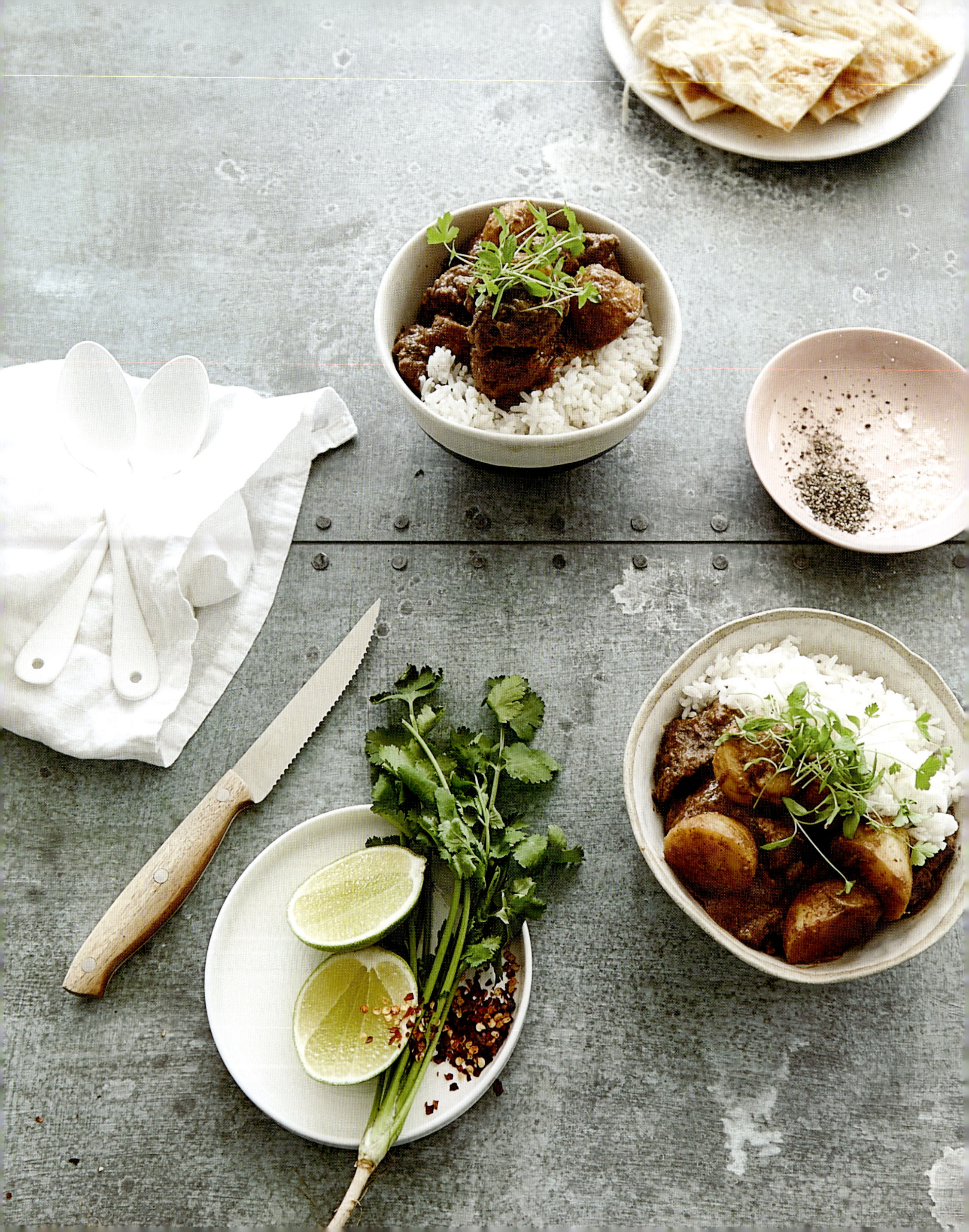

# massaman beef curry

**SERVES 8**

I fell in love with Massaman curry during my travels through Thailand, and am delighted that it is so easy to recreate at home. To my mind, it is the best of both worlds: it has all the richness of an Indian curry, but is lifted by the fresh Thai flavours. It is also mild and sweet, making this recipe a real crowd pleaser.

4 long red chillies, halved
2 brown onions, peeled and halved
4 garlic cloves, peeled
3cm piece galangal or ginger, peeled
1 lemongrass stalk, white part only, cut into 1cm pieces
160g roasted peanuts
200g water
50g stock concentrate (see page 190)
80g tamarind purée
60g fish sauce
20g coconut oil
15g coconut sugar
3 teaspoons coriander seeds
3 teaspoons cumin seeds
2 teaspoons ground cinnamon
Pinch ground cloves
400g can coconut cream
1kg beef chuck steak, cubed
1kg waxy new potatoes, halved
6 kaffir lime leaves

1. Preheat oven to 160°C.
2. Place chilli, onion, garlic, galangal or ginger, lemongrass, 80g peanuts, water, stock concentrate, tamarind purée, fish sauce, oil, sugar, coriander, cumin, cinnamon and cloves in TC bowl, purée for 30 seconds, speed 9. Scrape down sides.
3. Sauté for 10 minutes, steaming temperature, speed 2, MC removed and steamer basket on top to prevent splashes.
4. Add coconut cream, mix for 5 seconds, speed 4.
5. Place beef, potatoes and lime leaves in a large casserole dish. Pour over coconut mixture. Cover with a tight-fitting lid, place in oven and cook for 2 hours.
6. Remove lid and stir. Cook for a further 30 minutes, or until meat and potatoes are tender and sauce is thick.

Scatter with remaining peanuts and garnish with chilli flakes, fresh coriander, micro herbs, lime wedges or fried shallots. Serve with steamed rice or roti bread (see page 143).

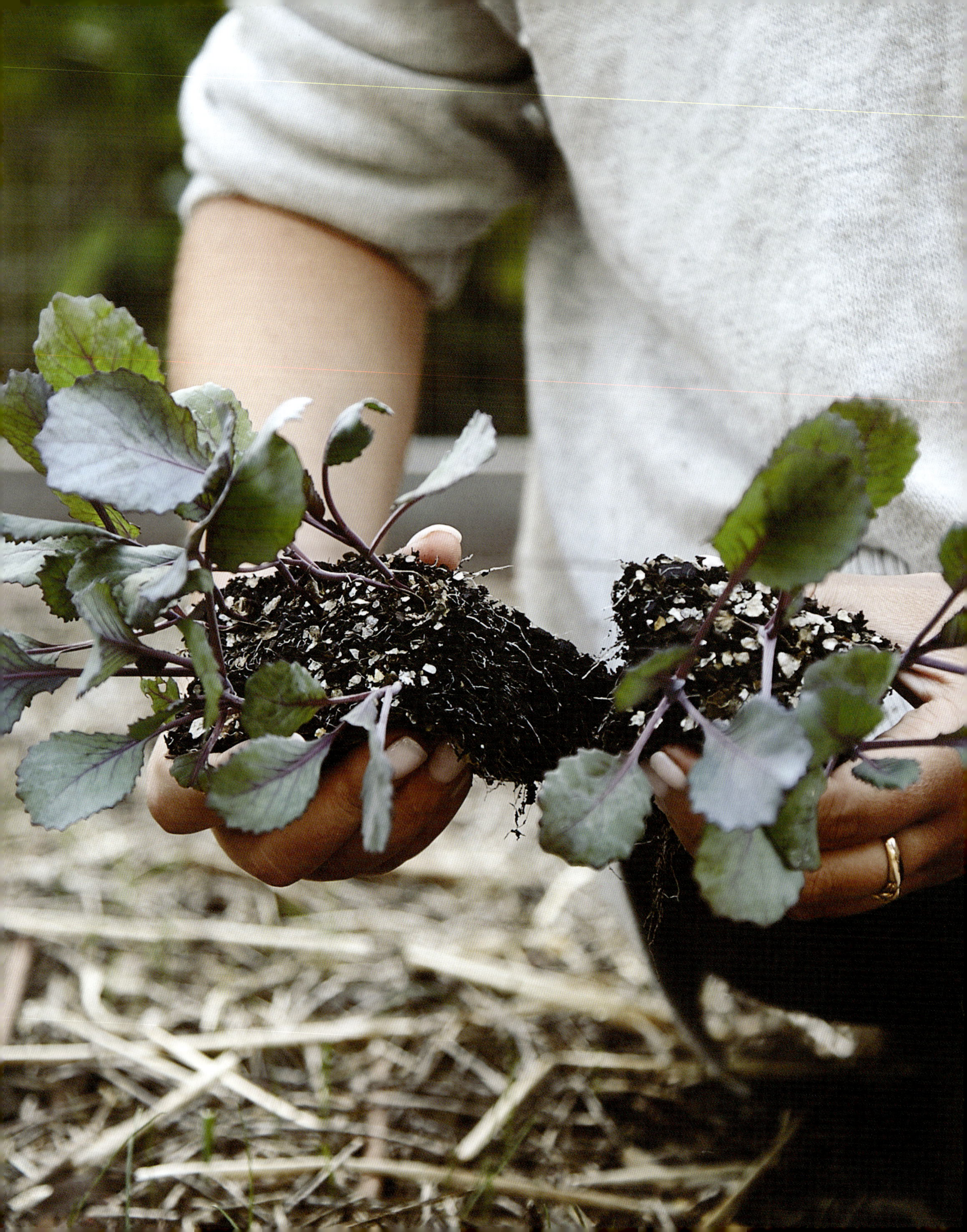

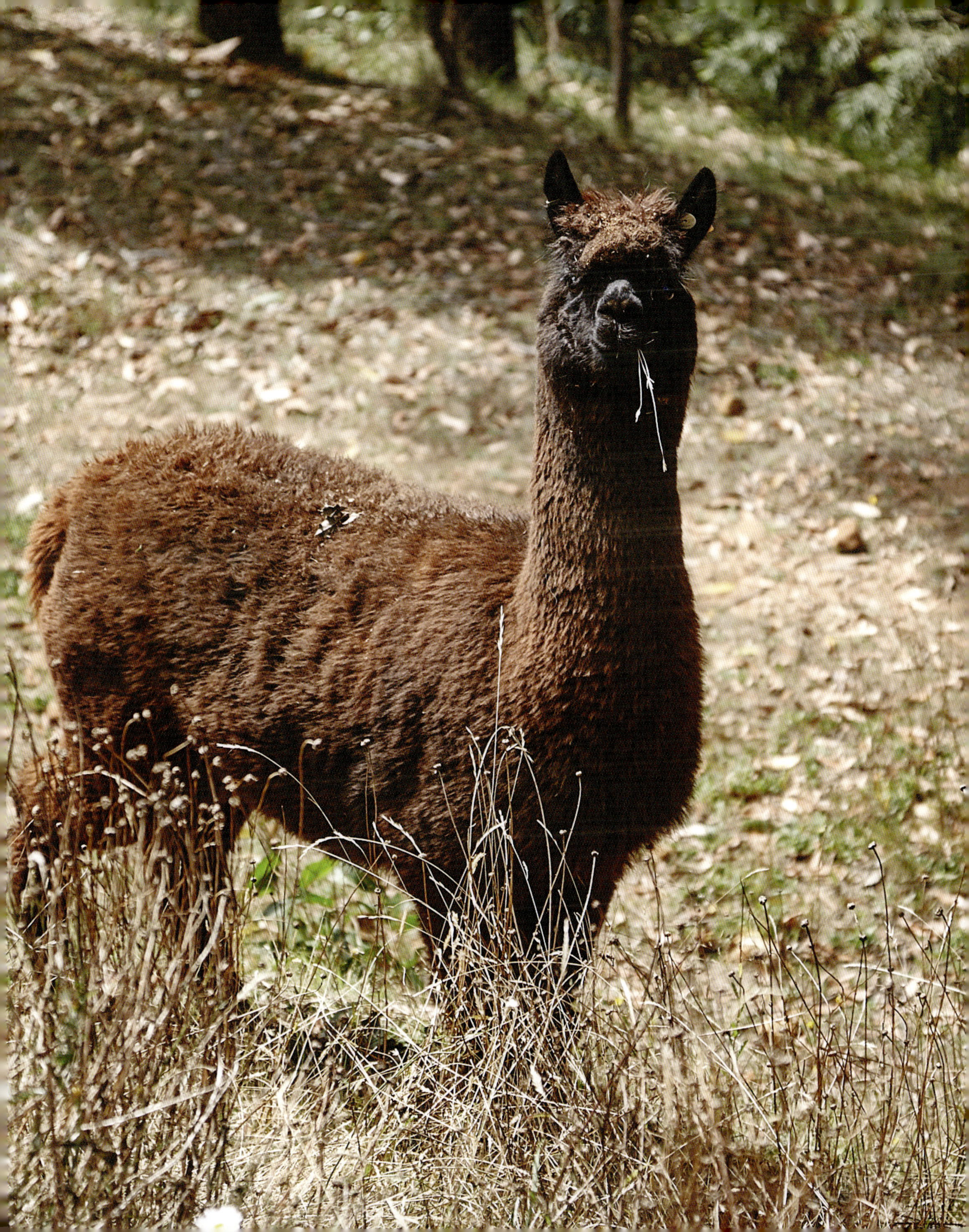

# bones about it

Whenever you've got bones left over from cooking, make a batch of bone broth. It's dead easy, chock full of nutrients and adds such amazing flavour wherever it is used. It is at the top of 'my waste not want not' mantra: take something destined for landfill and turn it into something truly nourishing – in this case, bone broth (or compost, my other great passion!).

We all know that for us to eat meat something had to die, and to respect this I believe we must make the most of everything that animal has given us, just like our ancestors did. The thought of these bones, jam-packed with precious nutrients, going into landfill is so sad – what a waste. Just like human bones, animal bones contain lots of calcium, magnesium, phosphorus and other essential minerals, as well as collagen and gelatine, which are great for digestion, gut health, inflammation, thyroid and your hair, skin and nails. By cooking these bones in water for a long period of time we are able to extract all these nutrients, resulting in a rich nutritious broth and bones that will literally crumble in your hand.

## HOW TO:

1. **COLLECT BONES**  These can be raw or cooked from any animal. It could be the leftover bones from beef ribs (see page 106), lamb shoulder (see page 108), lamb cutlets (see page 75), rotisserie chicken, chicken drumsticks, osso bucco, pork chops, fish carcasses etc. Just make sure all the bones you use are from one type of animal – you wouldn't mix beef and fish in one broth, for instance. Either use them to make a broth straight away or store them in ziplock bags in the freezer. This is also convenient if you only have a few bones – keep adding to your freezer bag until you've got at least a kilogram.

2. **FILL IT UP**  Place the bones in a large stockpot, casserole dish or slow cooker. Add enough cold water to completely cover the bones, plus a bit extra (approximately 2 litres of water to 1 kilogram of bones). Add a tablespoon of apple cider vinegar for every 2 litres of water. You can also add leftover veggie scraps such as celery tops, onion skins, garlic cloves and carrots, as well as fresh or dried herbs and spices, but I tend to keep my broth plain.

3. **COOK IT LOW AND SLOW**  Cook for between 12 and 72 hours – the longer the better! The exception here is fish bones, which only need 4–12 hours. If you are using a slow cooker (which I highly recommend), set it to low. If you don't have a slow cooker, bring the water to the boil on the stove, then reduce the heat to low so it is barely simmering and cover with a lid.

4   **STRAIN** Allow the broth to cool slightly then strain out all the bones, vegetables etc. I usually place a very large metal strainer over a large casserole dish and pour the contents of the pot into the second vessel, allowing the strainer to catch everything I don't want (be careful as the pot will be hot and heavy). Your broth is now ready! Discard or compost the leftover solids.

5   **STORE** You can use your broth straight away, but you'll probably have more than you need. I allow my broth to cool before ladling it into plastic containers to be frozen – usually in 1 litre batches for ease of use later on. You could also refrigerate it for up to 3 days.

6   **ENJOY** If frozen, allow your broth to defrost in the fridge. Depending on the bones you used, you might have a thick cap of fat on the top of your broth – if so, gently remove it and store it in the fridge or freezer, then use it to make amazing roast potatoes later (see page 178). If your bones contained a lot of gelatine, your broth may have actually turned to jelly once cooled – this is a good thing! It will return to liquid once warmed. Remember, your broth hasn't been salted, so you will need to season it with salt or stock concentrate (see page 190). Broth strength and flavour will vary greatly, depending on ingredients and cooking time. If yours is quite strong you might want to dilute it with extra water. Use it in risottos (see page 183), soups (see page 180), stews, curries, sauces or drink it on its own!

While there are many more techniques you can employ in your broth making I like to keep things as simple and straightforward as possible. For us at home, the easier it is the more often we are likely to do it – and that's what matters.

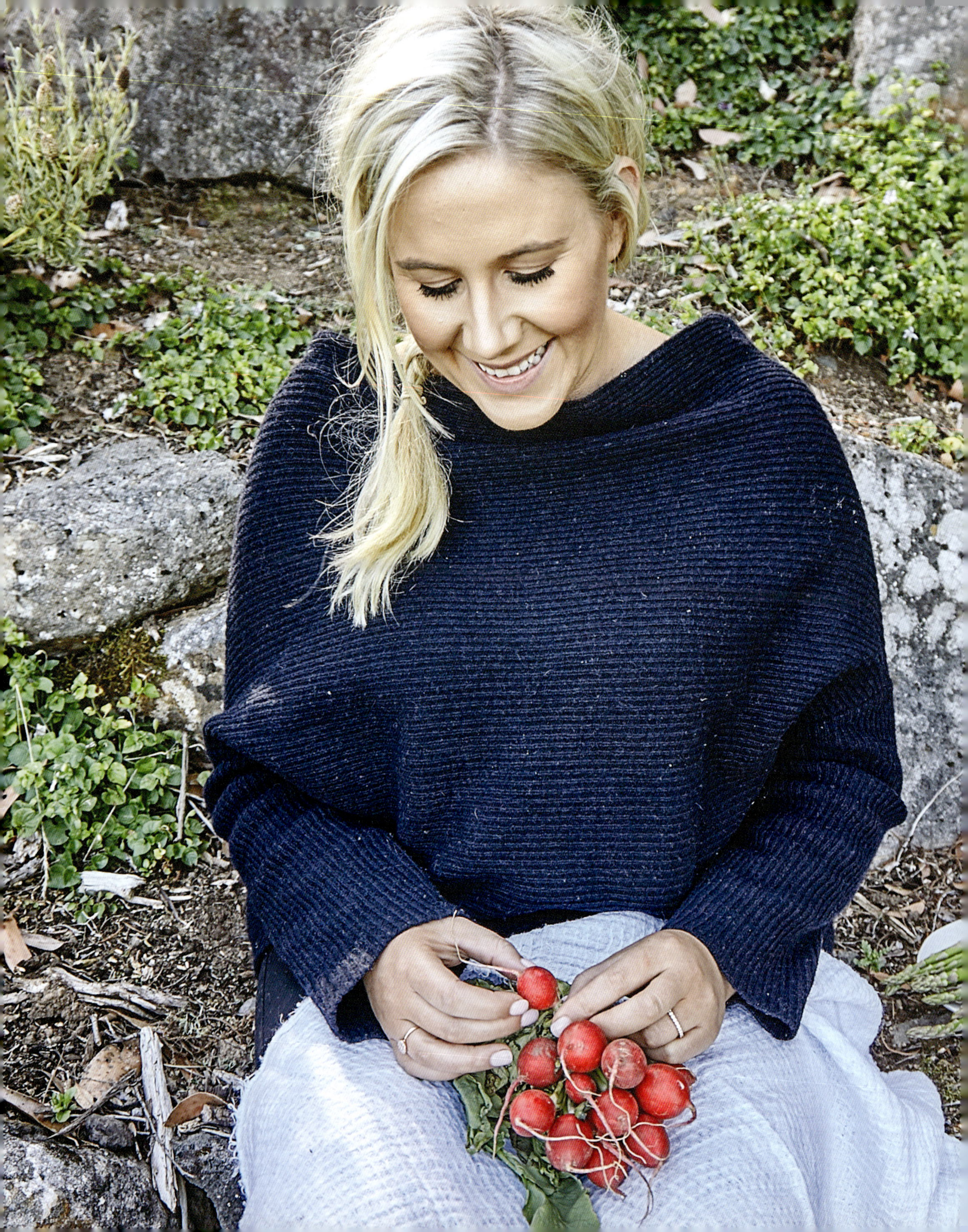

# super sides

Once you've got the main component of your meal sorted, you need to decide on your side dishes – although with side dishes as delicious as these, you might start thinking the other way around! I've included everything from fresh, light options through to downright decadent picks, so whatever you are in the mood for I've got you covered. Keeping these recipes separate means you can mix and match them with other dishes in this book, creating an exciting range of culinary possibilities.

# mashed potato

**SERVES 4**

This recipe always evokes fond family memories for me. My dad has always taken great pride in cooking the best steak I've ever tasted – so good, in fact, that's literally all he serves … just steak, on a plate! So when Dad says he's 'cooking dinner', I'll often whip up a batch of this mash. I love the way the soft pillowy potato soaks up all the delicious juices. Make no mistake, this mash is the ultimate indulgence – rich, silky and ever so creamy. It also makes the best topping for a shepherd's pie. Use the rich brisket ragù recipe as the base (see page 105).

1kg Dutch cream potatoes, peeled and chopped into 2–3cm pieces
2 teaspoons fine salt
250g milk
150g pouring cream

1. Insert butterfly into TC bowl. Add potato, salt, milk and cream, cook for 15–20 minutes, 100°C, speed 1.5, or until potato is soft and starting to break up, MC tilted to allow steam to escape.

2. Mash for 1 minute, speed 4.

Serve immediately or keep warm in a low oven or food warmer.

VARIATIONS: For a cheesy mash, add 100g grated cheese at step 2. You can also garnish the mash with a fresh herb that complements the flavours in the main dish.

SUPER SIDES

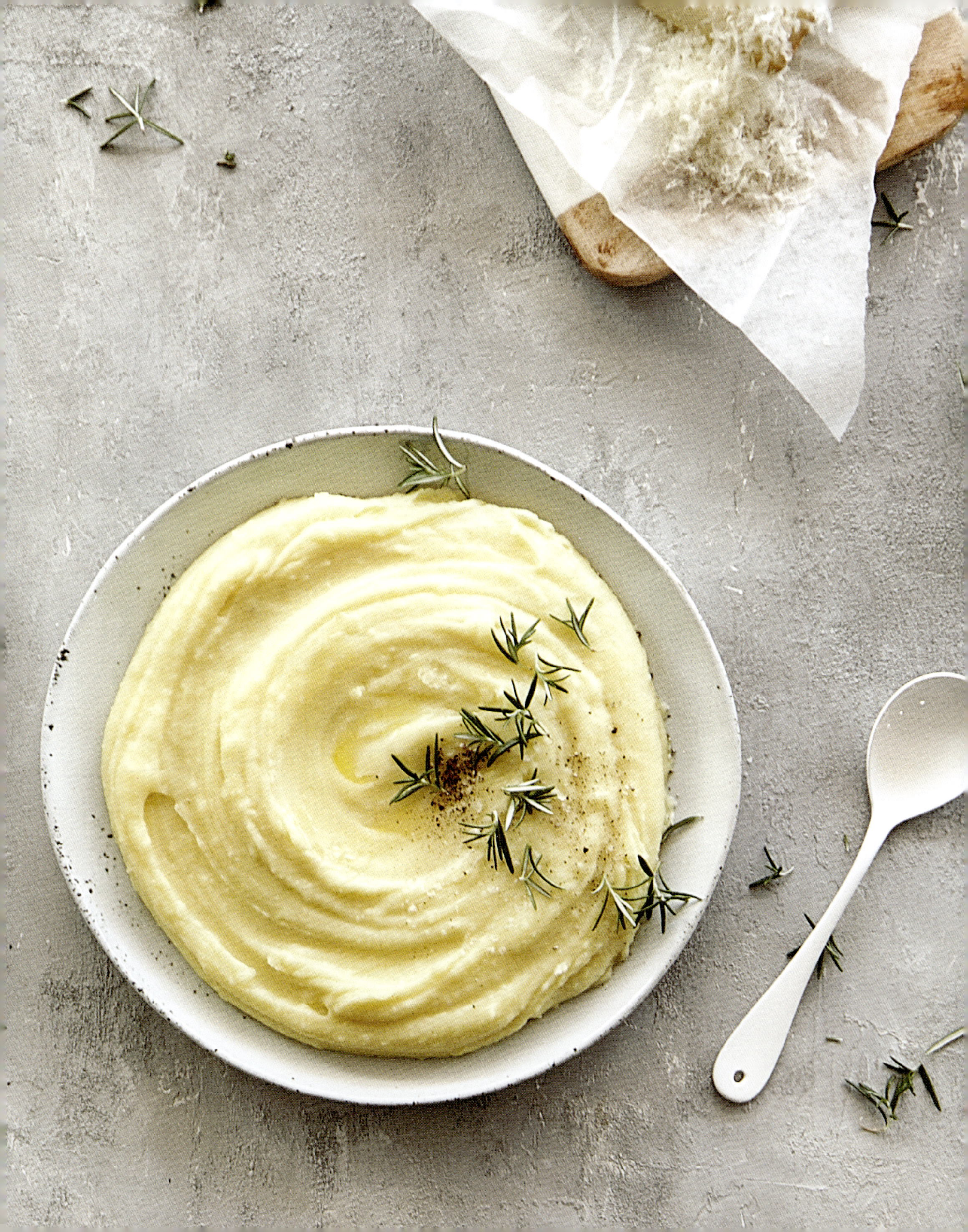

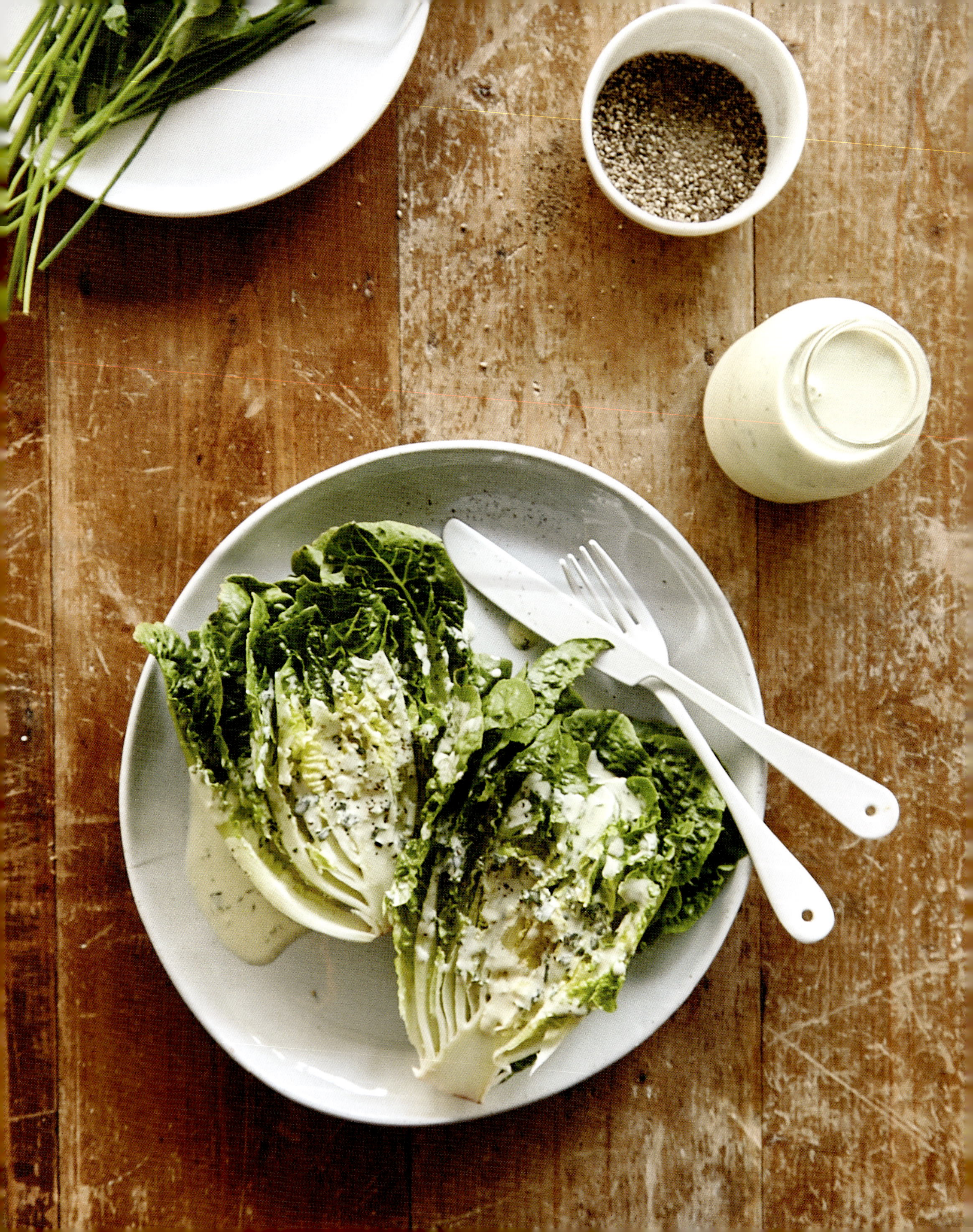

# crunchy salad with ranch dressing

**MAKES 2 CUPS**

A bowl of plain lettuce doesn't make the most exciting side dish, but smother it in ranch dressing and suddenly everyone's coming back for seconds! This delicious dressing makes it so easy to jazz up your greens, and even create a quick-fix meal – add a hard-boiled egg, shaved parmesan cheese and a cubed slice of grilled bread and you've got yourself a faux Caesar salad.

Handful fresh mint, chives or parsley
1 egg yolk
40g white balsamic vinegar or rice wine vinegar
30g Dijon mustard
½ teaspoon fine salt
½ teaspoon garlic powder
½ teaspoon onion powder
150g grapeseed oil or extra light olive oil
300g buttermilk
Crunchy leaves, to serve

1. Place herbs in TC bowl, chop for 3 seconds, speed 7.
2. Add egg yolk, vinegar, mustard, salt, garlic and onion powder, mix for 10 seconds, speed 4.
3. Continue mixing for 2 minutes, speed 4, while slowly drizzling oil onto the TC lid.
4. Add buttermilk, mix for 10 seconds, speed 4.

Store dressing in the fridge until ready to serve – it will continue to thicken as it chills. Keep refrigerated for up to 7 days. Drizzle over crunchy leaves just before serving.

NOTE: Cos, butter or iceberg lettuce, witlof or radicchio are my pick of crunchy leaves.

SUPER SIDES

# garlic pull-apart

**MAKES 1 LOAF**

I just love how this garlic bread neatly divides itself into 20 little pieces, each soft and fluffy on the inside while completely covered in garlicky buttery goodness. This loaf is at its best hot out of the oven, but in the unlikely event that you have leftovers wrap them in foil and warm at 150°C before serving.

500g baker's flour
1¼ teaspoons dried yeast
1¼ teaspoons fine salt
180g filtered water
180g milk
70g butter
Oil, for proving bowl
8 garlic cloves, peeled
Handful fresh parsley
50g macadamia oil

1. Place flour, yeast, salt, water, milk and 20g butter in TC bowl, mix for 6 seconds, speed 6.

2. Knead for 2 minutes, dough function.

3. Turn TC bowl upside down over an oiled bowl, allowing dough to drop out. Using a spatula, tuck the dough under itself to form a ball. Cover and position in a warm place for 1–2 hours, or until doubled in size.

4. Place garlic and parsley in clean TC bowl, chop for 3 seconds, speed 6. Scrape down sides.

5. Add macadamia oil and remaining 50g butter, heat for 3 minutes, 60°C, speed 2.

6. Once dough has doubled in size, tip out onto a clean work surface. Cut into 20 even-sized pieces.

7. Dip each dough piece into the butter mixture and place in a 680g bread tin. Place 10 balls of dough on the bottom of the tin, and then stack the remaining 10 on top and pour over any remaining butter mixture. Cover and position in a warm place for 30–60 minutes, or until dough has doubled in size again, rising approximately 2cm from the top of the tin.

8. Meanwhile, preheat oven to 175°C.

9. Once doubled in size, cover tin with foil. Bake for 30 minutes, then remove foil. Bake for a further 15 minutes, or until bread is golden and cooked through. Remove from tin immediately and dig in.

Individual pieces will simply pull apart from the loaf, no knife required.

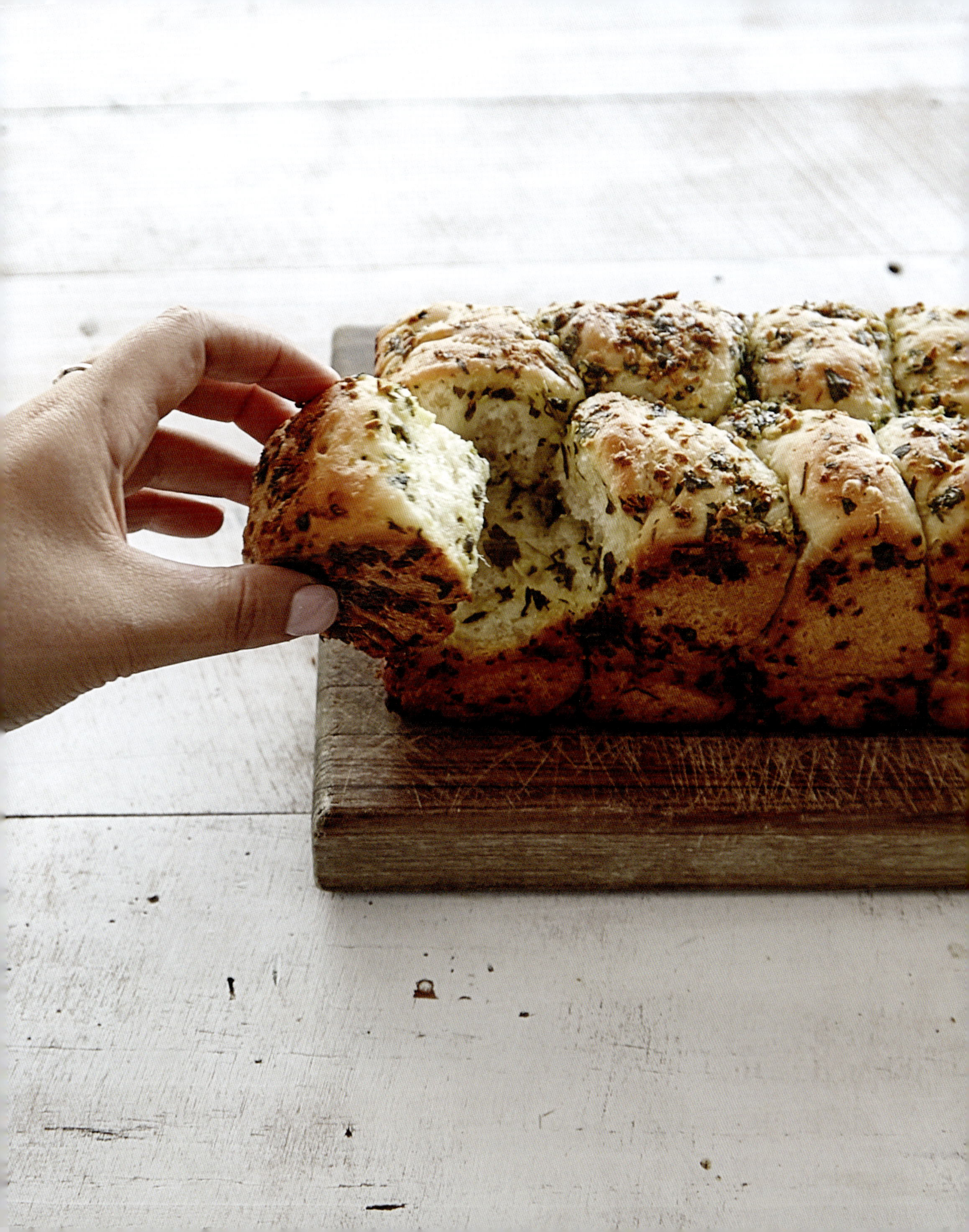

# pickled salad

SERVES 12

Barely a week goes by when I don't make a batch of this salad – I love having it on hand for quick lunches and dinners. Unlike most salads, this one actually improves with age! As the vinegar works its magic the vegetables begin to pickle, yet still maintain their crunch. I always make it at least 24 hours prior to serving, and then continue eating the leftovers for the next couple of days. It lends itself well to almost all cuisines, adding freshness to Mexican tacos, southern barbecues, burgers, Vietnamese noodles and Korean beef. This recipe makes a huge amount, but this is a good thing for this reason! If you've got a food processor now is the time to get it out; otherwise a mandolin slicer or julienne peeler will do the trick.

Large handful fresh mint
2 long red chillies, halved
200g white vinegar
2 teaspoons fine salt
1 teaspoon white or raw sugar
2 red onions, peeled, halved and thinly sliced
¼ white cabbage, thinly sliced
2 carrots, julienned
2 green apples, cored, julienned
1 cucumber, thinly sliced
1 bunch radishes, thinly sliced
Olive oil, to serve

1. Place mint and chilli in TC bowl, chop for 3 seconds, speed 6.

2. Add vinegar, salt and sugar, mix for 2 seconds, speed 6.

3. Place onion in a very large bowl. Pour over vinegar mixture, ensuring onion is as submerged as possible. Allow to stand for approx. 30 minutes (this is a good time to prepare the remaining vegetables).

4. Place cabbage, carrot, apple, cucumber and radish on top of onion and toss to combine, ensuring all vegetables have been coated in the vinegar. Serve immediately or, better yet, refrigerate for up to 3 days before serving. Ideally toss vegetables every 24 hours to redistribute vinegar.

Drizzle with olive oil just prior to serving.

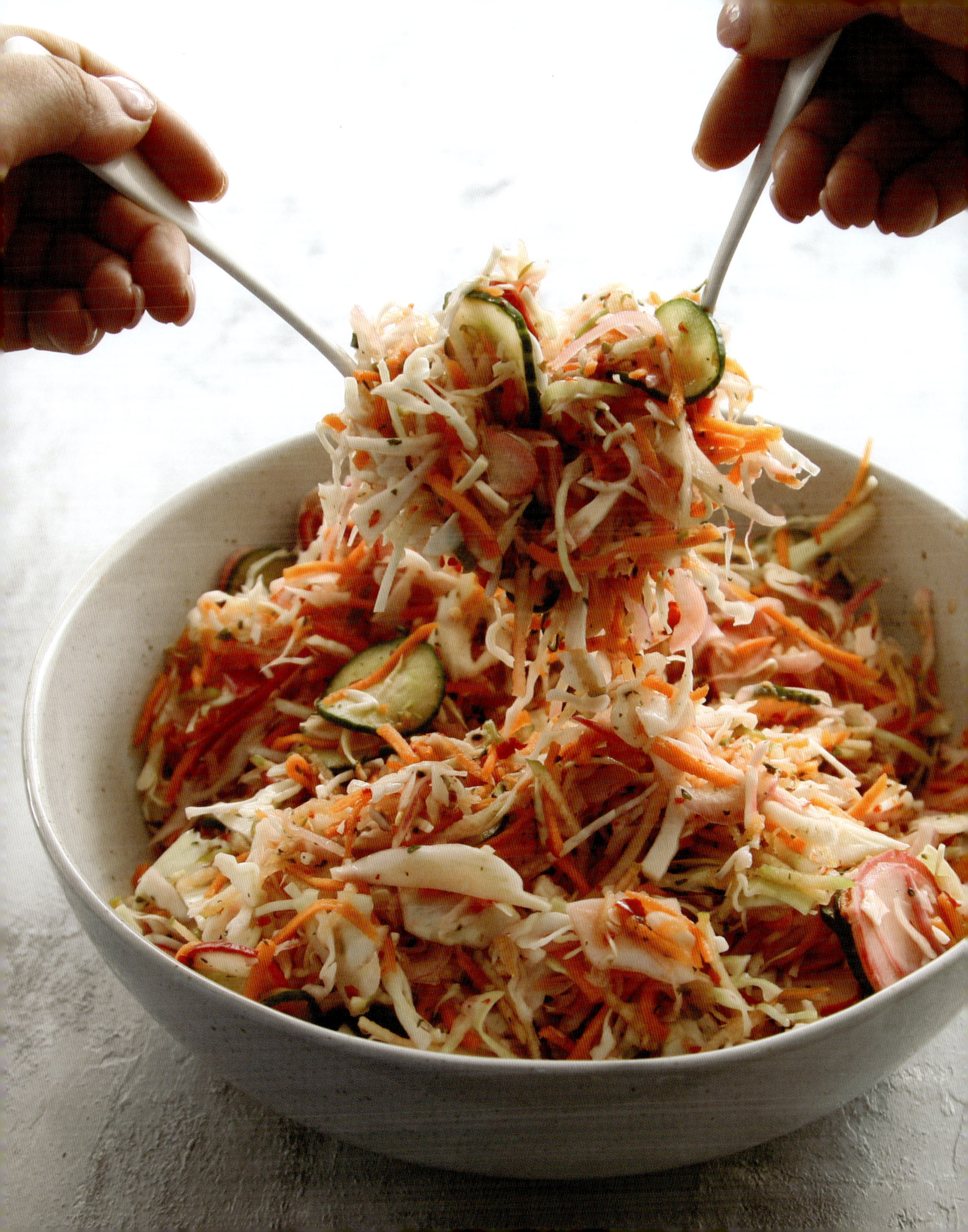

# soft polenta

**SERVES 6**

There is no better way to serve a rich ragù than on a bed of pillowy polenta. This is one of my favourite things to cook when entertaining in the cooler months as it is the ultimate comfort food. Of course that's not the only use for this creamy accompaniment; it also goes beautifully with sautéed mushrooms, wilted greens, hearty stews, roasted vegetables and grilled meats. Season with truffle salt to finish the dish to perfection.

750g water
250g milk
200g fine yellow cornmeal (see note)
40g butter
2 teaspoons fine salt

1. Insert butterfly in TC bowl. Add water and milk, heat for 12 minutes, 100°C, speed 3. During the last 2 minutes, slowly add cornmeal through the hole in the lid.

2. Cook for 45 minutes, 80°C, speed soft.

3. Add butter and salt, mix for 10 seconds, speed 3.

Garnish with infused oil, extra butter, cheese, truffle salt or micro herbs and serve immediately. As the polenta cools it becomes thick and gelatinous, eventually setting solid, which is great if you want to make polenta chips with the leftovers.

NOTE: Make sure you buy traditional cornmeal rather than instant polenta for this recipe.

VARIATION: For a cheesy polenta, add 100g grated parmesan or pecorino at step 3.

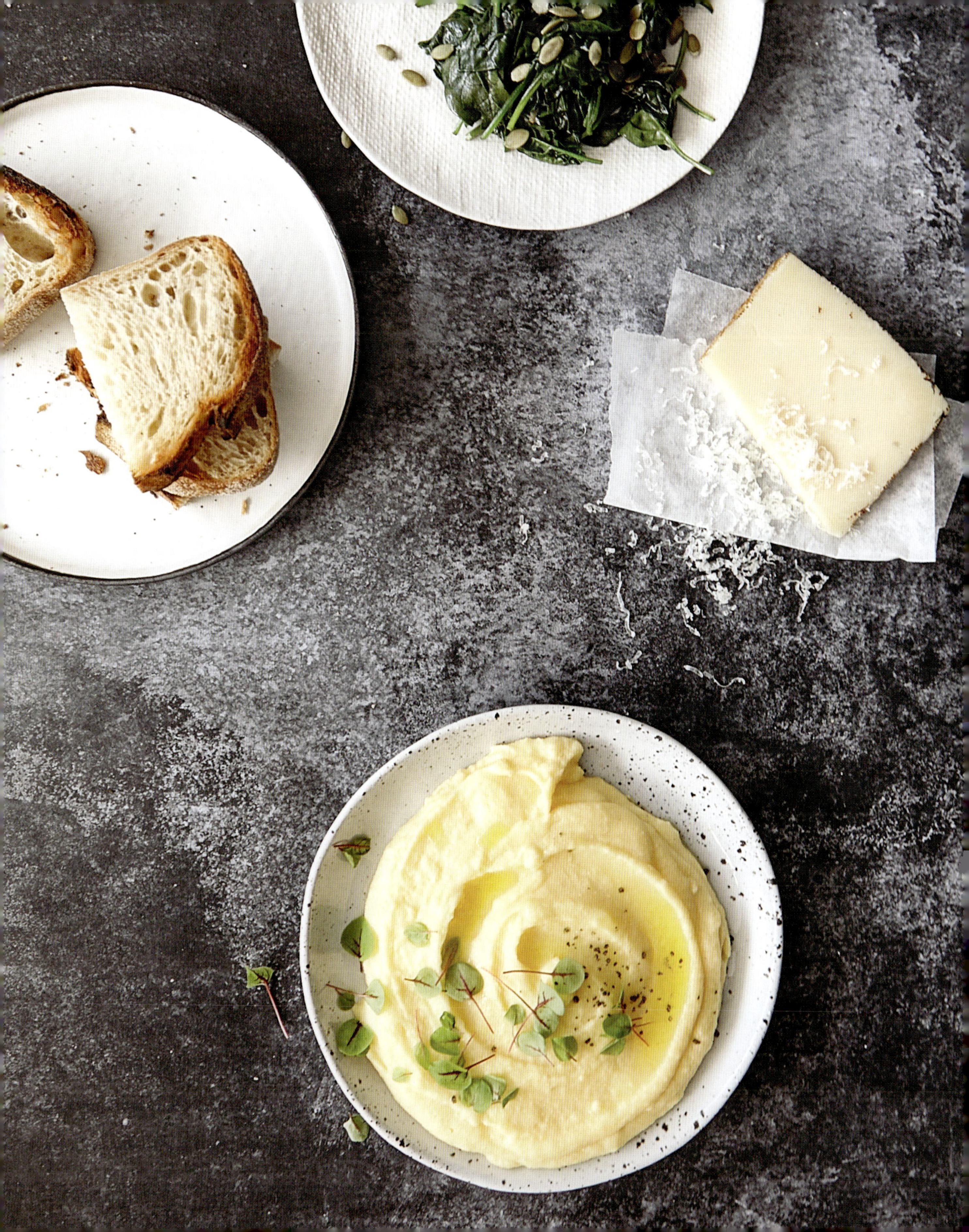

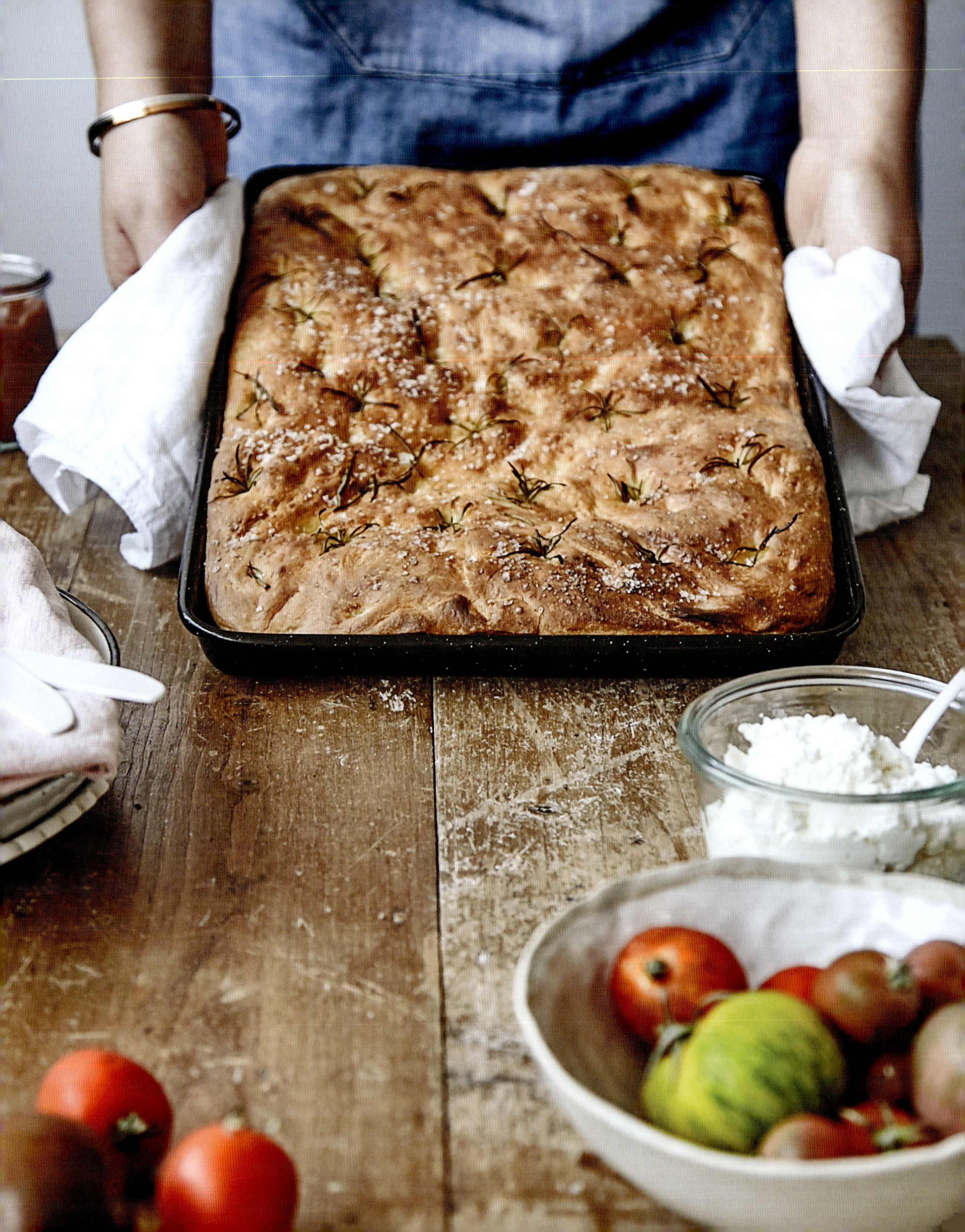

# focaccia

**MAKES 1 LOAF**

My love for homemade focaccia began in a little villa in the Tuscan countryside with a hundred-year-old wood-fired pizza oven. I would drown the dough in olive oil and cover it with rosemary (both the olives and herbs were grown mere metres from the kitchen), then slide the tray into the smoking brick chamber. With no way to measure temperature it was always a gamble, but somehow the final product was never anything less than extraordinary. While the home oven cannot quite replicate the complex flavours delivered by the coals, I guarantee this focaccia eaten fresh out of the oven will be better than anything you've ever bought.

680g baker's flour
470g cold filtered water
100g olive oil, plus extra for oiling
2 teaspoons dried yeast
2 teaspoons fine salt
Fresh rosemary
Salt flakes

1. Place flour, water, 50g olive oil, yeast and salt in TC bowl, mix for 6 seconds, speed 6.

2. Knead for 2 minutes, dough function. Transfer dough to a large oiled bowl and cover. Allow to stand for 2–3 hours, or until doubled in size.

3. Preheat oven to 220°C. Liberally grease a 35×20cm roasting tin with 25g olive oil.

4. Transfer dough to oiled tin and use hands to push it right into the corners. Use fingertips to make dimples across the surface of the dough (if sticking to hands, lightly oil the top of the dough first). Drizzle with remaining 25g olive oil. Sprinkle with fresh rosemary and salt flakes.

5. Bake for 25 minutes, or until focaccia is browned and cooked through. It should sound hollow when tapped. Transfer to a wire rack to cool for 15 minutes.

Serve warm – focaccia is best enjoyed soon after it is made.

NOTES: I never measure my olive oil – I simply ensure the tin and dough are completely coated – but I have included measurements for those who like more precise instructions.

In cold weather there's no need to use cold water – temperate water will ensure the dough rises in 2–3 hours.

# fresh charcoal pasta

SERVES 6

While fresh pasta may be a little more laborious than most of my recipes, the final product is worth every second. The flavour and texture is quite different from the dried varieties, making the meal seem more sumptuous somehow. The charcoal gives the pasta a striking black colour, but it is completely optional and may be left out. This is one of my favourite Saturday afternoon recipes, and it really helps to have two people on board – luckily my sister Loryn finds the act of rolling the pasta just as meditative as I do.

600g plain flour, plus extra for rolling
6 eggs
2 teaspoons fine salt
2 teaspoons food-grade charcoal (optional; see note)

1. Place all ingredients in TC bowl, knead for 2 minutes, dough function.

2. Tip out crumbly mixture onto bench and press into a disc. Wrap in cling film and rest for 20 minutes. If dough stays crumbly and doesn't come together, place back in TC bowl, add 2 teaspoons water and continue to knead for 30 seconds, dough function.

3. Cut dough into 8 equal pieces. Flatten each piece and flour both sides. Set pasta machine to the widest setting and feed through 1 piece of dough. Fold in half and repeat. Continue feeding dough through the widest setting (folding in half each time) until dough becomes silky and is uniform in shape (approx. 6 times).

4. Once silky, turn the machine to one setting narrower and feed dough through once. Turn one setting narrower again and repeat until the dough is desired thickness. Flour both sides of dough if it starts sticking to the machine or dragging. Repeat with remaining dough.

5. Run pasta through the fettuccine cutter, or leave as is and use for lasagne, ravioli, tortellini or cannelloni.

When ready to serve, cook pasta in salted boiling water until al dente. It will only take a couple of minutes.

NOTES: While it is possible to make fresh pasta using a rolling pin rather than a pasta machine, I never find this produces very good results and becomes more like hard labour than meditation.

Food-grade charcoal is available from good health food shops.

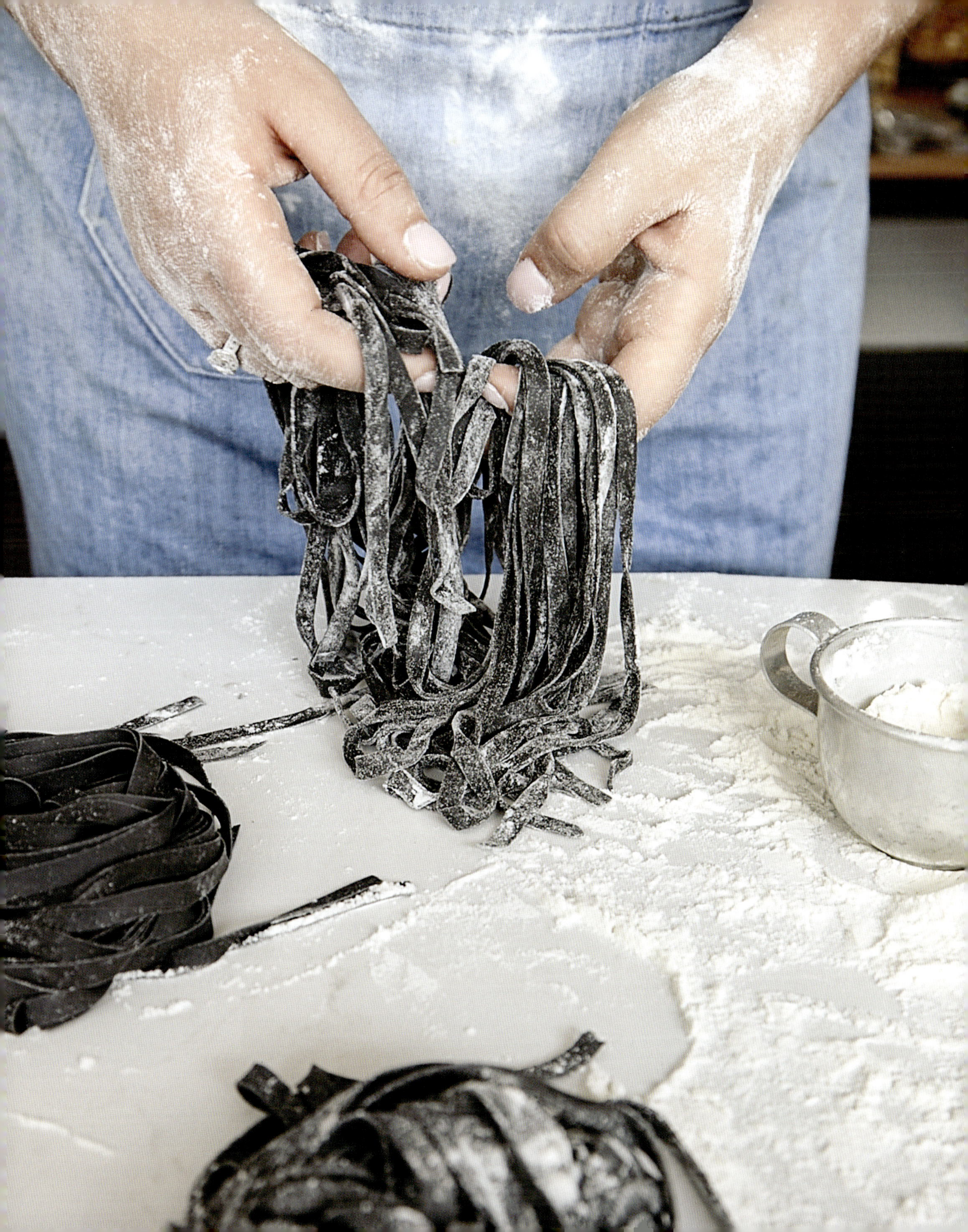

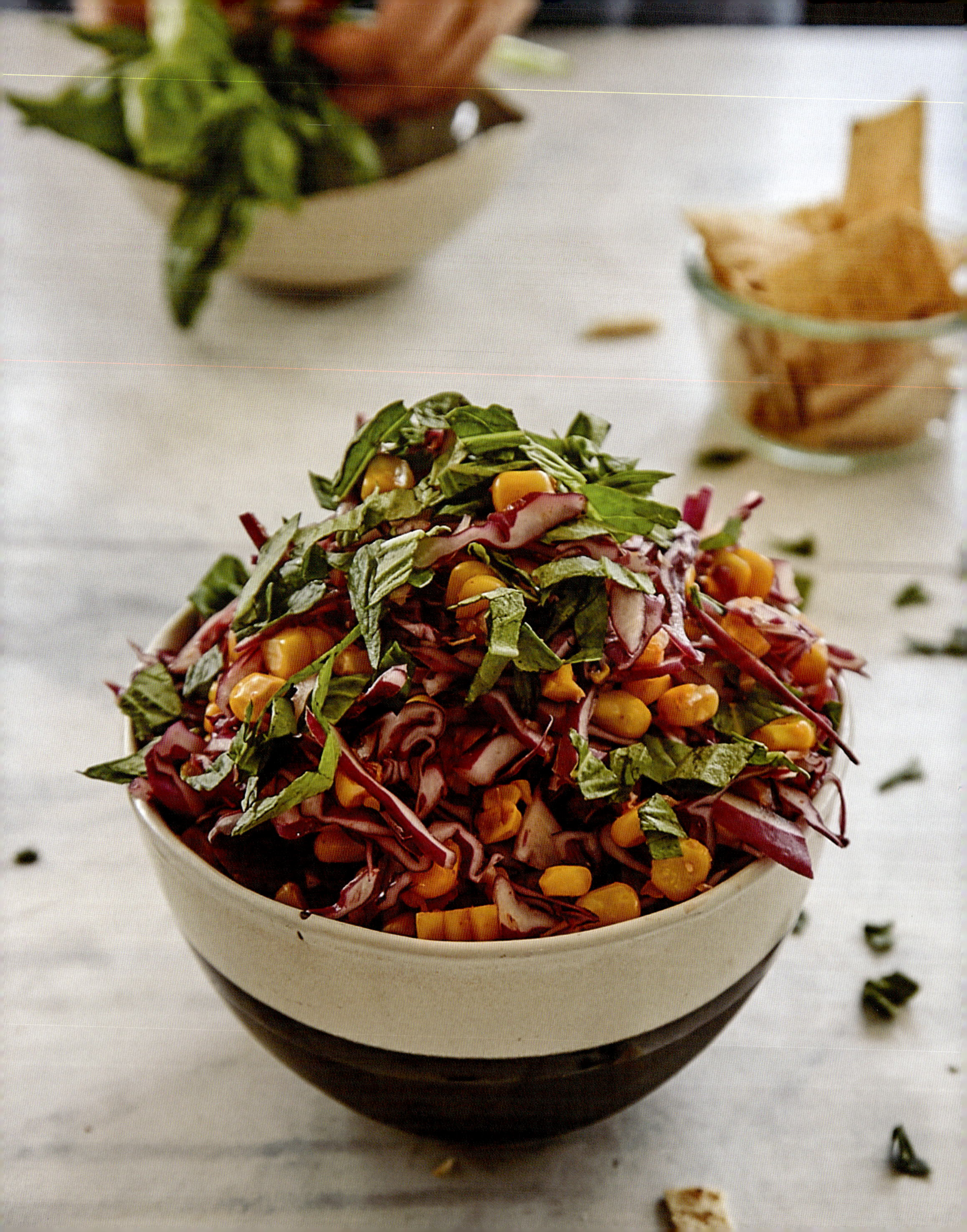

# mexican corn salad

**SERVES 6**

This vibrant salad has great flavours, colours and textures, making it a welcome addition to the weekly menu. While the corn and spices give it a Mexican feel, it accompanies a barbecued steak or pan-fried fish fillet just as well as it partners a quesadilla. Add some avocado, salad sprinkles (see page 251) and broken tortilla chips and you've got yourself an entire meal (perfect for meat-free Monday).

2 garlic cloves, peeled
2 teaspoons sweet paprika
1 teaspoon fine salt
½ teaspoon cayenne pepper
½ teaspoon dried thyme
1 red onion, peeled and halved
25g apple cider vinegar
25g white balsamic vinegar
20g olive oil
3 corn cobs, husks removed
¼ red cabbage, thinly sliced
Handful fresh basil leaves, roughly chopped

1. Place garlic, paprika, salt, cayenne pepper and thyme in TC bowl, chop for 7 seconds, speed 5.

2. Add onion, chop for 2 seconds, speed 5, or until roughly chopped.

3. Add vinegars and olive oil, mix for 2 seconds, speed 3. Set aside in a large bowl.

4. Place 700g water in TC bowl. Place corn in steaming tray and steam for 15 minutes, steaming temperature, speed 3, or until cooked.

5. Set corn aside and allow to cool for 15 minutes. Cut corn kernels off the cobs in strips and add to reserved spice mixture. Add red cabbage and basil and toss everything together until combined.

Serve immediately or refrigerate for up to 2 days. As this salad stores well it's a great one for lunchboxes.

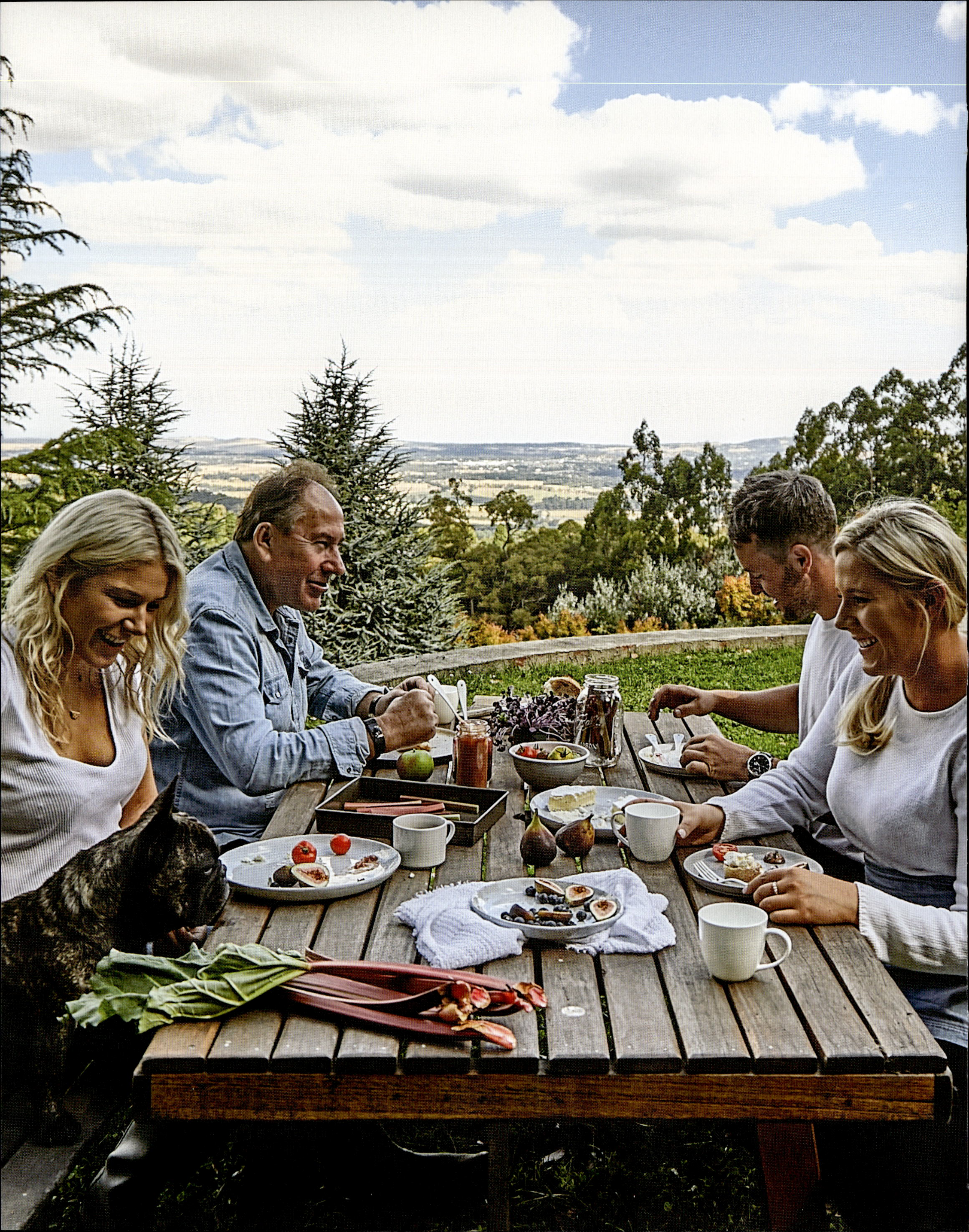

# easy entertaining

Given the choice I'd much rather eat at home, surrounded by friends and family, than at a fancy restaurant. Despite having to do the dishes, I always find these nights to be the most fun and authentic. I love the way good food brings people together, and this is never more true than with celebrations at home. Armed with a thermo cooker and a carefully selected menu, entertaining really can be easy! One of my favourite things to cook for a crowd is an Indian feast – so many of the components can be made in advance and it caters for almost all eating preferences. Individually, the recipes are accessible and achievable, but put together they create a spectacular feast. I've done all the planning for you, so now all you have to do is invite the guests and get cooking!

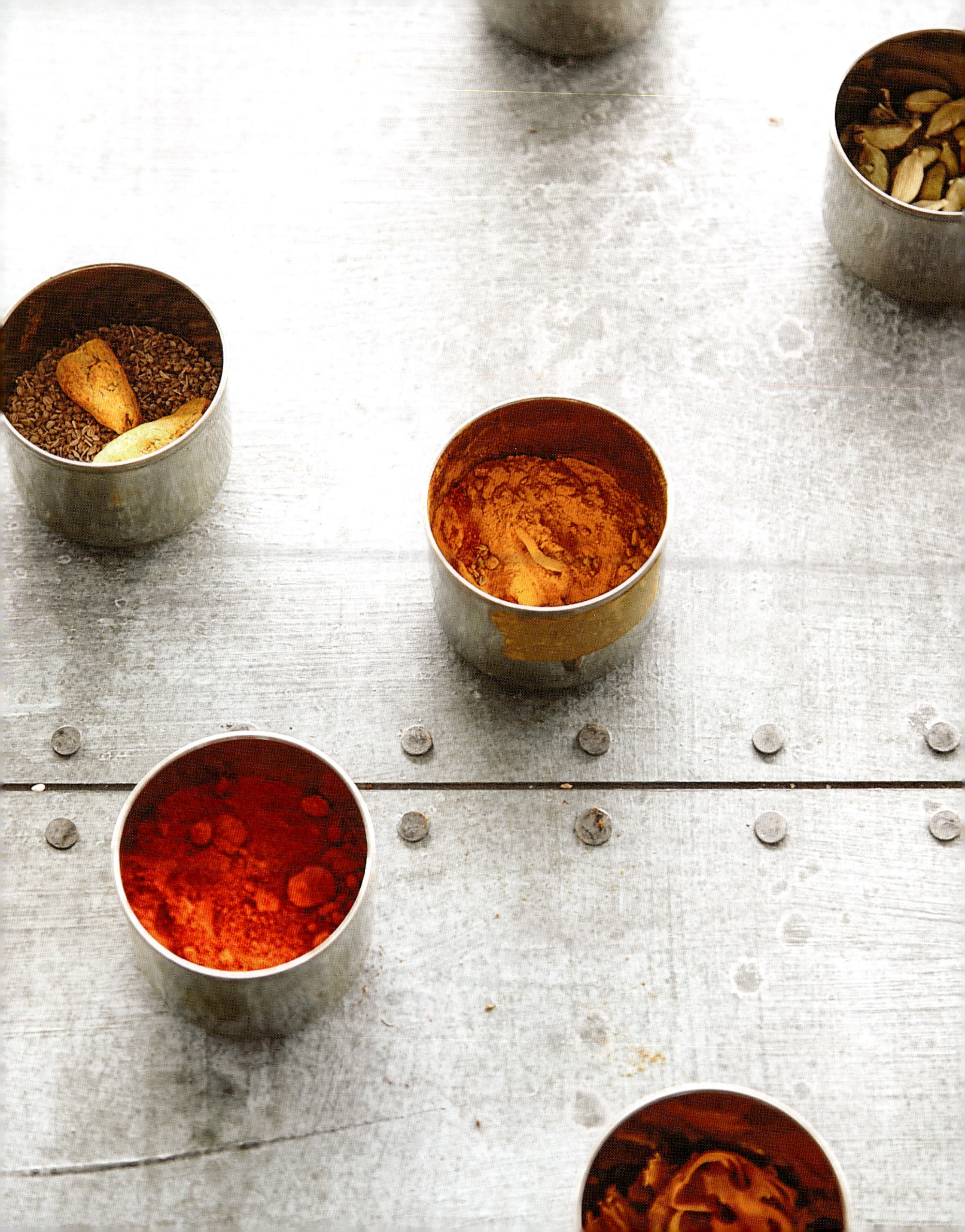

# indian feast

This is my menu for an Indian feast for ten. Feel free to cook every recipe or just some of them, or to substitute with other recipes – this is simply a guide to help with planning and preparation. There are vegetarian, vegan, dairy-free and gluten-free options, so no matter who your guests are everyone will be catered for without you having to prepare any special dishes. The only exception is dessert – you might also need to whip up a matcha parfait (see page 201) or peach and mango sorbet (see page 211) for any guests following a gluten-free, vegetarian or vegan diet. The most laborious of all the dishes is the roti bread, so if you are pushed for time you can either buy some ready-made or leave it out altogether and make a second batch of rice.

There are a lot of nuts in this menu, primarily used as thickeners. If you are feeding somebody with a nut allergy, omit the cashews and add extra coconut cream to the chickpea curry, beef curry and lassi. Simply leave the nuts out of the spiced rice.

## THE MAIN EVENT

chickpea curry
slow beef curry
roti bread
tamarind mint raita
spiced coconut rice
spiced cauliflower
mango chutney
coconut mango lassi

## SOMETHING SWEET

chai panna cottas

### SERVES 10

# chickpea curry

**SERVES 4**

This curry is probably the most well-tested recipe in the book – not because it needed it but because my sister Ellen loves it so much! While it fits perfectly as the vegan/vegetarian option at our Indian banquet, it also makes a convenient quick dinner option as you likely have most of the ingredients in your pantry already.

100g raw cashews
1 brown onion, peeled and halved
6 garlic cloves, peeled
3cm piece ginger, peeled
30g coconut oil
2 tablespoons curry powder
1 tablespoon ground turmeric
400g can diced tomatoes
400g can coconut cream
2 teaspoons fine salt
400g can chickpeas, rinsed and drained
100g baby spinach

1. Place cashews in TC bowl, mill for 20 seconds, speed 10. Set aside.

2. Without cleaning TC bowl, add onion, garlic and ginger, chop for 5 seconds, speed 5. Scrape down sides.

3. Add coconut oil, curry powder and turmeric, sauté 6 minutes, 100°C, speed 1.

4. Add tomatoes, coconut cream and salt, cook for 10 minutes, 100°C, speed 2, MC removed and steamer basket on top to prevent splashes.

5. Add chickpeas, spinach and milled cashews, combine using spatula and cook for a further 4 minutes, 100°C, reverse speed 2.

Serve with steamed basmati rice, roti bread (see page 143) or spiced coconut rice (see page 145).

NOTE: To keep the recipe short and sweet, we have just specified 'curry powder' here. It's essential to the success of the dish to use a very good quality purchased curry powder or, better yet make your own.

clockwise from top: tamarind mint raita *(see page 144)*, coconut mango lassi *(see page 149)*, spiced coconut rice *(see page 145)*, chickpea curry *(see opposite)*

# slow beef curry

**SERVES 10**

I love a slow-cooked curry – the flavour in this one is so rich and intense and the meat is so meltingly tender. And, unlike most dishes, the flavour actually improves with age! By slow cooking this beauty in the oven we've also freed up the thermo cooker, meaning you can get to work on steaming rice and vegetables, kneading roti dough, cooking chutneys, blending raitas, whipping up dessert or even getting tomorrow's breakfast started. This recipe is a favourite of mine, not just when I'm entertaining, but also for my Sunday cook-ups where I like to make big batches that can be frozen so I'm well-stocked with tasty homemade meals for when I don't have time to cook.

200g raw cashews
2 brown onions, peeled and halved
6 garlic cloves, peeled
20g coconut oil
2 tablespoons curry powder
1 tablespoon garam masala
1 teaspoon chilli flakes
400g coconut milk
80g stock concentrate (see page 190)
400g water
2kg chuck steak, cubed
500g frozen vegetables, defrosted (optional)

1. Preheat oven to 160°C.

2. Place cashews in TC bowl, mill for 20 seconds, speed 10. Set aside.

3. Place onion and garlic in TC bowl, chop for 5 seconds, speed 5. Scrape down sides.

4. Add coconut oil, curry powder, garam masala and chilli flakes, sauté for 10 minutes, 100°C, speed 2.

5. Add coconut milk, stock concentrate and water, mix for 10 seconds, speed 3.

6. Place beef in a large casserole dish and pour over coconut mixture. Cover dish with a tight-fitting lid and cook for 2 hours in the oven.

7. Remove lid and stir. Cook, uncovered, for a further 1 hour, or until meat is tender.

8. Add frozen vegetables (if using) and milled cashews and stir through. Cook for a further 15 minutes.

Serve immediately with rice, roti bread (see page 143) or steamed vegetables, or freeze in family-sized meal portions.

VARIATION: To keep this family friendly we have omitted fresh chilli, but for a spicier option add 2 green chillies at step 3.

clockwise from top: slow beef curry (*see opposite*), spiced cauliflower (*see page 146*), roti bread (*see page 143*), mango chutney (*page 148*)

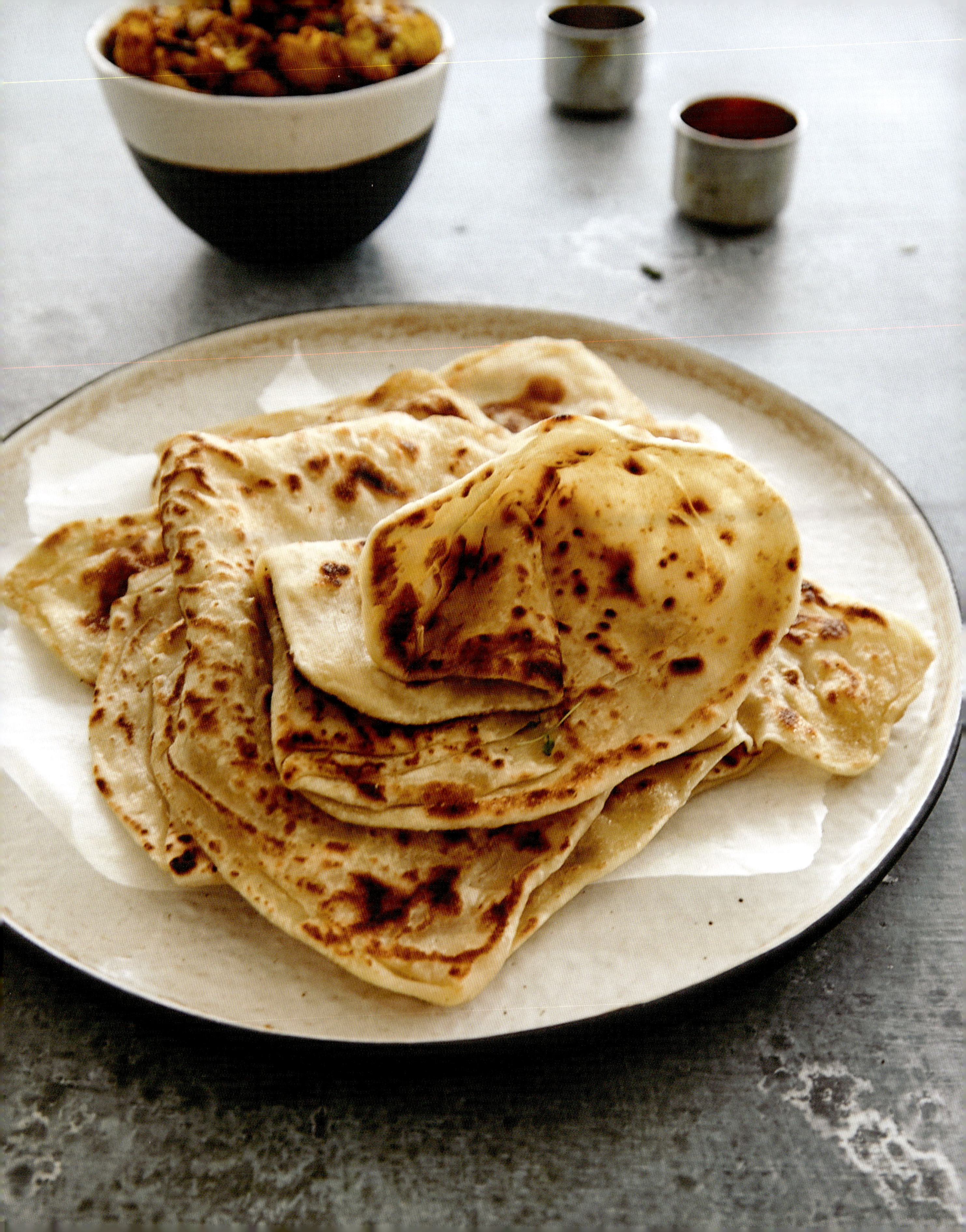

# roti bread

**MAKES 10**

This crispy, flaky, layered bread is the perfect vessel to mop up a delicious curry, but it's so good you might find yourself eating it straight from the pan! Don't stress about the shaping and folding – as long as you get lots of thin pastry layers separated by salty oily goodness it doesn't matter what shape it's in.

500g plain flour, plus extra for dusting
280g water
¼ teaspoon fine salt
80g butter, ghee or macadamia oil, melted
Salt flakes

1. Place flour, water and salt in TC bowl, mix for 10 seconds, speed 5.

2. Knead for 1 minute, dough function. Remove dough from TC bowl and divide into 10 small balls. Cover with a damp tea towel for 30 minutes.

3. Roll out a ball of dough into a thin square. Brush with melted butter, ghee or oil and sprinkle with salt flakes. Fold in half. Brush with butter, ghee or oil. Fold in half again to form a square and brush with butter, ghee or oil. Fold in half again and brush with butter, ghee or oil, then fold once more to form a small square. Lightly flour the folded square and then roll out thinly (about 1–2mm). Repeat with remaining dough.

4. Heat a large fry pan over medium heat (or 2 pans to reduce cooking time) and brush liberally with butter, ghee or oil. Add a single portion of dough and cook for 1 minute, then flip over and cook for another 1 minute. Continue flipping over every 1 minute until bread is cooked through and black spots have formed (about 4 minutes all up). Stack in a warm oven or food warmer. Repeat with remaining dough balls, adding a little butter, ghee or oil each time.

Serve warm.

VARIATION: For a dairy-free and vegan option use macadamia oil rather than butter or ghee.

# tamarind mint raita

**MAKES 3 CUPS**

During my travels around Sri Lanka I grew to love the frequent use of tamarind in pickles and chutneys. It has such a unique flavour that gives sweetness followed by a sour kick. The jarred purée is probably the easiest to find, either in supermarkets or Asian grocers, but if you don't have any replace it with a teaspoon of coconut sugar and the juice of one lime.

- 3 green chillies, halved and deseeded
- 2 green apples, quartered and cored
- 2 bunches fresh mint, leaves only
- 1 bunch fresh coriander, leaves only
- 400g thick Greek yoghurt
- 100g tamarind purée
- ½ teaspoon fine salt, or to taste

1. Place chillies in TC bowl, chop for 3 seconds, speed 6.
2. Add apple, mint and coriander, chop for 4 seconds, speed 6, or until finely chopped, assisting with spatula if necessary. Scrape down sides.
3. Add yoghurt, tamarind and salt, mix for 10 seconds, reverse speed 3, or until just combined.

Serve immediately or refrigerate for up to 5 days.

VARIATION: For a really spicy kick, don't deseed the chillies.

# spiced coconut rice

**SERVES 5**

My dear friend and curry connoisseur Claudette D'Cruz from No Worries Curries inspired this recipe – she often brings in delicious Indian dishes for us to try in the cooking school. This rice is so incredibly fragrant it will have your mouth watering, and the taste certainly won't disappoint. While this recipe has been designed to accompany a curry, after a long day it is really satisfying as a meal on its own eaten on the couch.

50g ghee, butter or macadamia oil
10 fresh curry leaves
4 dried red chillies
2 teaspoons mustard seeds
1 teaspoon cumin seeds
400g basmati rice, rinsed just prior to cooking
400g can coconut milk
300g water
2 teaspoons fine salt
100g roasted cashews or peanuts

1. Place ghee, butter or oil, curry leaves, chillies, mustard and cumin seeds in TC bowl, cook for 10 minutes, steaming temperature, speed soft.

2. Add rice, coconut milk, water and salt, cook for 10 minutes, 100°C, reverse speed 1.

3. Add nuts and fold through. Allow to stand for 10 minutes in TC bowl.

Serve warm with curry, tandoori meat, pan-fried tofu or vegetables.

NOTE: It is essential to allow the rice to stand for the specified time before serving as it continues to cook and absorb liquid.

VARIATION: For a dairy-free and vegan option use macadamia oil rather than ghee or butter.

# spiced cauliflower

+ BAKING

**SERVES 4**

I love the pops of flavour in this dish – the sweetness from the sultanas and the spice from the whole roasted seeds (of course, you can use ground spices if that's what you have in your pantry). For an easy weeknight meal, stir spiced cauliflower through coconut rice (see page 145) or plain basmati.

40g macadamia oil
2 teaspoons curry powder
1 teaspoon ground turmeric
1 teaspoon coriander seeds
1 teaspoon cumin seeds
1 teaspoon fine salt
1 head cauliflower, cut into small florets
60g sultanas or currants

1. Preheat oven to 200°C.

2. Place oil, curry powder, turmeric, coriander, cumin, salt and cauliflower in TC bowl, mix for 15 seconds, reverse speed 2, or until cauliflower is evenly coated.

3. Transfer to a roasting dish or lined baking tray and bake for 25 minutes, or until cauliflower is tender and browned at the edges, stirring after 15 minutes.

Toss through sultanas or currants and serve.

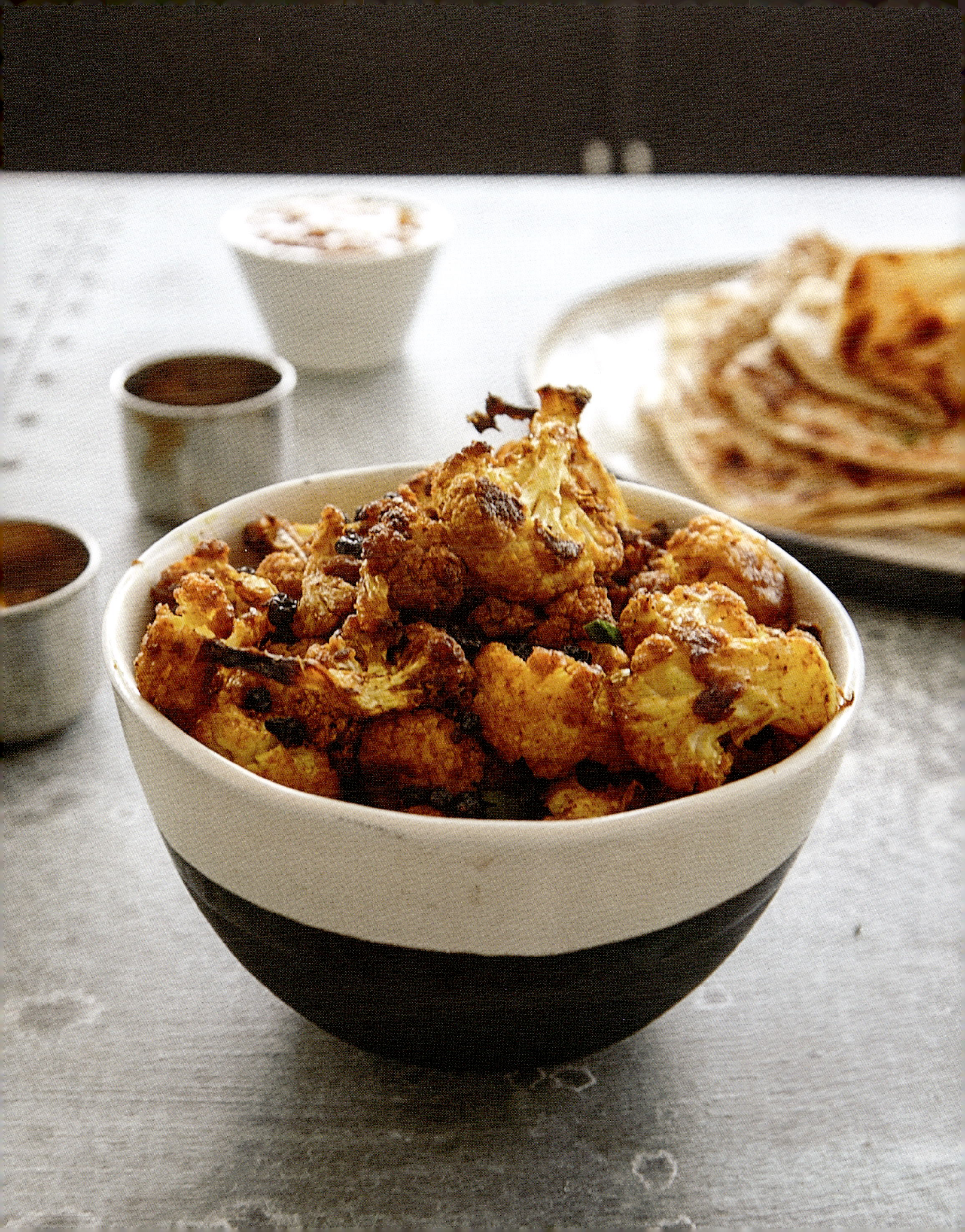

# mango chutney

**MAKES 4 CUPS**

I am yet to find something that this chutney doesn't pair well with. We've smeared it over sausage rolls, fritters, steak, burritos, savoury muffins, even avocado on toast! We've thinned it down and used it as a salad dressing and marinade. We've whisked it into scrambled eggs and frittata. And we're still not sick of it. So even though this recipe makes more than what you'll need for your Indian banquet, you'll thank me later!

1 brown onion, peeled and halved
2 garlic cloves, peeled
3cm piece ginger, peeled
1 green apple, peeled, cored and quartered
500g mango flesh (approx. 3 mangoes; see note)
400g can diced tomatoes
300g raw sugar
250g apple cider or white wine vinegar
1 teaspoon fine salt
1 teaspoon curry powder

1. Place onion, garlic and ginger in TC bowl, chop for 3 seconds, speed 6.

2. Add apple and mango, chop for 4 seconds, speed 4. Scrape down sides.

3. Add tomatoes, sugar, vinegar, salt and curry powder, cook for 45 minutes, steaming temperature, speed 1, MC removed and steamer basket on top to prevent splashes.

Pour into warm, sterilised jars and store in the fridge. It will keep for up to 12 months.

NOTES: Frozen mango can be used for this recipe; just make sure you defrost it first.

I always keep the empty glass jars when I finish things like mustard, coconut oil and tomato passata, and re-use them to bottle my homemade chutneys and other flavour makers. Give the jars a good clean out, removing all leftover food particles, then run through the dishwasher on the hottest cycle to sterilise. Alternatively, soak in boiling water for a few minutes. To remove pesky glued-on labels, coat in a mixture of equal parts bicarbonate of soda and olive oil and allow to stand for 30 minutes before scrubbing off with warm soapy water.

# coconut mango lassi

**SERVES 6**

After all the spicy and intense Indian flavours, you'll need something cooling to soothe the palate. A little sweet and a little salty, this lassi is just the thing. While traditionally made with yoghurt, I've opted for a dairy-free version by using coconut milk instead – not only does this mean all my guests can enjoy it, but the flavour combination of coconut and mango is one of my favourites.

**100g raw cashews**
**500g frozen mango, roughly chopped (see note)**
**400g can coconut milk**
**600g coconut water**
**½ teaspoon ground cardamom**
**¼ teaspoon fine salt, or more to taste**

1. Place cashews in TC bowl, mill for 20 seconds, speed 10.
2. Add mango and coconut milk, pulverise for 10 seconds, speed 9, assisting with spatula if necessary.
3. Add coconut water, cardamom and salt, purée for 1 minute, speed 9.

Pour into 6 glasses and serve. Store in the fridge if you're not enjoying it straight away – just give it a stir before serving.

NOTE: If you are buying mango already frozen, make sure it is Australian-grown mango as it always has the best flavour.

VARIATION: Cashews provide additional richness and creaminess, but they can be omitted for anyone with a nut allergy.

EASY ENTERTAINING

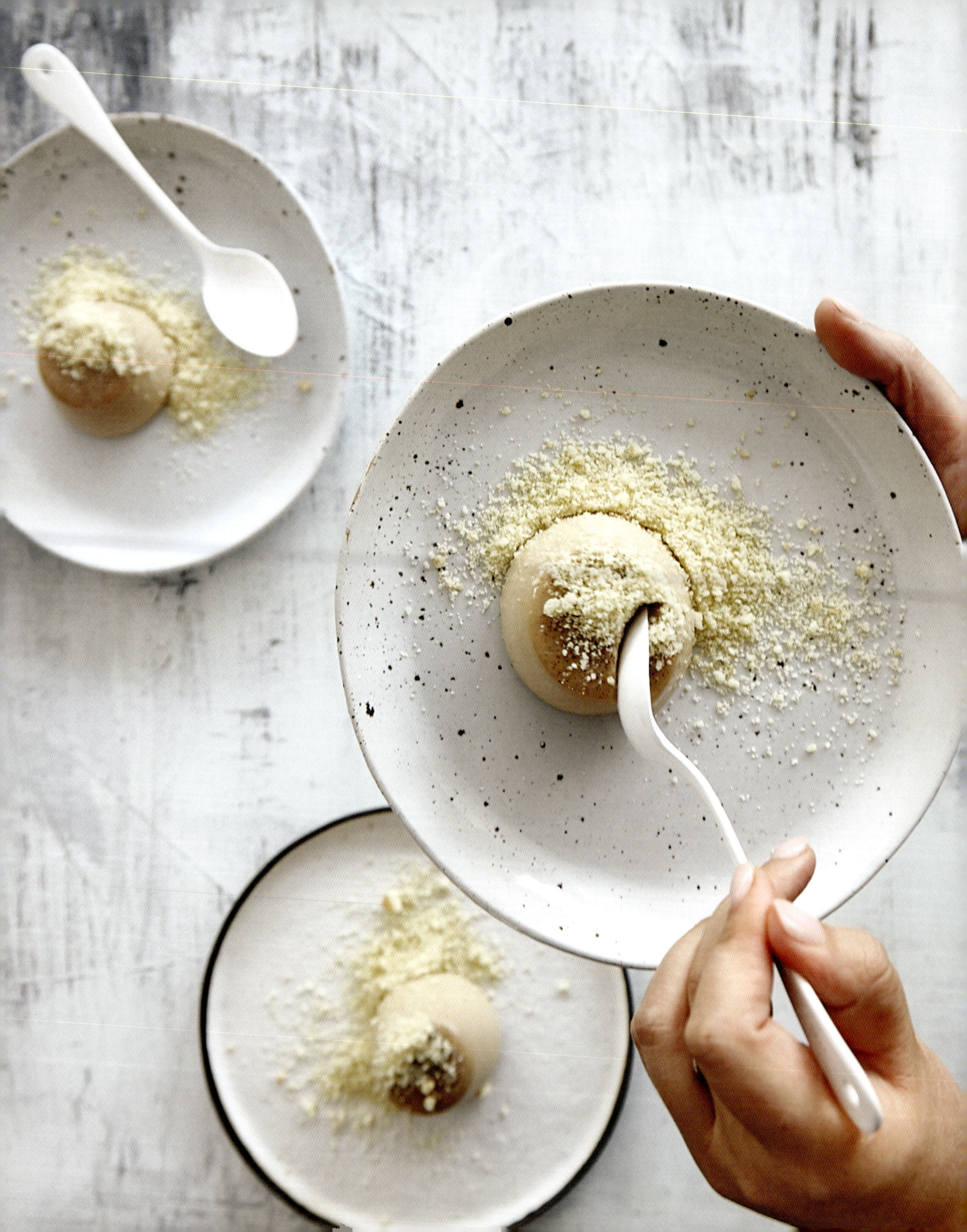

# chai panna cottas

**MAKES 10**

It wouldn't be an alyce alexandra cookbook without a panna cotta recipe! It truly is one of my favourite desserts, and this time I have combined it with one of my other great pleasures: chai tea. The result is a smooth and silky dessert with delicate spiced flavours – the perfect way to end our Indian feast, offering tea and sweets in one.

660g milk
4½ tablespoons loose black chai tea
65g raw sugar
1⅔ tablespoons powdered gelatine
330g thickened cream
1 teaspoon vanilla extract
5 plain sweet biscuits (such as shortbread, gingernuts or Anzac biscuits)

1. Place 500g milk and the tea in TC bowl, heat for 10 minutes, 90°C, speed 1. Allow to stand for 30 minutes.

2. Using a fine-mesh strainer, strain out the tea leaves and discard. Pour milk mixture into a clean TC bowl and add sugar. Heat for 5 minutes, 70°C, speed 1.

3. Meanwhile, place remaining 160g milk and gelatine in a cup or small bowl and stir to combine.

4. Add gelatine mixture to TC bowl, mix for 10 seconds, speed 4.

5. Add cream and vanilla, mix for 20 seconds, speed 2. Shake TC bowl from side to side to release any air bubbles. Pour mixture evenly into 10 silicone dariole moulds rinsed with cold water. Transfer moulds to an airtight container and refrigerate for a minimum of 6 hours.

6. Meanwhile, place biscuits in TC bowl, pulse three times on turbo speed, or until biscuits are a fine crumb. Set aside.

7. When ready to serve, sit moulds in a bath of lukewarm water (approx. 40°C, it is important not to use hot water) for around 4 minutes, or until panna cottas begin to pull away from the sides. Gently squeeze moulds to break the airlock and turn out onto individual serving plates.

Sprinkle with biscuit crumbs and serve.

NOTE: For a super-easy dessert, set the panna cotta mixture in little glass jars so there is no need to turn them out. Serve with spoons in the jars for a cocktail or picnic-style dessert.

VARIATION: Darjeeling makes a beautiful substitute for the chai.

# timeline

## 1–2 DAYS BEFORE

1. Check the ingredients list (see opposite) against the stock in your kitchen, then make a shopping list accordingly
2. Buy all the ingredients
3. Cook the mango chutney (see page 148) and store in glass jars in the fridge
4. Make the panna cottas (see page 151) and store in dariole moulds inside an airtight container in the fridge
5. Cook the slow beef curry (see page 140) in a flameproof casserole dish – allow to cool, then store in the fridge in the casserole dish (space permitting)

## DAY OF THE FEAST

1. Set the table
2. Crumble the biscuits to serve with the panna cotta (step 6, page 151) and store in an airtight container
3. Make the tamarind mint raita (see page 144) and store in the fridge
4. Make two batches of coconut mango lassi (see page 149) and store in jugs in the fridge
5. Make the roti bread dough and once rested, roll and shape (see page 143, steps 1–3). Brush each piece with macadamia oil and separate with sheets of baking paper. Cover dough with a damp tea towel and leave at room temperature until ready to cook
6. Coat the cauliflower in oil and spices (step 2, page 146) and transfer to a roasting tin – keep at room temperature until 1 hour before your guests arrive
7. Prepare ingredients for the chickpea curry (see page 138) and store in the fridge

## 1 HOUR BEFORE GUESTS ARRIVE

1. Preheat the oven to 200°C. Roast the cauliflower – once cooked, turn the oven off but leave the cauliflower in to keep warm (prop the door open for 5 minutes so the cauliflower doesn't continue to cook)
2. Meanwhile, cook the chickpea curry (see page 138) – transfer to a food warmer or pre-warmed casserole dish, cover and place on the table
3. Meanwhile, remove the beef curry from the fridge and reheat over low heat, stirring occasionally
4. Meanwhile, begin frying the roti bread (see page 143, step 4) – transfer to the oven to keep warm (the oven should be off but still warm from roasting the cauliflower)
5. Once the thermo cooker is free, cook the spiced coconut rice (see page 145) – allow to stand in the TC bowl until you are ready to serve
6. Transfer the mango chutney and raita to serving bowls and place on the table

## TO SERVE

1. Take the beef curry to the table in the casserole dish (use pot holders and place mats)
2. Take the cauliflower and bread to the table
3. Transfer the coconut rice from the TC bowl to a serving bowl and place on the table
4. Remove the jugs of lassi from the fridge, stir vigorously and place on the table

## AFTER THE MAIN

1. Sit the panna cotta moulds in a bath of lukewarm water
2. Turn out the panna cottas onto individual serving plates, sprinkle with biscuit crumbs and serve

# ingredients list

### FRIDGE

- 660g milk
- 400g thick Greek yoghurt
- 330g thickened cream
- 130g butter or ghee (or macadamia oil)
- 100g tamarind purée
- 2kg chuck steak

### FREEZER

- 1kg frozen mango flesh
- 500g mixed frozen vegetables

### PANTRY

- 500g plain flour, plus extra for dusting
- 500g raw cashews
- 400g basmati rice
- 5 × 400g cans coconut milk
- 2 × 400g cans diced tomatoes
- 400g can chickpeas
- 365g raw sugar
- 250g apple cider vinegar
- 100g roasted cashews or peanuts
- 60g sultanas
- 50g coconut oil
- 40g macadamia oil
- 5 plain sweet biscuits
- 4½ tablespoons loose black chai tea
- 1⅔ teaspoons powdered gelatine
- 1 teaspoon vanilla extract
- Fine salt

### SPICE RACK

- 4 dried red chillies
- 4½ tablespoons curry powder
- 1 tablespoon garam masala
- 2 teaspoons ground turmeric
- 2 teaspoons mustard seeds
- 2 teaspoons cumin seeds
- 1 teaspoon chilli flakes
- 1 teaspoon ground cardamom
- 1 teaspoon coriander seeds

### FRUIT AND VEGETABLES

- 4 brown onions
- 14 garlic cloves
- 6cm piece ginger
- 3 green chillies
- 3 green apples
- 3 mangoes (or 500g frozen mango flesh)
- 1 head cauliflower
- 100g baby spinach leaves
- 2 bunches fresh mint
- 1 bunch fresh coriander
- 10 fresh curry leaves

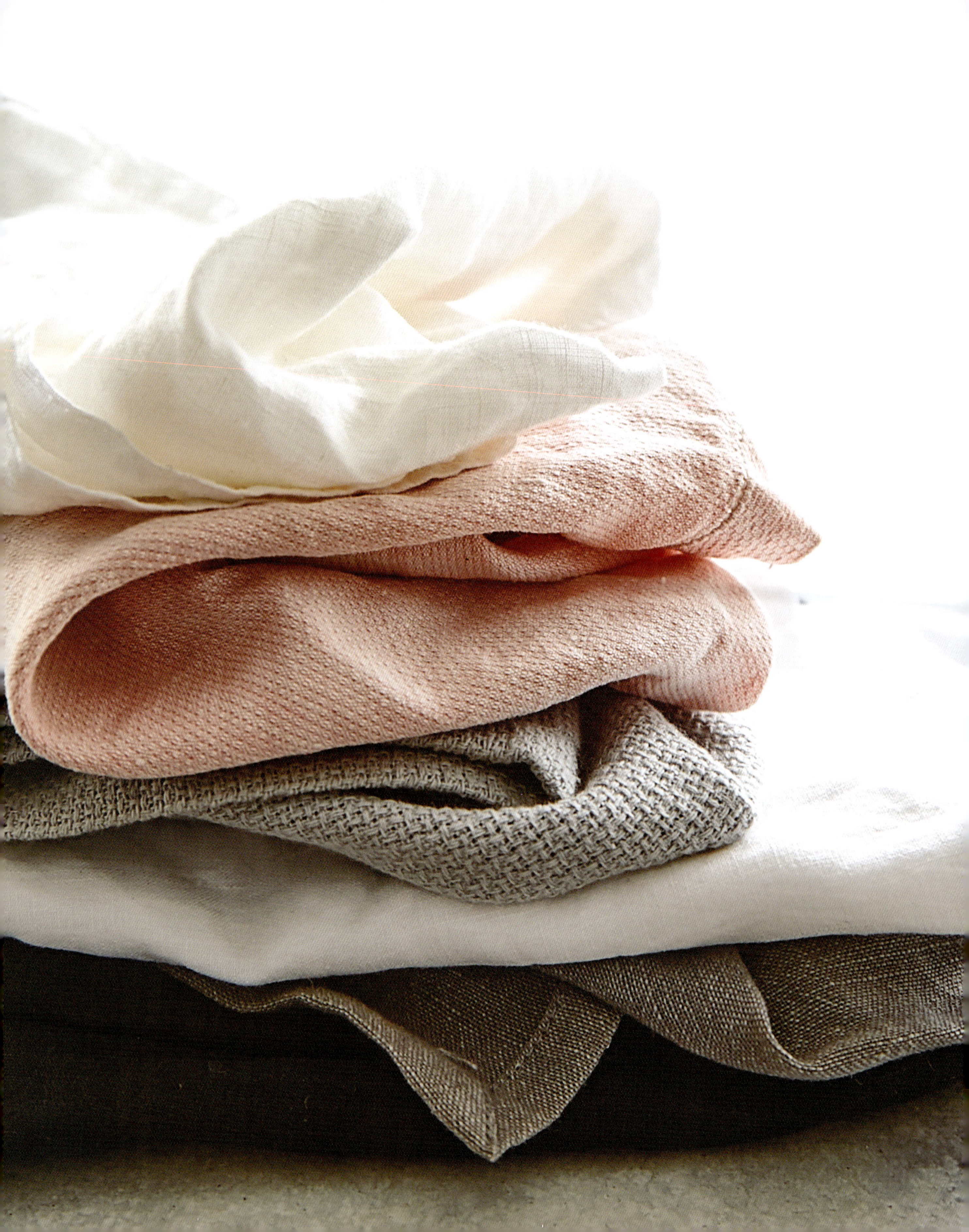

# how to make entertaining easy

- **STICK TO WHAT YOU KNOW**  Don't try something brand new for the first time – the threat of disaster is just too great! Either have a practice run beforehand (I'm sure you'll have some obliging taste testers) or cook something you are already comfortable with. This doesn't mean you need to dampen your creativity, simply play to your strengths – if you are a gun at risottos or cheesecakes, experiment with a new flavour combination.

- **MAKE A PLAN**  For larger events, I always write a plan, listing what needs to be done and when. This means you can go into auto pilot and work your way down the list, and no amount of distraction can derail you! It takes the pressure off as you know nothing will be forgotten, so you can simply focus on the food in front of you. My Indian feast timeline (see page 152) is a very thorough example of such a strategy, but even a few scribbled dot points will help keep you on track.

- **PREPARATION IS KEY**  Pick a menu that can be partially or entirely prepared in advance, leaving very little for you to do once your guests have arrived. Meals that need last-minute execution are usually out for me (think tempura); instead I opt for dishes that improve with age (such as ragù and curry), dishes that need to cool or are served cold (fresh bread, savoury tarts, noodle salads and panna cotta) or dishes that simply require assembly (fresh salads, cheese platters and oysters).

- **IT'S A FEAST, NOT A DEGUSTATION**  I like to lay out everything in the middle of the table banquet style and let people serve themselves – not only does this make it easier on the host, it also builds a sense of community around the table. Serve your curry in the casserole dish it was cooked in (put down a wooden board or place mat first), as this saves washing up later (win!) and keeps the food hot.

- **SKIP THE STARTERS**  I'm not really one for nibbles – why dull your appetite before all the best food is served? And laying out all the savoury food as soon as everyone arrives means I can sit down and relax with my loved ones. Mission accomplished.

After all, what is the point of all that good food if you can't enjoy the good company?

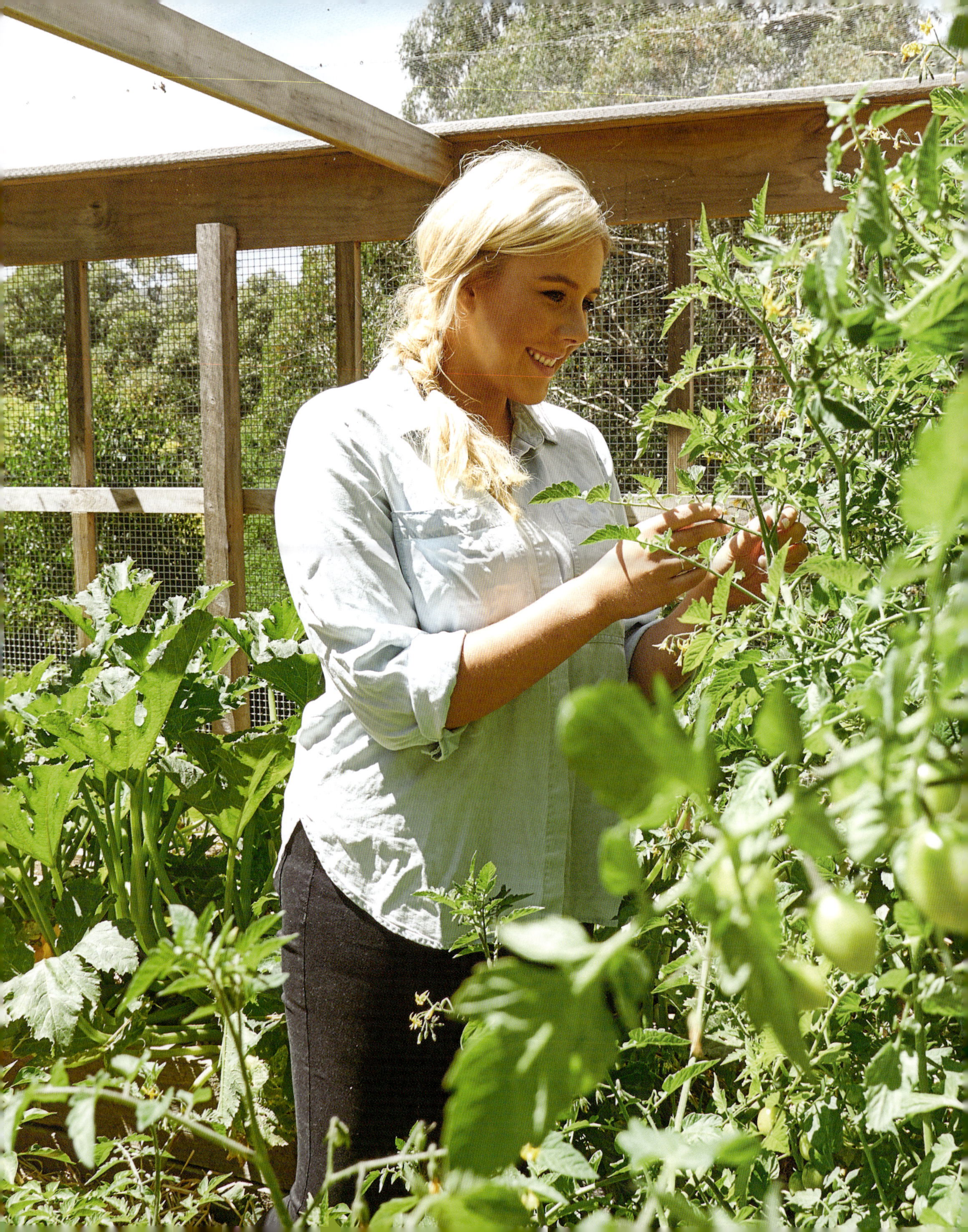

# waste not want not

To me, wasting food is a great insult – to the animals, to the farmers, to the environment, to all those who go without. So much of my home cooking really isn't based on recipes; it's more a matter of finding creative ways to use leftover ingredients and avoid waste. I have my go-to dishes for cleaning out the fridge, and it's these that I share in this chapter. More guides than recipes, focusing on the realities of life – you won't always have the perfect ingredients, but you can still whip up something delicious and nutritious with the bits and pieces you have on hand. It's all about cooking smarter, not harder, and getting creative with your cooking. Let me show you how ...

# almond coconut macaroons

+ BAKING

**MAKES 24**

So many of my favourite recipes require egg yolks (think rich ice creams, custards and savoury sauces), and I am often at a loss as to what to do with the whites! While pavlova is an obvious (and delicious) choice, for everyday fare I can't go past these biscuits. Caramelised on the outside and chewy in the middle, they are really simple to make. They also happen to be gluten free, dairy free and packed with wholesome ingredients, making them a real crowd pleaser when a sweet snack is in order. Now that I have my own chickens the wonder of the egg never ceases to amaze me, and there's no need for any part of it to ever be wasted.

180g shredded coconut
120g slivered almonds
100g white or raw sugar
4 egg whites (approx. 140g)
1 teaspoon vanilla extract
¼ teaspoon fine salt

1. Preheat oven to 160°C. Line a baking tray with baking paper or a baking mat.

2. Place coconut and almonds on lined tray and bake for 15 minutes, or until toasted and golden.

3. Place sugar in TC bowl, mill 10 seconds, speed 10. Scrape down sides.

4. Insert butterfly. Add egg whites, vanilla and salt, whip for 2 minutes, 37°C, speed 4.

5. Add toasted coconut and almonds, mix for 12 seconds, reverse speed 1. Mix in any loose ingredients with a spatula.

6. Place tablespoons of mixture on lined tray, leaving a 3cm space between each biscuit. Bake for 18 minutes, or until lightly browned.

Allow to cool completely on baking tray before transferring to an airtight container for storage.

NOTE: It is important when working with egg whites that the TC bowl is properly cleaned and dried first otherwise the egg whites won't whip properly. For best results, rinse it with a mixture of white vinegar and hot water to remove any traces of grease.

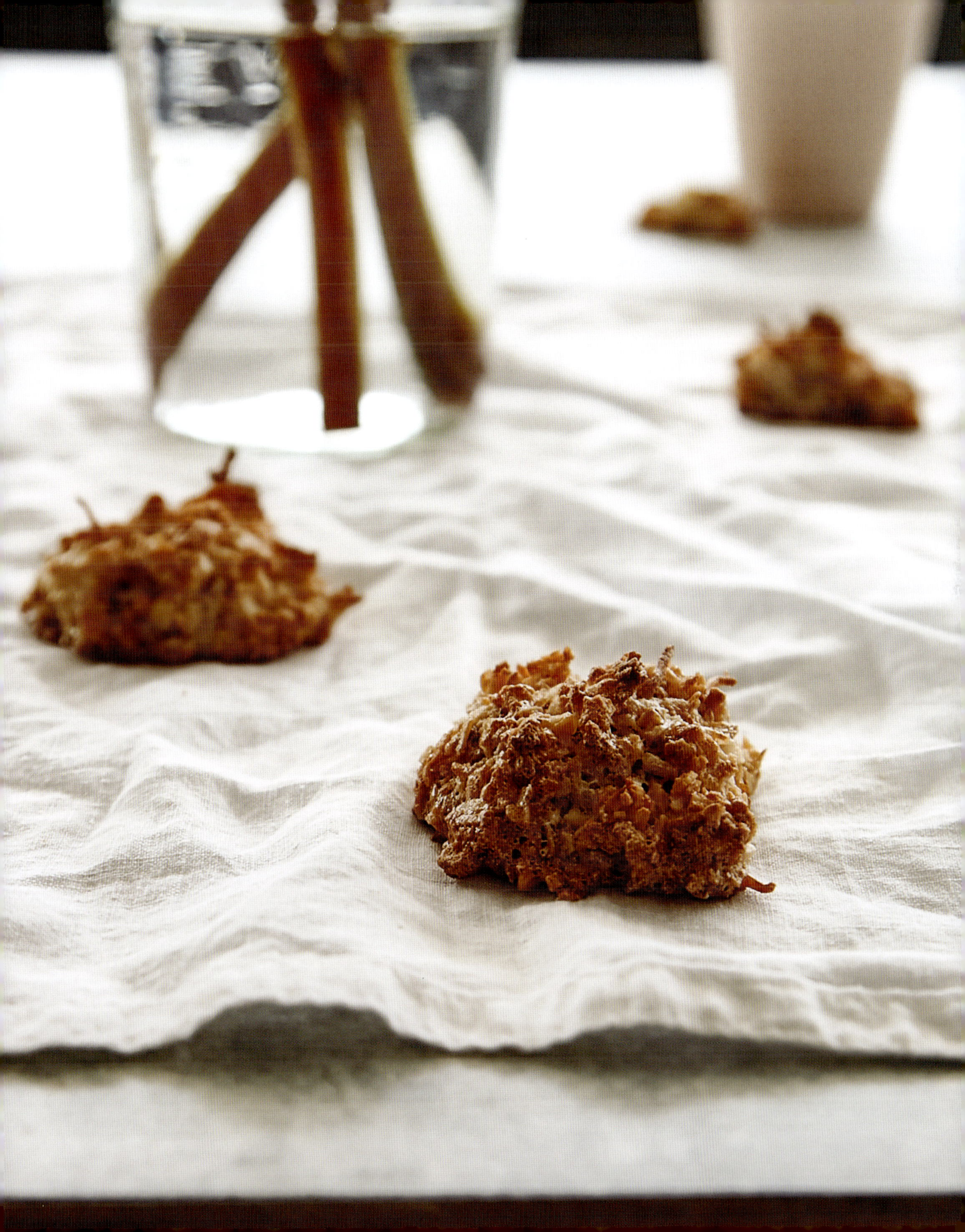

# ricotta cheese

+ DRAINING

**MAKES 300G**

In my view, anything produced by an animal is something to be highly valued, and milk is no exception. There is really no reason for it ever to be wasted – freeze it in ice-cube trays for making frappés and milkshakes, use it in smoothies for breakfast or custard for dessert, or, if you've got a lot of it in the fridge, make ricotta cheese. Still-warm homemade ricotta is vastly superior to anything you can buy – it's silky and creamy without a hint of sourness. And don't waste the leftover whey! It's very high in protein and blends seamlessly into smoothies, makes the fluffiest pancakes and can even be used as a starter in a whole range of fermented foods.

2 litres milk
1½ teaspoons fine salt
30g white vinegar, plus extra if needed

1. Place milk and salt in TC bowl, heat for 15 minutes, 100°C, speed 3. Check milk is registering 100°C, and if not, continue heating.

2. Meanwhile, line steamer basket with clean Chux, muslin cloth or paper towel, allowing to overhang.

3. Heat for a further 1 minute, 100°C, speed 2.

4. Add vinegar, stir for 5 seconds, speed 2. Allow to sit for 4 minutes.

5. Check that curds have formed – you should see the mixture separating into curds and whey. If a full separation hasn't occurred (whey should look yellow to green), add an additional 10g vinegar and mix for 5 seconds, speed 2.

6. Using a slotted spoon, scoop ricotta curds into the lined steamer basket. Fold over cloth or paper towel and pat down, flattening the curds. Allow to drain for 30 minutes (place basket in the sink or sit on top of a glass in a large bowl).

Remove cloth-wrapped cheese from basket and unwrap. Eat straight away or transfer to an airtight container and refrigerate until ready to serve. Consume within 4 days. I like to drizzle over a little honey or olive oil before serving.

NOTE: If you want to make a smaller batch with 1 litre of milk, halve the salt and vinegar and reduce the heating time to as long as it takes to reach 100°C.

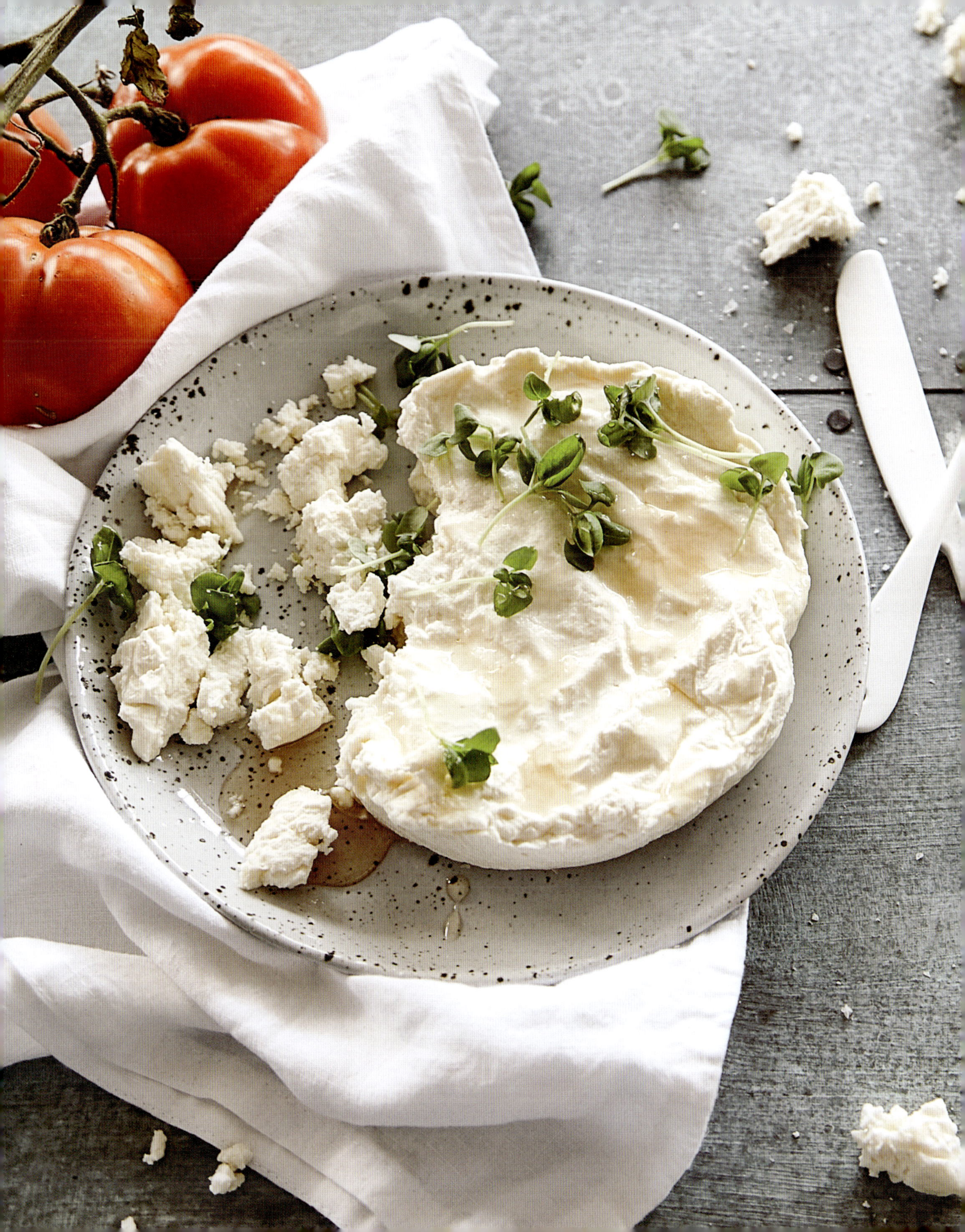

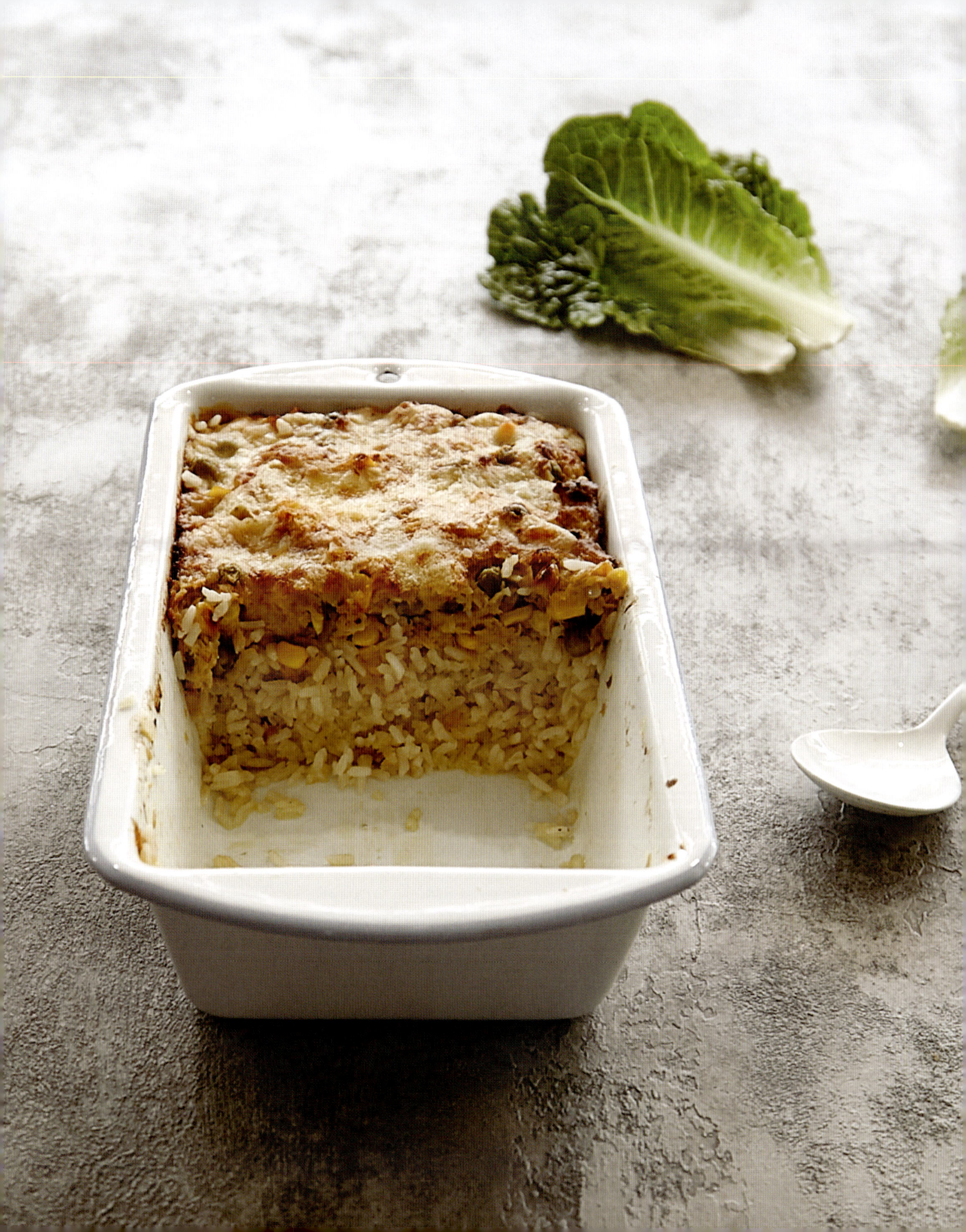

# tuna mornay bake

+ BAKING

SERVES 3

This dish instantly transports me back to my childhood; it was one of our favourite dishes and Mum would cook it regularly. Now as an adult I can see why she did – it's easy to whip up, super tasty and you probably already have most of the ingredients on hand. My preferred base is white rice, which is perfect as I always seem to cook far too much to accompany a curry! The excess rice is never wasted – I just store it in the fridge or freezer, ready for a tuna mornay makeover.

120g tasty cheese, roughly chopped
1 brown onion, peeled and halved
2 garlic cloves, peeled
20g olive oil
400g can tuna in oil
100g cream
200g mixed frozen vegetables
30g Dijon mustard
30g stock concentrate (see page 190)
3–4 cups cooked starch (such as Basmati rice, medium-grain white rice, sushi rice, brown rice, penne pasta, shell pasta, mashed potato)

1. Preheat oven to 180°C.
2. Place cheese in TC bowl, grate for 4 seconds, speed 8. Set aside.
3. Place onion and garlic in TC bowl, chop for 5 seconds, speed 5. Scrape down sides.
4. Add olive oil, sauté for 5 minutes, 100°C, speed 1.
5. Add drained oil from tuna, cream, frozen vegetables, mustard, stock concentrate and 50g of cheese, cook for 5 minutes, 100°C, reverse speed 1.
6. Add tuna, fold through using spatula.
7. Spread starch over base of a small casserole dish or loaf tin and pour tuna mixture over top. Sprinkle with remaining grated cheese. Bake for 20 minutes, or until cheese is bubbling and golden.

Serve hot immediately, however it is still delicious cold the next day. You can re-heat it (covered) in a moderate oven.

WASTE NOT WANT NOT

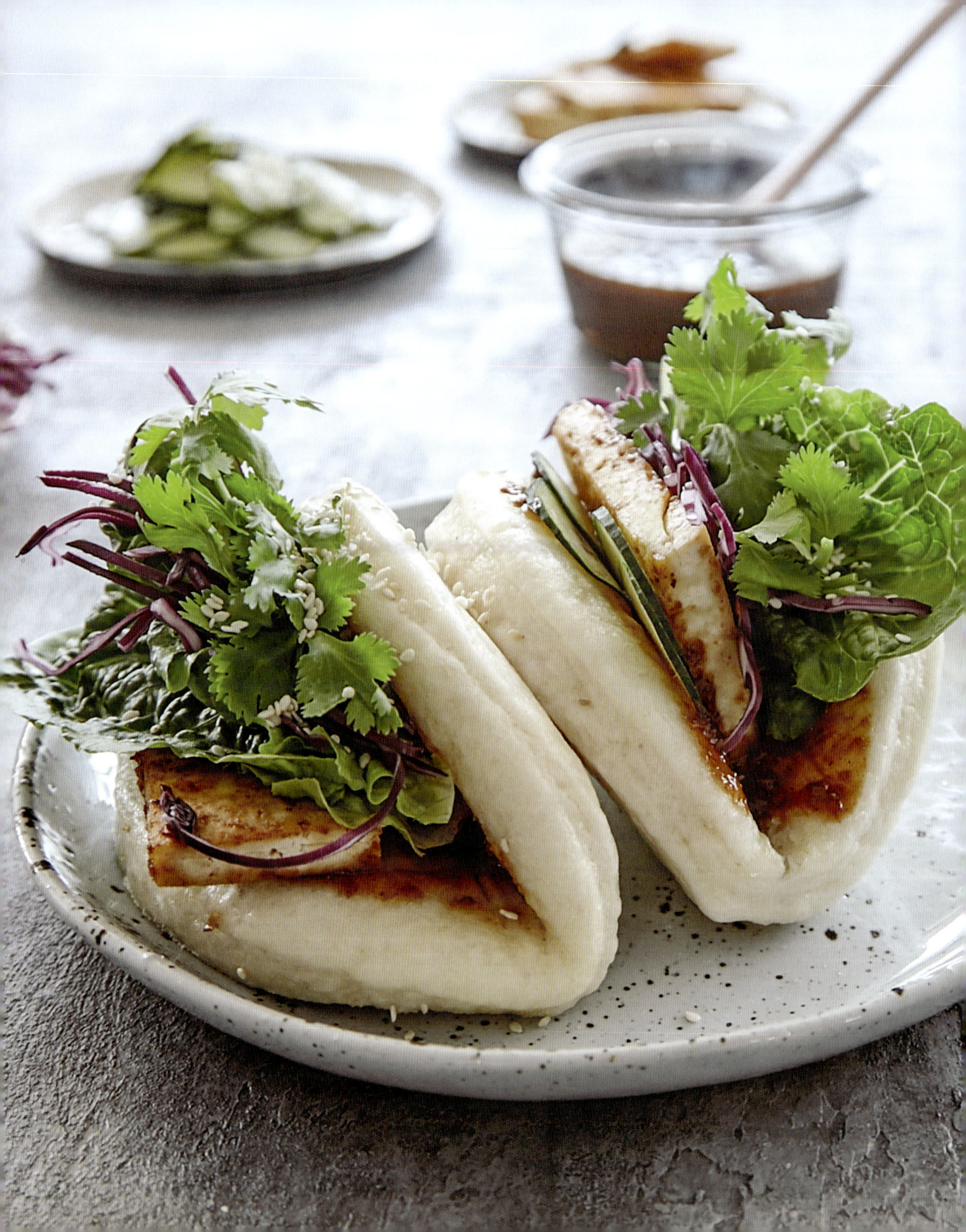

# anything goes baos

MAKES 10–12

Baos might be one of those things you thought you'd never cook at home, but really they are easier than they look! Just make sure you get started on this recipe early as the dough does take a while to rise. They're a great way to use up leftover meat and veggies, as a little bit goes a long way inside these soft and fluffy buns.

| INGREDIENT: | WHY NOT TRY: |
| --- | --- |
| 500g ultra white flour | Or plain flour |
| 250g warm water | |
| 40g white sugar | Or caster sugar |
| 20g oil, plus extra for oiling and brushing | Rice bran, macadamia, grapeseed, extra light olive or any neutral tasting oil |
| 1½ teaspoons dried yeast | |
| 1½ teaspoons baking powder | |
| ½ teaspoon fine salt | |
| 2 cups cooked meat or tofu, shredded or thinly sliced | Korean beef ribs (see page 106), char siu, barbecued duck, steamed chicken, pork belly, fried tofu |
| 2 cups vegetables, shredded or thinly sliced | Pickled salad (see page 124), kimchi-kraut (see page 236), cabbage, cucumber, chilli, spring onion, carrot, radish, lettuce |
| Handful fresh herbs | Mint, coriander, Thai basil, Vietnamese mint |
| Sesame seeds, to serve | |
| Hoisin sauce (see page 224), to serve | |

*continued →*

# anything goes baos continued

1. Place flour, warm water, sugar, oil, yeast, baking powder and salt in TC bowl, mix for 10 seconds, speed 6.

2. Knead for 2 minutes, dough function. Transfer dough to an oiled bowl, cover and set aside for 2–3 hours, or until doubled in size.

3. Transfer dough to a lightly floured bench or baking mat and roll out to approx. 8mm thick. Using a round cutter (approx. 10cm diameter), cut out 5–6 rounds. Roll remaining dough into a ball and set aside.

4. Fill TC bowl with 700g water. Heat for 8 minutes, steaming temperature, speed 3, or until steaming temperature is reached.

5. Meanwhile, brush the top of the dough rounds with oil and lightly roll into slight oval shape. Fold in half lengthways.

6. Place baos in steaming tray, utilising steaming tray insert. Steam for 8 minutes, steaming temperature, speed 3. Meanwhile, roll out remaining dough and repeat the process to give you another 5–6 baos.

7. Cover cooked baos in foil to keep warm while cooking remaining baos for 8 minutes, steaming temperature, speed 3. Check water in TC bowl and top up if it is getting low.

While baos are still warm, gently split open at the seam and fill with meat or tofu, vegetables and herbs. Sprinkle with sesame seeds and serve with hoisin sauce.

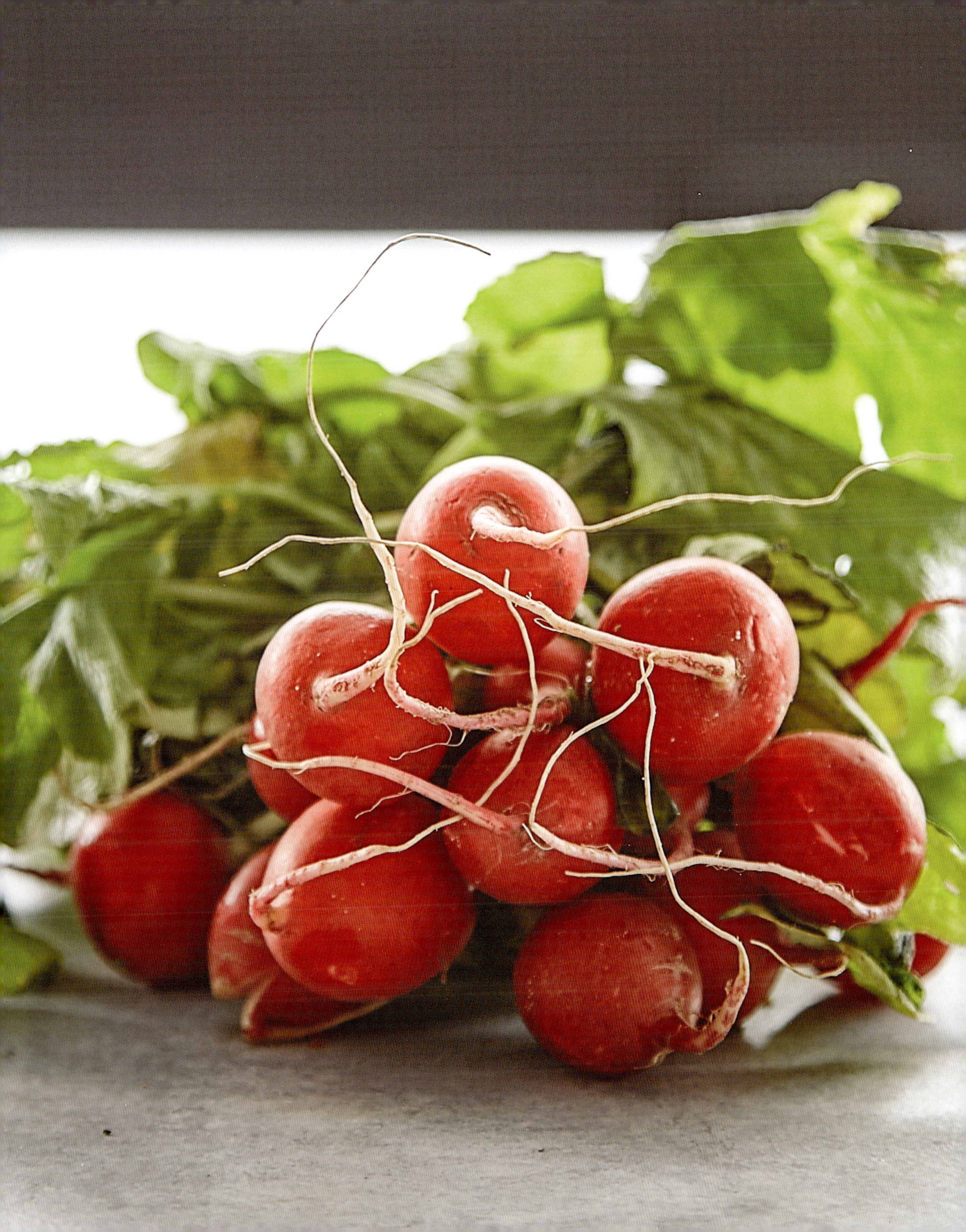

# herb vinaigrette

**MAKES 1 CUP**

We always seem to end up with more herbs than we need. Turning them into this tangy vinaigrette not only creates an easy way to incorporate them into a range of dishes, it also extends the shelf life way beyond what the veggie drawer can offer. Change the herbs to suit what you are cooking: try basil with summer salads and cheese, mint with lamb or Greek dishes, dill with fish, rosemary with roast vegetables, coriander with Mexican or Thai food, and marjoram with rich meats.

| INGREDIENT: | WHY NOT TRY: |
| --- | --- |
| 2 handfuls fresh herbs | Basil, parsley, mint, coriander, rosemary, thyme, dill, marjoram |
| 120g olive oil | Or macadamia oil |
| 100g vinegar | White wine vinegar, red wine vinegar, white balsamic vinegar, apple cider vinegar |
| 2 teaspoons Dijon mustard | |
| 1 teaspoon fine salt | |

1. Place herbs in TC bowl, chop for 2 seconds, speed 8.
2. Add oil, vinegar, mustard and salt, mix for 30 seconds, speed 4. Transfer to a glass jar and refrigerate until ready to serve.

Shake or stir before using. The vinaigrette will keep in the fridge for up to 2 weeks.

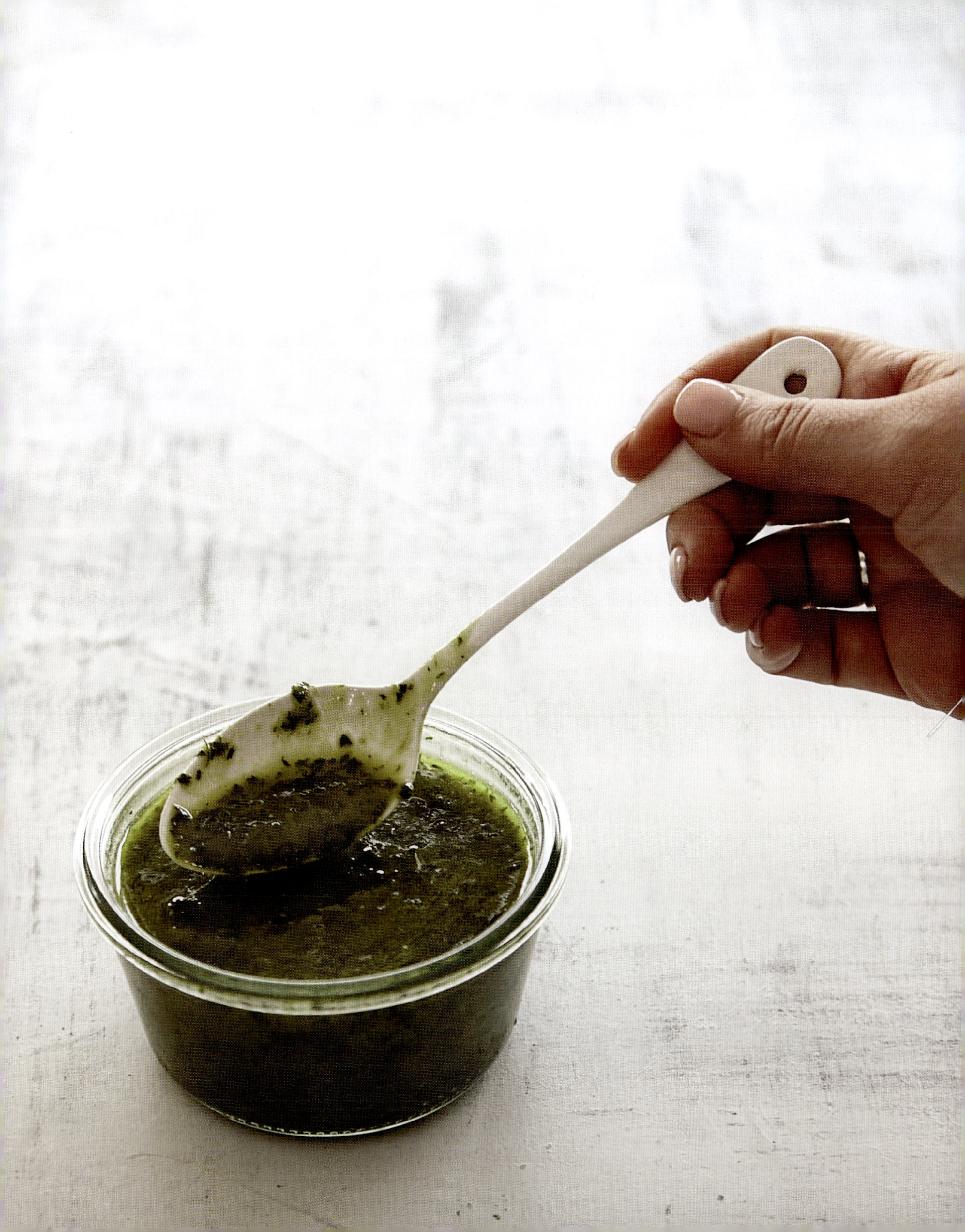

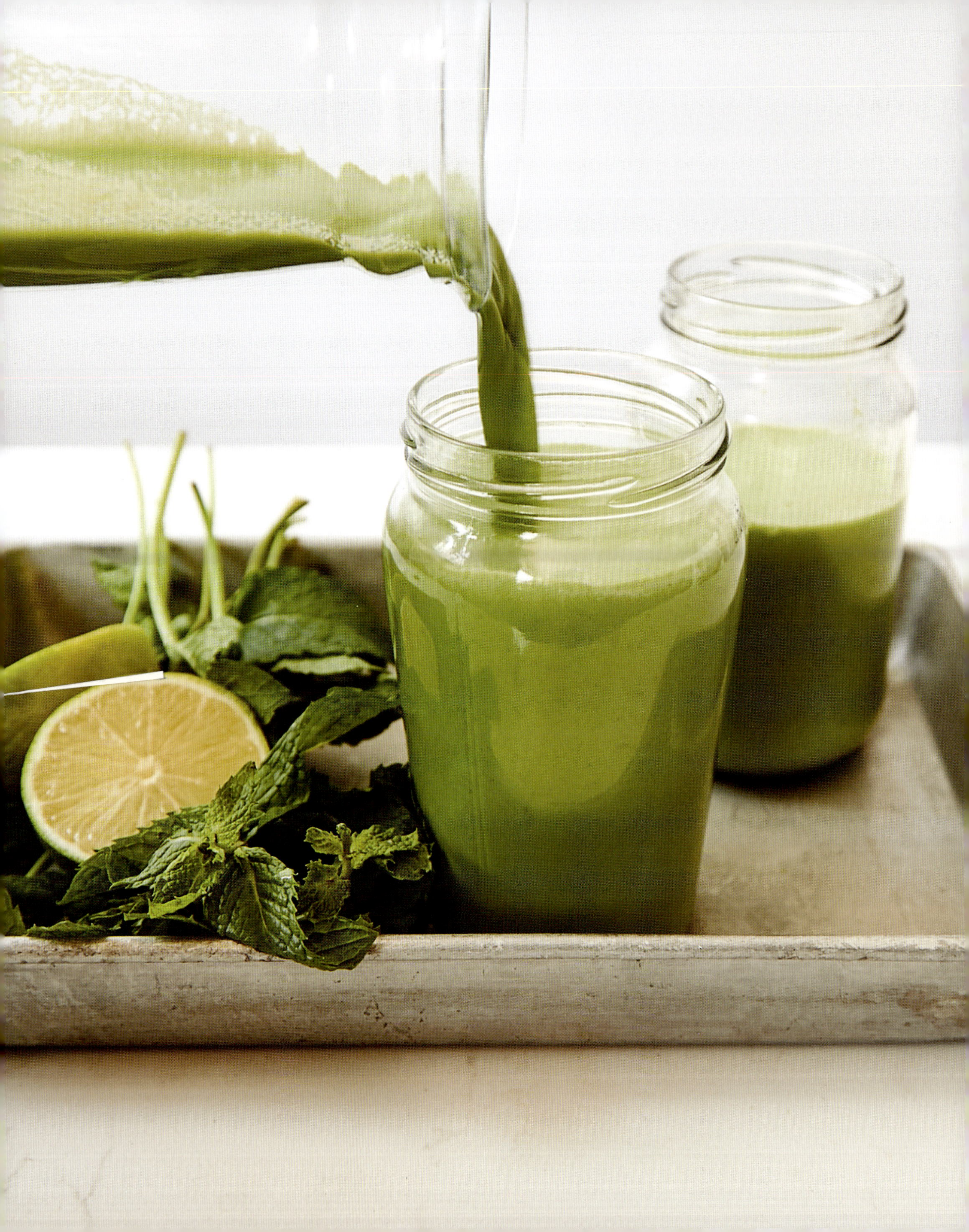

# clean green smoothie

SERVES 2

Green smoothies are the backbone of my kitchen – I am always whipping up a quick concoction to drink on the go, whether it be for breakfast, lunch, an afternoon snack, or occasionally dinner! I love the convenience and also the health benefits, but most of all I love the fact that I can throw in any old scraps of fruit and vegetable and that these won't be wasted. I never actively shop for my smoothie ingredients, rather I raid the fridge and the freezer. That's why instead of offering another green smoothie recipe, I've written my 'green smoothie guide'. This is the formula I use to make a delicious green smoothie every time, no matter what I have on hand. In my opinion, thermo cookers make the smoothest and creamiest green drinks, but there is definitely an art to it beyond throwing in all the ingredients!

| INGREDIENT: | WHY NOT TRY: |
| --- | --- |
| 40g nuts or seeds (optional) | Almonds, cashews, macadamias, hazelnuts, chia seeds, pumpkin seeds, sesame seeds, flaxseeds, sunflower seeds |
| 150g frozen fruit | Banana, mango, avocado, berries, peach |
| 100g leafy greens | Spinach, lettuce, bok choy, kale, beetroot leaves, celery leaves, rocket |
| 100g fresh vegetables or fruit, roughly chopped | Carrot, beetroot, celery, fennel, pineapple, apple, watermelon, papaya, apricots |
| 20g sweetener (optional) | Honey, rice malt syrup, pure maple syrup, coconut nectar, molasses |
| 2 teaspoons superfoods (optional) | Protein powder, cacao powder, green powder, bee pollen, green algae powder, vitamin C powder, acai powder, purple corn extract, green olive extract, gelatine |
| 750g liquid, plus extra if needed | Almond milk, cow's milk, thin yoghurt, macadamia milk (see page 18), soy milk, coconut milk, chia milk, coconut water, cooled tea, whey, fruit juice, kombucha, water |

continued →

# clean green smoothie continued

1. Place nuts or seeds (if using) in TC bowl, mill for 20 seconds, speed 9.

2. Add frozen fruit, leafy greens, fresh vegetables or fruit, sweetener (if using), superfoods (if using) and 50g of liquid. Pulverise for 30 seconds, speed 9.

3. Set timer for 1 minute, speed 9, while slowly adding the remaining 700g liquid onto the TC lid. Check the consistency; if it is too thick add more liquid and mix for a further 20 seconds, speed 9.

Serve immediately or pour into an insulated bottle to sip throughout the day.

NOTE: If you are using chia seeds in your smoothie, you will need to consume it immediately as it will continue to thicken the longer it sits.

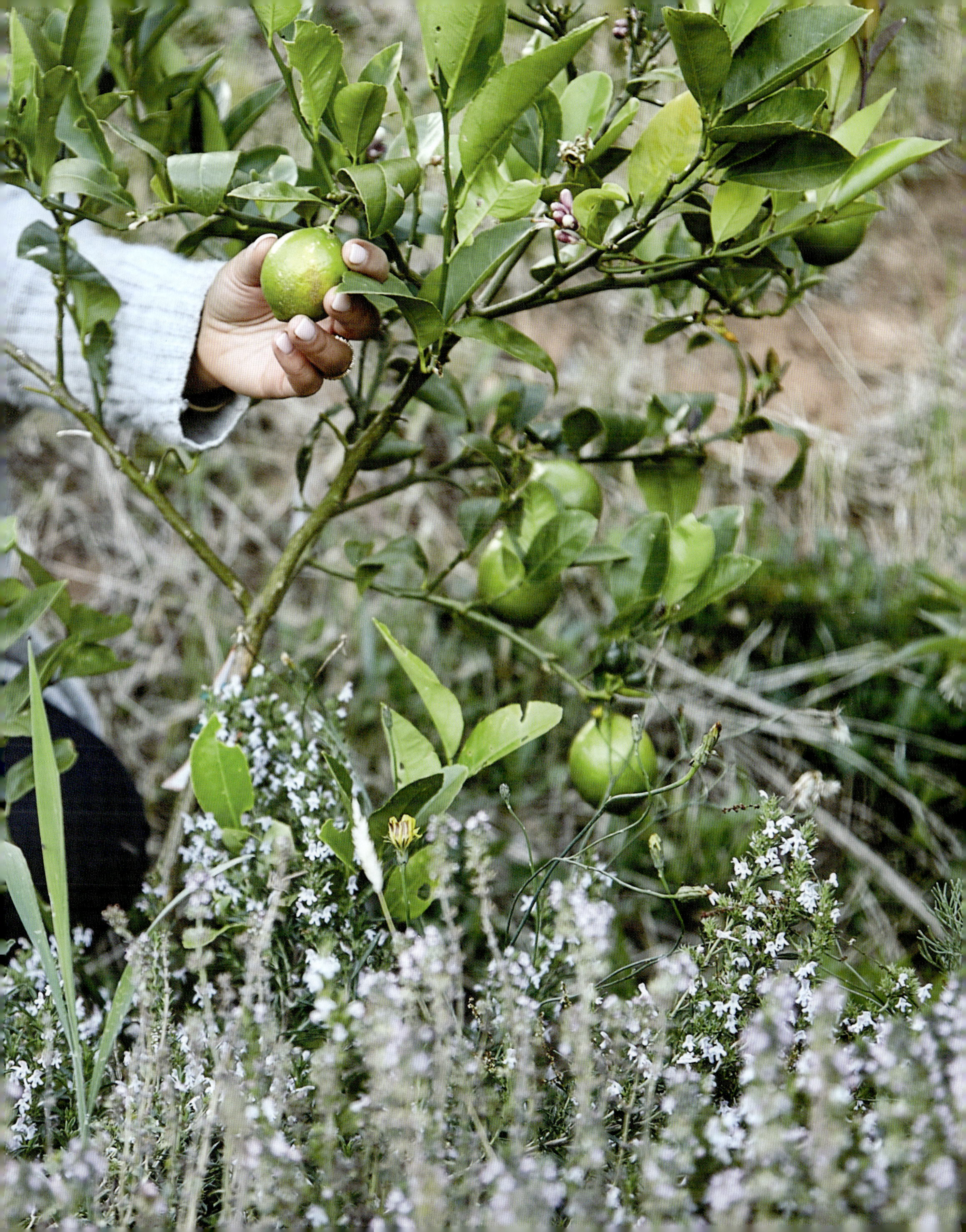

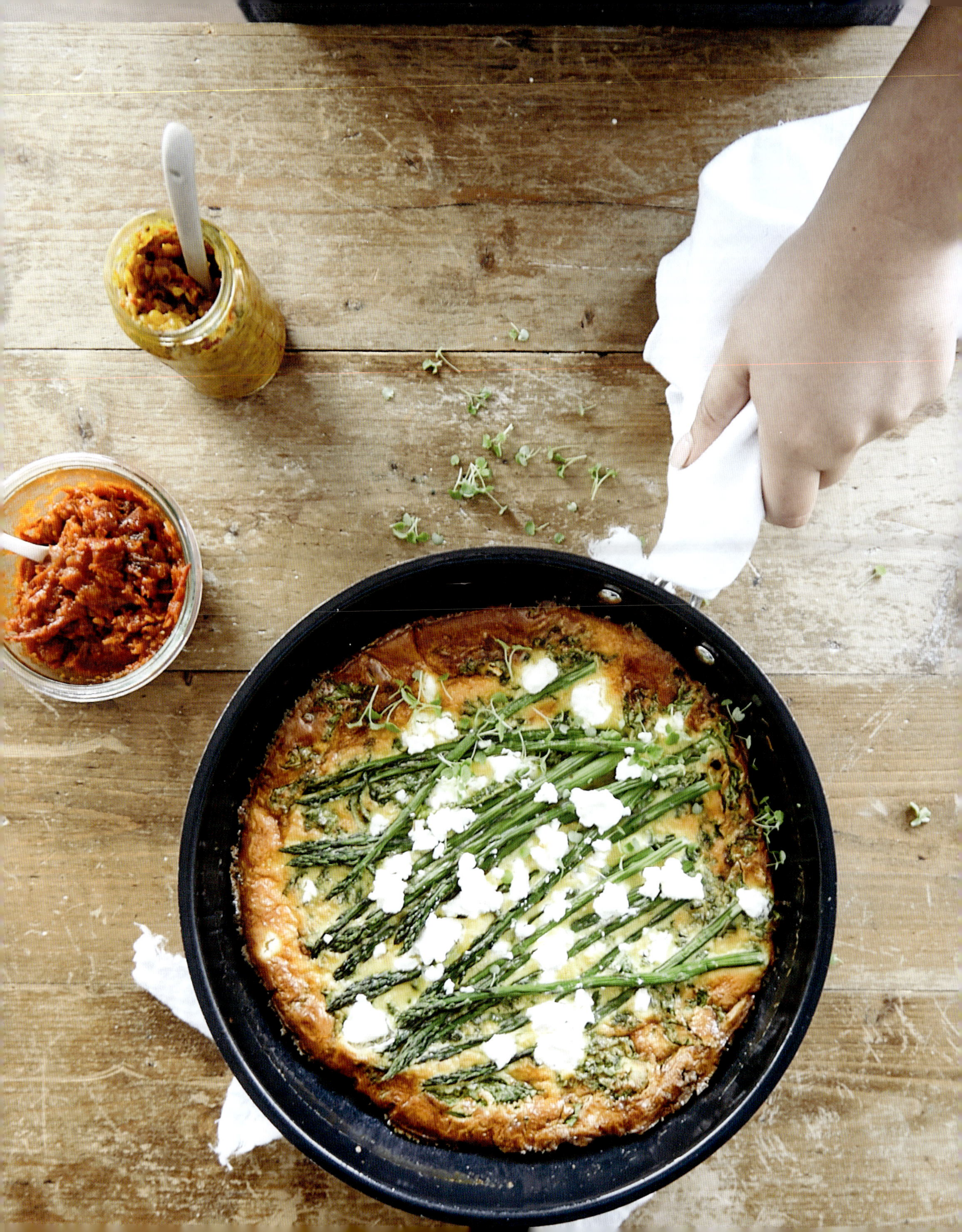

# frugal frittata

SERVES 5

A frittata is hands down my favourite way to use up leftovers ... not only are they really tasty, but you can serve them for breakfast, lunch and dinner. And all the times in between! They are delicious cold and you can cut the slices as little or as large as you like, making them perfect for lunchboxes, afternoon snacks, picnics, long car trips or finger food with drinks. In the spirit of 'waste not' I urge you not to throw your egg shells in the rubbish. They contain so many precious nutrients and it's a terrible shame for these to simply rot in landfill. Compost them instead, and use the nutrients to grow more food. Even a small worm farm in the corner of the garage makes a difference.

| INGREDIENT: | WHY NOT TRY: |
| --- | --- |
| 20g fat | Olive oil, macadamia oil, butter, ghee, lard, drippings (see page 178) |
| 4 cups ready-to-eat leftovers, cut into 2cm pieces | Steamed or roasted pumpkin, steamed broccoli, beans or asparagus, sautéed mushrooms, roasted potatoes, tomatoes, carrot or sweet potato, spinach, kale, spring onions, roast beef, roast chicken, pulled pork, smoked trout, smoked salmon, fried tofu, shredded chicken, steak, sausages, meatballs (see page 80), rissoles, shredded lamb (see page 108), salami, olives |
| 10 eggs | |
| 100g cream | Any type is fine |
| 1 teaspoon salt | Flavour bomb salt (see page 246) or fine salt |
| 100g cheese, grated or crumbled | Blue, feta, mozzarella, tasty, cheddar, parmesan, gorgonzola |

*continued →*

WASTE NOT WANT NOT

# frugal frittata continued

1. Preheat grill to medium.

2. Heat fat in a 28cm fry pan over medium heat. Add leftovers, sauté for 5 minutes, moving frequently, until heated through.

3. Meanwhile, place eggs, cream and salt in TC bowl, mix for 10 seconds, speed 4.

4. Reduce heat under pan to medium–low and pour egg mixture evenly over leftovers. Cook for 7 minutes, or until outer egg mixture sets.

5. Sprinkle or dot with cheese, then place fry pan under grill for 5 minutes, or until frittata is set and golden.

6. Allow to cool slightly before placing a large plate over the top of the fry pan and quickly flipping upside down. Gently lift off pan, and use a second plate to flip frittata back over. Alternatively, use an egg flip to serve individual wedges straight from the pan.

Serve with a side salad and chutney (see pages 239–240).

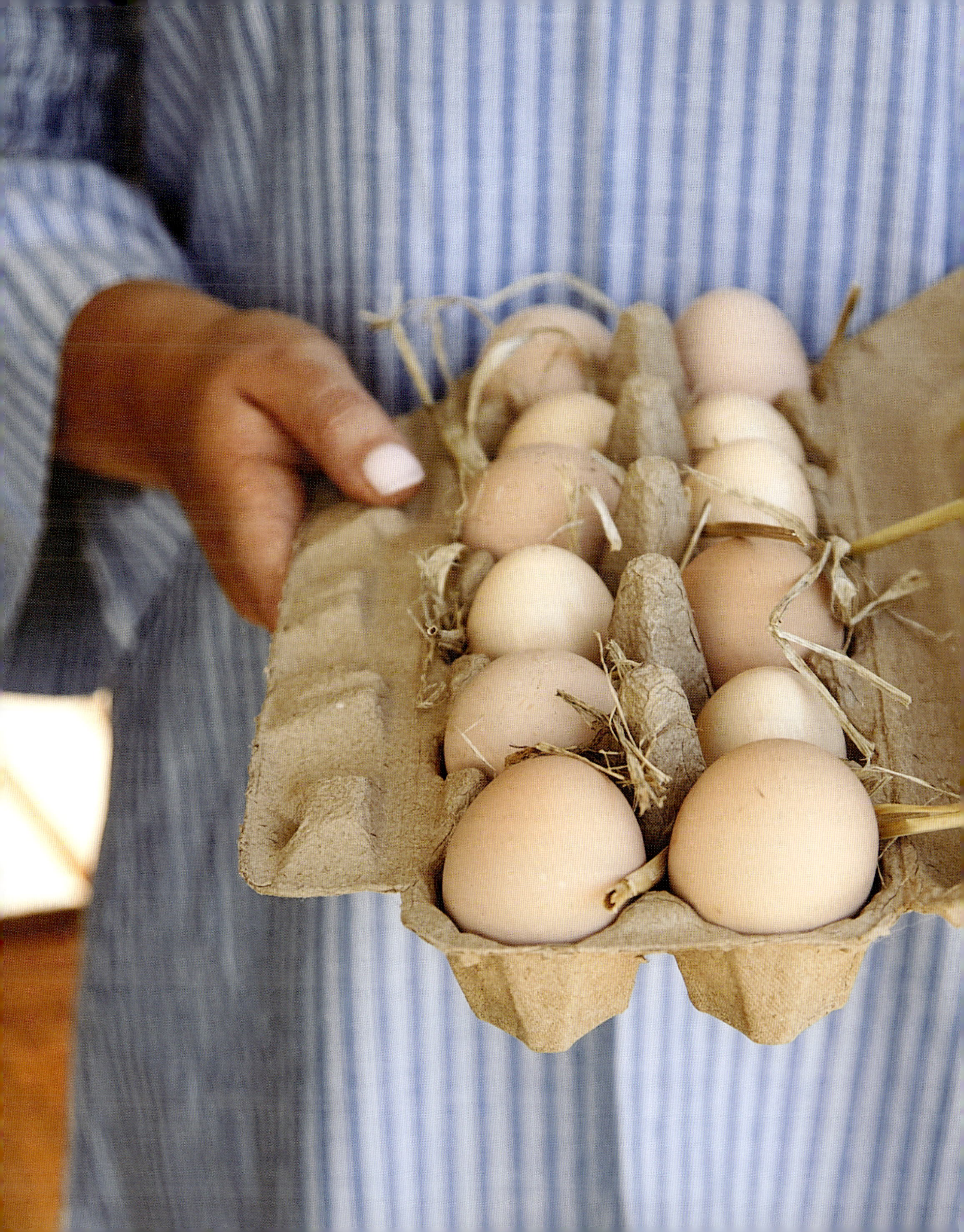

# roast potatoes

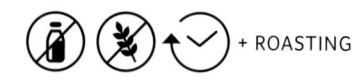

+ ROASTING

### SERVES 6

Crisp on the outside and fluffy on the inside, who can resist a perfect roast potato? The trick, I believe, is to steam them first and then roast them in animal fat. But how much of this precious substance do we simply wash down the sink these days? Think about the oil left in the pan after frying bacon or sausages, the fat and juices that collect in the bottom of a roasting tin after a Sunday roast. These remnants are full of flavour, not to mention vitamins and minerals, and shouldn't be wasted. My solution is to collect the leftover fat and pan juices in a little jar and store it in the freezer. The next time roast potatoes are on the menu I simply pull out the jar and there's my cooking oil. Voila!

| INGREDIENT: | WHY NOT TRY: |
| --- | --- |
| 1kg potatoes | Either new potatoes, quartered, or any larger roasting potato, cut into 2cm pieces |
| 80g fat | Dripping from roast beef, pork, lamb or chicken, the fat skimmed off the top of stocks (see page 115), the pan oils left from fried bacon, chorizo, speck, pancetta, sausages, chops or lamb cutlets |
| 1 teaspoon salt | Flavour bomb salt (see page 246) or fine salt |

1. Preheat oven to 210°C.
2. Fill TC bowl with 500g water. Place potatoes in steaming tray and steam for 18 minutes, steaming temperature, speed 3, or until just tender. Set aside.
3. Place fat and salt in TC bowl, heat for 2 minutes, 60°C, speed 2.
4. Add potatoes, mix for 3 seconds, reverse speed 3, or until evenly coated. Spread out potatoes evenly in large roasting tin and roast for 25 minutes, or until golden.

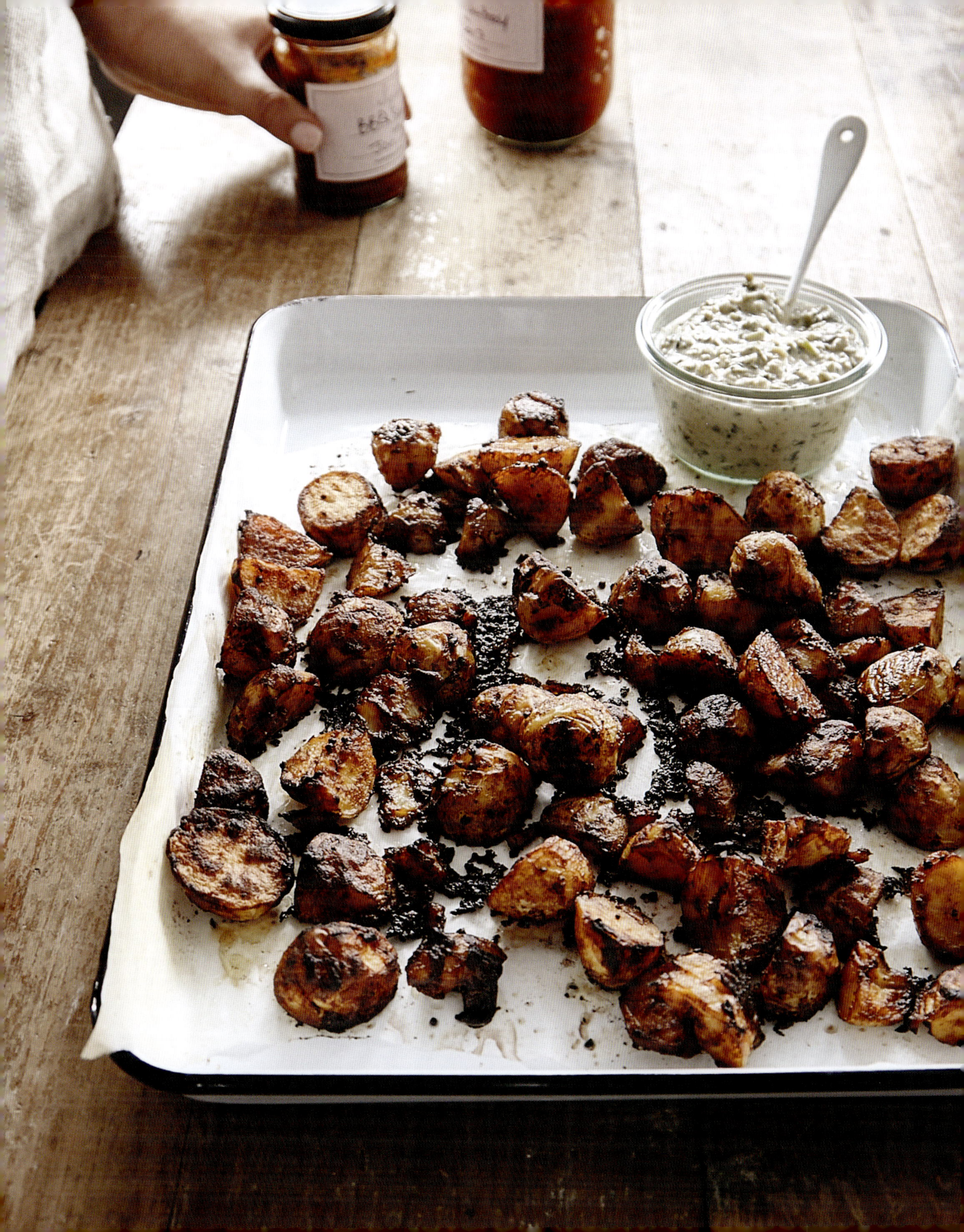

# noodle curry soup

SERVES 3

Whether it's homemade or takeaway, here's a great way to turn leftover curry into a delicious meal for three, without feeling like you are eating the same meal twice. You might even find yourself cooking a little extra curry just so you can make this soup the next day, and this is definitely a good move.

| INGREDIENT: | WHY NOT TRY: |
| --- | --- |
| 200g noodles | Udon, vermicelli, fresh egg, soba, spaghetti |
| 400g can coconut milk | |
| 400g curry | Any curry with beef (see pages 111 and 140), pork, chicken, fish, prawn, vegetables, tofu |
| 3 cups diced or sliced vegetables | Spinach, coral lettuce, bok choy, pak choy, snow peas, capsicum, carrot, spring onion, bean sprouts, steamed broccoli, pumpkin, sweet potato and/or beans, defrosted frozen peas and/or corn |
| Fresh herbs | Mint, Vietnamese mint, coriander, basil, Thai basil, parsley |
| Garnish | Coconut flakes, fried shallots, chilli flakes, fried garlic, roasted peanuts or cashews, lime wedges |
| Saltiness, to taste | Fish sauce, soy sauce, tamari, stock concentrate (see page 190), salt flakes, flavour bomb salt (see page 246) |

1. Prepare noodles according to packet instructions.
2. Meanwhile, place coconut milk in TC bowl, heat for 6 minutes, steaming temperature, speed 3.
3. Add curry, heat for 5 minutes, steaming temperature, reverse speed 1.
4. Meanwhile, divide vegetables and cooked noodles among 3 serving bowls.

Pour over soup mixture, top with herbs and your choice of garnish. Add saltiness to taste.

VARIATION: Even if you don't have any leftover curry you can still make this – add 2 cans of coconut milk and curry paste, to taste.

WASTE NOT WANT NOT

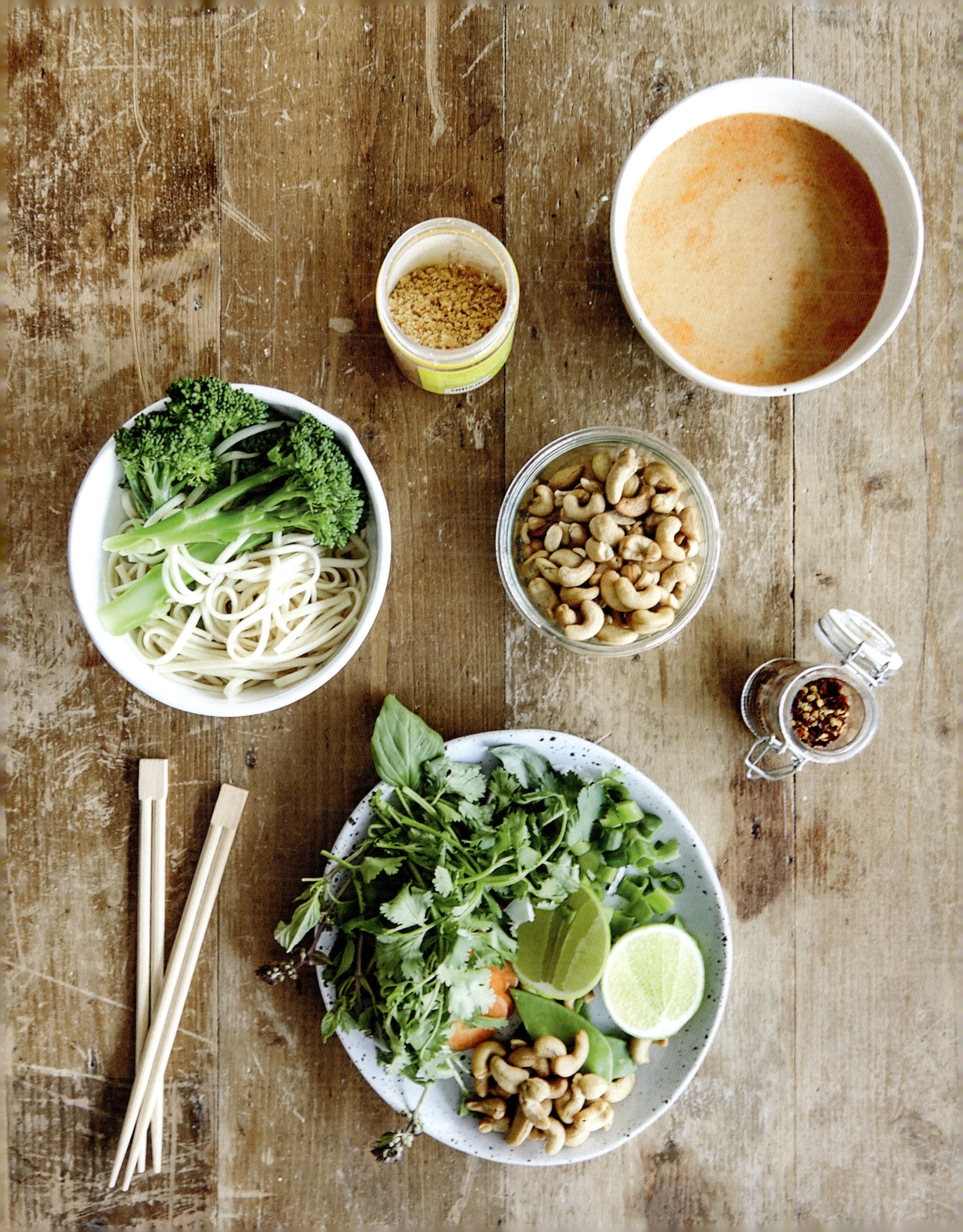

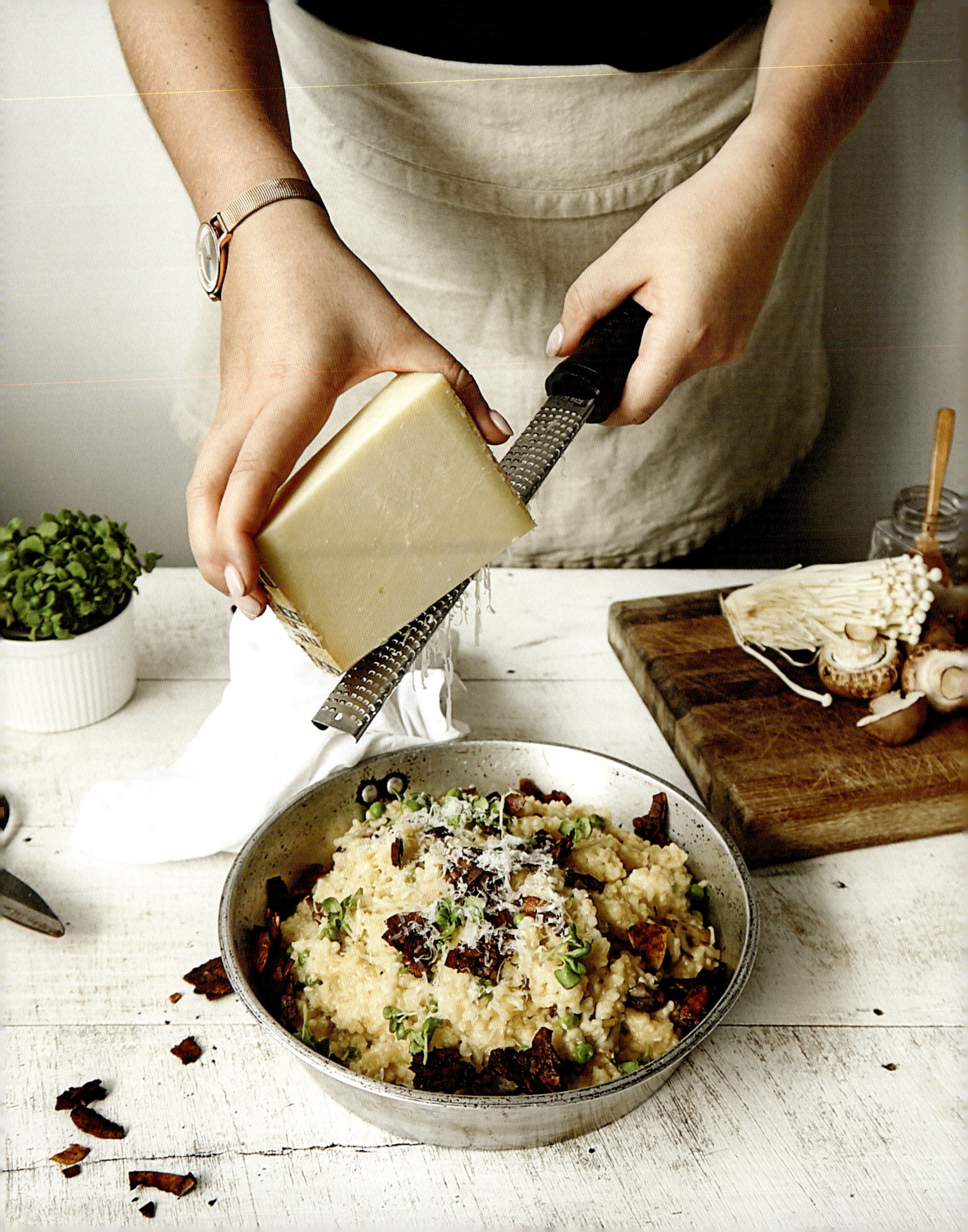

# 'the' risotto

**SERVES 4**

This is the only risotto recipe you will ever need. Pick your ingredients based on what's in the fridge and tailor the flavours to your family's preferences. Just so we're clear, I don't want you turning the oven on just to roast a bit of pumpkin! Maybe you've got leftovers from last night's roast dinner, or you've got muffins baking so you sneak in a tray of veggies. Maybe you've got a tiny bit of leftover meat sauce that didn't fit in your lasagne. Or maybe you're steaming eggs for tomorrow's lunch and you pop the steaming tray on top filled with that lonely head of broccoli. It's all about getting creative and cooking smarter.

| INGREDIENT: | WHY NOT TRY: |
|---|---|
| 1 onion, peeled and halved | Brown or white onion, leek, red Asian shallots |
| 2 garlic cloves, peeled | |
| 40g olive oil | |
| 300g Arborio rice | |
| 800g stock | Chicken stock, vegetable stock or 750g water and 50g stock concentrate (see page 190 and 114) |
| 120g white wine | Or additional stock |
| 1½ cups ready-to-eat vegetables | Spinach, chopped tomatoes, roasted pumpkin or cauliflower, sautéed mushrooms, defrosted frozen peas or corn, steamed asparagus, beetroot or broccoli, grated zucchini |
| ½ cup ready-to-eat meat, or extra vegetables | Roast lamb (see page 108), cooked prawns, beef ragù (see page 105), shredded chicken, fried chorizo, bolognaise sauce |
| 40g dairy | Butter, mascarpone, grated cheese, cream |
| Toppings | Greek feta, ricotta cheese (see page 160), burrata, fresh mint, basil or parsley, toasted pine nuts (see note page 94), olives, pesto, rocket, facon (see page 230) |

*continued →*

# 'the' risotto continued

1. Place onion and garlic in TC bowl, chop for 5 seconds, speed 5. Scrape down sides.

2. Add oil, sauté for 5 minutes, 100°C, speed 1.

3. Add rice, sauté for 2 minutes, 100°C, speed 1.

4. Add stock and wine, cook for 13 minutes, 100°C, reverse speed 2.

5. Add vegetables, meat (if using) and dairy, combine using a spatula. Cook for 3 minutes, 100°C, reverse speed 2. Allow to stand for 5 minutes before serving.

Divide evenly among 4 bowls and add toppings.

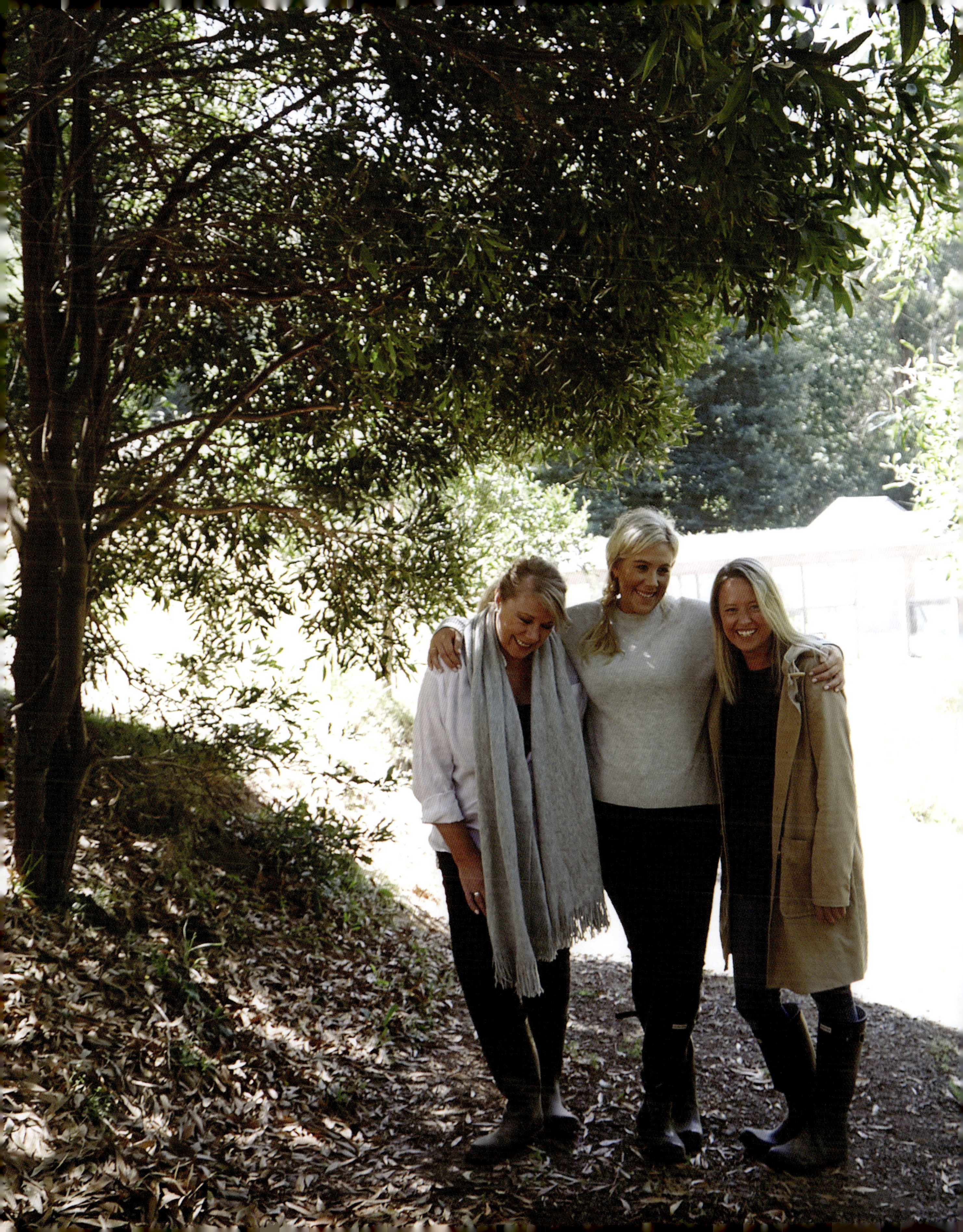

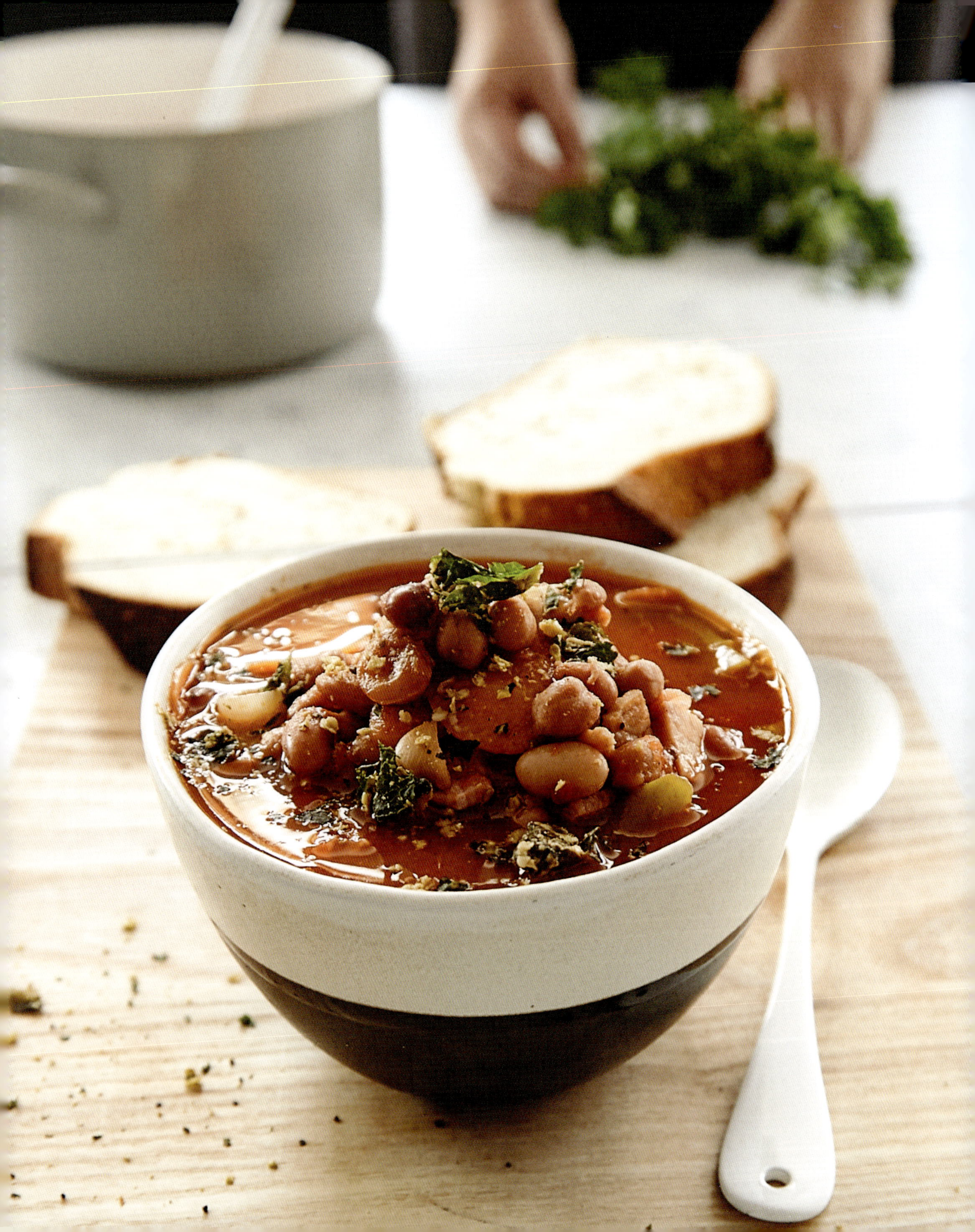

# money-saving minestrone

**SERVES 4**

This simple soup is nourishing and nurturing. It's great Friday night fare, using up all the bits and pieces left in the fridge after a busy week. It also costs next to nothing to make, proving that eating well doesn't have to be expensive.

| INGREDIENT: | WHY NOT TRY: |
| --- | --- |
| 1 onion, peeled and halved | Red onion, white onion, brown onion, golden or red Asian shallot, leek |
| 2 garlic cloves, peeled | |
| 20g fat | Olive oil, meat drippings, butter, ghee, macadamia oil |
| 4 cups raw vegetables, sliced or diced | Capsicum, carrot, celery, corn kernels, green beans, peas, snow peas, potato, zucchini, sweet potato, kale, broccoli, mushrooms, spinach |
| 400g can diced tomatoes | |
| 600g liquid | Water with 20g stock concentrate (see page 190), chicken stock, vegetable stock, beef stock (see page 114) |
| 20g stock concentrate (see page 190) | Or a stock cube |
| 1 cup ready-to-eat starch (optional) | Canned beans (rinsed and drained), cooked lentils, cooked rice, cooked noodles, cooked pasta |
| 1 cup ready-to-eat meat, shredded or diced (optional) | Roast lamb (see page 108), poached chicken, beef ragù (see page 105), salami, fried bacon |
| Toppings, to serve (optional) | Chilli flakes, grated or shaved cheese, fresh parsley, fresh basil, kale chips |
| Bread, to serve | Or gluten-free bread |

*continued →*

# money-saving minestrone continued

1. Place onion and garlic in TC bowl, chop for 5 seconds, speed 5. Scrape down sides.

2. Add fat, sauté for 5 minutes, 100°C, speed 1.

3. Add vegetables, tomatoes, liquid and stock concentrate, cook for 12–20 minutes, 100°C, reverse speed soft, or until vegetables are just cooked.

4. Add starch and meat (if using), cook for 2 minutes, 100°C, reverse speed soft.

Divide soup among 4 bowls, add toppings (if using) and serve with a slice of crusty bread.

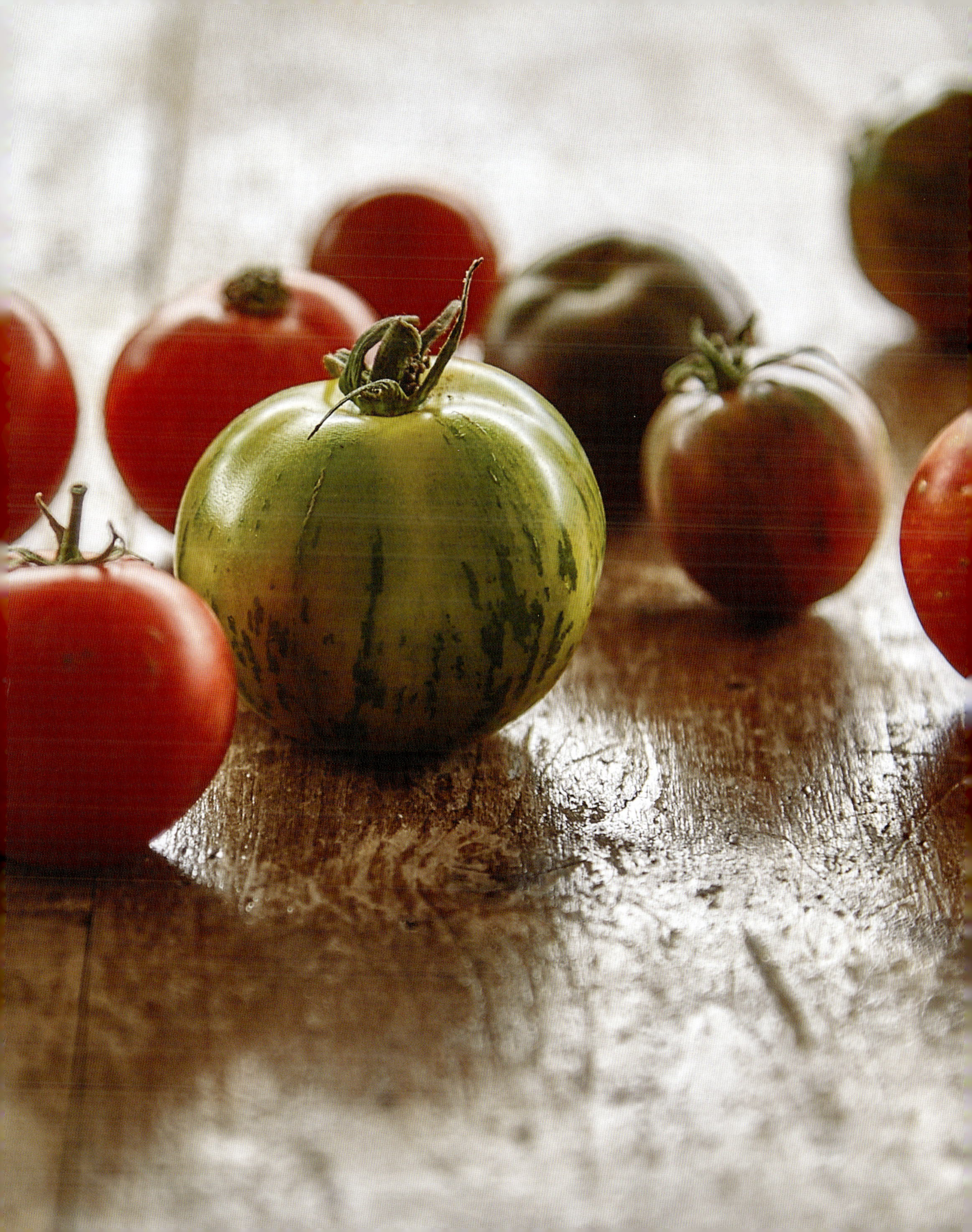

# stock concentrate

MAKES 1 LITRE

Stock concentrate is a staple in most savoury thermo cooker recipes, and for good reason – the salt lifts all the flavours in the dish and the herbs and vegetables add extra seasoning. Use it wherever you would usually use salt, a stock cube or liquid stock. Add a tablespoon to pasta sauces, soups, risottos, gravies, curries or stews. But you don't need a recipe! And you certainly don't need to shop for the ingredients. This is the ultimate 'clean out the veggie drawer' guide – simply use whatever odds and ends are left in the fridge. Think of the times you've bought a bunch of spring onions and only used a couple, a bunch of herbs and only used a few sprigs, or a kilo of pumpkin but only needed 800 grams. Or when you've bought a punnet of tomatoes for a salad, but never got around to making it; the tomatoes might not be looking their freshest for a salad but they will be perfectly fine blended and cooked into a stock concentrate.

| INGREDIENT: | WHY NOT TRY: |
| --- | --- |
| 600g vegetables, roughly chopped | Use a variety – carrots, celery, pumpkin, zucchini, capsicum, sweet potato, rocket, spinach, lettuce, spring onions, tomatoes, cabbage, broccoli (stalks), asparagus (woody ends) |
| 1 onion, peeled and halved | Red onion, white onion, brown onion, golden or red Asian shallot, leek |
| 2 garlic cloves, peeled | |
| 2 handfuls fresh herbs | Use a variety – basil, parsley, mint, coriander, rosemary, thyme, dill, marjoram |
| 150g coarse salt | |
| 50g olive oil | |

1. Place vegetables, onion, garlic and herbs in TC bowl, chop for 6 seconds, speed 7, assisting with spatula. Scrape down sides.
2. Add salt and oil, cook for 20 minutes, 100°C, speed 2.
3. Purée for 1 minute, speed 9.

Allow to cool before transferring to sterilised jars (see note page 148) and storing in the fridge for up to 3 months.

NOTE: If preferred, you can freeze stock concentrate in ice-cube trays and simply pop out a cube on demand for an approximate tablespoon.

WASTE NOT WANT NOT

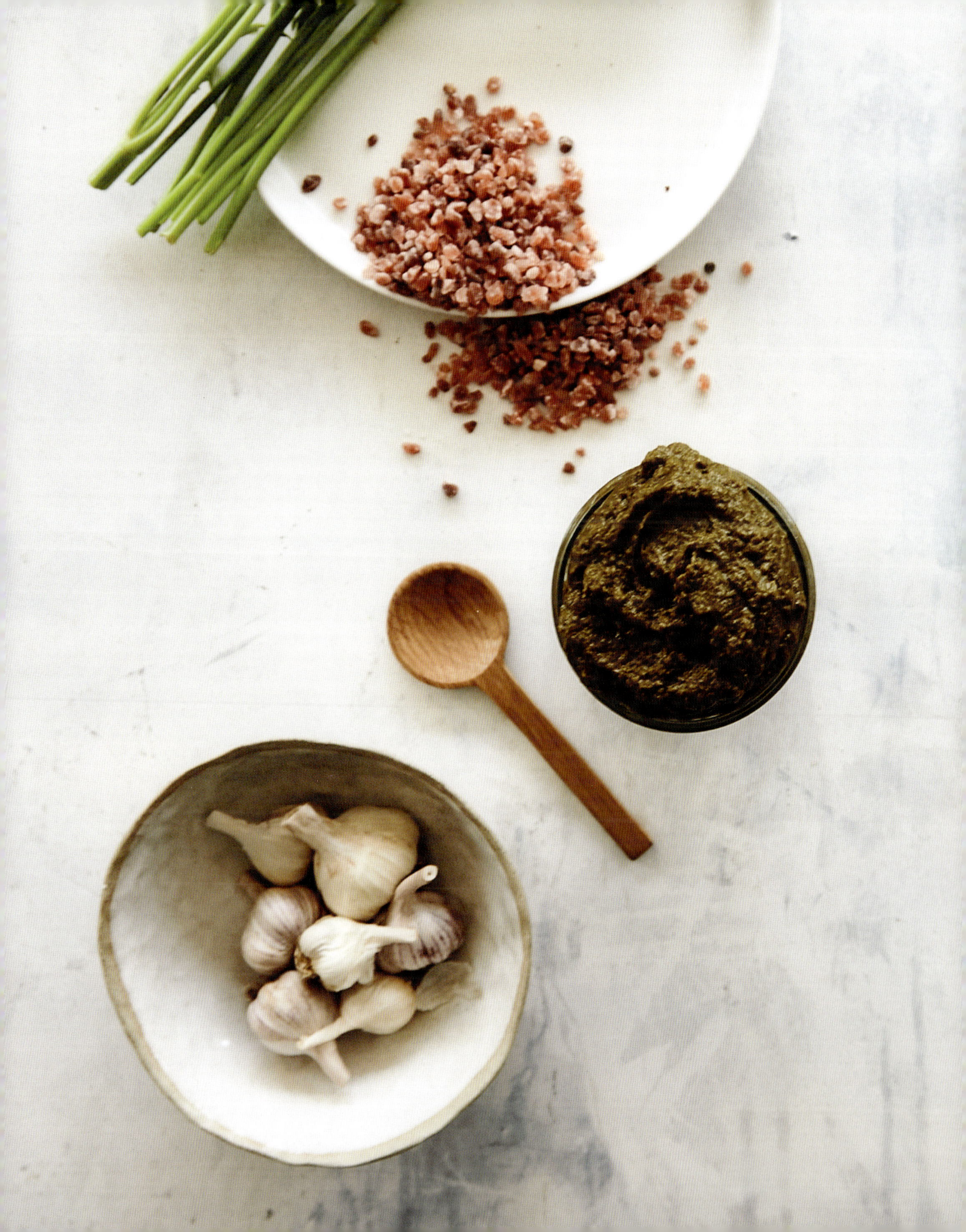

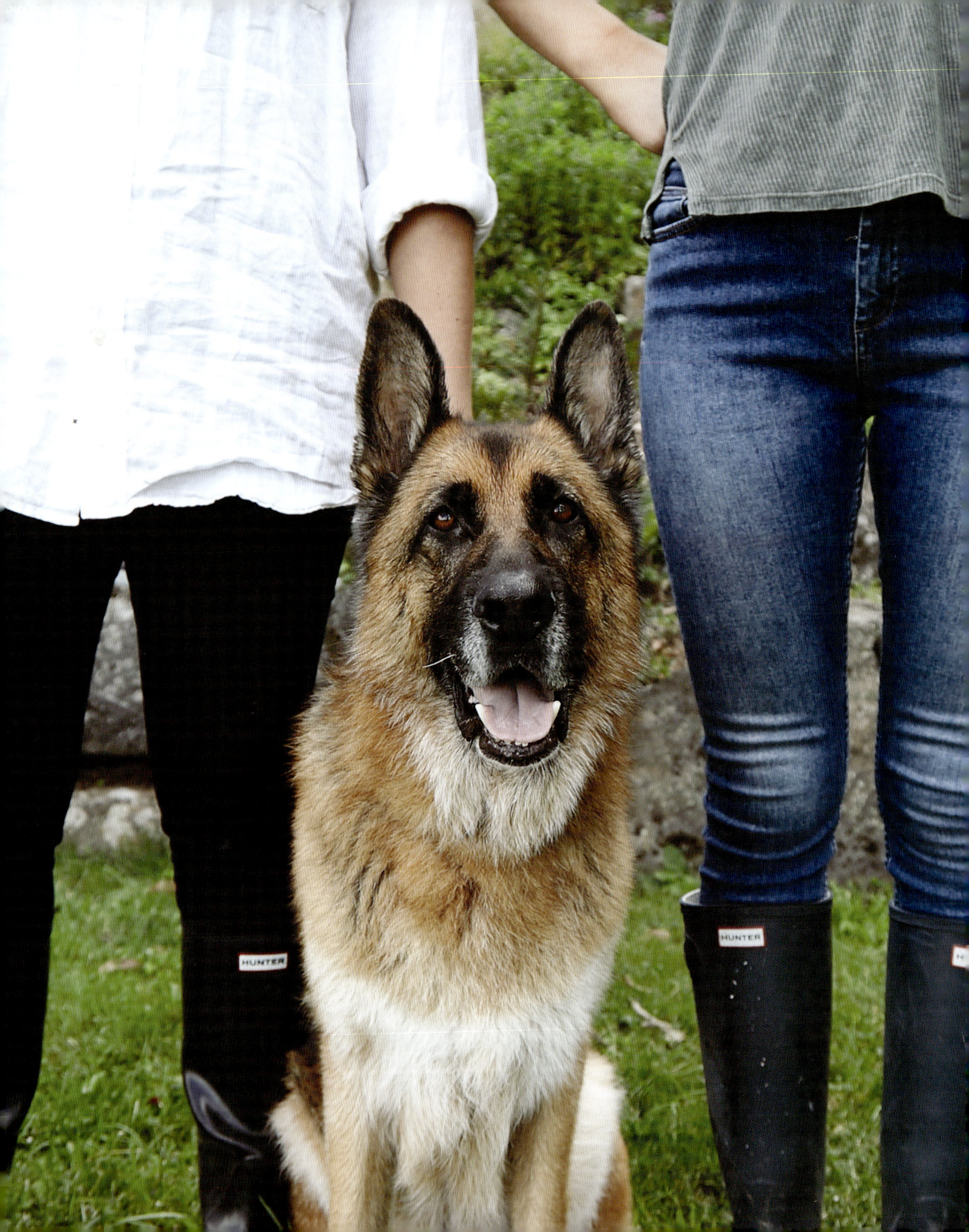
HUNTER
HUNTER

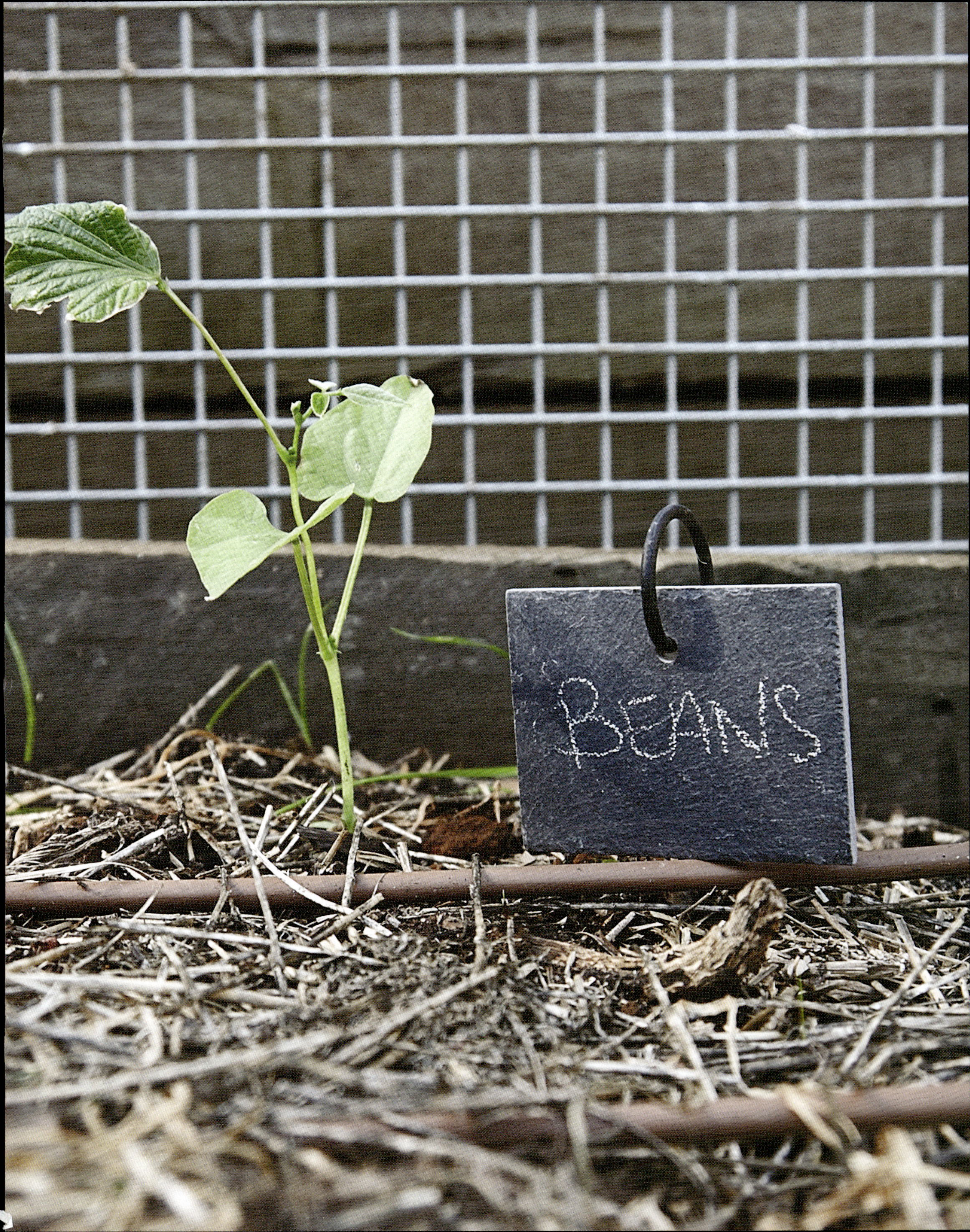
BEANS

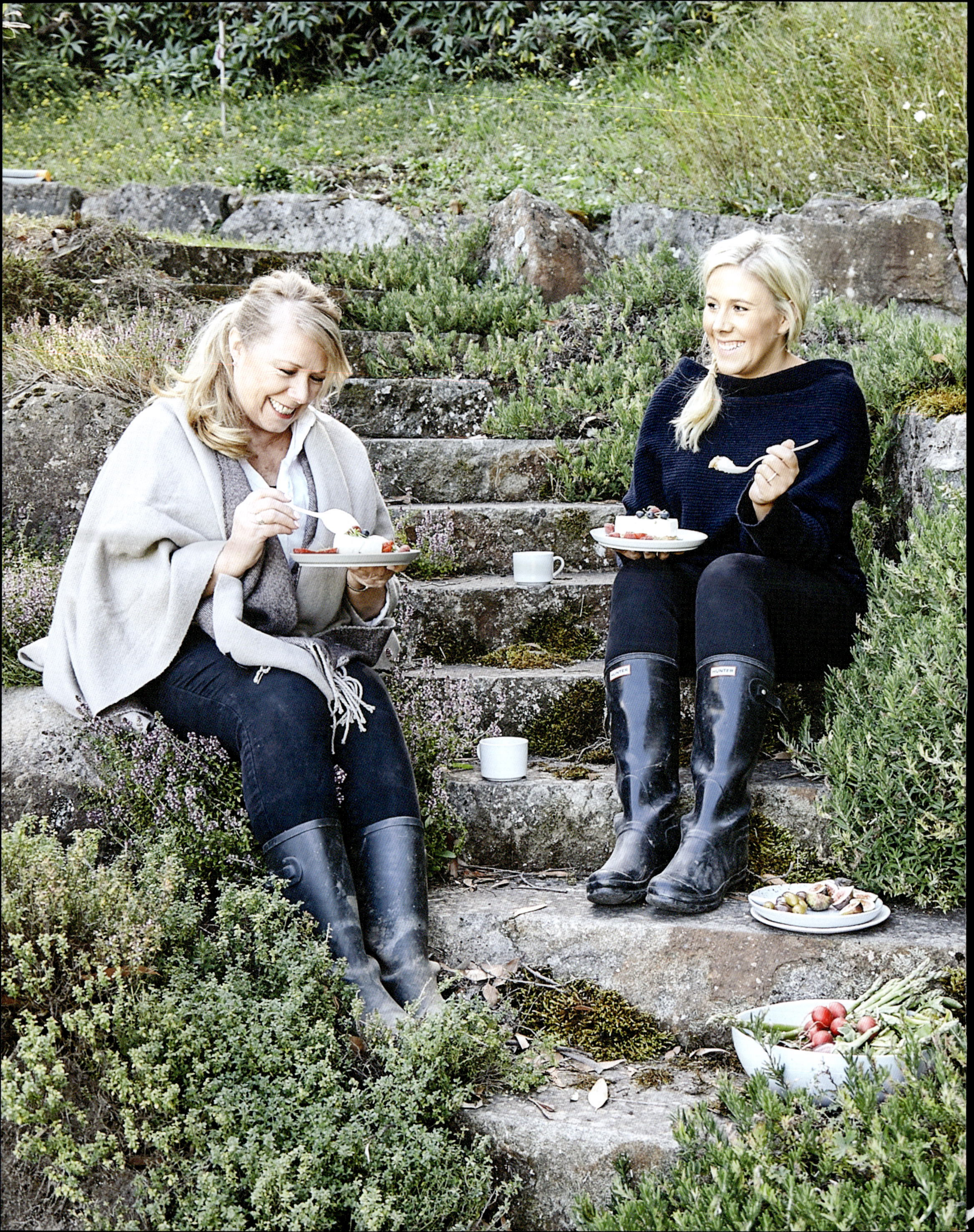
HUNTER

# homemade is best

I believe homemade is always best, and this is especially true of sweet treats. They are such a joy to make, and are usually accompanied by a sense of occasion. I like to keep things simple when it comes to sweets – a few quality ingredients combined creatively is all you need. Here we've got recipes for every occasion and every palate, from the ultra-decadent to the fresh and fruity. With a thermo cooker and such easy recipes, why would you not cook them yourself?

# individual dark chocolate cakes

+ BAKING

**MAKES 12**

… that just happen to be vegan! These are so rich, fudgy and delicious that it's almost impossible to believe there are no eggs, butter, milk or even chocolate in the recipe. My sister Ellen thought all her Christmases had come at once! Kudos to Nigella for the inspiration.

1 vanilla bean, halved
200g brown sugar
220g plain flour
60g cocoa powder
2 teaspoons instant coffee granules
1½ teaspoons bicarbonate of soda
½ teaspoon fine salt
300g boiling water
60g macadamia oil
20g dark rum
1 teaspoon apple cider vinegar

1. Preheat oven to 170°C.

2. Place vanilla bean and sugar in TC bowl, mill for 15 seconds, speed 10.

3. Add flour, cocoa, coffee granules, bicarbonate of soda and salt, sift for 5 seconds, speed 6.

4. Add boiling water, oil, rum and vinegar, mix for 30 seconds, speed 3. Scrape down sides and base of TC bowl.

5. Mix for a further 10 seconds, speed 3, or until combined and smooth.

6. Divide mixture evenly among 12 silicone bar moulds (approx. 90ml each; see note). Lightly tap moulds on bench to remove any air bubbles.

7. Bake for 15 minutes, or until a skewer inserted just comes out clean. Allow to cool for 10 minutes before pushing up from the bottom of the moulds and removing cakes. Cool completely on a wire rack.

Serve just as they are, or frost with coconut caramel (see page 254) or a simple chocolate ganache. If desired, garnish with dried rose petals (pictured).

NOTE: If you don't have silicone bar moulds you can make the cakes in a muffin tin but you may need to increase the cooking time. Test with a skewer – they are ready when it comes out clean.

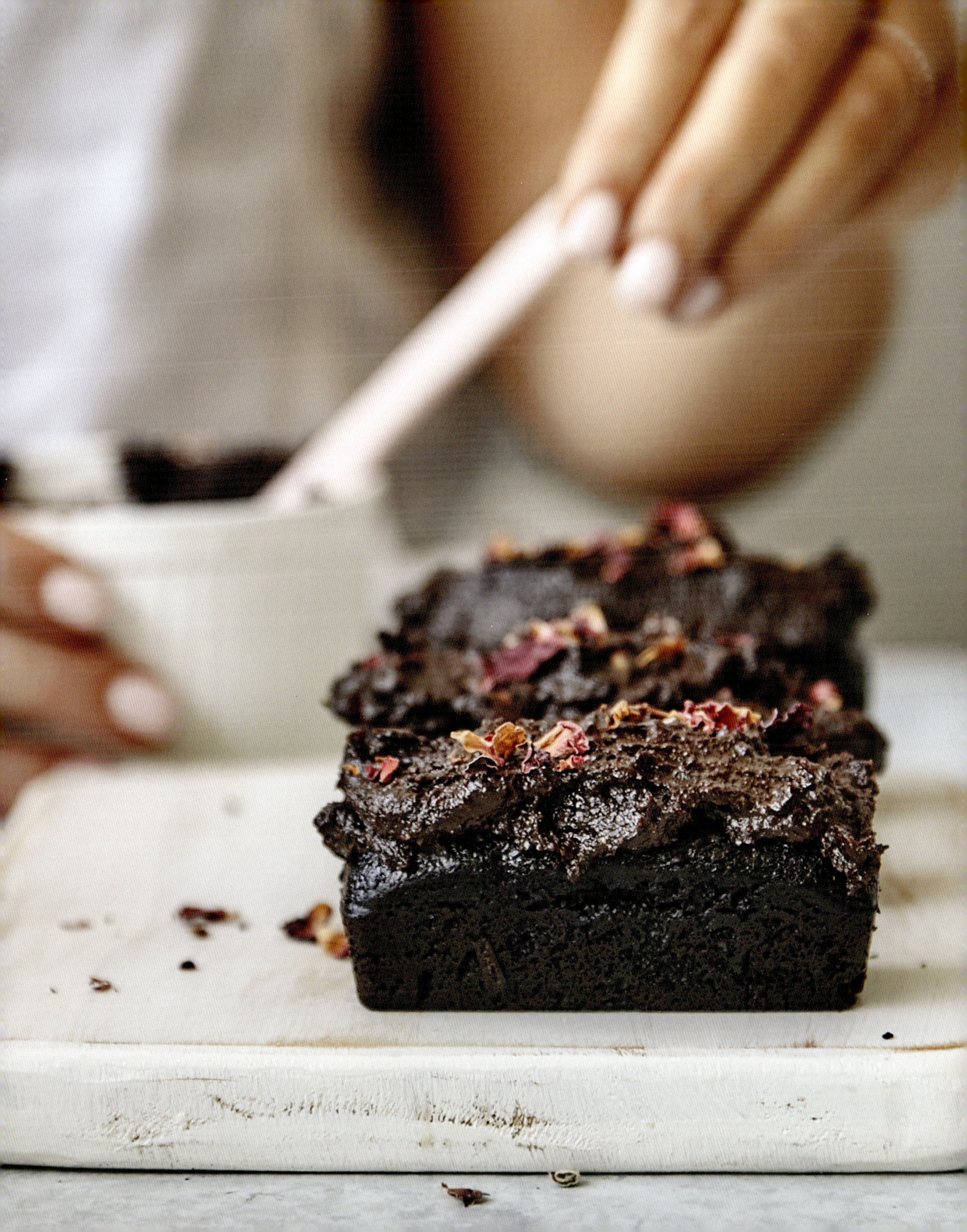

# butterscotch ice cream

+ FREEZING

**SERVES 6**

There's no hiding how much I love homemade ice cream, but sometimes at the end of the day even the thought of emulsifying something for a minute in the thermo cooker seems like a real effort. That's why I love this ice cream – you can scoop it out and serve it straight from the freezer (even if it's been in there for months!). The sweet and creamy butterscotch flavour is so decadent you'll only need a small scoop ... maybe.

90g golden syrup
50g dark brown sugar
500g thickened cream
240g sweetened condensed milk
160g evaporated milk
1 teaspoon vanilla extract

1  Place golden syrup, sugar and 100g cream in TC bowl. Cook for 5 minutes, 90°C, speed 4.

2  Add condensed milk, evaporated milk, vanilla and remaining 400g cream. Mix for 30 seconds, speed 4.

3  Pour mixture into a shallow container, cover and freeze for a minimum of 8 hours.

Serve scoops straight out of the container.

VARIATION: Sprinkle lightly with salt flakes before serving for a 'salted caramel' version. For a truly decadent ice-cream dessert, drizzle over some quick toffee sauce (see page 252) before serving.

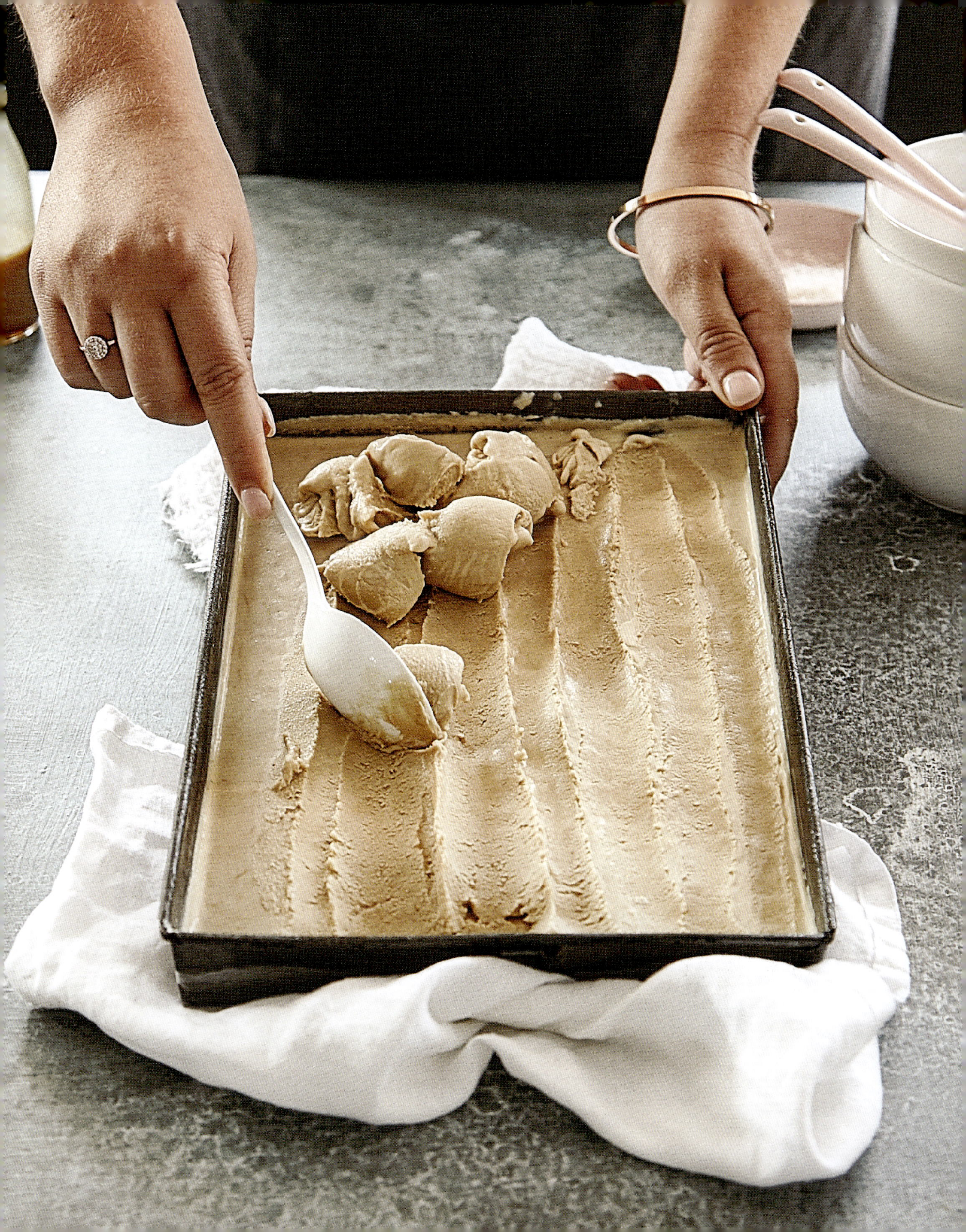

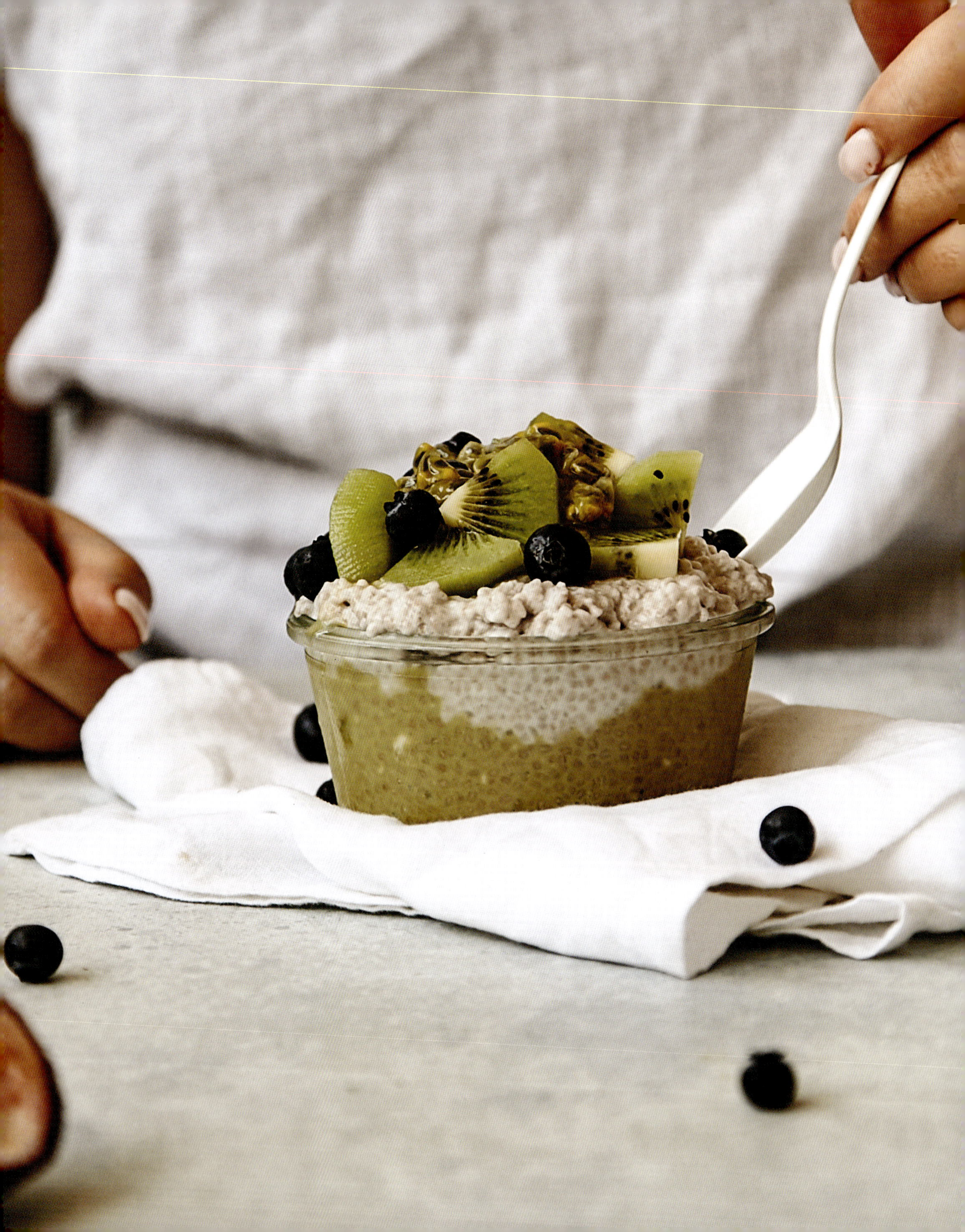

# matcha passionfruit chia parfait

+ REFRIGERATION

**SERVES 6**

This is the healthiest of desserts; in fact, it makes an equally good breakfast! It's thick, creamy and decadent, but contains no dairy, eggs or thickeners. The matcha gives it a sophisticated flavour, while the passionfruit cuts through the richness and adds an intoxicating perfume. Assemble the parfait in glasses or jars to show off the pretty layers.

50g raw sugar
800g canned coconut milk
120g chia seeds
1 tablespoon matcha green tea powder
6 passionfruit

1. Place sugar in TC bowl, mill for 10 seconds, speed 10. Set aside approximately half.

2. Add 400g coconut milk and 60g chia seeds, mix for 5 seconds, reverse speed 4. Set aside.

3. Without cleaning TC bowl, add reserved sugar, remaining 400g coconut milk and 60g chia seeds, and matcha powder. Mix for 5 seconds, reverse speed 4. Set aside separately. Refrigerate both mixtures for a minimum of 4 hours.

4. When ready to serve, divide matcha chia mixture among 6 glasses or jars. Top each with pulp of half a passionfruit, then spoon in coconut chia mixture. Finish with remaining passionfruit.

Serve just as they are or, if you want to gild the lily, garnish with fresh berries, slices of mango or kiwi fruit or edible flowers.

# anzac biscuits

**MAKES 24**

An oldie but a goodie, and who doesn't love an Anzac biscuit? Crunchy around the edges and chewy in the middle. But what I love most about these biscuits is how quick and easy they are – no refrigerating the dough, rolling or shaping with cookie cutters. You can have a warm cookie in your hand in less than 30 minutes. Perfect.

120g raw sugar
250g butter, roughly chopped
180g golden syrup
120g brown sugar
1 teaspoon bicarbonate of soda
270g plain flour
160g rolled oats
120g desiccated coconut

1. Preheat oven to 160°C. Line 3 baking trays with baking paper or baking mats.
2. Place raw sugar in TC bowl, mill for 10 seconds, speed 10. Scrape down sides.
3. Add butter, syrup and brown sugar, heat for 3 minutes, 100°C, speed 3.
4. Add bicarbonate of soda, flour, oats and coconut, mix for 10 seconds, reverse speed 4. Mix in any loose oats and coconut with a spatula.
5. Place golf-ball-sized balls of dough on lined trays 10cm apart and flatten slightly. Bake for 15–20 minutes, or until golden. Allow to cool on baking trays for 15 minutes before transferring to a wire rack to cool completely.

Store in an airtight container for up to 1 month. Great for lunchboxes as they are both egg and nut free.

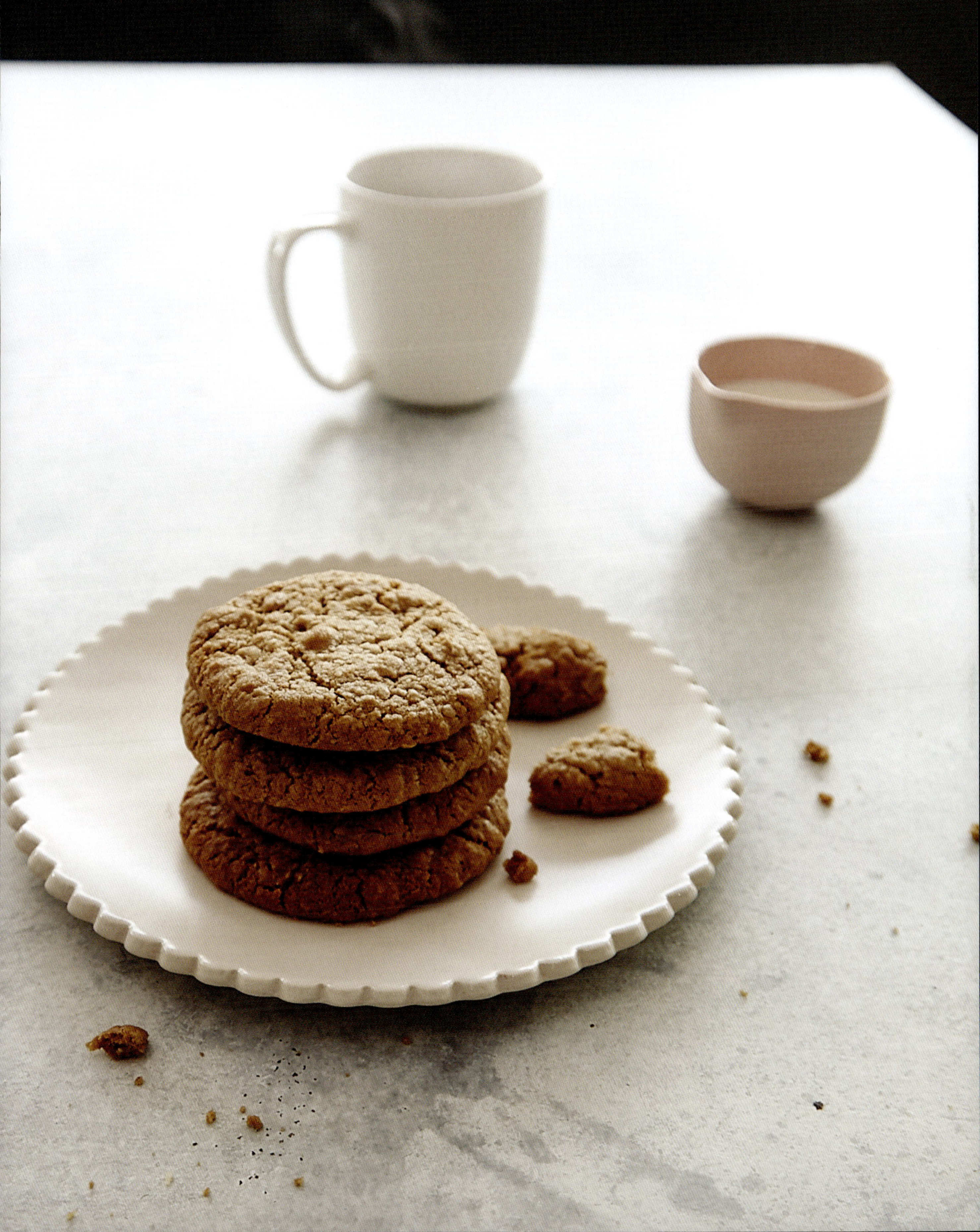

# choc macadamia cookies

**MAKES 14**

This is what a good cookie is all about: a soft and chewy chocolate base studded with buttery, crunchy macadamia nuts. It's decadent, it's amazing, and you might just have the ingredients on hand right now ...

150g butter, chilled and roughly chopped
250g brown sugar
1 teaspoon vanilla extract
1 egg
180g plain flour
30g cocoa powder
½ teaspoon baking powder
Pinch salt
100g raw macadamia halves

1. Preheat oven to 160°C. Line a baking tray with baking paper or a baking mat.

2. Place butter, sugar and vanilla in TC bowl, mix for 30 seconds, speed 6. Scrape down sides.

3. Add egg, mix for 10 seconds, speed 4.

4. Add flour, cocoa, baking powder and salt, mix for 30 seconds, speed 3. Scrape down sides.

5. Add macadamias, mix for 20 seconds, reverse speed 3.

6. Roll mixture into golf-ball-sized balls. Place on lined tray 5cm apart and press down to flatten slightly. Bake for 15–20 minutes, or until cookies are just beginning to crisp up around the edges. They should still be soft and fragile. Allow to cool on baking tray for 15 minutes before transferring to a wire rack to cool completely.

Store in an airtight container for up to a week and try not to eat them all at once!

NOTE: If it is a really warm day or your butter is soft, chill the mixture in the fridge for 15 minutes before rolling it into balls.

VARIATION: For double choc chip cookies, replace the macadamia nuts with dark chocolate chips.

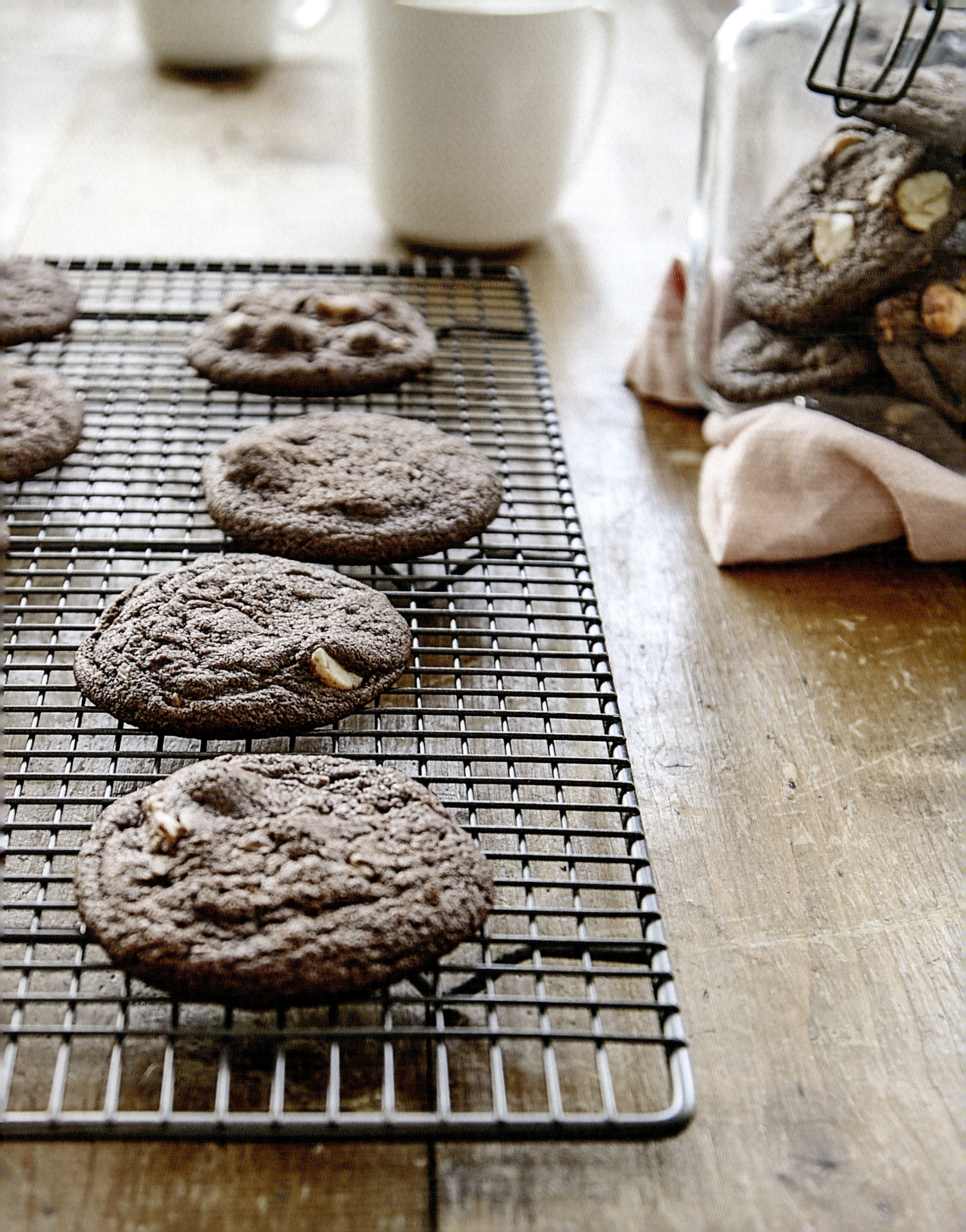

# individual 'baked' cheesecakes

**SERVES 8**

I love how these little steamed cheesecakes perfectly replicate their baked counterparts without going anywhere near the oven. They really are impressive, yet the method is foolproof, making this a recipe you've got to try. My mum and I had a little too much fun testing a range of different flavours, but in the end we decided to keep it simple and let you decide by varying the toppings and accompaniments. That way, once you've mastered the basic recipe the possibilities are virtually endless.

60g Anzac biscuits (see page 202), roughly broken
100g coconut sugar or brown sugar
1 tablespoon cornflour
250g cream cheese, roughly chopped
250g fresh ricotta (see page 160), roughly crumbled
2 eggs
Butter, softened, for greasing

1. Place biscuits in TC bowl, mill for 12 seconds, speed 7, or until fine. Set aside.

2. In a clean TC bowl place sugar, cornflour, cream cheese, ricotta and eggs, blend for 10 seconds, speed 4. Scrape down sides.

3. Warm mixture for 3 minutes, 70°C, speed 3.

4. Scrape down sides and blend for 10 seconds, speed 4.

5. Generously grease 8 silicone dariole moulds with butter, then add a tablespoon of biscuit crumbs and roll around to evenly coat the bottom and sides. Divide cheesecake mixture evenly among the moulds, filling to 1cm from the top.

6. Assemble cheesecakes in steaming tray, cover with a double layer of paper towel lengthways, making sure all cheesecakes are covered to keep condensation from dripping onto the cheesecakes while cooking.

7. Place 700g of water in TC bowl, steam for 20 minutes, steaming temperature, speed 3, or until mixture has set and springs back when touched.

8. Allow cheesecakes to stand for 20 minutes, then remove from moulds by inverting moulds onto a board. Leave to cool completely before transferring to a storage container – the cooler they are, the less fragile they will be. Refrigerate for a minimum of 4 hours before serving.

Serve drizzled with caramel sauce (see page 252, pictured), berry coulis, passionfruit curd or chocolate ganache, or top with a scoop of ice cream – strawberry or vanilla, or try butterscotch (see page 198) with a sprinkling of sea salt flakes.

NOTES: To ensure this recipe is gluten free, use a pure cornflour, and gluten-free biscuits.

If you are not using homemade ricotta, make sure you buy fresh ricotta from the deli rather than the ricotta sold in punnets at the supermarket. This has a more watery consistency than deli ricotta, meaning the cheesecakes won't set properly.

VARIATION: The Anzac biscuits can be replaced with any sweet biscuit, homemade or purchased.

# cheat's vanilla slice

**MAKES 12**

As kids, we always made vanilla slice using lattice biscuits rather than puff pastry. It is certainly easier to make and serve that way, and I actually prefer the crunch of the biscuit with the oozy creamy custard ... although that might just be the nostalgia talking. A little tip: to make them easy to eat slice horizontally through the custard, splitting the slice into two halves, each with a crunchy biscuit base and custard topping.

100g raw sugar
900g milk
5 eggs
170g cornflour
2 teaspoons vanilla extract
300g thickened cream
24 lattice biscuits

1. Place sugar in TC bowl, mill 10 seconds, speed 9.

2. Add milk, eggs, cornflour and vanilla, cook for 10 minutes, 90°C, speed 4. Pour into a container, cover and refrigerate for a minimum of 8 hours.

3. Insert butterfly in TC bowl. Add cream, whip for 10 seconds, speed 4, or until cream just clings to the sides of the TC bowl. Be careful not to overwhip. Remove butterfly and scrape down sides.

4. Cut cold custard into 10 pieces and add to TC bowl. Mix for 45 seconds, speed 5, assisting with spatula, or until just smooth (avoid overmixing or custard will become too thin). If the mixture appears to be 'stuck' and no longer processing, remove lid and scrape down sides before continuing.

5. Line a 20×15cm roasting tin or cake tin with baking paper with plenty overhanging the sides. Layer 12 lattice biscuits tightly across the bottom of the lined tin and spread custard thickly and evenly over biscuits. Top with the remaining 12 lattice biscuits, lining up with the ones on the bottom. Refrigerate for 1 hour.

6. Using the sides of the baking paper, lift slice out of tin. Use a knife to cut through custard in between each biscuit stack, being careful not to break biscuits.

Serve slices as they are or dusted with icing sugar.

NOTE: Ideally, the slices should be served 1 hour after assembly, but if you need to make them further in advance allow them to stand at room temperature for 15 minutes prior to serving. After 24 hours the biscuits will soften and lose their crunch, but they will retain their shape and of course will still be absolutely delicious.

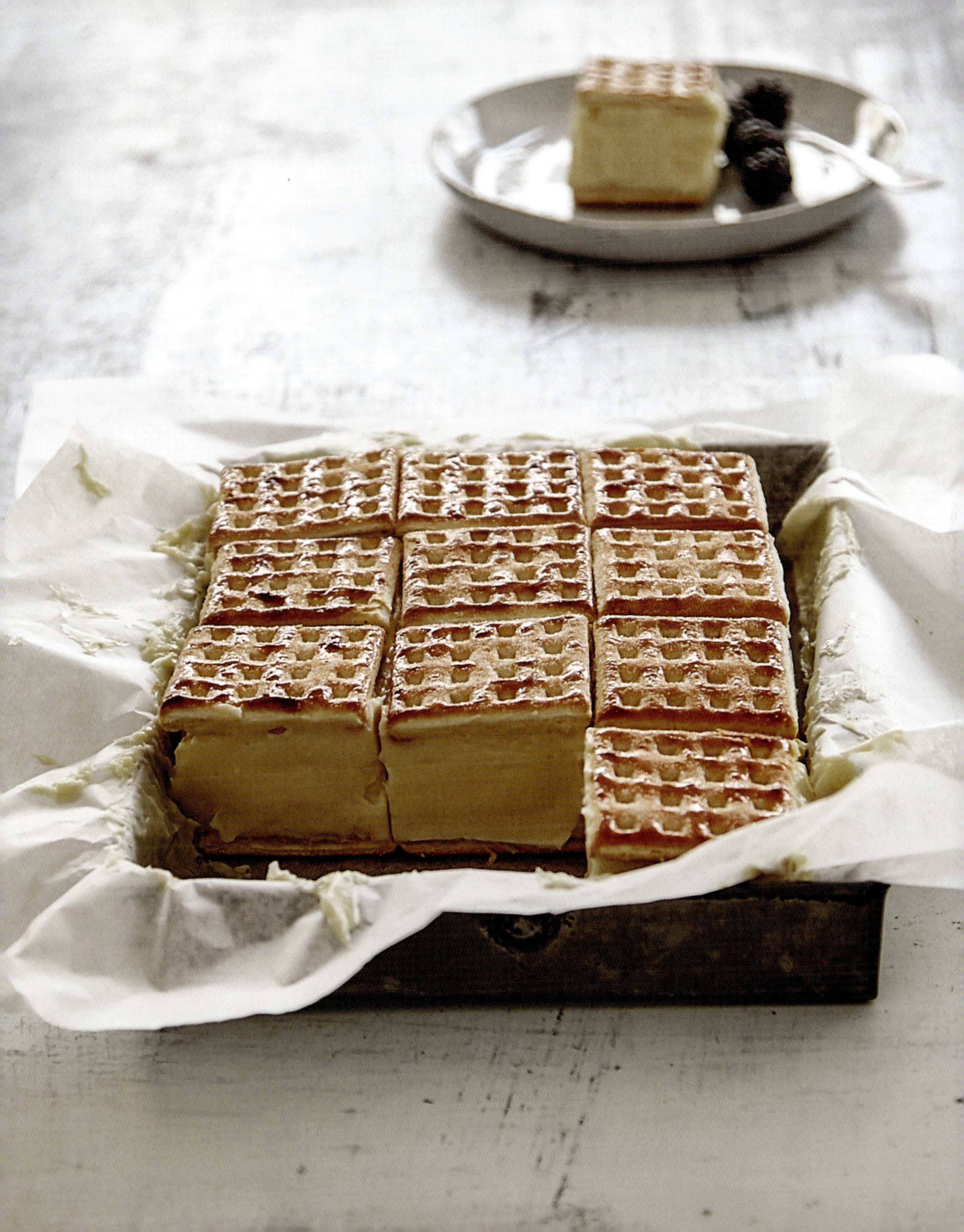

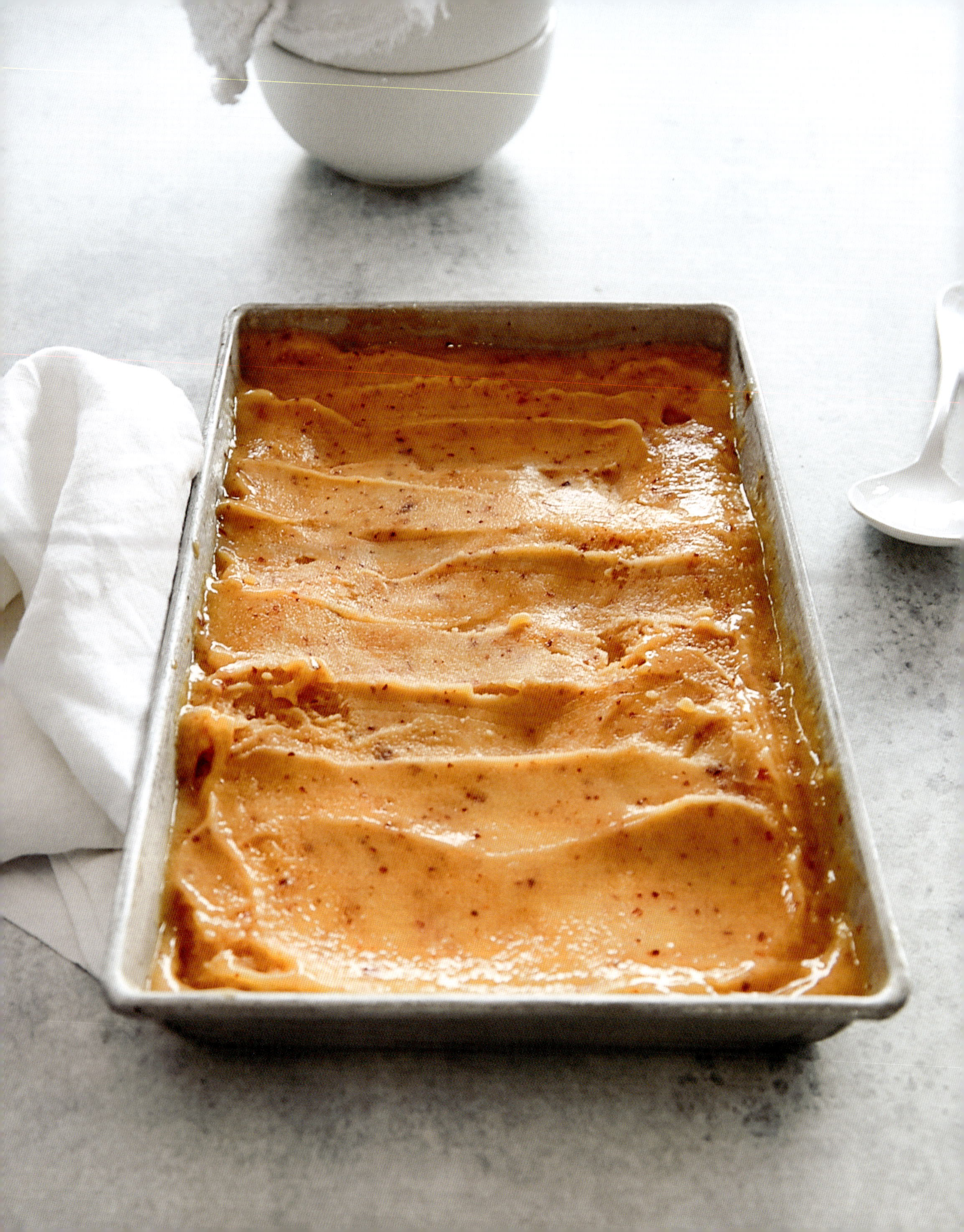

# peach and mango sorbet

+ FREEZING

**SERVES 4**

This vibrant sorbet is smooth and creamy yet fresh and flavoursome. During summer, get in the habit of freezing mangoes and peaches when they are ripe and juicy so you can enjoy this delicious sweet treat long after the sunshine has gone.

30g raw sugar, or to taste
2 mangoes, roughly chopped and frozen
2 peaches, roughly chopped and frozen
1 lime, juice only

1. Place sugar in TC bowl, mill for 10 seconds, speed 9.

2. Add mango, peach and lime juice, pulverise for 10 seconds, speed 9, or until powdery, assisting with spatula if necessary.

3. Mix for 30 seconds, speed 6, or until mixture becomes smooth and creamy, assisting with spatula if necessary. Once desired consistency is reached, stop processing.

Serve immediately or freeze in a shallow container for up to 2 hours.

# yoghurt cheesecake

SERVES 10

The first time I attempted a yoghurt cheesecake was for my partner Alex's birthday, and I took a gamble that the cream cheese would make the mixture firm enough to hold. I was wrong, and the whole thing was an embarrassing, melting mess on the plate. I learnt two things from my mistake: firstly, add gelatine; and secondly, don't try a new recipe for a special occasion! On the upside, the flavour was divine and it was the perfect end to a big meal – decadent but with a refreshing lightness, thanks to the yoghurt and fruit. So I persevered with the recipe and it's a good thing too, as it may just be my favourite cheesecake yet.

90g raw almonds
35g raw sugar
70g plain flour
70g butter, at room temperature
150g thickened cream
1½ tablespoons powdered gelatine
380g cream cheese, roughly chopped
600g Greek yoghurt
120g thin honey, plus extra to serve
1 vanilla bean, seeds scraped
Fresh fruit, to serve

1. Preheat oven to 180°C. Line the base and sides of a 23cm springform tin with baking paper.

2. Place almonds and sugar in TC bowl, mill for 20 seconds, speed 10.

3. Add flour and butter, mix for 5 seconds, speed 8. Press mixture firmly into the base of lined tin. Bake for 15 minutes, or until golden. Allow to cool completely.

4. In a clean TC bowl place cream and gelatine, heat for 4 minutes, 70°C, speed 3.

5. Add cream cheese, mix for 6 seconds, speed 6. Scrape down sides.

6. Add yoghurt, honey and vanilla seeds, mix for 15 seconds, speed 5, or until just smooth. Pour mixture over cooled base, then smooth the surface. Lightly tap tin on bench to remove any air bubbles. Refrigerate for a minimum of 6 hours.

To serve, carefully release side of tin and remove baking paper, then transfer cheesecake to a serving platter. Top with fresh fruit and drizzle with extra honey.

NOTE: The honey to serve is not just a garnish – it's also for sweetness. Go heavy handed!

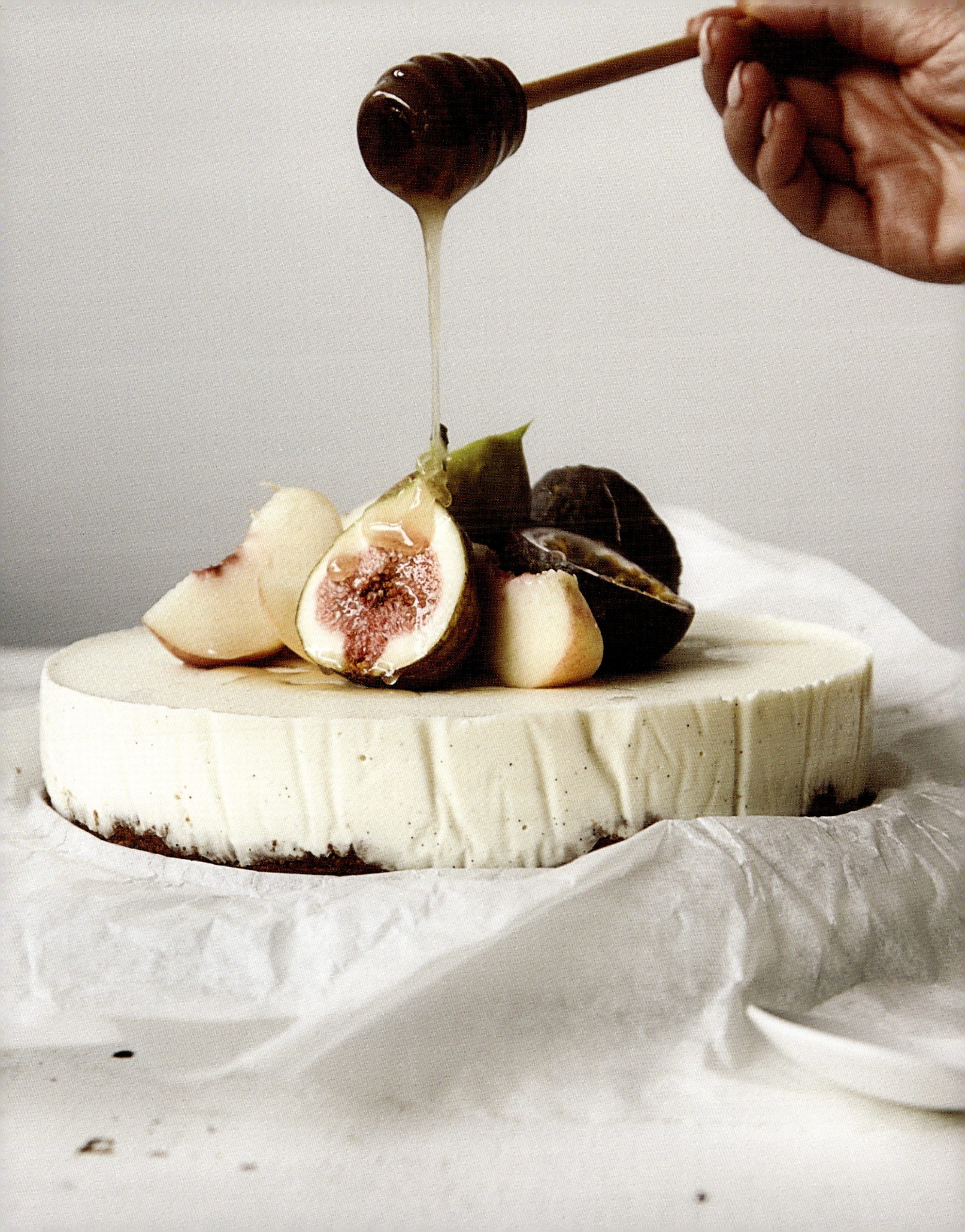

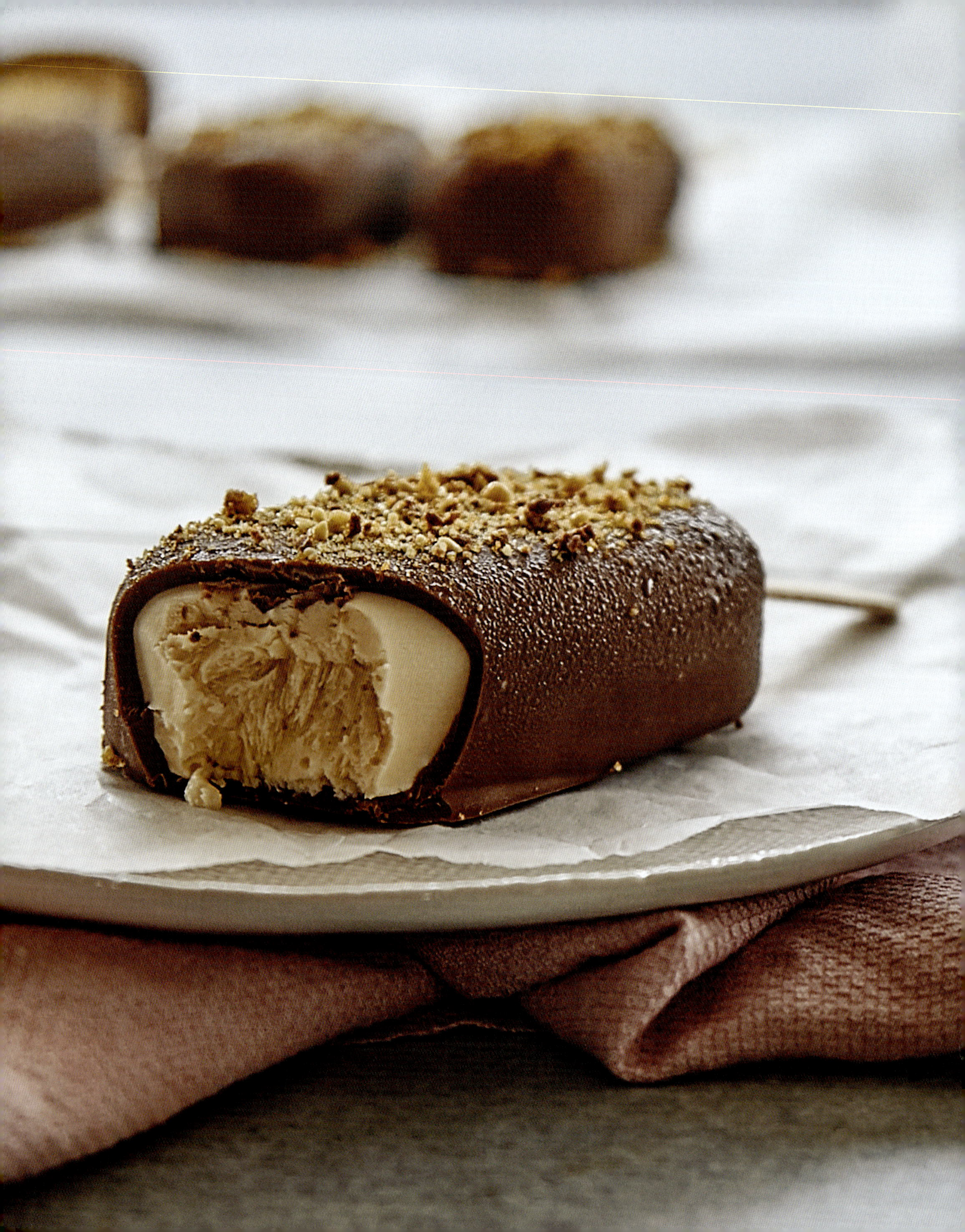

# peanut butter choc pops

**SERVES 6**

I just love these – the combination of peanuts, chocolate and honeycomb is such a winner. They look so impressive but are really easy to make; the key is to work quickly as the chocolate will set almost as soon as it touches the ice cream.

220g thickened cream
180g sweetened condensed milk
100g evaporated milk
100g unsweetened peanut butter (see note)
20g honeycomb, roughly broken
400g milk chocolate buttons
10g macadamia oil

1. Insert butterfly into TC bowl. Add cream, condensed milk, evaporated milk and peanut butter to bowl, whip for 30 seconds, speed 4. Divide mixture evenly among 6 popsicle moulds and insert wooden sticks. Freeze for a minimum of 8 hours.

2. Place honeycomb in clean TC bowl, mill for 2 seconds, speed 7, or until fine but still with some texture. Set aside.

3. Place chocolate and macadamia oil in clean TC bowl, melt for 3 minutes, 50°C, speed 1. Scrape down sides.

4. Mix for 30 seconds, speed 4, or until smooth. Transfer to a tall, narrow glass.

5. Remove ice creams from moulds and place on a lined baking tray. Working quickly, dip ice cream in chocolate so completely coated, allowing excess chocolate to drip back into glass. Return to baking tray and immediately sprinkle with honeycomb. Repeat with remaining ice creams, then return to freezer.

Freeze for a minimum of 1 hour before serving.

NOTES: You can use either smooth or crunchy peanut butter for this recipe, depending on whether you want a smooth or textured ice cream.

You will probably have leftover chocolate. Allow it to set hard before returning to your pantry or add milk and make an indulgent hot chocolate (see page 219).

# boozy berry fool

+ REFRIGERATION

**SERVES 6**

My grown-up take on simple berries and cream, this dessert can be made entirely in advance and served straight from the fridge – the perfect way to end a long evening. I love the whipped mascarpone cream, but if you prefer an airier dessert leave it out and double the cream. The gelatine gives the berry mixture a little bit of stability, making it easy to achieve height and texture when assembling.

140g port, sherry, brandy or other liquor
1 teaspoon powdered gelatine
250g frozen raspberries
80g raw sugar
500g mixed fresh berries, strawberries quartered
250g mascarpone cheese
250g thickened cream

1. Combine liquor and gelatine in a cup. Set aside.
2. Place raspberries and sugar in TC bowl, cook for 6 minutes, 100°C, speed 1, MC removed.
3. Add liquor and gelatine mixture, mix for 20 seconds, speed 3.
4. Place fresh berries in a small bowl and pour over hot mixture. Refrigerate until completely cool, minimum 4 hours.
5. Meanwhile, insert butterfly into clean TC bowl. Add mascarpone and cream, whip for 10 seconds, speed 4, or until smooth and just beginning to cling to the sides of the bowl. Refrigerate until ready to serve.

To serve, either layer berries and cream in glasses or swirl together.

NOTE: Add layers of sponge for a modern version of a trifle, or blind bake a sweet tart shell, then fill the cooled shell with berries and cream (pictured page 6).

VARIATION: For a family-friendly version, replace the liquor with fruit juice.

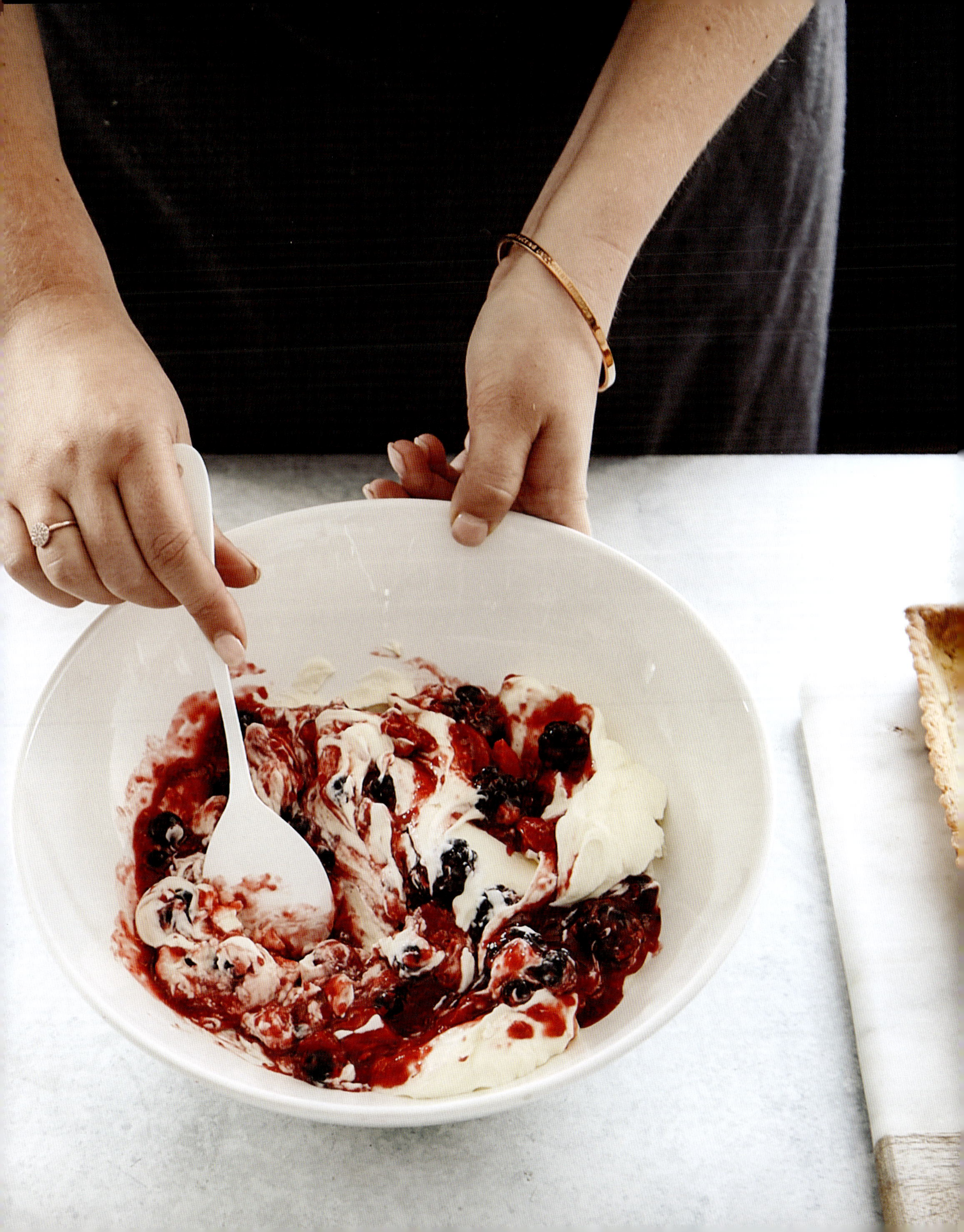

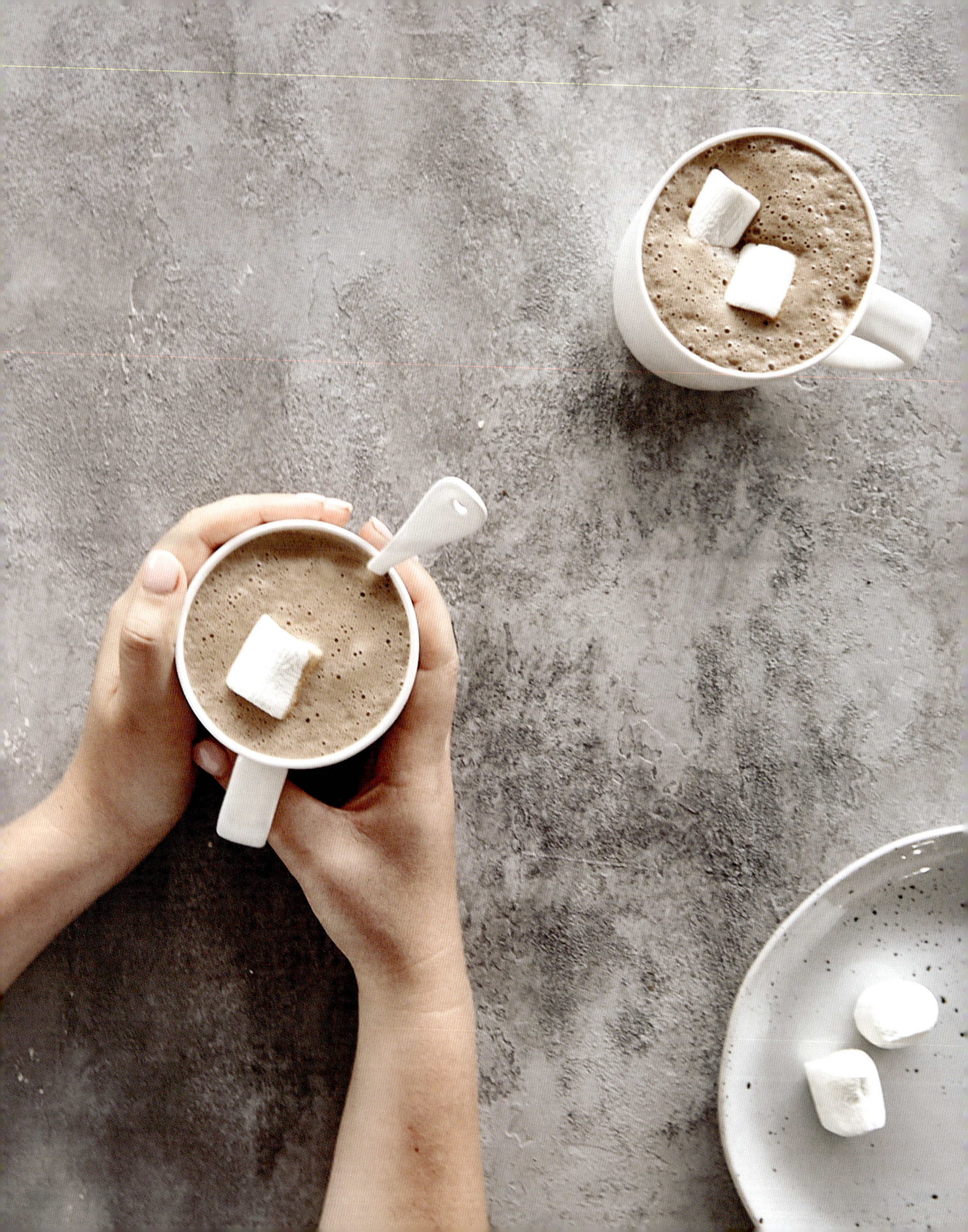

# after-dinner mint hot chocolate

SERVES 2

I love a creamy cocktail just as much as I love dessert, and this decadent recipe allows me to enjoy them both in one delicious serve. I can't think of a more delightful way to finish a meal, except maybe this and a slice of cheesecake ...

80g dark chocolate (70% cocoa solids), roughly broken
360g milk
80g pouring cream
80g peppermint schnapps

1. Place chocolate in TC bowl, grate for 5 seconds, speed 8.
2. Add milk and cream, heat for 6 minutes, 70°C, speed 3.
3. Add schnapps, froth for 1 minute, slowly increasing from speed 1 to 9, MC tilted to allow steam to escape.

Pour into 2 large mugs and serve immediately, with marshmallows, if desired.

NOTE: This recipe can easily be increased to serve 4 — just double the ingredients and cook for 10 minutes at step 2.

VARIATION: Any liquor can be used in this recipe. Try Baileys Irish Cream, Kahlúa, whisky or rum. For a non-alcoholic version, omit the schnapps, increase the milk to 440g and add 4 drops of food-grade peppermint essential oil.

# pretty as a picture

We want you to be proud of your dish as you carry it to the table, so we asked our food stylist Loryn to share her simple tips for making your food look as good as it tastes.

- **CHOOSE YOUR CROCKERY WISELY** Serve colourful food on white plates – you don't want the two competing for attention.

- **SPRINKLE AND DRIZZLE** If the dish is looking a little bland, sprinkle something over the top to add some interest. It can be anything that will complement the flavours on the plate: herbs, nuts, seeds, coconut, cheese, pepper, salt flakes, pomegranate molasses, olive oil, balsamic reduction, fried shallots, chilli flakes, rose petals, icing sugar, fairy floss … you name it!

- **GO ASYMMETRIC** When garnishing, get a little creative with placement. Don't just sprinkle herbs all over the place (although I admit, I can be a little heavy-handed with the micros) or place a neat pile in the middle. If you're serving a curry, for example, perhaps try a big bunch of herbs in the corner and then some chilli and fried shallots piled on top with a lime wedge on the side. It's not the nineties anymore – there's no need for the mandatory sprig of curly parsley.

- **CREATE TEXTURE** Never flatten out your food (unless it is a tart or cake of course!). So often people serve risotto or a salad in a bowl and flatten the whole thing out; all this does is make the food look mushy and removes visual interest. Texture is so important so give the dish some height and variation.

- **K.I.S.S.** Never underestimate the power of keeping it simple. Food itself can be so beautiful – the colours, the textures, the variation – and occasionally we forget that. Sometimes the best styling is no styling at all.

- **EMPLOY DISTRACTIONS** *However*, sometimes food just isn't that attractive, and this is when I pull out what I call the 'distraction technique', which means serving it with colourful garnishes and lots of little side dishes and accompaniments on a large wooden or marble board. When the food itself isn't so easy on the eye, make the whole experience beautiful.

- **COLOUR IS EVERYTHING** When you've got green soup, don't just garnish it with more green. Add some black (cracked pepper) or white (cream). If you're unsure, dig out the colour wheel from high school art class (all jokes aside); you want to choose colours that are either complementary (either side of your main colour) or contrasting (on the opposite side).

- **INVEST IN PLAIN CUTLERY AND CROCKERY** Then add excitement with cheaper elements like napkins and salad servers. I wish I could buy a whole new set of plates and cutlery every season, but boy what a waste! So to keep things on trend, I purchase classic serving dishes, platters and crockery and add flair with small serving plates, ramekins, serving spoons and so on.

- **CLEAN UP YOUR SLOPS** Simple.

Remember … it doesn't have to be perfect. It's the imperfections of home-cooked food that makes it so real and unique. If your cake cracks on top, embrace it – it will still taste amazing. All the food in this book is real food, no fancy tricks, cooked exactly as the recipe says. Sometimes we cook something for a photoshoot and it doesn't go 100% to plan, but we don't recook it (who has time for that?). The show must go on, just as it does in your home kitchen. We either embrace that little crack on the cake, or hide it and highlight something else.

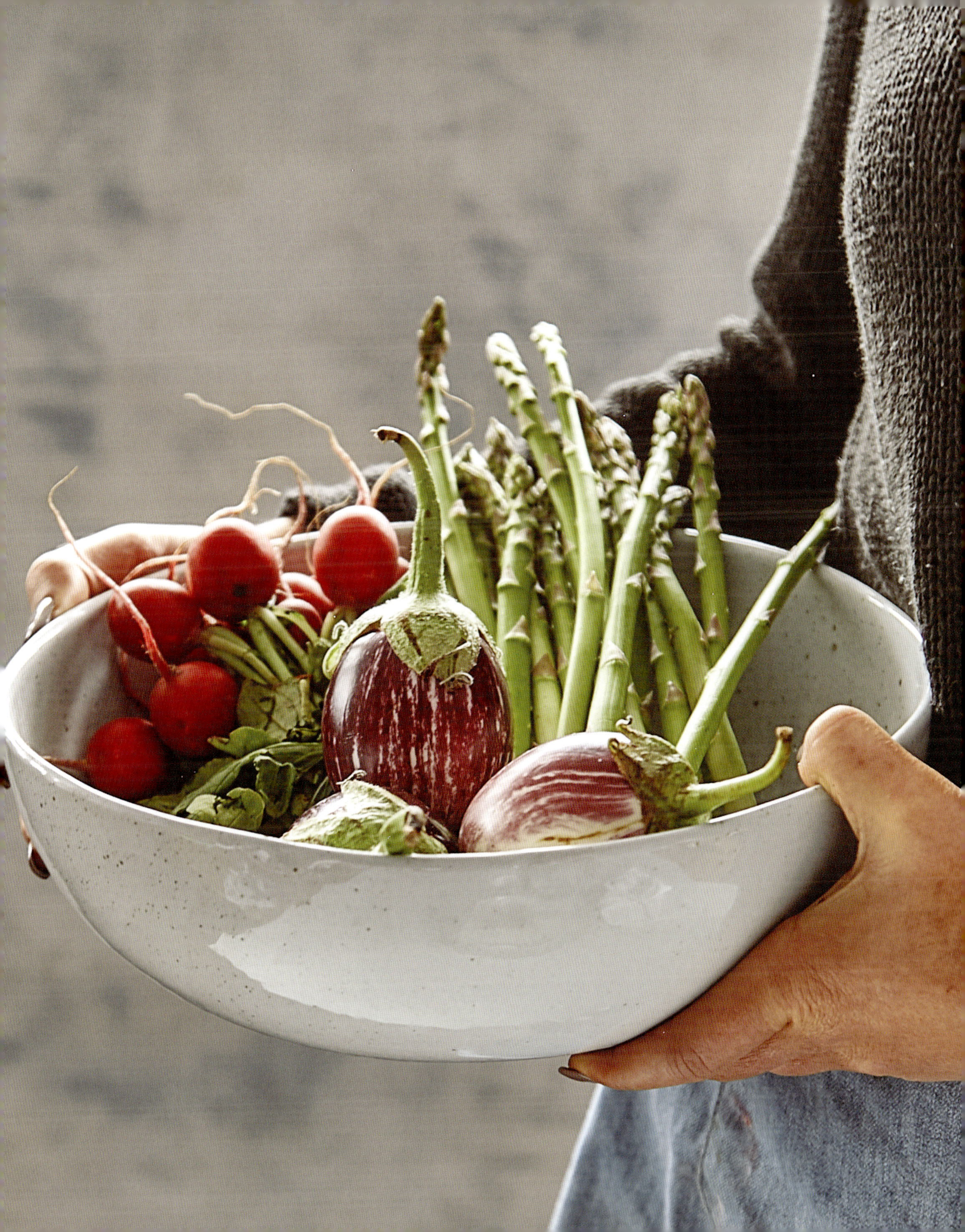

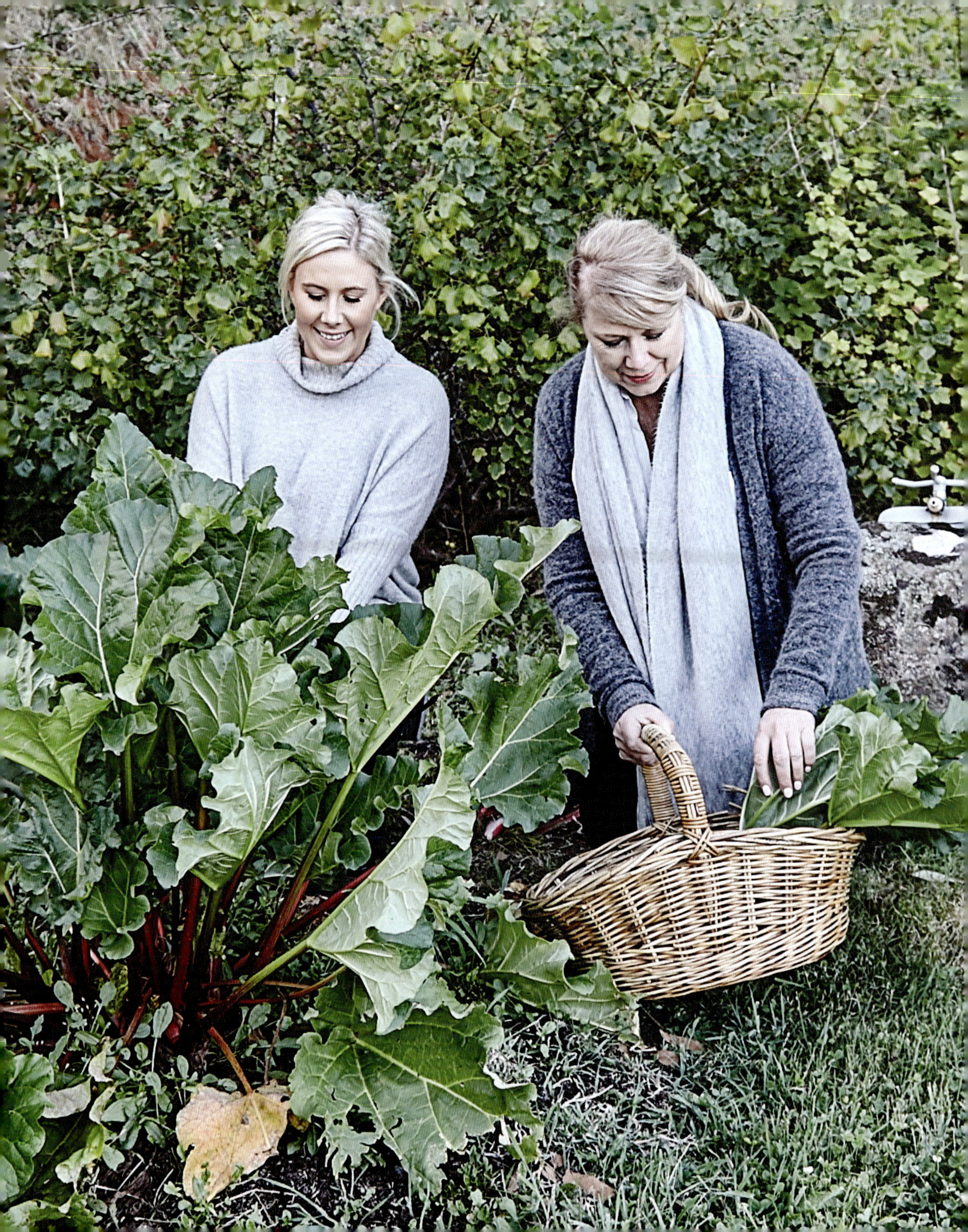

# flavour makers

The flavour makers are my secret weapon to creating amazing meals with very little effort. It's astonishing what a good sauce, chutney, salt or sprinkle can do to an otherwise lacklustre meal. These are investment recipes – make them when you've got a little extra time on your hands and enjoy the rewards for months to come as they add an instant injection of flavour to so many dishes. This is where the thermo cooker really shines, stirring and controlling temperature while you are free to do other things. If you grow your own produce, these recipes are a great way to use up the surplus; but if not, buy fruit and veg at the height of its season to lock it in at its best and cheapest. These recipes are also my pick for edible gifts as most have a long shelf life. Everyone is so busy these days, so taking the time to make something for someone is such a beautiful way of expressing love and gratitude.

# healthy hoisin

**MAKES 2 CUPS**

My mum Janene has a great knack for making healthier swaps when cooking, and this recipe is the perfect example. It tastes like the delicious sweet hoisin sauce we know and love, but without all the dubious ingredients. Given it only takes 15 minutes to make you can whip it up on demand to accompany rice paper rolls and dumplings, toss through noodles and stir-fries, or slather on burgers and meats.

4 garlic cloves, peeled
2 long red chillies, halved
1 teaspoon Chinese five-spice powder
50g macadamia oil
250g miso paste (see note)
160g pure maple syrup
60g rice vinegar
40g molasses

1. Place garlic and chilli in TC bowl, chop 4 seconds, speed 6. Scrape down sides.

2. Add five-spice powder and oil, cook 4 minutes, 100°C, speed 1.

3. Add miso paste, maple syrup, vinegar and molasses, mix 5 seconds, speed 5. Scrape down sides.

4. Cook 6 minutes, 100°C, speed 2, MC removed.

5. Replace MC and blend for 30 seconds, speed 8. Pour into a sterilised jar (see note page 148), cool and refrigerate.

Store in the fridge for up to 4 weeks. Pictured here served with our soft and fluffy baos (see page 165).

NOTE: For this sauce to be gluten free, you'll need to use a miso paste made from soybeans, chickpeas, brown rice or adzuki beans.

FLAVOUR MAKERS

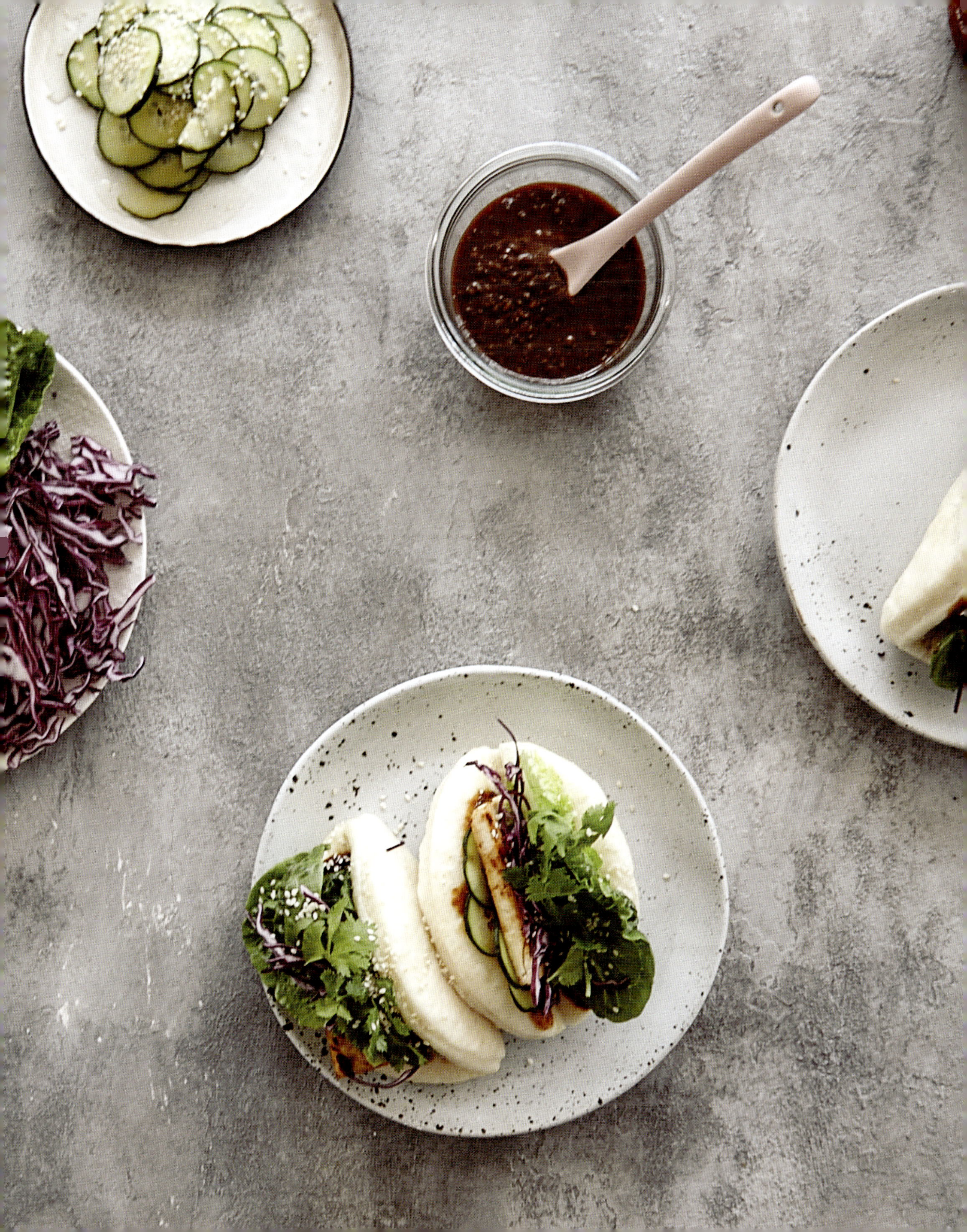

# herbed mayo

**MAKES 1 CUP**

This mayo is tangy, sweet and full of flavour. Serve it with homemade sweet potato fries (pictured) and polenta chips, slather it on burgers and sandwiches, and toss it through coleslaws and potato salads. I've included my pick of herbs, but you can use whatever you have on hand.

200g grapeseed oil
50g olive oil
Small handful fresh chives
Small handful fresh basil
Small handful fresh parsley
1 egg yolk
30g apple cider vinegar
30g Dijon mustard
10g honey
1 teaspoon fine salt
1 teaspoon onion powder
1 teaspoon garlic powder

1. Weigh grapeseed and olive oils into a small jug. Set aside.
2. Place herbs in TC bowl, chop for 4 seconds, speed 7, or until finely chopped.
3. Add egg yolk, vinegar, mustard, honey, salt, onion powder and garlic powder, mix for 10 seconds, speed 4.
4. With blade continuing to run on speed 4, slowly drizzle the oils onto TC lid. Continue to mix for 2 minutes, speed 4, until thickened.

Serve immediately or refrigerate in an airtight container for up to 5 days.

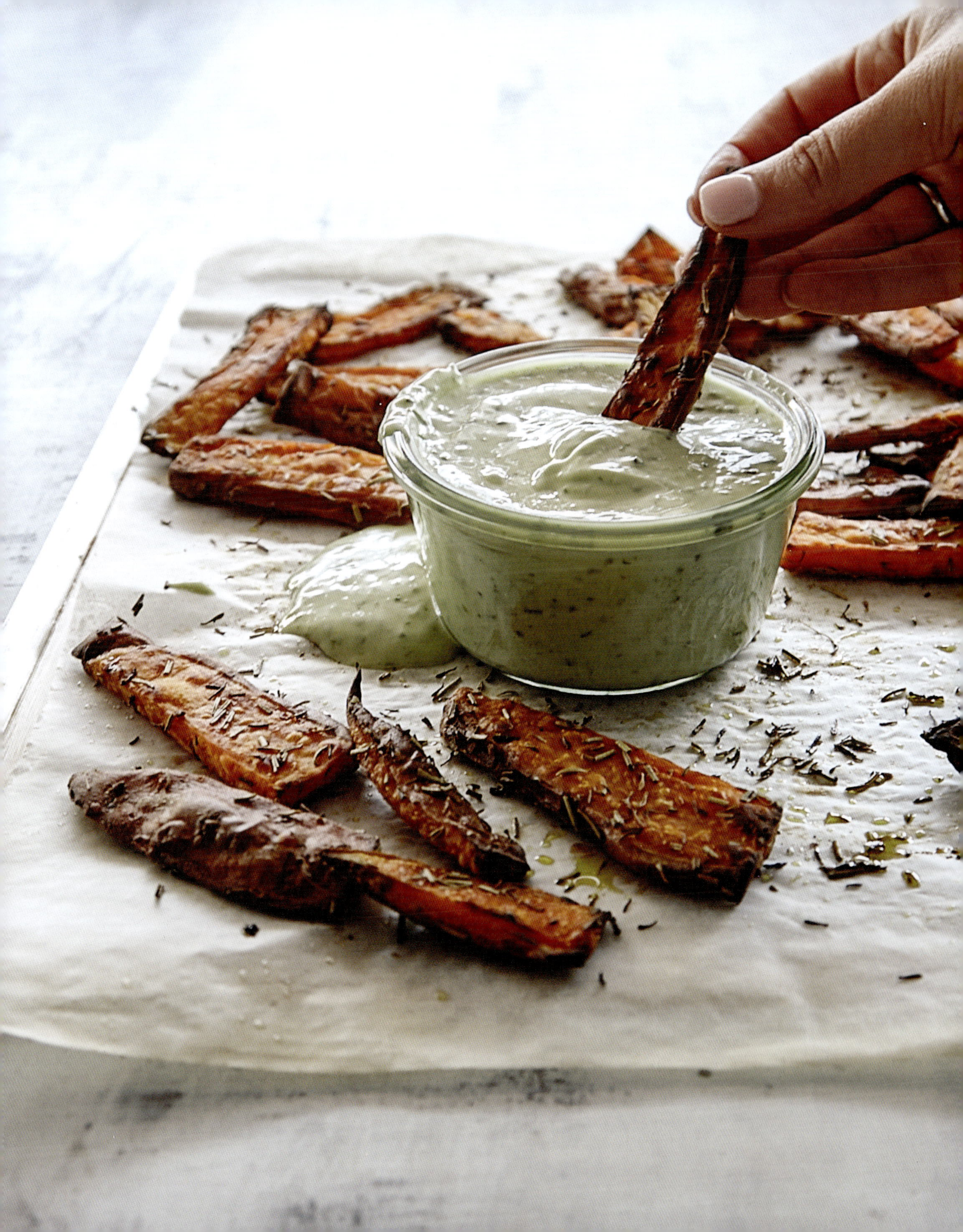

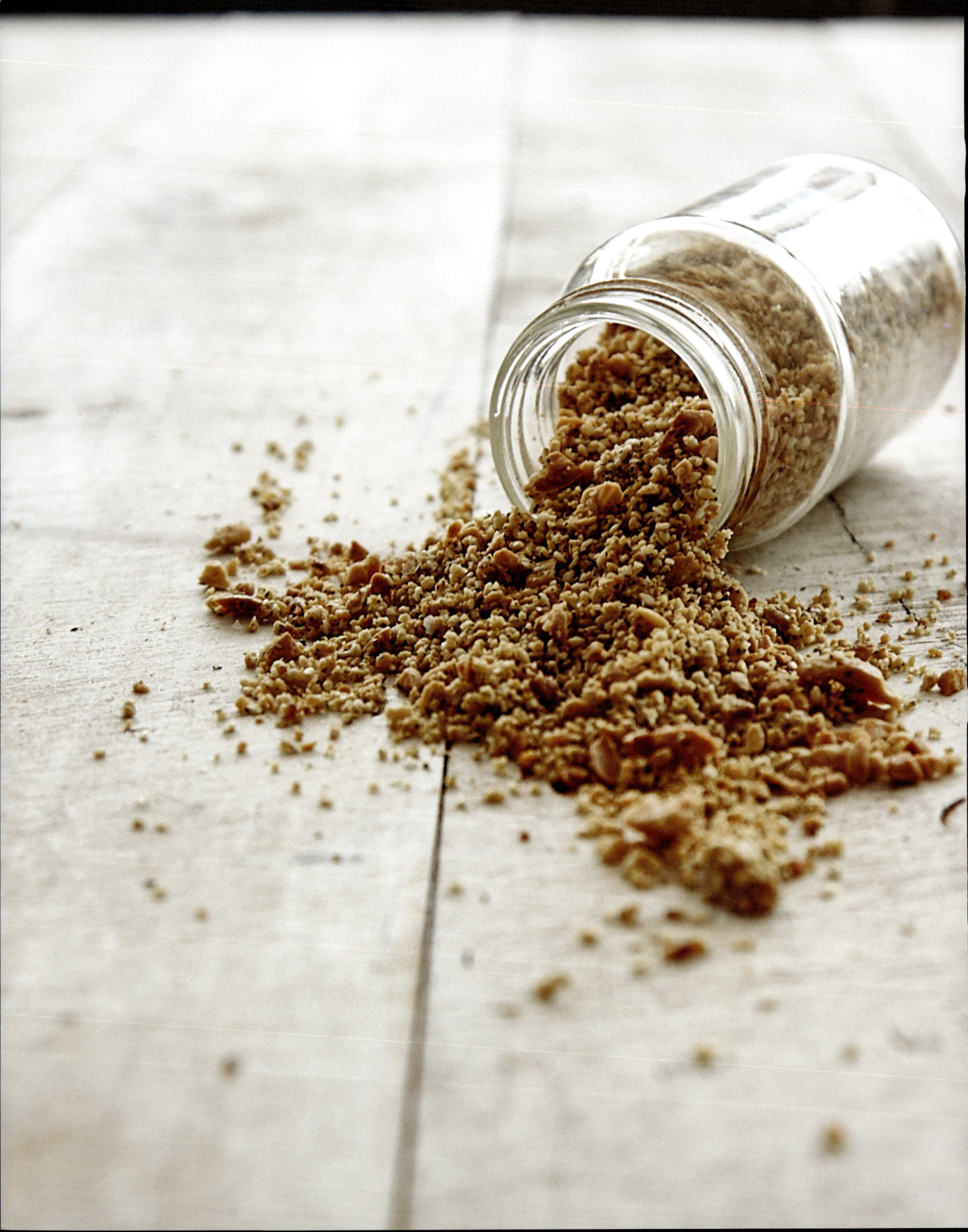

# lemon myrtle dukkah

**MAKES 1 CUP**

This is my mum Janene's invention, and I love how she's put an Australian twist on a classic Egyptian recipe by incorporating the lemon myrtle, a Queensland native. Sweet, salty, citrussy and spicy, this is a winning combination. Sprinkle it over salads and grilled meats, use it to crust lamb cutlets and chickpea fritters, or just serve it simply with crusty bread and olive oil.

80g sesame seeds
65g raw macadamia nuts
75g blanched almonds
1 teaspoon chilli flakes
2 teaspoons ground dried lemon myrtle (see note)
1½ teaspoons salt flakes

1. Preheat oven to 170°C.
2. Place sesame seeds and macadamia nuts on a baking tray. Place almonds on a separate baking tray. Place both trays in oven for 9 minutes, or until golden. Remove from oven and allow to cool for minimum 10 minutes.
3. Place sesame seeds, macadamia nuts and chilli flakes in TC bowl. Mill for 4 seconds, speed 6.
4. Add almonds, lemon myrtle and salt, mill for 2 seconds, speed 5, or until fine but still with some texture.

Store in an airtight container in the fridge for up to 6 months.

NOTE: Look for dried lemon myrtle in the spice section of specialty grocers and delicatessens, or order online – the flavour is truly unique.

# facon

**MAKES 3 CUPS**

Fake bacon = facon, and this version really is as good as the real thing! Salty, slightly sweet, crispy on the outside and chewy in the middle. I cannot get enough of this stuff and sprinkle it on everything. Literally.

80g coconut oil
80g tamari
20g pure maple syrup
4 tablespoons nutritional yeast flakes (see note page 251)
1 teaspoon sweet paprika
1 teaspoon liquid smoke (preferably hickory; see note page 246)
240g coconut flakes

1. Preheat oven to 150°C. Line 2 baking trays with baking paper or baking mats.
2. Place all ingredients in TC bowl, warm 2 minutes, 50°C, speed 1. Tip mixture onto lined trays and spread out evenly.
3. Bake for 15 minutes, or until the mixture on the very edges of the trays turn dark golden, then turn off oven. Allow mixture to cool completely inside the oven – do not open door during this time.

Store in an airtight container for up to a month. In really warm weather, store it in the fridge. Pictured here with wilted greens and Mexican hollandaise (see page 28).

VARIATION: If you can't find liquid smoke, use 1½ tablespoons smoked paprika instead.

FLAVOUR MAKERS

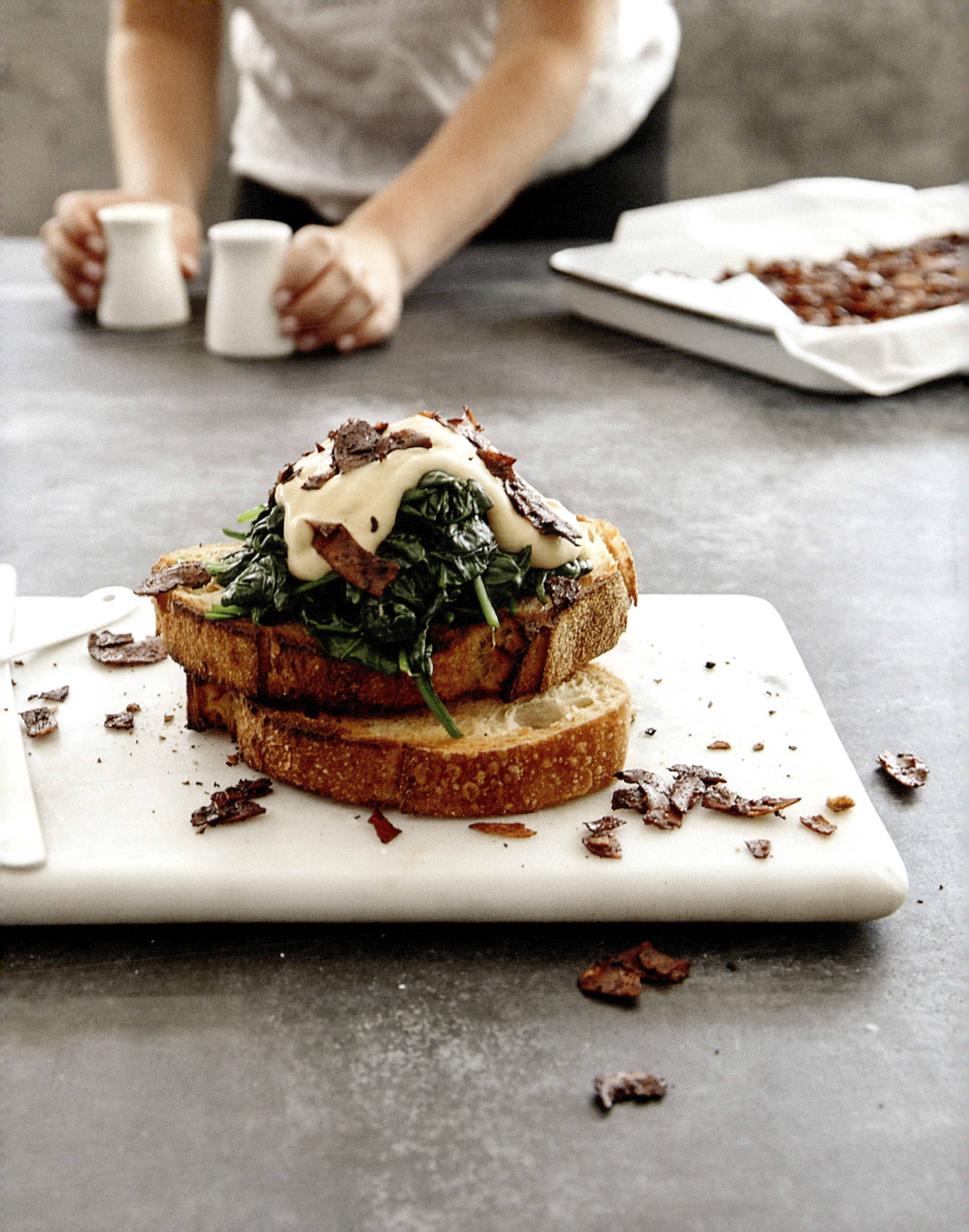

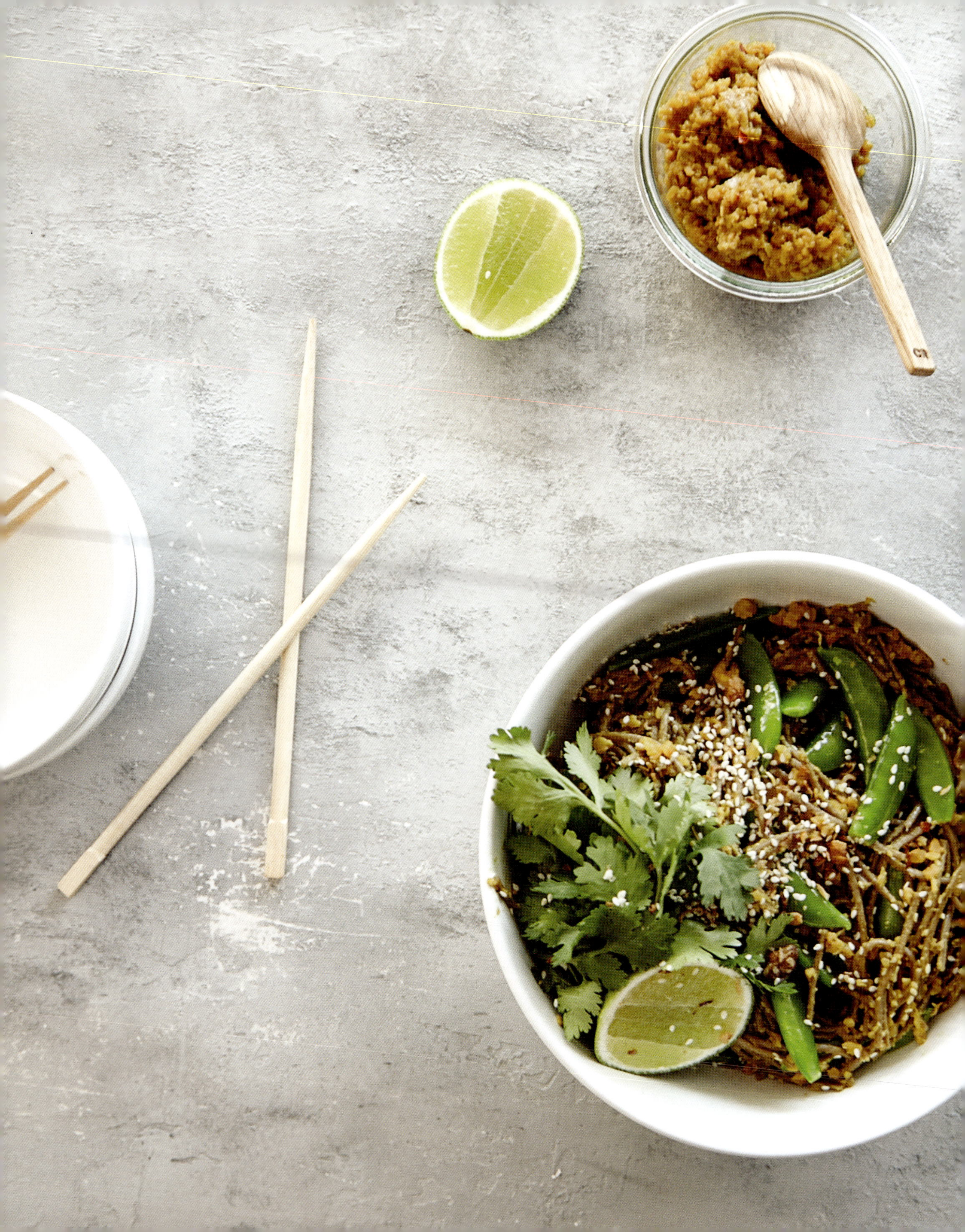

# satay sauce

**MAKES 2 CUPS**

Creamy, salty, spicy, sweet and sour, this sauce is so addictive you'll be eating it off the spoon! Serve it as a dipping sauce for vegetable crudités, meat skewers and flatbread, or thin it down with water or extra peanut oil and use it as a base for sautéing meat, fish, tofu or vegetables. For a quick meal, toss through soba noodles and steamed veggies (pictured).

1 long red chilli
2 garlic cloves, peeled
200g roasted peanuts
20g brown sugar
½ teaspoon ground cumin
½ teaspoon ground turmeric
100g coconut milk
50g peanut oil
20g shoyu or tamari
10g fish sauce
2 teaspoons tamarind purée

1. Place chilli and garlic in TC bowl, chop for 5 seconds, speed 5.
2. Add peanuts, chop for 3 seconds, speed 6.
3. Add sugar, cumin, turmeric, coconut milk, peanut oil, shoyu or tamari, fish sauce and tamarind purée, cook for 5 minutes, 80°C, reverse speed 2.

Serve hot or cold. The sauce will thicken as it cools.

NOTE: Depending on the type of nuts used, you may need to add salt to this recipe. Try it after step 3 and season to taste.

VARIATION: For a vegetarian and vegan alternative, omit the fish sauce and add a teaspoon of stock concentrate (see page 190) instead.

# barbecue sauce

**MAKES 1 LITRE**

While barbecue sauce is completely at home with steaks, sausages and burgers, its uses certainly don't end there. It is delicious stirred through shredded meats, used as a marinade, added to meatballs, drizzled over burritos and quesadillas, tossed with a cobb salad, stirred through baked beans – you can even use it on a pizza instead of tomato paste! The rich smokiness of this sauce also adds a meaty flavour to vegan and vegetarian dishes – try brushing it over tofu or mushrooms before you grill them.

6 garlic cloves, peeled
2 brown onions, peeled and halved
40g olive oil
800g canned diced tomatoes
180g malt or apple cider vinegar (see note)
150g brown sugar
100g Worcestershire sauce (see note)
1 tablespoon smoked paprika
2 teaspoons Dijon mustard
2 teaspoons fine salt

1. Place garlic and onion in TC bowl, chop for 5 seconds, speed 5. Scrape down sides.

2. Add oil, sauté for 6 minutes, 100°C, speed 1.

3. Add tomatoes, vinegar, sugar, Worcestershire sauce, paprika, mustard and salt. Cook for 40 minutes, steaming temperature, speed 2, MC removed with steamer basket on top to prevent splashes.

4. Purée for 30 seconds, speed 6.

Pour into warm sterilised jars (see note, page 148) and allow to cool completely before serving. Store in the fridge for up to 6 months. Pictured with beetroot burgers (see page 100).

NOTE: For a vegetarian and vegan barbecue sauce, ensure your Worcestershire sauce does not contain anchovies. For a gluten-free option use apple cider vinegar.

VARIATION: If you happen to have liquid smoke on hand, add ½ teaspoon at step 4 before puréeing for a truly smoky barbecue sauce.

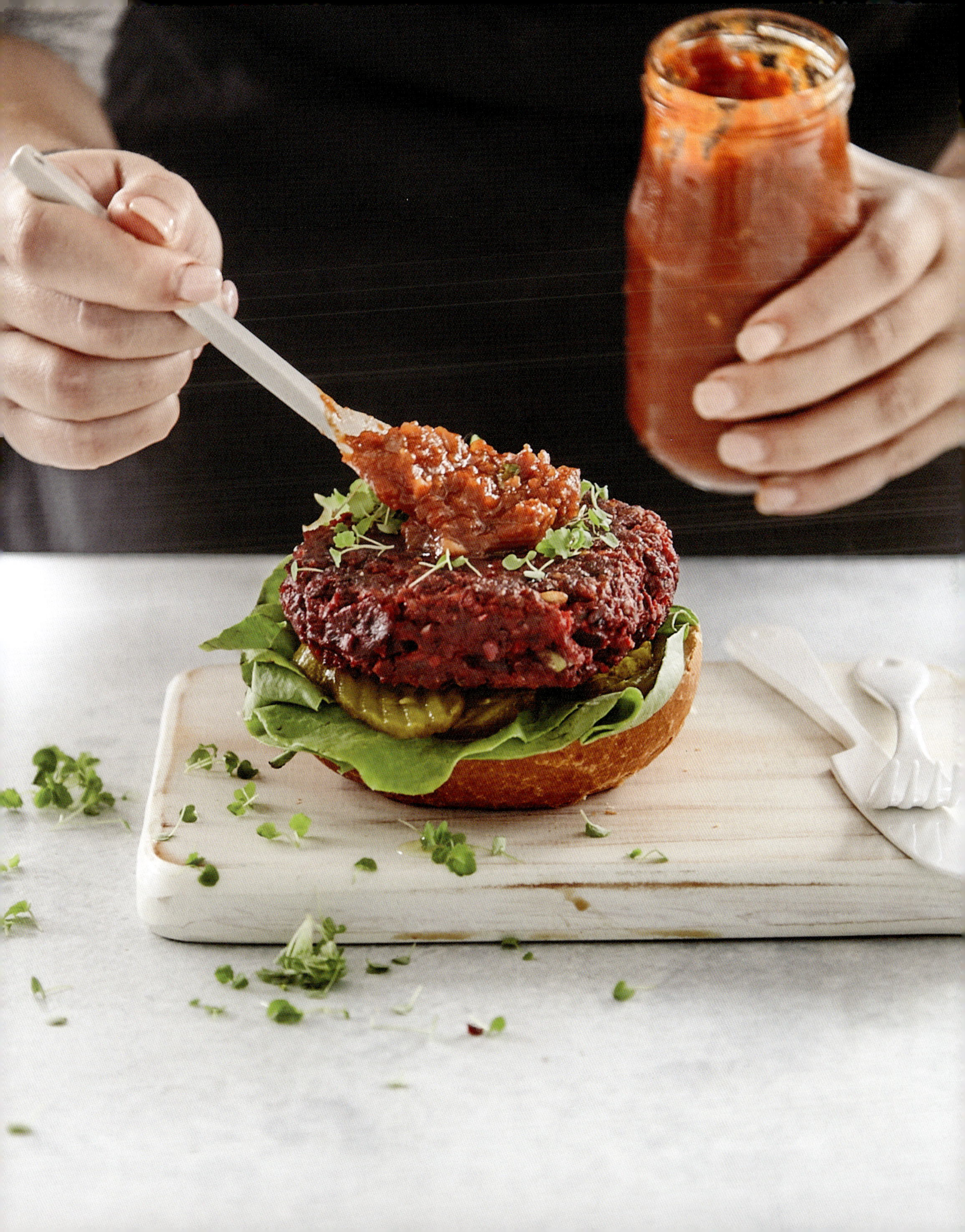

# easy kimchi-kraut

**MAKES 6 CUPS**

I'm sure this recipe doesn't even come close to the 'proper' way of making kimchi, but it's easy and it works (and that's what matters to me!). It's more like a sauerkraut with kimchi flavours. A thermo cooker makes the whole process much quicker by removing the laborious step of manually massaging the cabbage for 10–20 minutes to break it down. Serve a tablespoon of this with anything and everything savoury – it adds a big hit of flavour and your gut will love you for it.

1 green apple, cored and quartered
4cm piece ginger, peeled
4 garlic cloves, peeled
30g tamari
1½ tablespoons fine salt
2 teaspoons dulse flakes
Chilli flakes, to taste
½ small white cabbage, thinly sliced (or ¼ large cabbage)
2 carrots, julienned

1. Place apple, ginger and garlic in TC bowl, chop for 5 seconds, speed 5.
2. Add tamari, salt, dulse flakes, chilli flakes and as much cabbage as will fit in TC bowl, knead for 1 minute, dough function.
3. Top up with as much cabbage as will fit, knead for 1 minute, dough function.
4. Top up with remaining cabbage, knead for 1 minute, dough function.
5. Add carrot, knead for 1 minute, dough function.
6. Squish the entire mixture (including all liquid) into a pickle press. Place the lid on and tighten the press down until the vegetables are firmly compacted and the liquids rise above the press, completely submerging the vegetables. If there isn't enough liquid, wait 30 minutes and tighten again. If you don't have a pickle press, use a large glass jar with a weight inside to push the vegetables down and keep submerged under the liquid. Special dunking weights can purchased, or use a small cup, bowl or plate.
7. Allow to sit, undisturbed, at room temperature but out of direct sunlight for between 2 and 14 days. Taste every few days until it is to your liking. The longer it sits the less salty it will be and the pickled flavour will become stronger.

Transfer vegetables to a sterilised jar (see note page 148), seal and refrigerate until ready to serve. Fermented vegetables can be kept in the fridge for up to a year and improve with age.

NOTE: It is essential that the vegetables are completely submerged in the liquid, otherwise mould may grow on the top. If mould does grow, discard all the vegetables and start again. Next time, knead the vegetables for longer and add more salt. Bubbles, white foam and white scum may form on top of the liquid – this is completely normal. Lift it off with a spoon once the fermentation process has finished.

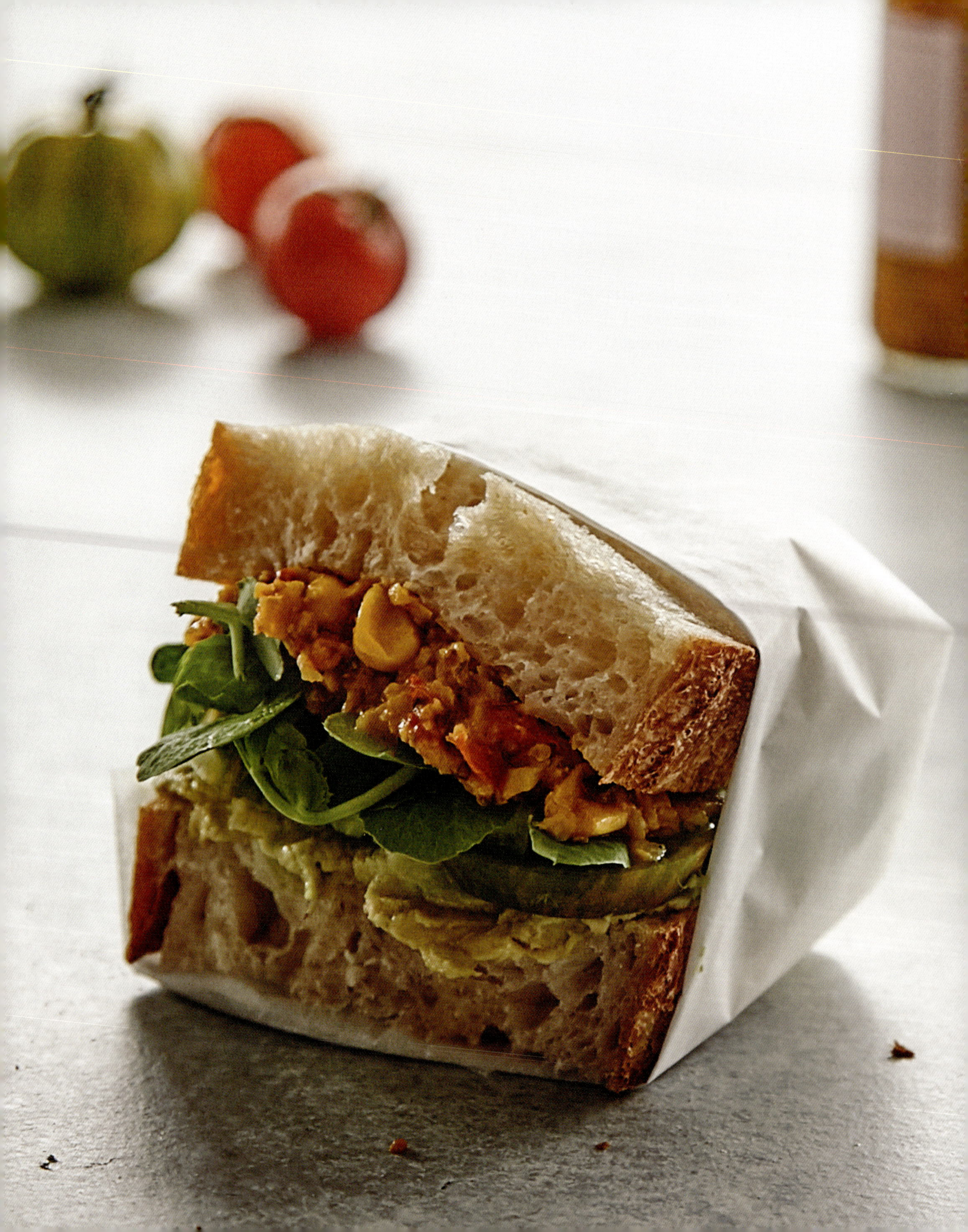

# corn and mustard chutney

**MAKES 4 CUPS**

This delicious condiment contains plenty of veggies and is low on sugar compared with most chutneys, relying instead on the natural sweetness of the corn. Perfect to make at the height of summer when zucchini, capsicum and corn are at their best and readily available. It's particularly good as a spread on toast and sandwiches, along with avocado, roast meats or cheese. A jar of this never lasts long in the AA office fridge, especially when we are testing new bread recipes. Mmm!

2 brown onions, peeled and halved
40g olive oil
2 zucchini, quartered
1 red capsicum, quartered and seeds removed
500g fresh or frozen corn kernels, defrosted if frozen
200g wholegrain mustard
100g raw sugar
50g apple cider vinegar
50g Dijon mustard
2 teaspoons curry powder
2 teaspoons fine salt
1 teaspoon ground turmeric

1. Place onion in TC bowl, chop for 5 seconds, speed 5. Scrape down sides.

2. Add oil, sauté for 6 minutes, 100°C, speed 1.

3. Add zucchini and capsicum, chop for 5 seconds, speed 6, or until coarsely grated.

4. Add corn, wholegrain mustard, sugar, vinegar, Dijon mustard, curry powder, salt and turmeric, mix for 8 seconds, reverse speed 4.

5. Cook for 30 minutes, steaming temperature, reverse speed 2, MC removed and steamer basket on top to prevent splashes.

6. Chop for 2 seconds, speed 6.

Transfer to sterilised jars (see note page 148). Store in the fridge for up to a month. Serve with cheese, savoury pastries or roast meats, or spread thickly on sandwiches or toast.

from left to right: tomato chutney *(see opposite)*, caramelised orange balsamic *(see page 243)*, rhubarb and ginger relish *(see page 242)*

# tomato chutney

**MAKES 2 CUPS**

Naturally you can serve this classic chutney in the usual way as an accompaniment to barbecued meats, pies, sausage rolls, fries and the like, but it also adds a great flavour to soups, stews and sauces and can be spread as a base on homemade pizzas. Use it in much the same way you would tomato paste.

- 2 brown onions, peeled and halved
- 4 garlic cloves, peeled
- 40g olive oil
- 1.2kg tomatoes, roughly chopped
- 50g red wine vinegar
- 40g brown sugar
- 1 tablespoon sweet paprika
- 1 teaspoon fine salt
- ½ teaspoon chilli flakes, or to taste
- 50g sultanas (optional)

1. Place onion and garlic in TC bowl, chop for 5 seconds, speed 5. Scrape down sides.
2. Add oil, sauté for 5 minutes, 100°C, speed 1.
3. Add tomato, vinegar, sugar, paprika, salt and chilli, cook for 1 hour, steaming temperature, speed 2, MC removed and steamer basket on top to prevent splashes.
4. Stir through sultanas (if using) and transfer chutney to a sterilised glass jar (see note page 148).

Store in the fridge for up to 6 months.

NOTE: This is a thick chutney, but if you prefer a more liquid consistency just reduce the cooking time by 10 minutes at step 3. To make a smooth tomato sauce, purée for 30 seconds, speed 8 after step 3.

# rhubarb and ginger relish

**MAKES 4 CUPS**

My garden lovingly provides me with kilos of blushing pink rhubarb stalks every week during the warmer months, which is a good thing, given how much of this relish we go through! Although it's sweet and jam-like in consistency, the rhubarb adds a sour edge and the ginger offers a real kick, firmly identifying this as a savoury condiment. It pairs best with heavier foods such as with steak, sausages, rissoles, pies, curries, sweet potato fries and toasted sandwiches, and it works beautifully on a cheese platter.

1 brown onion, peeled and halved
6cm piece ginger, peeled, or to taste
800g rhubarb, 500g roughly chopped into 5cm pieces and 300g cut into 1cm pieces
350g raw sugar
250g apple cider vinegar
1 teaspoon fine salt

1. Place onion and ginger in TC bowl, chop for 5 seconds, speed 5.
2. Add 500g rhubarb cut into 5cm pieces, sugar, vinegar and salt, cook for 30 minutes, steaming temperature, speed 1.5, MC removed and steamer basket on top to prevent splashes.
3. Add remaining 300g rhubarb cut into 1cm pieces, cook 5 minutes, 100°C, reverse speed 1.5.

Transfer relish to warm, sterilised jars (see note page 148) and store in the fridge for up to 6 months.

# caramelised orange balsamic

**MAKES 2 CUPS**

I'm sure I've doubled my intake of leafy greens since introducing this balsamic reduction into my diet – it just makes everything taste so good! Toss it with rocket leaves and a splash of olive oil and you've got the perfect side salad, or bulk it up with feta, toasted almonds and roasted vegetables for an awesome vegetarian meal. Then of course you can drizzle it over pasta, pizza, stews, roasts, cured meats, cheeses and bruschetta as a finishing vinegar, or serve it with oil as a dipping sauce with crusty bread. Room for dessert? Try dotting it over berries and ice cream for an amazing sweet finish. If you were to make only one 'flavour maker' for your store cupboard, this would definitely be it (which is convenient, as it's also one of the easiest).

**700g balsamic vinegar**
**300g orange juice**
**150g brown sugar**

1. Place all ingredients in TC bowl, cook for 40 minutes, steaming temperature, speed 2, MC removed and steamer basket on top to prevent splashes.

   Allow to cool before transferring to a sterilised jar (see note page 148). Store in the fridge for up to 3 months.

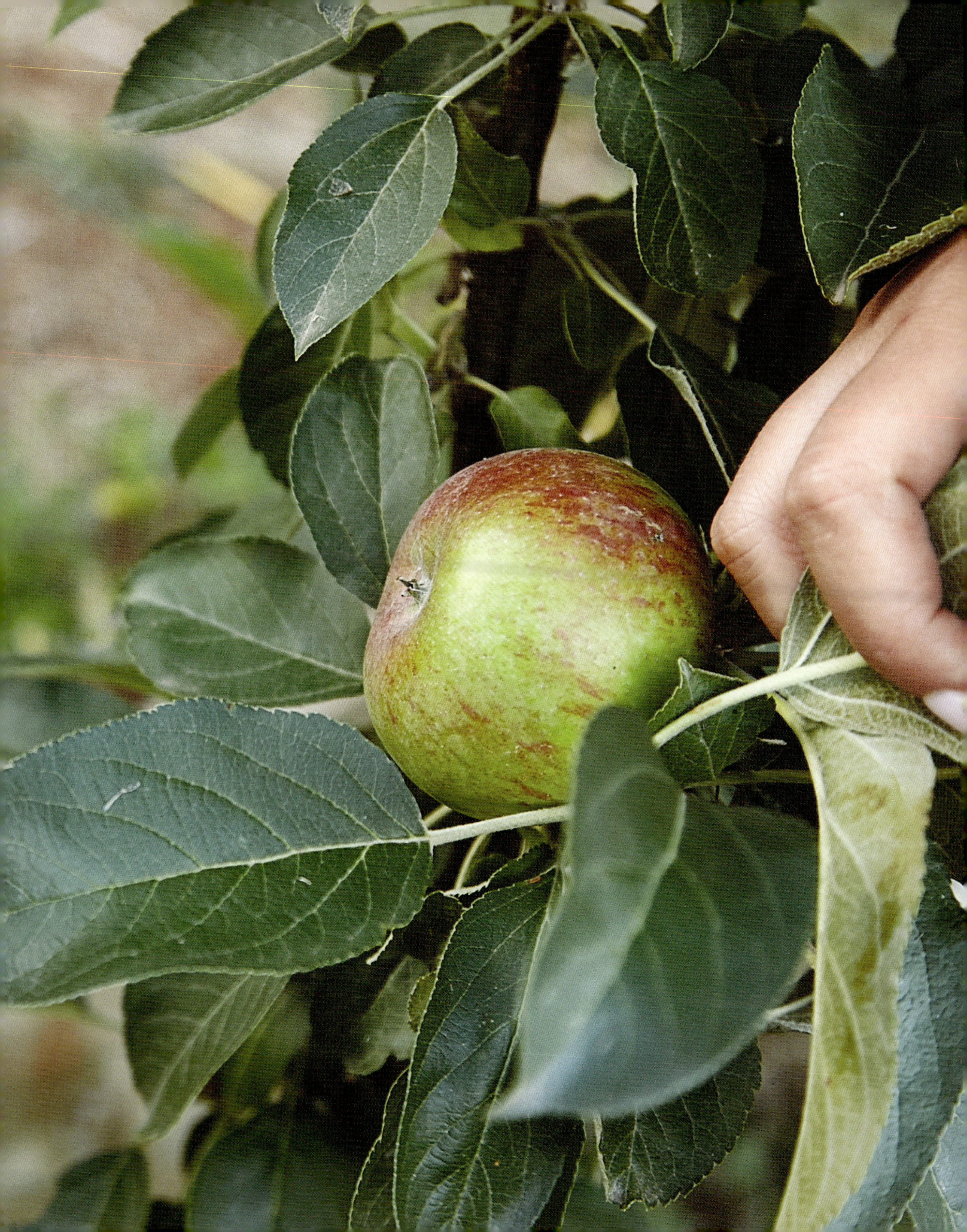

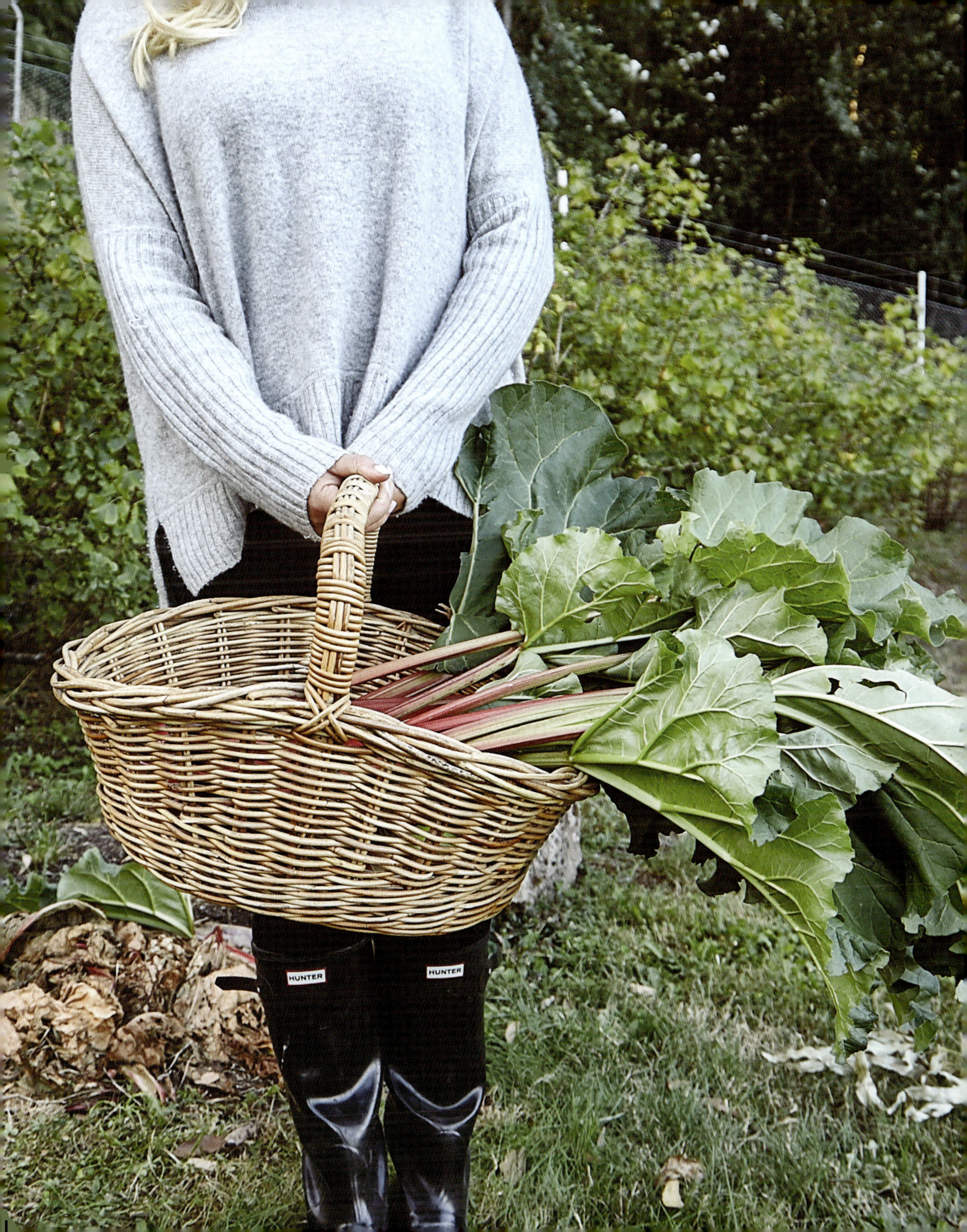
HUNTER
HUNTER

# flavour bomb salt

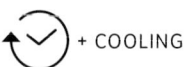

+ COOLING

**MAKES 1 CUP**

Use this anywhere you would use regular salt. Not only will it enhance all the existing flavours, it adds its own umami seasoning (sans MSG). Make it in bulk to give as an edible gift – just be prepared for requests for top-ups. This stuff is seriously addictive!

200g coarse salt
2 garlic cloves, peeled
1 tablespoon coriander seeds
1 tablespoon mustard seeds
2 teaspoons chilli flakes
20g tamari
½ teaspoon liquid smoke (see note)

1. Preheat oven to 95°C. Line a baking tray with baking paper or a baking mat.

2. Place all ingredients in TC bowl, mill for 5 seconds, speed 9. Spread out over lined tray.

3. Bake for 10 minutes, then turn off oven. Allow mixture to cool completely inside the oven.

4. Once cool, transfer to clean TC bowl and mill for 5 seconds, speed 6.

Store in an airtight jar. It will keep for up to a year. If you find it starts to clump together over time, just put it back in the TC bowl and mill for 5 seconds, speed 6.

NOTE: Liquid smoke can be found in specialty grocers or purchased online. It literally tastes and smells like smoke in a bottle, adding amazing depth of flavour to savoury dishes.

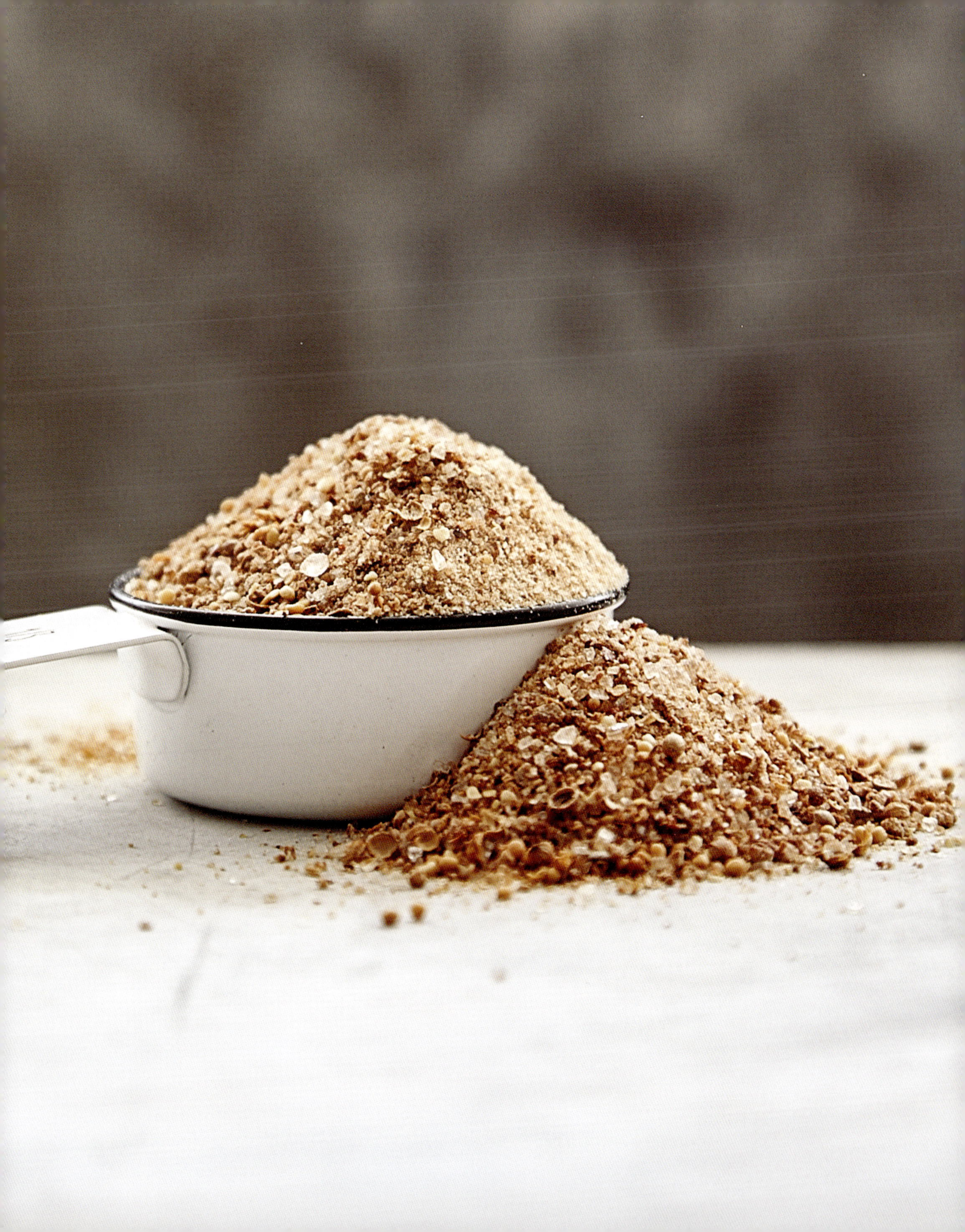

# garlic cubes

+ FREEZING

**MAKES 10 CUBES**

Golden sautéed garlic does so much more for a dish than raw garlic can. But there are times when I simply don't have the time or patience to sauté a clove or two for a dish, especially if the rest of the ingredients just need assembling rather than cooking. My solution: get organised on the weekend and batch cook your garlic, then freeze it in cubes for whenever garlic is needed – tossed through pasta, added to salad dressings, spread on toast or homemade pizza bases, melted onto steamed corn and other steamed vegetables, or stirred through mashed potato, or any soup or sauce.

**20 garlic cloves, peeled**
**150g olive oil**

1  Place garlic in TC bowl, chop for 4 seconds, speed 6. Scrape down sides.

2  Add oil, sauté for 15 minutes, 100°C, speed 1, MC removed. Divide oil and garlic evenly among 10 ice-cube holes and freeze until ready to use.

Once frozen, you can pop out the garlic cubes and store in a ziplock bag in the freezer until needed.

FLAVOUR MAKERS  248

clockwise from top: salad seed sprinkles *(see page 251)*, garlic cubes, *(see opposite)*, meyer lemon infused oil *(see page 250)*

# meyer lemon infused oil

+ COOLING

**MAKES 1 CUP**

When you begin to grow your own food, you quickly realise that a tomato is not simply a tomato and a lemon is not simply a lemon! There are hundreds of varieties of each fruit and vegetable, yet only a couple of each are widely available commercially. And unfortunately the chosen few don't seem to have been selected for their flavour, but rather because they transport and store well. Luckily, the highly fragrant Meyer lemon is often available in specialty grocers during the colder months. It has a sweet and complex flavour, adding character that the standard astringent lemon cannot match. This infused oil is a beautiful way to capture all these qualities, virtually offering Meyer lemon on tap! Drizzle it over pasta, salads, steamed vegetables, quiches, savoury tarts and seafood.

**250g olive oil**
**2 Meyer lemons, rind only**

1. Place oil and rind in TC bowl, infuse for 20 minutes, 80°C, speed soft. Pour into a jar and leave to cool and further infuse for 12 hours.

2. Strain oil through a sieve to remove rind and transfer to a sterilised bottle (see note page 148).

Store oil in the fridge but stand at room temperature for 15 minutes prior to serving.

NOTE: Pure olive oil solidifies when refrigerated, which is why it is important to bring it to room temperature before serving.

VARIATION: If Meyer lemons are unavailable, use the more common varieties of Eureka or Lisbon, or even oranges or grapefruit.

# salad seed sprinkles

+ COOLING

**MAKES 4 CUPS**

I love having these salad sprinkles on hand as they lift the most mundane of meals by adding both flavour and texture. The tamari and yeast flakes give that all-important umami flavour, while the toasted seeds add incredible crunch. Sprinkle over leaf salads, coleslaws, roasted vegetables, Asian greens, frittatas and scrambled eggs, or simply eat a handful as a satisfying snack!

150g pumpkin seeds
150g sunflower seeds
100g sesame seeds
25g poppy seeds
25g flaxseeds
25g chia seeds
20g macadamia oil
20g tamari
20g apple cider vinegar
1 tablespoon nutritional yeast flakes (see note)
2 teaspoons sweet paprika
1 teaspoon smoked paprika
1 teaspoon fine salt
½ teaspoon chilli flakes (optional)

1. Preheat oven to 140°C.
2. Place all ingredients in TC bowl, mix for 20 seconds, reverse speed 3. Spread the mixture across 2 large baking trays or roasting tins.
3. Bake for 10 minutes, then turn off oven. Allow mixture to cool completely in the oven – do not open door during this time.

Once cooled, transfer to an airtight jar or container and store for up to a month.

NOTE: Nutritional yeast flakes are little yellow flakes available from health food stores, full of B vitamins, minerals and protein, and with a suprisingly authentic cheese flavour. Not to be confused with baker's or brewer's yeast!

FLAVOUR MAKERS

# quick toffee caramel sauce

**MAKES 1½ CUPS**

This really is the quickest, easiest, no-fail caramel sauce, and is my go-to flavour maker to drizzle over puddings, ice cream, custard, pancakes, apples or roasted bananas. I think it might become yours too.

120g pouring cream
90g golden syrup
70g brown sugar
50g butter
30g honey

1  Place all ingredients in TC bowl, cook for 7 minutes, 90°C, speed 4.

Serve hot from the TC or let it cool and serve cold. Store in the fridge for up to a month (not that it will last that long!). If you want to, reheat it in the TC for 5 minutes, 90°C, speed 4.

from left: quick toffee caramel sauce *(see opposite)*, coconut caramel *(see page 254)*, raspberry, rhubarb and vanilla jam *(see page 255)*

# coconut caramel

**MAKES 1 CUP**

This coconut caramel is thick, creamy and delicious but completely dairy free. It has a great texture that's suitable for icing and filling baked desserts, layering in parfaits, drizzling over custards and ice creams, and dipping fresh fruit into (try slices of green apple for an afternoon sweet treat). It can even be used as a dairy-free tea and coffee creamer or milkshake flavourer.

**100g coconut sugar**
**15g kuzu (see note)**
**1 vanilla bean, halved (optional)**
**400g can coconut cream**

1. Place sugar, kuzu and vanilla bean (if using) in TC bowl, mill for 40 seconds, speed 10. Scrape down sides and lid.

2. Add coconut cream, cook for 20 minutes, steaming temperature, speed 3, MC removed and steamer basket on top to prevent splashes.

For a warm, runny sauce serve immediately, or transfer to a glass jar and refrigerate until completely cool for a thicker caramel.

NOTE: Kuzu root, available from health food stores, is a healthy cooking starch that beautifully thickens soups, stews, sauces and desserts.

# raspberry, rhubarb and vanilla jam

**MAKES 5 CUPS**

Combining these three ingredients will give you jam perfection. The raspberries offer a sweet flavour and brilliant ruby hue, the rhubarb adds a contrasting tartness and creates a great texture, and the vanilla subtly perfumes the jam, decorating it with tiny black seeds. Much, much more than a simple condiment for toast, try stirring it through yoghurt, cream or ice cream, sandwiching it between sponge cakes, or tossing it with sliced apples or peaches for an impressive pie filling or crumble base. It's amazing what you can create in very little time when you've got some quality flavour makers on hand.

400g raw sugar
1 vanilla bean, halved
500g rhubarb, ends trimmed, cut into 5cm pieces
1 lemon, peeled, pith and pips removed
500g frozen raspberries
100g water

1. Place sugar and vanilla bean in TC bowl, mill for 20 seconds, speed 9.

2. Add rhubarb and lemon, chop for 5 seconds, speed 7.

3. Add raspberries and water, cook for 30 minutes, steaming temperature, reverse speed 1, MC removed and steamer basket on top to prevent splashes.

4. Check volume of jam in the TC bowl — you want approx. 1.25 litres (use markers on the inside of the bowl). If not at this level, continue cooking for a further 5–10 minutes, steaming temperature, reverse speed 1, MC removed and steamer basket on top to prevent splashes.

Pour into hot, sterilised jars (see note page 148) and store in the fridge.

VARIATION: For a low-carb, sugar-free option, replace the raw sugar with xylitol.

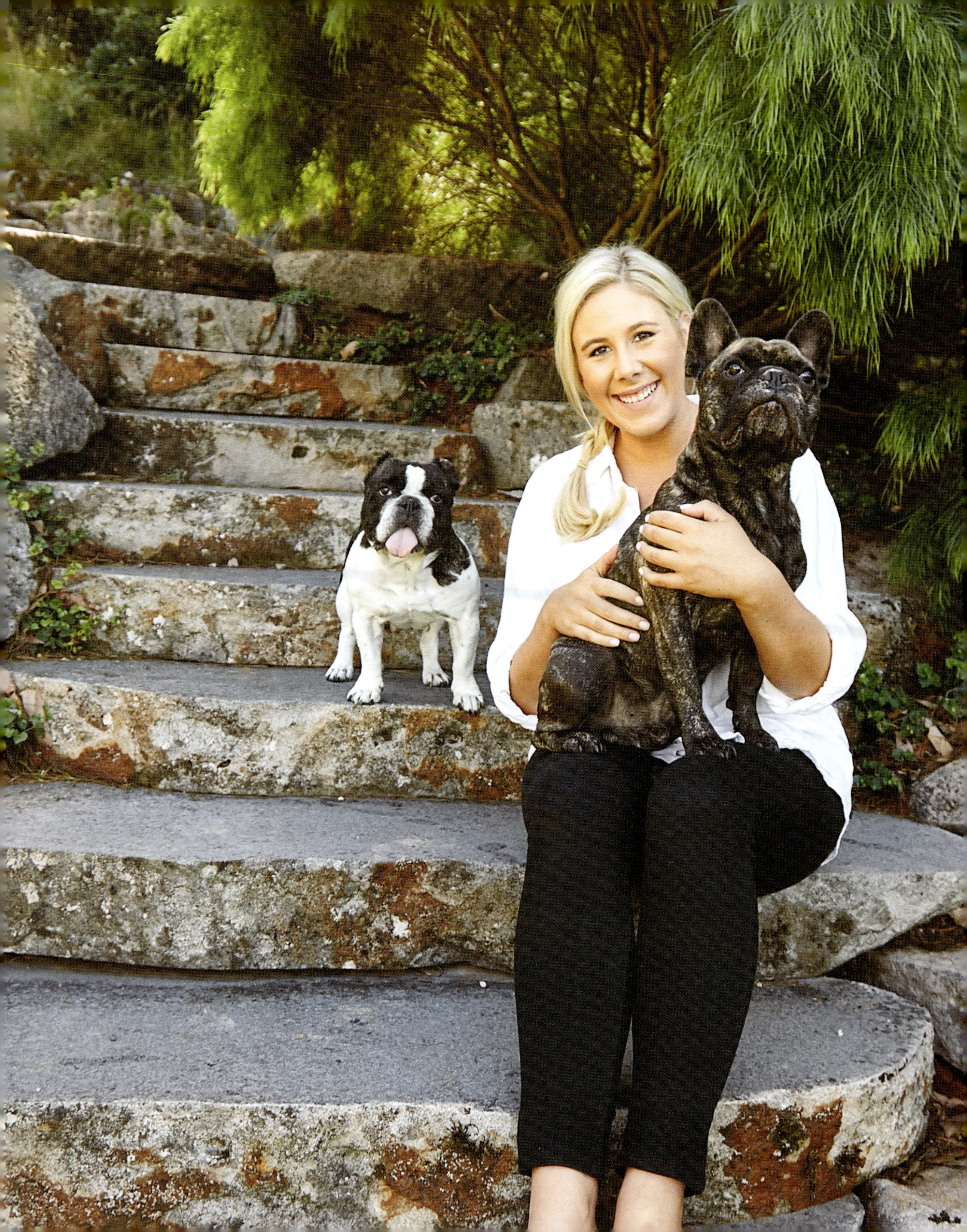

# acknowledgements

A more accurate name on the cover of this book would be 'team alyce alexandra', for there are so many people who contributed to making it all that it is. Directly, a tribe of talented individuals have worked so hard; and indirectly, many people have been so accommodating as I put my life on hold, giving everything to these pages. I am so grateful to you all.

**My publisher Katrina:** a huge thank you for believing in me, for without your spruiking this book would not exist. Thank you for letting me run with my vision and supporting me every step of the way. It has been a humbling experience, and one for which I am eternally grateful.

**My editor Rachel:** thank you for your brilliant editing, and for knowing exactly the right words to express what I am thinking. You have worked tirelessly and been such a great support – I have so appreciated your warmth, kindness and humour, even when we were both working much later than we should have been!

**My designer Emily:** I sincerely appreciate your commitment to making this book flawless – you've perfectly captured me and my vision and I couldn't be more thrilled with the outcome. Thank you!

**The Penguins:** as a writer it doesn't get any better than having Penguin Random House publish your work, and I sincerely appreciate all those behind the scenes who have made this book possible. Thank you all for believing in me and my work, especially Cate who was the very first person to champion this book.

**My mum Janene:** throughout this entire process you have quietly supported me in so many ways, from developing recipes, washing dishes and shopping at markets to shovelling straw and curling hair. I don't think you appreciate just how much of a difference you have made, but it means the world to me.

**My dad Alex:** you have given me everything I need to live my dreams – most importantly, your steadfast love and support. Thank you for getting behind everything I take on in life, no matter how crazy, and for doing literally anything you can to help.

**My sister Ellen:** you have backed us every step of the way and provided so much comfort and counsel. Your enthusiasm has been a breath of fresh air and your assistance has been invaluable, for a tripod cannot stand on two legs. Thank you for everything.

**My partner Alex:** thank you for silently picking up all the pieces after the whirlwind while this book has been my everything. Your love, support and assistance means so much to me ... and the chickens and the alpacas!

**The AA team Sally, Pauline, John, Ellen and Janene:** your passion and enthusiasm for all that we do and the big smiles on your faces each day make work such a joy. You've all gone above and beyond during the production of this book, and Loryn and I couldn't be more appreciative or proud of our team.

**My cheerleader Craig:** not only have you been our unofficial brand ambassador, but you've also been a great support to both the business and me personally. Thank you for lending a hand wherever needed, from washing dishes and packing orders to brainstorming chicken coops.

**My recipe testers Pauline, Craig, Tess, Karen, Kaye, Tim and Tash:** my secret squirrel army – thank you so much for generously offering your time and for all your lovely feedback.

**My customers:** throughout my cookbook journey there have been so many amazing customers who have shown such excitement and commitment towards my brand, and I cannot thank you all enough for the support. I am truly humbled, for without all you wonderful people I would never have had the privilege of writing my seventh book.

**My friends:** thank you all for your endless encouragement, advice and enthusiasm, and so many laughs along the way. While I have not had enough time to spend with you during this project, you all mean the world to me. A special shout out to Poppy for her superb modelling skills, and for always saying exactly what I need to hear.

**To so many others:** more than I can mention here, but thank you to Con for being our location shoot assistant, Khaye for all the help and interest in the kitchen, Hello Coffee Apollo Bay for the coconut chips, Trish for looking after all my babies, and to all those real food crusaders who inspire me. Of course, I can't forget about all the animals that have offered me such love and joy – the dogs Spencer, Chelsea and Duke, the alpacas Kath and Kim, and the chickens Bluey, Sasha, Whitey, Mo, Lilo, Marci, Eunice and Pip.

Finally, one person who deserves more praise and acknowledgement than I can find the words to express is **Loryn** – my sister and the brains and brawn behind the alyce alexandra operation. It is your creative genius that breathes life into my words and recipes, your innovation that inspires me, and your belief in me that propels me forward. I couldn't have more admiration, respect and love for you – thank you for everything.

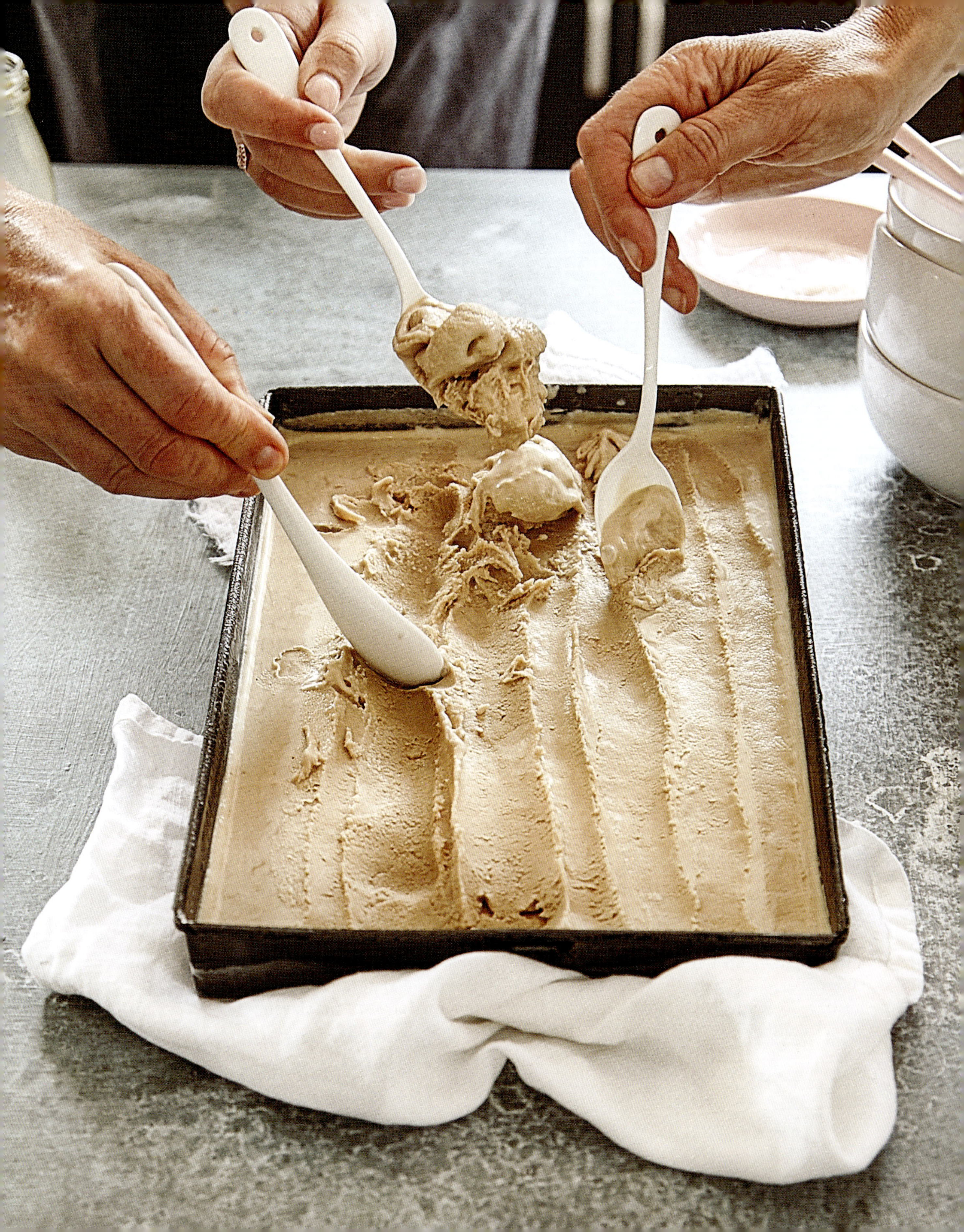

# index

## a
after-dinner mint hot
   chocolate  219
almond coconut macaroons  158
anything goes baos  165
anzac biscuits  202
apricot delights  38

## b
bake, tuna mornay  163
balls, chocolate cookie dough  32
balsamic, caramelised orange  243
baos, anything goes  165
barbecue sauce  234
beef
   korean beef ribs  106
   massaman beef curry  111
   moreish meatballs  80
   rich brisket ragù  105
   slow beef curry  140
beetroot burgers  100
berries
   boozy berry fool  216
   raspberry, rhubarb and vanilla
      jam  255
biscuits
   anzac biscuits  202
   choc macadamia cookies  204
black bean
   rice and black bean burritos  78
bolognaise, mushroom  90
boozy berry fool  216
bread
   cheese and vegemite scrolls  40
   focaccia  129
   garlic pull-apart  122
   lazy breakfast loaf  16
   roti bread  143
breakfast latte  22

brisket, rich ragù  105
burgers, beetroot  100
burritos, rice and black bean  78
butterscotch ice cream  198

## c
cakes
   individual 'baked'
      cheesecakes  206
   individual dark chocolate
      cakes  196
   yoghurt cheesecake  212
caramel
   coconut caramel  254
   quick toffee caramel sauce  252
caramelised orange balsamic  243
cauliflower, spiced  146
chai panna cottas  151
cheat's vanilla slice  208
cheese and vegemite scrolls  40
cheesecake
   individual 'baked'
      cheesecakes  206
   yoghurt cheesecake  212
cheese, ricotta  160
chia
   matcha passionfruit chia
      parfait  201
   pink chia puddings  11
chickpea curry  138
chilli
   chilli olive spaghetti  94
   chilli soy oysters  56
   garlic chilli sardines on toast  76
choc macadamia cookies  204
chocolate
   after-dinner mint hot
      chocolate  219
   choc macadamia cookies  204
   chocolate cookie dough balls  32

fudgy chocolate fig slice  51
individual dark chocolate
   cakes  196
peanut butter choc pops  215
chutney *see also* sauces
   corn and mustard chutney  239
   mango chutney  148
   tomato chutney  241
clean green smoothie  171
coconut
   almond coconut
      macaroons  158
   coconut caramel  254
   coconut mango lassi  149
   coconut yoghurt  24
   spiced coconut rice  145
coffee
   breakfast latte  22
   lavender coffee tonic  46
concentrate, stock  190
cookies *see also* biscuits
cookies, choc macadamia  204
corn
   corn and mustard chutney  239
   mexican corn salad  133
crackers, cranberry and
   hazelnut  44
cranberry and hazelnut crackers  44
creamy
   creamy tomato and basil
      spread  52
   creamy zucchini soup  68
crispy kale fritters  15
crunchy
   crunchy maple pecan
      clusters  12
   crunchy salad with ranch
      dressing  121
cubes, garlic  248
curried lentil 'sausage' rolls  98

curry
    chickpea curry 138
    fresh green curry 93
    massaman beef curry 111
    noodle curry soup 180
    slow beef curry 140

## d

dips
    creamy tomato and basil spread 52
    extra-punchy hummus 37
    green olive dip 43
    herbed mayo 226
dressings *see also* sauces
    caramelised orange balsamic 243
    crunchy salad with ranch dressing 121
    herb vinaigrette 168
drinks
    after-dinner mint hot chocolate 219
    breakfast latte 22
    coconut mango lassi 149
    lavender coffee tonic 46
    loryn's tropical 'juice' 48
    macadamia milk 18
dukkah, lemon myrtle 229

## e

easy kimchi-kraut 236
eggs
    frugal frittata 175
    potato, mint and fried egg salad 71
extra-punchy hummus 37

## f

facon 230
fig
    fudgy chocolate fig slice 51
flavour bomb salt 246
focaccia 129
fool, boozy berry 216
fresh
    fresh charcoal pasta 130
    fresh green curry 93
frittata, frugal 175
fritters, crispy kale 15
frugal frittata 175
fudgy chocolate fig slice 51

## g

garlic
    garlic and white wine mussel pots 67
    garlic chilli sardines on toast 76
    garlic cubes 248
    garlic pull-apart 122
ginger
    rhubarb and ginger relish 242
green
    clean green smoothie 171
    fresh green curry 93
    green olive dip 43

## h

healthy hoisin 224
herbed mayo 226
herb vinaigrette 168
hoisin, healthy 224
hollandaise, mexican 28
honey porridge 21
hot chocolate, after-dinner mint 219
hummus, extra-punchy 37

## i

ice cream
    butterscotch ice cream 198
    peanut butter choc pops 215
individual
    individual 'baked' cheesecakes 206
    individual dark chocolate cakes 196
infused oil, meyer lemon 250

## j

jam, raspberry, rhubarb and vanilla 255
'juice', loryn's tropical 48
juices *see also* drinks

## k

kale, crispy fritters 15
kimchi-kraut, easy 236
korean
    korean beef ribs 106
    korean rice bowl 60

## l

lamb
    lamb shoulder with salsa verde 108
    lamb with herby yoghurt lentil salad 75
lassi, coconut mango 149
latte, breakfast 22
lazy breakfast loaf 16
lemon
    lemon myrtle dukkah 229

meyer lemon infused oil 250
lentil
    curried lentil 'sausage' rolls 98
    lamb with herby yoghurt lentil salad 75
loaf, lazy breakfast 16
loryn's tropical 'juice' 48

## m

macadamia milk 18
macaroons, almond coconut 158
mango
    coconut mango lassi 149
    mango chutney 148
    peach and mango sorbet 211
mashed potato 118
massaman beef curry 111
matcha passionfruit chia parfait 201
mayo, herbed 226
meatballs, moreish 80
mexican
    mexican corn salad 133
    mexican hollandaise 28
meyer lemon infused oil 250
milk
    breakfast latte 22
    macadamia milk 18
minestrone, money-saving 187
mint
    after-dinner mint hot chocolate 219
    potato, mint and fried egg salad 71
    tamarind mint raita 144
money-saving minestrone 187
moreish meatballs 80
mornay, tuna bake 163
mushroom
    mushroom bolognaise 90

one-bowl mushroom spaghetti 65
mussel pots, garlic and white wine 67
mustard
    corn and mustard chutney 239

## n

noodle curry soup 180
nuts
    cranberry and hazelnut crackers 44
    crunchy maple pecan clusters 12
    sweet and spicy nuts 35

## o

oil, meyer lemon infused 250
olives
    chilli olive spaghetti 94
    green olive dip 43
one-bowl mushroom spaghetti 65
oysters, chilli soy 56

## p

panna cottas, chai 151
parfait, matcha passionfruit chia 201
pasta
    chilli olive spaghetti 94
    fresh charcoal 130
    one-bowl mushroom spaghetti 65
    tuna mornay bake 163
peach and mango sorbet 211
peanut butter choc pops 215
pecan, crunchy maple clusters 12
pickled salad 124

pink chia puddings 11
polenta, soft 126
pops, peanut butter choc 215
porridge, honey 21
potatoes
    mashed potato 118
    potato, mint and fried egg salad 71
    roast potatoes 178
puddings, pink chia 11
pull-apart, garlic 122
pumpkin, thai soup 88

## q

quick toffee caramel sauce 252

## r

ragù, rich brisket 105
raita, tamarind mint 144
ranch dressing, with crunchy salad 121
raspberry, rhubarb and vanilla jam 255
relish *see also* chutney
relish, rhubarb and ginger 242
rhubarb
    raspberry, rhubarb and vanilla jam 255
    rhubarb and ginger relish 242
ribs, korean beef 106
rice
    korean rice bowl 60
    rice and black bean burritos 78
    spiced coconut rice 145
    sushi mash-up 96
    'the' risotto 183
    tuna mornay bake 163
rich brisket ragù 105
ricotta cheese 160

risotto, 'the' 183
roast potatoes 178
roti bread 143

## s

salads
    crunchy salad with ranch dressing 121
    lamb with herby yoghurt lentil salad 75
    mexican corn salad 133
    pickled salad 124
    potato, mint and fried egg salad 71
    vietnamese trout salad 62
salad seed sprinkles 251
salsa verde, with lamb shoulder 108
salt, flavour bomb 246
sardines, garlic chilli on toast 76
satay sauce 233
sauces
    barbecue sauce 234
    healthy hoisin 224
    herbed mayo 226
    lamb shoulder with salsa verde 108
    mexican hollandaise 28
    quick toffee caramel sauce 252
    satay sauce 233
sausage rolls, curried lentil 98
savoury summer tart 54
scrolls, cheese and vegemite 40
seafood
    chilli soy oysters 56
    garlic and white wine mussel pots 67
    garlic chilli sardines on toast 76
    tuna mornay bake 163
    vietnamese trout salad 62

slice
    cheat's vanilla slice 208
    fudgy chocolate fig slice 51
slow beef curry 140
smoothie
    clean green smoothie 171
    smoothie bowl 27
soft polenta 126
sorbet, peach and mango 211
soups
    creamy zucchini soup 68
    money-saving minestrone 187
    noodle curry soup 180
    thai pumpkin soup 88
spaghetti
    chilli olive spaghetti 94
    one-bowl mushroom spaghetti 65
spiced
    spiced cauliflower 146
    spiced coconut rice 145
spread, creamy tomato and basil 52
spreads *see also* dips
sprinkles, salad seed 251
stock concentrate 190
sushi mash-up 96
sweet and spicy nuts 35

## t

tamarind mint raita 144
tart, savoury summer 54
thai pumpkin soup 88
'the' risotto 183
toffee caramel sauce, quick 252
tofu
    fresh green curry 93
tomato
    creamy tomato and basil spread 52

tomato chutney 241
tonic, lavender coffee 46
tropical 'juice' 48
trout, vietnamese salad 62
tuna mornay bake 163

## v

vanilla
    cheat's vanilla slice 208
    raspberry, rhubarb and vanilla jam 255
vietnamese trout salad 62
vinaigrette, herb 168

## y

yoghurt
    coconut yoghurt 24
    lamb with herby yoghurt lentil salad 75
    yoghurt cheesecake 212

## z

zucchini, creamy soup 68

VIKING

UK | USA | Canada | Ireland | Australia
India | New Zealand | South Africa | China

Penguin Books is part of the Penguin Random House group of companies whose addresses can be found at global.penguinrandomhouse.com.

Penguin Random House Australia

First published by Penguin Random House Australia Pty Ltd, 2017.

Text copyright © Alyce Alexandra 2017
Photography copyright © Loryn Babauskis 2017
Design © Penguin Random House 2017

The moral right of the author has been asserted.

All rights reserved. Without limiting the rights under copyright reserved above, no part of this publication may be reproduced, stored in or introduced into a retrieval system, or transmitted, in any form or by any means (electronic, mechanical, photocopying, recording or otherwise), without the prior written permission of both the copyright owner and the above publisher of this book.

Photographer and food stylist: Loryn Babauskis
Publisher & project manager: Katrina O'Brien
Designer: Emily O'Neill
Editor: Rachel Carter

Printed and bound in China by 1010 Printing International Ltd

National Library of Australia
Cataloguing-in-Publication data:

Alexandra, Alyce, author.
Everyday thermo cooking / Alyce Alexandra; photographer: Loryn Babauskis.
9780143784456 (paperback)

Thermomix (Kitchen appliances)
Kitchen appliances.
Food processor cooking.
Cooking.

Other Creators/Contributors:
Babauskis, Loryn, photographer.

penguin.com.au